WHO'S WHO
IN POPULAR MUSIC

The British Music Scene

Compiled by

Sheila Tracy

WORLD'S WORK

Copyright © 1984 Sheila Tracy
Designed by Victor Shreeve
Published by World's Work Ltd.
The Windmill Press, Kingswood, Tadworth, Surrey
Filmset in Optima by August Filmsetting, Haydock
Printed in Great Britain by Billing & Sons Limited, Worcester.
0 437 17601 0

Contents

Acknowledgements

I would like to thank the record companies, agents, managers and their secretaries who supplied me with a lot of the necessary information for this book. And a particular 'thank you' to everyone who took the time and the trouble to talk to me, which eased my task considerably. My grateful thanks too for all her hard work, to my research assistant Amanda Easterbrook and to my husband John Arnatt, for putting up with having no one to talk to for the past six months!

Introduction

The Concise Oxford Dictionary defines popular music as; 'songs, folk tunes etc not seeking to appeal to refined or classical taste.' Another way of saying music for the unrefined masses! But even we in the masses have our likes and dislikes. Some people are into pop, others into jazz, the majority, I would suspect, wander along whistling a happy tune somewhere between the two. That's what is known as MOR, middle of the road. I've tried to cater for all three of these categories.

Not all the people in this book are stars, but all of them play an important role in the overall British music scene, in the recording and television studios, on radio and the musical stage. They are intended to be a representative cross section of the best of the current British music makers. I have exercised a certain amount of licence regarding the term British, as you will find several Americans, Canadians and at least one Australian, all of whom have lived and worked in Britain for many years, which I feel is a fair qualification.

MOIRA ANDERSON
'There I was, back on the school bus . . .'
BORN: 5th June in Kirkintolloch, Scotland. Father a deep sea diver. **EDUCATED:** Aire Academy. Royal Scottish Academy of Music, studying singing, piano and clarinet. From the age of seven she sang with the Kirkintolloch Junior Choir, with whom she travelled to Canada, Denmark and Holland.
FIRST JOB: Music teacher in a school, for two years.
Her first break came when she auditioned for BBC Scotland and was given her first broadcast shortly afterwards. Her first television appearance was in 1960 on the famous *White Heather Club*. Was given her own television series in Scotland which was eventually networked, and from then Moira Anderson became a household name. 1970 turned out to be *her* year. She appeared in the first of many Royal Command Performances; headlined a summer show at Blackpool and starred in her own show at the London Palladium. She also received the OBE. She has won Scotland's Singer of the Year Award, and in 1982 was awarded the British Academy of Song writers, Composers and Authors Gold Star.

■ Highspot of career: 'Receiving the OBE in 1970'. ■ A moment to remember: 'When I auditioned for the BBC, I was still working as a school teacher. I got a letter saying I would be put on a list of people to be considered for broadcasts, but shortly afterwards producer Ian McFaddyen rang me and asked me if I could possibly get to Glasgow that evening to sing in the show at the Glasgow Empire as someone had been taken ill. "But I've never been on a variety stage in my life," I said. "Never mind about that, just get there," was the reply. It was such a big thrill for me to sing in that marvellous theatre even although it was only for one night. I came home so elated, and there I was the next morning back on the school bus!' ■ Likes: Good conversation and good food.
■ Dislikes: Smoking, and people who leave litter around.
■ Married to Dr Stuart Macdonald, and lives in Strathclyde.

JULIE ANDREWS (Julia Wells)
'Stopping the show at 12 years old with an F above high C . . .'
BORN: 1st October 1935 in Walton-on-Thames, Surrey. Father a woodwork and metalwork teacher. **EDUCATED:** Various schools around the country while touring with her mother and step-father. Cone-Ripman School, London.
Her mother was the part-time pianist at an evening dance school and would take Julie with her so that she saw dancing and heard music before she could walk and talk. Her first performance on any stage was as Nod in the dancing school's production of *Winken, Blinken and Nod* at the age of three and when the buttons on her pyjamas came undone in the middle of the performance, she carried on! It was in the summer of 1939 that her mother Barbara Wells played piano for a summer show at Bognor Regis. On the same bill was a Canadian Vaudeville entertainer Ted Andrews and shortly afterwards, she divorced Ted Wells and married Ted Andrews.
Julie was five years old when her mother remarried and her name was changed legally to Julie Andrews. Ted and Barbara Andrews became a well known variety act in the 40s and Ted Andrews was quick to spot the obvious potential of his step-daughter's voice. He arranged for her to have singing lessons with Madam Lillian Stiles-Allan. She had to practise for half an hour a day and later recalled: 'It seemed much longer than that. I loathed singing and resented my step-father asking me to perform. But he was a good disciplinarian and I was grateful later that he had made me take singing lessons.' Over the years she developed perfect pitch. 'I'm firmly convinced one can develop perfect pitch, you don't have to be born with it.' She made her first professional performance on stage with her parents at the age of 10, standing on a beer crate in order to reach the microphone to sing her solo. 'It was such immense fun that I did it several times more during the school holidays and on the odd Tuesday night when it wasn't desperately important. My mother played the piano and my step-father sang. Once in a while I joined him in a duet, it must have been ghastly but it

seemed to go down all right.' In 1947, Ted Andrews, playing golf with Val Parnell, persuaded him to listen to Julie's voice. He was so impressed that he booked her for his new review *Starlight Roof* which was about to open at the London Hippodrome, starring Pat Kirkwood, Vic Oliver and Fred Emney. On the opening night, soaring with the greatest of ease to the F above top C in Titania's aria from *Mignon*, she stopped the show. Many years later she said: 'I never really stopped working after that, except for the odd holiday once in a while.' For the next few years she appeared in variety and pantomime all over the country and in 1954 got her first really big break when she was offered the part of Polly Browne in the Broadway production of the hit London musical, *The Boy Friend*. She almost turned it down: 'I had toured on my own all around Britain, but suddenly the idea of leaving my home and family for two years in America was too much.' She asked her real father's advice and Ted Wells told her to see America while she had the chance. She took it but, still afraid of being homesick, stuck out for a one-year contract instead of the usual two. She opened on Broadway in September 1954 in *The Boy Friend* and the critics loved her. And that one-year contract she had insisted upon was to bring her an even bigger success. Because of it she was able to accept the next big offer that came her way, to play Eliza in Alan Jay Lerner's and Ernest Loewe's musical of George Bernard Shaw's *Pygmalion*. Just 19 months after her Broadway debut, she opened to rave reviews in what was destined to be one of *the* great musicals of the 20th century, *My Fair Lady*: a triumph she was to repeat in London two years later. Ten days after the Broadway opening, the cast assembled at 10 o'clock on a Sunday morning to record the songs for what was to become the best-selling original-cast album ever. Fourteen hours later, at midnight, it was finished. It was on 8th August 1959 that she sang the role of Eliza for the last time after 1,000 performances in 3,000 hours over three years. 'You don't want to go on, but suddenly you don't want to go either. The old firm, the old job becomes very dear.' But her voice in those three years had taken a belting and it wasn't helped when her tonsils were removed. It was an anxious time, but in just over a year she was back on Broadway playing Queen Guinevere to Richard Burton's King Arthur, in *Camelot*, her third Broadway success in a row. Having played Eliza in both the Broadway and London productions of *My Fair Lady*, it was unthinkable that she wouldn't land the film role. But the unthinkable happened. With no film experience behind her, she was passed over by Jack Warner for the more experienced Audrey Hepburn. But she had her revenge and her reward. The reward was the title role in Walt Disney's *Mary Poppins*, which she couldn't have done if she had been filming *My Fair Lady*; the revenge was winning an Oscar for her very first film when Audrey Hepburn wasn't even nominated. At the award's ceremony in Hollywood, accepting her Oscar, she thanked Jack Warner 'for making it all possible'. Having made her film debut in a musical, she proved she could tackle a straight role in *The Americanisation of Emily*. Then came *The Sound of Music* which she viewed with something less than enthusiasm. 'After all what can you do with nuns, seven children and Austria?' Answer: make one of the biggest money-spinning movies of all time! It was to be her greatest film success, a success that wasn't to be repeated in her other film roles. *Thoroughly Modern Millie* was treated fairly kindly by the critics, but her portrayal of Gertrude Lawrence in *Star* was

considered by them to be an unmitigated disaster. It didn't do too well at the box office either. Her other films include *Torn Curtain Hawaii, Darling Lili* directed by Blake Edwards whom she was to marry and the *Tamarind Seed* in which she co-starred with Omar Sharif and which was also directed by Blake Edwards. She put her Mary Poppins image well and truly behind her when she appeared topless in another of Blake Edwards' films, *Victor Victoria* in 1982. Although her albums have sold consistently well over the years, she has never been hit-parade material. Perhaps her meticulous diction is far too precise for *Top of the Pops*. She once said, 'I have to be very careful about singing contemporary songs. I've been told I have clear diction and unless the lyrics are very interesting, it sounds quite wrong. I can't sing oh-wo-wo-wo, now can I? It's absurd. Lovely when other people do it, but when I do it, it's just awful.'

■ A moment to remember: Eleven weeks spent in the Alps shooting *The Sound of Music* when some of the younger children lost their first teeth during the filming and a local dentist had to work all night making a false set of children's teeth so that filming could continue without great big gaps in the wrong places which would show up on the wide screen. ■ Likes ice cream and reading poetry. ■ Married to Blake Edwards, has one daughter, Emma, from her marriage to Tony Walton, three adopted children, and lives in California.

COLIN ANTHONY
'A tour to remember with the Beatles . . .'
BORN: Bath, Somerset. Father a fire/ambulance man. **EDUCATED:** Moorfields Junior School. Bath Art School. West of England College of Art. Private tuition in piano and singing. Guildhall School of Music. **FIRST JOB:** Fronting his own band at the Storyville Club, Cologne and Frankfurt, Germany. In 1979 sang the lead role in the rock musical *Rock-a-bye-Becket* at

the Cockpit Theatre in London. He made his first broadcast many moons ago on the *Dave Lee Travis Show* on Radio 1 with Colin Anthony's Cycles. Since then has sung with all the BBC Orchestras in London and the regions and can be heard regularly on just about every music programme broadcast on Radio 2. Has also sung extensively on the Continent, including the British entries in the Nordring Radio competitions and was one of the winning team in Belgium in 1983. As well as doing a lot of radio, he tours with his own small band which he has been fronting since the mid 60s. Not only in the UK but also in America and Europe. 'We supported many of the headliners on tours throughout the 60s including the Beatles, Duane Eddy, Johnny and the Hurricanes.' As a soloist he has appeared in many Song Festivals including the Charleville Song Contest in Cork which he won in 1981. He's also a talented song writer and has had many songs published, several of which he has sung himself on the air. Many of his songs are written in collaboration with Shadows' (qv) keyboard player Cliff Hall. Has written, produced and performed two albums, *Empty Spaces* and *Live Colin Anthony*.

■ Highspot of career: 'Supporting the Beatles on one of their early tours of the UK. *From Me To You* hit the No. 1 spot during that tour, which was quite exciting.' ■ A moment to remember: 'I walked on stage in Malmo, Sweden, facing an audience to perform a new song. The programme was going out "live" to eight countries. When I put the ear-phones on they immediately fell apart around my head – the sound-pieces around my chest. I couldn't hear a thing! Ahhh!'
■ Likes music and sailboarding. ■ Married to Karen, has one son, Nicholas, and lives in Surrey.

THE BARRON KNIGHTS
'A highly polished stage act . . .'

Butch Baker
BORN: 16th July 1941, in Amersham, Buckinghamshire. (Nearly in a taxi!) Father a factory worker. **EDUCATED:** Cedars Grammar School, Leighton Buzzard. Schoolboy fights and playing rugger resulted in a broken nose. 'I look like the founder member of the British echelon of the Mafia!' His father, a keen guitarist, gave him a banjo for his eighth birthday. He also plays the guitar. **FIRST JOB:** Working in the advertising department of an engineering magazine. He gave his first public performance at Marsworth Village Hall. Has been with the Barron Knights right from the start in 1960.

■ Highspot of career: Joining the Barron Knights. ■ Likes Cornwall and the Lake District. Dislikes selfishness and unkindness. ■ Married to Christine, has two sons and one daughter and lives in Bedfordshire.

Dave Ballinger
BORN: 17th January 1939 in Slough, Buckinghamshire. **EDUCATED:** Slough Tec. & College of Further Education. Took up the drums as a hobby while at college and then joined a local group, playing semi-professionally. **FIRST JOB:** An apprentice coppersmith. Made his first public appearance at the Slough Adelphi. Turned professional in 1961 and joined The Wanted Five, appearing at the London Palladium. He then joined the Barron Knights but left them for 12 months in 1963 when the urge to travel led him to work as a floating musician on cruises. He rejoined the group in January 1964.

■ Likes high tech and life in the country. Dislikes 'people leaving our gate open and letting the dog out'. ■ Married to Lucille, has two daughters and one son and lives in Bedfordshire.

Duke D'Mond (Richard Eddie Palmer)

BORN: 25th February 1943 in Dunstable, Bedfordshire. Father a printer. **EDUCATED:** Priory, Dunstable, where he sang in the choir and boxed in the school team along with Toni Avern, the group's manager. Was welterweight champion of the school. **FIRST JOB:** An electrotyper and stereotyper. He quit a six-year apprenticeship, when in his final year, to join the Barron Knights. First sang in public at a cinema in Rushden, Northamptonshire.

■ Highspots of career: Appearing on *Sunday Night at the London Palladium*. ■ Likes parrot seed and dog biscuits. Dislikes learning to talk and being clipped. ■ Married to Pauline, has one daughter and lives in Bedfordshire.

Pete Langford

BORN: 4th October 1943 in Durham. **EDUCATED:** 'Pass.' **FIRST JOB:** A packer in a sewing machine warehouse where an accident cost him the end of one finger (from then on he played nine-finger guitar). Took up music seriously when he was 16, running a semi-pro group called the Zodiacs. Made his first public appearance at Hockliffe Methodist Church. He joined the Barron Knights from his job in the sewing machine warehouse.

■ Highspot of career: *Call Up The Groups* reaching the No. 2 spot in the charts in 1964. ■ Likes spring. Dislikes the French on a ski holiday. ■ Married to Veronica, has one daughter and lives in Bedforshire.

Barron Antony Osmond

BORN: 15th June 1934 at RAF Abingdon, Berkshire. Father an RAF Officer. **EDUCATED:** Churchers College, Petersfield, where he studied piano. **FIRST JOB:** Engine fitter in the RAF at 16. His first posting as a boy apprentice was to near Oxford and he earned pin-money by playing harmonica with a local group and by singing calypsos and folk songs in coffee bars. Students in Oxford elected him a member of the Heritage Society, something of an honour for a non-student. He became Pole Vault Champion in the RAF and was posted to the Far East where he made his first broadcast while in Malaya. In his spare time became a cartoonist. After being demobbed he took a job in Bedfordshire delivering bread, but dreamt of becoming a professional musician and so decided to form a group and on 5th October 1960 the Barron Knights were born.

■ Highspot of career: Opening the *Beatles Christmas Show* at Finsbury Park Empire in 1963. ■ Likes considerate drivers. Dislikes being kept waiting in a crowded bar. ■ Is single and lives in Bedfordshire.

The Barron Knights' first engagement after their formation in 1960 was at the Locarno Ballroom in Coventry when they earned the princely sum of 30s. shared between them! They were always more concerned with putting on a show than doing a straightforward presentation of their songs, with the result that their numbers often had comedy or visual appeal. They became adept at parodying the acts of the day and in 1964 they made a record doing just that. It took them an hour to put together, one session to record but four months to get it released. Parodying other people's songs meant copyright problems. 'We were beginning to give up hope,' says Barron Antony Osmond, 'The people we had to get permission from were endless – music publishers, artists, managers. We kept changing things, but eventually reverted to our original tape.' When it was eventually released, *Call up the Groups* shot to No. 2 in the charts. The Barron Knights had arrived and they've been there ever since, the same five original members, a lot older and a lot greyer but with one of the most polished stage acts in the world today. Their hits have been numerous and they have several Gold Discs to their credit. In 1978 they were awarded the Golden Nationwide Award for being Family Entertainers of the Year. Long may they continue.

■ A moment to remember: 'During our tour of Australia, the Australian tour manager, Chris Cunningham, had the habit of referring to distances between each and every job as "about an hour". Obvious this became increasingly amusing especially as we left for some jobs three or four hours beforehand. The real crunch came when we had to fly from Sydney to Perth and back to Sydney to perform a one-night engagement (almost 6,000 miles in all). Upon our return Chris enquired, "how long did you play?" "About an hour," was the reply in harmony – 2 days 11 hours less than the journey!'

SHIRLEY BASSEY
'An unscheduled quick change . . .'

BORN: 1937 in Cardiff. Father a merchant seaman. **FIRST JOB:** Wrapping chamber pots in a factory where the supervisor would get fed up with her singing while she worked and tell her to 'belt up'!

As well as wanting to be a singer she had many ambitions. 'Every year I wanted to be something different, an air hostess, a nurse, a model . . . . I wanted to wear beautiful clothes as I always had my sister's hand-me-downs.' At 15 she was singing in working men's clubs around Cardiff and one night while standing in for someone who was sick, was heard by a producer who was putting on a show in London. 'He said, "I want that girl in my show"; it was like the films!' Made her first trip to London for an audition which she passed and at 16 joined the chorus of a touring revue. She never looked back. Michael Sullivan became her manager and soon she was working the Variety circuit. Jack Hylton when he first saw her reacted with 'Just another bloody singer', but he soon realized her potential and she made her West End debut at the Adelphi Theatre. Her appearance at London's Café de Paris caused a sensation and shortly afterwards she made her first visit to America to appear in Las Vegas. Her first record to enter the charts was *Banana Boat Song* in 1957 and it looked as if it might be a one-hit wonder because it was almost two years before *Kiss Me Honey Honey Kiss Me* reached the No. 4 spot and sparked off a whole string of chart successes which lasted through the 60s and into the 70s. A dynamic performer on both stage and television, she has retreated into semi-retirement in recent years, but in 1984 made something of a comeback with her recording of the theme song of the film *Champions*, returning to the UK from her home in Switzerland to give her first television interview for 10 years. She still has many fans, who must have been infuriated to hear that the most successful

remedy for frightening the pigeons away from Liverpool airport, where they were hazardous to aircraft, was to play Shirley Bassey's *Big Spender* at full blast through outside speakers. No other singer was so effective!

■ A moment to remember: Famous for her fabulous gowns, which are literally made around her, she tells the story of the night something went wrong. 'As I hit a top note, my strap broke and out came my left boob. I didn't miss a beat as I kept my hand there and looked to the wings to ask for another dress but there wasn't anybody there. So I sang,

"Will somebody please bring me another dress"; but nobody did and I finished the song still holding on. My husband who was sitting in the audience suddenly realized what was wrong and got them to bring another dress to the side of the stage. I said to John Barry who was playing for me at the time, "Busk it, I'm off', and I did the quickest change I've ever done in my life. I came on in another gown and everyone applauded; they didn't know what had happened, they just thought I was showing off that I had more than one gown!' ■ Has two daughters, Sharon and Samantha, one son, Mark, and one grandson, Luke. Lives in Switzerland.

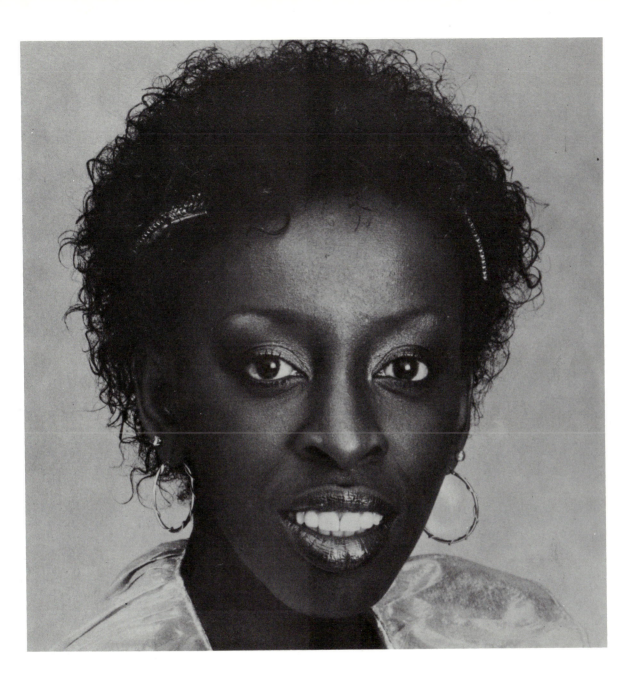

MADELEINE BELL
'A tap on her shoulder . . .'

BORN: 23rd July 1942, in Newark, New Jersey, USA. Father a floral decorator. **EDUCATED:** Miller Street School, Newark, South Side High School, Newark. **FIRST JOB:** A meat wrapper in a supermarket at 16. 'The day I left school I got a job'. She started singing in churches and on street corners. Joined her first gospel group at 14 and did gospel gigs at weekends. Made her first broadcast with a gospel group in a church where there was a radio broadcast every Sunday night. She came to the UK in 1962 in a musical called *Black Nativity*.

Made her first broadcast here on *Saturday Club* with Brian Matthew in 1964. Joined the vocal group Blue Mink in October 1969 and stayed with them for almost five years. Is now one of this country's top session singers and broadcasts regularly with the BBC Radio Orchestra/Radio Big Band. Programmes include the *Joe Loss Show, Nordring Radio Festival 1981*, and she is heard on many of Radio 2's music programmes including *Big Band Special*.

■ Highspot of career: 'I was appearing in a charity show at the Theatre Royal, Windsor and after the first half I had changed ready for the finale and was standing side stage watching Morecambe and Wise when somebody came through the door behind me and tapped me on the shoulder. It was Prince Charles and he said how pleased he was to meet me. That for me, being an American, was a very exciting moment.' ■ A moment to remember: 'In 1981 I did a thirteen-week series on Radio 1 on Sundays from 10am to 12 noon. I was also appearing at the Talk of the Town which meant that I didn't get home until 4am on a Sunday morning, so I gave up all idea of going to bed and sat up answering my fan mail, then took a long bath and left for the studio at 7.30am. One Sunday, Paul Williams said to me "You're sounding really tired, what you should do is to smile when you talk into the microphone." So, there I was with a big grin prancing around the studio to make myself sound awake . . . and it worked!' ■ Likes eating, cooking and watching television. Dislikes getting up in the morning and phoney people who are always posing. 'I don't like to be seen too much, maybe that's why I've never become a big star.' ■ Lives in Middlesex.

CILLA BLACK (Priscilla White)
'As a kid I was flash and a ham and always knew I was going to be a star . . .'
BORN: 27th May 1943 in Liverpool. Father a docker. **EDUCATED:** St Anthony's School, Liverpool. Anfield Commercial College. 'I always took part in all the school concerts. I was flash and I was a ham. I wouldn't have liked me as a child at all and I wouldn't like my children to be like I was.' **FIRST JOB:** Typist in

a Liverpool office. 'I always knew I was going to be a star, but I thought I had better get a job to fill in until my Fairy Godmother came along, so I took a year's secretarial course. I also took up the Dictaphone and became quite good at that.' It was while she was on the secretarial course at Anfield that she started going to youth clubs such as the Iron Door and the Cavern. 'My girl friend used to pester the groups who were playing there to let me sing with them. She only did it because she wanted an excuse to meet them!' Around this time, Cilla became friendly with Ringo Starr, 'I used to tint his Mum's hair for her. If I couldn't be a singer, I was going to go in for hairdressing and own a chain of hairdressing salons. I used to experiment on Ringo's Mum and she never, ever complained! Funnily enough it was John Lennon, who I didn't know very well, who mentioned my name to Brian Epstein, and I actually did my audition with the Beatles.' Her change of name from White to Black was an accident. She was always known as Cilla, but a local rag, the Mersey Beat, printed her name as Cilla Black. 'My father was horrified because he thought I was going to be a big star— well I'd been telling him that for years—and no one would ever know I was his daughter! But I liked Black better than White, so I kept it and strangely enough it led to a change of nickname for Dad. He was always known down at the docks as "Shiner" because he was so particular about his boots, and after I had my first hit they started calling him "Frustrated Minstrel" because he didn't know whether he was Black or White!' Her first job as a professional singer was at a Beatles concert in Southport, where she stood in for the Fourmost who couldn't appear because they were doing a television show. 'My boyfriend Bobby (Willis) took me there on the bus. I wore my own frock and I didn't know anything about stage make-up. Bobby didn't know anything about stage lighting and when the stage manager asked him for a lighting plot, he thought he was asking for a light for his cigarette! We were very green.' Three months later after turning professional, she became the first girl to capture the No.1 spot in the charts in two years, *Anyone Who Had a Heart,* which sold 100,000 copies in one day, was followed three months later by another No.1, *You're My World.* That same year, 1964, saw her starring at the London Palladium, and appearing in the Royal Variety Show. 1965 brought a series of overseas tours to Australia, New Zealand and America, and her pantomime debut as Little Red Riding Hood at the Wimbledon Theatre. Her film debut in *Work . . . is a Four Letter Word,* in 1967, turned out to be a one-off although she did try her hand at acting again in the mid 70's with a situation comedy series. *Cilla's World of Comedy.* But it was as hostess of her own TV variety shows that she found most success, winning the *Sun's* Top Female Television Personality Award for five consecutive years. Although her records no longer feature in the hit parade, her album, *The Very Best of Cilla Black,* released in 1983, earned her a Double Platinum Disc, proving how popular she has remained. Her infectious personality, Liverpool accent and her entire lack of 'side', has guaranteed her successful transition from pop star to entertainer.

■ Highspot of career: 'The most exciting moment for me, has to be meeting the Queen at my first Royal Command Performance. I've done many since, but I shall never forget that one. I remember, as a kid, waving to the Queen when she came on a visit to Liverpool, and I was always convinced she was waving back to me. But to actually shake hands with her; and I remember the conversation we had so clearly. Colour television had just started and we talked about the make-up you needed to wear for colour as opposed to black and white. It was a very thrilling evening.' ■A moment to remember: 'For me, Birmingham, next to Liverpool, is the most marvellous city as the people there are very funny. When I was playing in *Jack and the Beanstalk* at the Hippodrome at Christmas 1983, at one point in the script I had to say, "I don't know where I am", and a voice from the audience shouted, "You're in the Hippodrome". But the best bit came at the end of one particular evening, when, with the giant quivering before me because I've beaten him and have him at my mercy, I ask the audience, "What shall we do with him?" and a little voice piped up, "Why don't you sing to him." I didn't really know which way to take that!' ■Likes beetroot, 'We grow it in the garden and I bottle it and eat it six or seven times a day. I love the smell of the vegetables growing in the garden, I even enjoy peeling potatoes, Bobby thinks I'm mad.' ■Dislikes people smoking in lifts. ■Married to Bobby Willis (who is her manager), has three sons, Robert, Benjamin and Jack, and lives in Buckinghamshire.

DAVID BOWIE (David Jones)
'Tremendous creative talent . . .'
BORN: 8th January 1947 in Brixton, London. **EDUCATED:** Bromley High School. He played tenor sax in a group at school. He also got into a fight which damaged an eye; the subsequent operation left him with a paralysed pupil. **FIRST JOB:** Commercial artist. Formed his first professional group at 17, Davie Jones and the King Bees, and with them made his first record. Other groups followed, the Manish Boys and the

Lower Third, none particularly successful. He was then forced to change his name to avoid confusion with Davy Jones of the Monkees. He chose Bowie after the famous knife of that name. 'I was always very solitary and insular as a teenager. I put a shell around myself, felt very uneasy expressing my emotions. I was very English, I had a rein on my emotions, was very easily flustered, tight lipped I guess. When I did start expressing myself, it came out with such an explosion that it sent me right over the top.' Greatly influenced by actor/singer/composer Anthony Newley, whose work he admired, he released a series of pop love songs as a solo artist. He then became interested in Buddhism, dropped out of the music scene altogether and opened up an Arts Lab in Beckenham. But the urge to perform proved too strong, and he joined Lindsay Kemp's mime company which was to prove to be quite an influence on his future career. While still running his Arts Lab, he wrote and recorded *Space Oddity*, which gave him his first hit, reaching No.5 in the charts in October 1969. It was to be another three years before his next hit single, and a lot of people thought he was a one-hit wonder, but Bowie, at first disillusioned by pop stardom, decided to take the pop world by storm, by being more outrageous than anyone else and so Ziggy Stardust was born. What he created was an international sensation and from then on Bowie could do exactly what he wanted to do and could make the kind of records he wanted to make. A man of tremendous creative talent who took the gamble of playing the pop scene at its own game and winning 'hands down'. Throughout 1972 and 1973 Bowie and his entourage toured Europe, America and Japan culminating in a concert at the Hammersmith Odeon in July 1973 where he announced his retirement. It lasted for precisely a year and having got his breath back, Bowie was back in business. A TV Special led to an album, *Diamond Dogs* which in turn led to another USA tour and another album *Young Americans* which produced two hit singles, the title track and *Fame* which gave him his first No. 1 in America. Meanwhile, in the UK, *Space Oddity* was re-released and made the No.1 spot in the UK charts 6 years and 63 days after its first appearance at No.5! That same year, Bowie made his film debut in Nicholas Roeg's *The Man Who Fell to Earth* about a visitor from another planet who tries to colonize Earth, but his powers are destroyed and he ends an alcoholic cripple. Technically brilliant, the film failed to attract both critics and public alike, but it established Bowie as a competent actor and an invitation to play the title role in the *Elephant Man* on Broadway followed. He moved back to Europe in 1976, living for a while in the Turkish quarter of Berlin. His next film *Just a Gigolo* was made in West Germany and once again drew adverse criticism, although Bowie himself emerged without much harm done, because 1983 saw him co-starring with Catherine Deneuve in *The Hunger* and with Tom Conti in *Merry Christmas Mr Lawrence*. 1983 also saw him back at the top of the charts with the title track from the album *Lets Dance*. Rather like a terrier who takes a rat by the scruff of its neck, shaking it and doing what he will with it, David Bowie has swept through more than a decade of pop music, from hard rock to disco and has established himself as one of the most influential pop stars of the 70s. It will be fascinating to see what he achieves in the 80s.

■Highspot of career: His six month stint in the *Elephant Man* on Broadway. 'After doing the *Elephant Man* all that time I

felt I could handle anything. It was wonderful to do a performance like that without any aid, no whisky, no vodka, no drugs.' ■Likes Gilbert and Sullivan, and skiing. Dislikes the trappings of the pop world. ■Has one son and lives in Switzerland.

ELKIE BROOKS
'In this business you've got to be very positive . . .'
BORN: 25th February, 1945 in Salford, Lancashire. Father a baker. Left Salford at 15 to try her luck in London. **FIRST JOB:** Singing with a dance band. She fronted the jazz-rock line up Dada before moving on to Vinegar Joe, which she describes as a 'real good bread and butter gigging band'. Unfortunately their records didn't sell and they broke up. 'I was a wreck. I was really heartbroken because I'd been totally immersed in what I'd been doing. I started to write songs because when you're indecisive and you have no direction, a lot seems to come out.' A contact in Georgia led to her moving to America and becoming a backing singer for the Southern rock band Wet Willie. She stayed a year and had a wonderful time. 'I'm your definitive group member. I like the companionship, the whole experience of being on the road, the road games, the booze, the lousy rooms, everything.' Back in the UK she continued touring in cabaret and in the mid 70s got herself a recording contract with A & M which led to the release of her first album, *Rich Man's Woman* including some of her own songs she'd written over the previous couple of years. It also provided her with a single *He's a Rebel*, which made no impression on the charts. It was to be another two years before she had her first hit, In 1977 song writers Lieber and Stoller produced her album *Two Days* which entered the charts, but not before two singles had been released from it, giving her her first two Top 10 entries; Elkie's own *Pearl's a Singer* No.8 and *Sunshine after Rain*, No.10. The following year *Lilac Wine* made it into the Top 20 likewise *Shooting Star* in the album charts. Almost three years elapsed before any further recording success came her way. Then in November 1981 came the chart busting album *Pearls*, going triple Platinum with an astonishing 59 weeks in the album charts reaching the No.2 spot. Her chart success led to a sell-out tour of the UK in the spring of '82 and in November of that year *Pearls II* almost did as well as its predecessor, making it to No.5 in the album charts and giving her a hit single with *Nights in White Satin*. 'To be a woman in this business you've got to be very positive and have an incredible personality, twice as much as a guy, It's so easy for a woman to fall into the "nice lady" bag. I like to think of myself not necessarily as aggressive on stage but as strong and sure of myself. I hope to come over the same way on record. I just sing how I feel.

■A moment to remember: 'Those years on the road. They were very, very hard for me and I wouldn't want to have to do it over again. But it just wasn't my turn at the wheel before. I needed to go through all those things to develop the enthusiasm, energy and confidence that I have now.' ■Likes and dislikes . . . 'far too many to list!' ■Married to Trevor Jordan, has one son, Jermaine, and lives in London and Devon.

BROTHERHOOD OF MAN

'After 12 successful years we can afford to be a bit choosy . . .'

Martin Lee

BORN: 26th November 1946 in Surrey. Father a bookbinder. **EDUCATED:** 'All over.' When he was nine years old the family went to Australia for five years. He played guitar with several groups while still at school. **FIRST JOB:** Upholsterer.

■Likes exotic food. 'When I first joined Brotherhood of Man I was a very plain eater, very much an egg and chips man and would never touch a pizza or Chinese or Indian. Now I love them all.' Dislikes washing his hair every morning.   ■Married to Sandra Stevens and lives in Surrey.

Sandra Stevens

BORN: 23rd November 1948 in Leeds. **FIRST JOB:** Secretary. Before joining Brotherhood of Man she sang with the bands of Joe Loss and Ken Mackintosh. Also made many broadcasts with the Northern Dance Orchestra and was the resident singer at the Wakefield Theatre Club.

■Married to Martin Lee and lives in Surrey.

Nicky Stevens

BORN: 3rd December 1948 in Carmarthen, Wales. Father a professional musician. Originally trained as a classical singer, at 15 she was touring the Continent as a singer and then became resident vocalist at a Welsh night club. She also worked in cabaret in South Africa before joining the group.

■Married to Alan Johnson and lives in Buckinghamshire.

Barry Upton

BORN: 25th February 1952. Father a draughtsman. **FIRST JOB:** Draughtsman. He is the newest member of the group, having first joined their backing band.

■Single and lives in Bedfordshire.

Lee Sheriden

Original member of the group who left temporarily to concentrate on writing in 1982. With Martin Lee and Tony Hiller, their manager, has been responsibile for writing most of their hit songs.

■Married to Pat, has two daughters and lives in Berkshire.

In 1969 Tony Hiller wrote a song *Love One Another* for an international song competition and wanted to form a group with a name to fit the song, so he got together four session singers and called them Brotherhood of Man. Following the competition, they recorded another of Tony's songs, *United We Stand*, which early in 1970 reached No.10 in the charts. After that the group just fizzled out, but around that time Tony Hiller met Martin Lee and Lee Sheriden, two other songwriters and they joined forces, not only to write songs, but also with the purpose of re-forming Brotherhood of Man. They scored their first hit in 1975 with *Kiss Me Kiss You Baby*, which was a million seller in Europe, topping the charts in Scandinavia, Germany, Holland and France. But it was in 1976 that they really took off in the UK by winning the Eurovision Song Contest with *Save Your Kisses for Me* which remained at No.1 for six weeks, earning them a Platinum Disc. They had another No.1 the following year with *Angelo*, and over the next few years had many more chart entries. Their *B for Brotherhood*, *20 Greatest* and *Sing 20 Number One*

Hits also did well in the album charts. They've toured Australia, the Middle and Far East and now, after 12 successful years, can afford to be choosy, according to Martin Lee: 'We don't like doing summer seasons. We did one in 1983 and it was a disaster. They always try to put a square peg into a round hole, they want you to do things their way, and with us it just doesn't work, we like to do things our own way. Our writing is probably the most important side of our career now. We write songs for a whole lot of people other than ourselves. It's often difficult to keep track of who's recorded what. I've been writing songs since I was 12 years old and I often come across an old demo record, play it and think, listen to that, it's too much!'

■Highspot of career: Winning the Eurovision Song Contest in 1976. ■A Moment to remember: 'When we won the Eurovision Song Contest at The Hague in Holland in 1976, all hell broke loose after the competition was over. There were a million photographers and a million reporters swarming all over the place, so they hustled us down to a room in the basement to give us a breather before the press call. Suddenly we look around and Sandra is missing. Tony panics thinking she had been kidnapped and all the security guards are put on alert to stop anyone leaving the building until she has been found. Pandemonium reigns for the next quarter of an hour with no sign of Sandra. Then the door opens and in she walks. "What's wrong?" she asks in amazement. 'I've only been to the loo and on the way back a photographer called Peter grabbed me and wanted me to pose for some photographs for his magazine." So this guy had nobbled her while all the rest of the world's press were waiting upstairs. We became very friendly with Peter after that. He was Dutch and we did a lot of work with him. He was really magic.'

MAX BYGRAVES (Walter Bygraves)

'I wanna tell you a story . . .'

BORN; 16th October 1922 in Rotherhithe, London. Father a professional boxer. **EDUCATED:** St Joseph's, Rotherhithe. As a kid he would sit in the 'gods' at the New Cross Empire watching such stars as Max Miller and Billy Bennett. Entered a children's talent contest at the same theatre singing *It's My Mother's Birthday Today* and won. Dressed in his father's cap and long trousers, he borrowed a friend's dog as a prop which was a master stroke. When the dog 'performed' on stage at the end of young Walter's song, it brought the house down! 'I had never heard laughter like it before. I knew when I left the theatre that night, all I ever wanted was to hear an audience laugh like that again.' **FIRST JOB:** Crawford's Advertising Agency, High Holborn, carrying copy to various Fleet Street newspapers. Also worked as a carpenter building an air raid shelter at the Crosse & Blackwell factory in

Bermondsey. Volunteered for the RAF at $17\frac{1}{2}$ and served five years as a fitter. On his first evening in the NAAFI, did an impression of Max Miller and from then on was known as Max. Appeared in many shows while in the RAF and in 1942 married WAAF, Blossom Murray. His demob in 1945 found him working on a building site and hating every moment, but he was also playing a few British Legion and Working Men's Clubs in the London area. A chance meeting with an ex-RAF colleague led to an audition for the BBC and his first broadcast. This in turn led to an offer of a 16-week Moss Empire tour. In May 1946 he opened at the Sheffield Empire. It was the first step on a ladder that was to lead right to the top. Has starred on many occasions at the London Palladium; played the Palace in New York with Judy Garland which was followed a few months later by a six-week season with her show in Hollywood. Has made many tours of Australia which has become a second home to him, and appeared in no less than 18 Royal Command Performances. His recording career came about when he sang a song with 'Archie' in the long running radio series of the 50s, *Educating Archie*. His first big hit was *Cowpuncher's Cantata* in 1952, followed by *Gilly Gilly Ossenfeffer Katzenellen Bogen by the Sea* and *Heart of my Heart* which were both Top 10 entries. Other hits in the 50s included his own composition *You Need Hands* which won him the Ivor Novello Award in 1958. He has written many songs over the years, and when he wrote his autobiography in 1976, wrote the perfect song to go with it, *Back in my Childhood Days*. Having had considerable success with singles up to the beginning of the 70s when *Deck of Cards* was a Top 20 entry, he hit on the idea of an album of sing-along songs after his mother complained she couldn't listen to the radio anymore because of the twanging guitars and words she couldn't understand. *Sing Along with Max* was not a great success . . . at first, but the Australians loved it and awarded him a Gold Disc which was flown over to be presented on his television show, *Max*, which was running at the time. After the presentation, MD Geoff Love suggested Max sing a medley of songs from the album which up until then had sold very few copies in the UK. So, with Bob Dixon at the piano, he did just that. The next day the telephone started to ring in record shops around the country. The record company couldn't press the records quickly enough. Within four weeks of that television show, he had won himself another Gold Disc, this time in the UK. It was to be the first of several, as sing-along album followed sing-along album, all of them high in the charts. His next television series became *Singalongamax* which sold even more albums. Then came *Singalongparty Song*, *Singalongxmas* and *100 Golden Greats*, even the change of title didn't make any difference, it reached No. 3 in the charts. His 1984 album has him singing *Family Favourites* and provided he doesn't run out of songs, he's found a market for life! His films include *Charley Moon,* 1953; *A Cry from the Streets,* 1957; *Spare the Rod*, 1961. His autobiography *I Wanna Tell You a Story* was published in 1976 and his first novel, *The Milkman's on his Way*, in 1977. In 1973 was named Variety Club of Great Britain Show Business Personality of the Year. Was awarded the OBE in 1982.

■ Highspot of career: 'Is something I didn't do! I was appearing on *Sunday Night at the London Palladium* and seated in Claridges Hotel watching me was Alfred Hitchcock who was over in London making what turned out to be his last film, *Frenzy*. You see, you never know who's watching you. Anyway, he liked what he saw, looked at copies of all my old films and asked me to play the part of the murderer in *Frenzy*. When all the contracts had been agreed, I had to get out of two weeks at the Golden Garter in Manchester and they had sold so many tickets that they wouldn't release me, so I lost the film. But being asked by Hitchcock to star in one of his films has to be a highspot. Another was being asked to a private lunch with the Queen at Buckingham Palace.' ■ A moment to remember: 'About 18 months before he died, I was sitting with Tommy Cooper in a pub when someone came over to ask for our autographs. This chap said, like they all do, "I wanna tell you a story". After he'd gone Tommy said to me, "Did you ever actually say, I wanna tell you a story, because I never said 'Just like that'. People would come up to me after a show and get quite annoyed because I hadn't said. 'Just like that', but I didn't say

it, because I didn't know how to say it!" And it's true, neither of us originated those sayings. They were invented for us by the impressionists! Mind you we made good use of them afterwards!' ■ Likes every kind of food (apart from escargots), good plain cooking, ale and cider. Dislikes politicians. 'I don't trust them'. ■ Married to Blossom, has two daughters, one son and five grandchildren. Lives in London and Dorset.

CHAS AND DAVE
'We want people to have a good time . . .'

Chas (Charles Hodges)
BORN: 28th December 1943 in Edmonton, London. Father, who died when Chas was four, played the mouth organ. Mother, Daisy, played piano in pubs. **EDUCATED:** Eldon Road School, Edmonton. At the age of six was given his first guitar, known as Rosie, by an uncle. Taught himself to play by listening to records and picking out the guitar part. Much later taught himself to read music. At 15, needing a new guitar to play gigs, the only way he could afford one was to win the money in a talent contest. He was given a lift to the pub where the contest was being held, but got lost in the fog on the way so missed it. But his mother, worried about him, set out for the pub, entered the contest on piano and won. So he was able to buy his guitar after all! At 18, standing in for Jerry Lee Lewis at rehearsals for a show in Edmonton, he got so carried away he started impersonating his idol. At that moment Jerry Lee Lewis came into the hall and said, 'What the hell do you need me for when you've got him?' **FIRST JOB:** Watch repairer, but he got the sack because he kept falling asleep. He joined Mike Berry and the Outlaws, who on one occasion were topping a bill which included an unknown group from Liverpool called the Beatles. Also played with Cliff Bennett and the Rebel Rousers.

■ Likes rock 'n' roll, some Country music, pie and mash.
■ Married to Joan, has two daughters, Juliet and Kate, one son, Nick and lives in Hertfordshire.

Dave (Dave Peacock)

BORN: 24th May 1945 in Ponders End, London. **EDUCATED:** Elmer Road School, Ponders End. His father bought him his first guitar for 30s. from Woolworths when he was six. 'The first music I heard was my Uncle Bill playing the banjo at parties and I was mad about that sound.' It was Uncle Bill who gave him his first lessons on the banjo. **FIRST JOB:** Sign writer. He joined a group called the Rolling Stones who deciding that was a stupid name, changed it to the Raiders! Also played with a Country & Western line-up, the Tumbleweeds.

■ Likes rock 'n' roll, some country music and stewed eels. ■ Married to Sue and lives in Hertfordshire.

Mick Burt

BORN: 23rd August 1938. **FIRST JOB:** Plumber. Was a drummer with Cliff Bennett and the Rebel Rousers at the same time as Chas was with them, but when the group folded, he left the business and went back to being a plumber. Asked to join Chas and Dave in 1975, he remains very much in the background of the trio.

■ Married to Wendy, has one son and one daughter and lives in Middlesex.

Chas and Dave first met in 1961 when Chas was with Mike Berry and the Outlaws and Dave was with the Raiders, and Brian Juniper, another member of the Raiders, gave Chas a lift one night after he'd missed the last bus home. They found they had a lot in common musically but it was to be 10 years before, disillusioned with the pop scene, they joined forces in 1972 to write and perform the kind of songs they had both grown up with in sing-songs around the piano at home. They played gigs with Chas on guitar and Dave on bass in such pubs as The Prince of Wales Gravesend, The Essex Arms in the East End and Cooks Ferry Inn at Edmonton. Having built up quite a following in the London area, they released their first album, *One Fing and Annuver* in 1975. It included a song called *Gertcha*. That same year they invited Mick Burt to join them on drums to make it a trio although they decided to go on calling themselves Chas and Dave. It was a chance encounter in an Islington pub that put them into a different league. An advertising agency executive happened to hear them singing *Gertcha*. With the new Courage Beer campaign in the planning stages, it seemed to be the perfect song. The rest is history. *Gertcha* became a nationwide catchword and the song released as a single entered the charts. Twenty years after their first meeting, Chas and Dave were on their way. 'We were never pushing to become famous, we just thought we'd make a living,' said Chas. 'We wanted to write songs and pay the rent. We weren't making a dash for stardom,' said Dave. Their first Top 10 entry was *Rabbit* in 1980, released on their own record label, Rockney. Women's Libbers described it as a sexist song, so they promptly wrote *Beer Belly* to compensate! 1982 was a good year with *Ain't No Pleasing You* reaching the No.2 spot in the charts and their own Christmas Day television show which was so successful that they were given their own Saturday night series in the summer of 1983. But it's not only Cockney audiences who are bowled over by Chas and Dave. They made their first tour of Australia in 1983 and returned down under in 1984; the same year they made a hit with the Arabs in the Middle East! After more than a decade of playing everthing from old people's homes to a Christmas season at London's Dominion Theatre, they sum up their success quite simply: 'We want people to have a good time. Basically, that's what it's all about.'

■ A moment to remember: Touring the country in their none too clean white Range Rover, they were flagged down by the police one night, who were on the lookout for a similar vehicle. 'When they realized who we were, they wouldn't let us go until we'd sung *Gertcha* and autographed their note books!'

ANGELA CHRISTIAN
'Please say hello to the ansaphone . . .'

BORN: 20th April 1948 in Edgware, Middlesex. Father a caterer. **EDUCATED:** Grammar school, Twickenham. Secretarial college in Kingston, Surrey and Torquay, Devon. Had no formal musical training but sang in local choirs. Taught herself to play the guitar. **FIRST JOB:** Resident singer/guitarist with a trio at the Imperial Hotel, Torquay in 1965. Also spent a year singing at the New Stanley Hotel in Nairobi and six months in a hotel in Bahrain. Toured with the Syd Lawrence Orchestra for a year and has also appeared with the Don Lusher Big Band. Made her first broadcast, she thinks, in March 1966 in an OB from the Imperial Hotel, Torquay with the Steven Evans Trio for *Swingalong* on the BBC Light Programme. Broadcasts regularly with the BBC Radio Orchestra, BBC Big Band and the Brian Dee Trio.

■ Most exciting moment of career: 'My first "live" concert for radio, part of the BBC Festival of Light Music from the Royal Festival Hall in June 1979, with the Syd lawrence Orchestra. Also my trip to Nairobi.' ■ Likes reading, sewing and dressmaking. Dislikes housework, tripe and onions, and people who hang up without saying anything when her Ansaphone answers the telephone. ■ Is single and lives in Avon.

TONY CHRISTIE (Tony Fitzgerald)
'Oh that Tony, he can make that voice talk . . .'
BORN: 25th April 1943 in Conasborough, Nr. Doncaster. Father an accountant. **EDUCATED:** Various schools in Conasborough area. Taught himself to play piano and guitar and sang in both school and church choirs. 'I was a good Catholic boy and sang at Mass every Sunday.' **FIRST JOB:** A wages clerk in a steel works. At the age of 17 formed a singing duo with a friend performing Everley Brothers songs in local clubs. 'Our first paid job was singing in a club near Conasborough on the same bill as comedian Norman Collier. We were terrible; very inexperienced and amateurish.' After a couple of years he went solo, did a BBC audition and made his first broadcast for producer Ron Belchier. 'I was very much in awe of Ron as he was the sound effects man on the *Goon Show*, and that used to be my favourite show. When I first went solo, I didn't like it. I missed the company of working with someone else and also the backing groups in the clubs were so bad. So for a time I formed my own group.' He changed his name to Christie after seeing the film *Darling*. 'I fell in love with Julie Christie!' It was while he was doing The Blackpool Command Show in 1967 that he was 'discovered' by Harvey Lisberg, the manager of 10CC and Herman's Hermits. In 1970 he was offered a recording contract and the following year had his first hit *Las Vegas*. Then came *What I did for Maria* which got to No.2 in the charts and *Is this the Way to Amarillo*. He became very popular on the Continent, particularly in

Germany and Spain, and also had hit records down-under, in Australia and New Zealand. He has two Gold Discs, several Silver ones and a Platinum Album.

■ Highspots of career: 'My very first record, although at the time I really didn't appreciate it. It all happened so quickly and then I was off touring the world. But now I'm doing a lot of writing with Peter Callander who wrote a lot of my early hits, and I've done an album on which 10 out of the 12 songs were mine.' ■ A moment to remember: 'I came off stage in Dublin one night and I overheard one of my fans, who was queueing to get my autograph, say to one of the musicians who was passing, "Oh that Tony, he can make that voice talk." And also in Dublin (this is turning into an Irish joke) a man once said to me, "With a voice like that, you'll never have to work." ■ Likes nice wine. Dislikes toilet seats that don't stand up by themselves, it makes it a very difficult operation!' ■ Married to Sue, has a son, Sean, two daughters, Antonia and Sarah, and lives in the West Midlands.

PETULA CLARK
'From child star to international stardom . . .'
BORN: 15th November 1932 in Epsom, Surrey. Father a male nurse. **EDUCATED:** Moor Lane Elementary School, St Bernard's, Surbiton. Romanoff, Surbiton. 'I got my first radio series when I was nine years old, and the producer, Cecil Madden, thought I should go to a better school than Moor Lane, so that's when I moved to St Bernard's in Surbiton. I also took dancing lessons with Gladys Dare, but I was never very good and I still can't dance very well.' **FIRST JOB:** She was working on radio at nine and made her film debut at 12 in *A Medal for the General*, but she can't really remember how it all came about. 'My mother was Welsh, so we went to chapel and I sang in the choir. I used to sing around the house a lot and sang in school concerts. But what I do remember, very vividly, is the first time I sang with an orchestra. The performance was at Bentalls in Kingston, and after being used to singing with only a piano, there was this marvellous sensation of being backed by a full orchestra. It was tremendous experience and one I have never forgotten.' She was put under contract by J. Arthur Rank and made several pictures, among them *The Card*, in which she gave Alec Guinness his first screen kiss. Like all child stars she was longing to be given more adult roles and wanted desperately to grow up. 'At 17 I was still in ankle socks, but yearning with all my heart to be beautiful and mysterious like Ingrid Bergman!' She had several hit records throughout the 50s, but it was the move to France at the end of the decade that was to bring her international stardom as a singer. Recording company PR executive Claude Wolff became her manager and also married her and groomed her for a world-wide market. Early in 1965 she made the top of the American charts with *Downtown* and won her first Grammy. Three weeks later she again hit the No.1 spot with *My Love* and won another Grammy for *I Know a Place*. For the remainder of the 60s her records invariably did better in the States than in the UK. She spent a fair amount of her time in America making many television appearances, including three of her own network specials, among them the now legendary hour with Harry Belafonte. She also guested on the Flip Wilson, Carol Burnett, Dean Martin, Glen Cambell and Andy Williams Shows, and stopped the show at the 1971 Academy Awards

singing *For All We Know*, which won Song of the Year honours. Her popularity in America led to her being cast opposite Fred Astaire in *Finian's Rainbow* in 1968 and the following year, back in the UK, she co-starred in a musical version of *Goodbye Mr Chips* with Peter O'Toole. She sings all over the world, recently breaking the 44-year house record for attendance at the Empire Room of New York's Waldorf Astoria. She has won French awards, German awards, Italian awards, British awards, American awards, her favourite being the time she was named 'First Lady of Memphis'; and they're all stored away in a little cubby hole in her home in Switzerland. 'Well, I have to keep them somewhere!' She is the first to admit she's happiest when working in front of an audience and 1981 found her re-creating the role of Maria in a revival of *The Sound of Music* in London, playing to packed houses for more than year. Her ambition is to star in a really good modern musical. 'What I am looking for is a sensational play with good contemporary music.' Petula Clark is something of a show business phenomenon; a child star at 10, she has never relinquished her hold on an audience and, now in her 50s, she is an international star of considerable standing. The secret of her success has undoubtedly been the fact that she has never allowed herself to be typecast. Her tremendous versatility has allowed her to move with the times. One tends to forget that she was turning out hit records a couple of generations ago, as she is essentially a modern singer, and there is no greater compliment one can pay her than that.

■ Highspots of career: 'There have been so many of them; from the time I sang in a charity concert at the Royal Albert Hall in London when I was 10, to receiving a standing ovation at the Academy Awards ceremony in Los Angeles in 1971—it's very difficult to pick out just one.' ■ A moment to remember: 'One night during *The Sound of Music*, I was making my entrance after the honeymoon, when for the first time the audience sees me wearing smart clothes. Well, the door opened I stepped through, tripped and fell flat on my face. The rest of the cast looked at me aghast. The audience were totally confused, trying desperately to remember whether that happened in the original show and the film. I managed to struggle to my feet and there I was, with my hat over one eye and my stockings all laddered, I must have looked a sight. But when we'd all got over the shock of it, of course, we had a fit of hysteria and the audience, who by that time had realized it was an accident, were marvellous. I really hurt myself that night too!' ■ Likes the sun and good French cooking. Dislikes cigarette smoke and snobs.
■ Married to Claude Wolff, has two daughters, Barbara and Kate, and one son, Patrick, and lives in Switzerland.

TAMMY CLINE
'Top Country award five years in a row . . .'
BORN: 16th June, 1953 in Hull, Humberside. (It was Yorkshire then!) Father a builder. EDUCATED: David Lister School, Hull. 'I didn't like music much while I was at school, although they had a folk band which I sang with.' FIRST JOB: Canteen assistant at the Hull Daily Mail. She then worked in the Reckett's factory in Hull. While there, she went to a pub one night with a girl friend where there was a resident band, The Falcons. They were asking for volunteers to come up on the stage and sing and her friend persuaded her to have a go. The result was that the band offered her a job! After a few

months of getting up at 7.30am to work in the factory, having got to bed at 3am after singing with the band, she decided to pack in the day job. 'I was only working three or four nights a week with the band, but still earning more money than I earned at the factory. Meanwhile she had married Rod Boulton, the guitarist with the Falcons, and together they formed a duo, Tammy and Dave Cline. In order to get a chance to audition for the Wembley Festival, they joined a local band, Uncle Sam, but every time they entered the talent competitions that would have gained them entry to Wembley, they came third. However, she was beginning to gain recognition in country music circles and was soon being offered radio and television dates, as a solo artiste. Her first big break came with an appearance on ITV's *Search for a Star*. 'That was the happiest and saddest week of my life. I was treated like a queen all week, with glamorous dresses to wear, like I had never worn before. When the show finished on Saturday night and the audience had left, I went into my dressing room and the beautiful dresses and shoes had gone and I just stood there in my bra and pants and felt like crying!' Backed by her own group The Southern Comfort Band, she has become one of the UK's top country singers over the past few years, and has now made several appearances at the Wembley Festival. She has been named Best British Female Country Vocalist of the Year five years in succession, 1980 through to 1984. In July 1984 represented Britain at the International Country & Western Music Association Awards Gala in Fort Worth, Texas.

■ Highspot of career: 'I've always had two ambitions, to go to America and sing in Nashville. In 1980 I was invited to represent Britain at the International Fan Fair Show in Nashville, so I achieved both those ambitions at the same time. I shall never forget that night. I had to sing in front of an audience of 20,000 and I was so frightened that my husband literally had to push me onto the stage. But once I was there, it was fabulous. I only sang four songs and I could have carried on for ever. It was just incredible.' ■ A moment to remember: 'I once did a television show with Eddie Braben and Eli Woods, and a few weeks later, I was asked to go back and do the rest of the series. As far as I knew I was just singing a song as I had done before, but when I started to sing this slow ballad on the first of the shows, the audience began to laugh and I couldn't think why. I thought perhaps my knickers were falling down, but I looked over my shoulder and there were Eddie Braben and Eli Woods doing a comedy routine while I was singing and they hadn't even told me about it. Of course I fell apart! But from then on that was the routine each week, although I had to keep a straight face, which wasn't easy. But it was good fun, once I knew what was going on!' ■ Likes driving (she's recently passed her test), and Indian food. ■ Dislikes housework, 'but I can't bear a scruffy house. I don't like people who assume that because you're a female vocalist, you're going to hate every other female vocalist.' ■ Married to Rod Boulton, has one daughter Melanie, one son Richard and lives in Humberside. 'But I'm Yorkshire not a Humbersider!'

COLORADO
'Country music is not as narrow as it used to be . . .'

Gordon Davidson (Gordy)
(Vocals, guitar, mandolin)
BORN: 2nd November 1956 in Dornoch, Sutherland, Scotland. Father a shopkeeper. EDUCATED: Dornoch Primary School; Dornoch Academy. Started playing guitar at 14 and mandolin at 17. FIRST JOB: Crofter. Founder member of Colorado. Runs a small croft of some 30 acres on the hills

overlooking Durnoch on which he rears sheep and grows hay, potatoes and turnips. 'We can be down in the South of Scotland in five hours and in London in 12 and I've no intention of leaving my croft for life in a city. I'd rather sacrifice a day's travelling time and live where I do.'

■ Likes fresh air, animals, playing darts. ■ Dislikes big cities, cold weather and fish dishes. ■ Is a bachelor and lives in Sutherland.

Geordie Jack
(Vocals, guitar, fiddle)
BORN: 20th April 1950 in Dingwall, Scotland. Father a labourer. EDUCATED: Golspie High School. Started playing acoustic guitar when he was eight years old. Took up the fiddle in 1981. FIRST JOB: Travelling salesman. He was also a shop manager before opening his own music shop in Golspie which he still runs. Founder member of Colorado.

■ Likes the cinema, cheery faces and happy people. ■ Dislikes changing his guitar strings and packing his suitcase. ■ Married to Irene, has two sons, Kevin and Trevor, one daughter, Kimberley, and lives in Sutherland.

David Duncan (Dado)
(Vocals, bass guitar)
BORN: 9th January 1956 in Golspie, Sutherland. EDUCATED: Golspie Primary School; Golspie High School. Learnt to play most brass instruments at school and took up bass guitar in 1974. FIRST JOB: Baker. (He went into music for the dough!) Founder member of Colorado.

■ Likes fry-ups, Indian food, darts and lager. ■ Dislikes unpunctuality, smoking in confined spaces and pubs that serve whiskies in tiny one-sixth of a gill measures. ■ Married to Shona and lives in Sutherland.

Allan Thompson (Tomp)
(Steel guitar)
BORN: 17th December 1950 in Elgin, Morayshire. EDUCATED: Elgin Academy. Started playing guitar in 1970 and took up the steel guitar eight years later. FIRST JOB: Lorry driver. Joined Colorado in June 1983.

■ Likes darts, golf, fishing, sunshine and walking his dog. ■ Dislikes bein cooped up in the van. ■ Is a bachelor and lives in Morayshire.

Finlay Grant
(Drums, vocals)
BORN: 8th July 1950 in Elgin, Morayshire. EDUCATED: Elgin Academy. Started playing drums at 14. Was a session drummer in London before joining Colorado in January 1984.

■ Likes working with wood and cooking pizzas. ■ Dislikes the cold and mean people. ■ Is a bachelor and lives in Morayshire.

It all started at a talent competition in a Country Club in Inverness in 1978. An unknown group, New Release were on the list of contestants. When they turned up in their white suits, they announced themselves as Colorado, having decided on a name change en route to the club. They won that night and have been winning awards ever since. 'We never really intended to get into Country music as there's not many musicians to pick from. We originally planned a five-piece band with trumpet and saxophone, but when Dado who played trumpet had teeth trouble, he switched to bass, we recruited a steel guitar and sort of drifted into Country. In a small country area like ours (they all originally came from Golspie, Sutherland) you have to be versatile because you have to cater for all ages, but the requests for Country music became so popular it just seemed to grow from there. We enjoy the Country music we've gotten into and we've never tried to be Western or American.' Perhaps that's why they are so popular with Americans. After coming second in the Marlboro Talent Contest at Wembley in 1979, they backed Box Car Willie on both his 1980 and 1981 European tours. This led to an invitation to appear at the Grand Ole Opry in Nashville in June 1981, the first Scottish act to appear at that world famous venue. In 1982 they chalked up another first by venturing behind the Iron Curtain to top the bill in Budapest. Described once as 'a splendid example of well groomed young manhood', their suits and frilly shirts drew a few whistles from the crowd accustomed to seeing their stars in T shirts and jeans! 1983 found them back in the States representing Britain at the International Fan Fair in Nashville and the International Country & Western Music Association Awards Gala in Fort Worth, Texas to which they returned in 1984. Their highly acclaimed LP *Tennessee Inspiration* recorded on their first visit to Nashville, was followed in the spring of 1984 by the album *Colorado*. Winners of the British Country Music Association's Best Group Award for three successive years, 1981–'83, they also won the Wembley Festival Award for Best British Group in 1983 and the Silk Cut Award for the Best British Group in 1984. They are heard regularly on Radio 2's *Country Club*. 'Country music is not as narrow as it used to be. A lot of barriers have come down and now it ranges right across the board. People used to think Country music was a bit hick, second class citizen's music, well that barrier has been knocked down as well. We like to think of ourselves as ambassadors for the North of Scotland.

■ Highspot of career: Playing the Grand Ole Opry in Nashville in 1981 and playing before 30,000 enthusiastic Hungarians in Budapest in 1982. ■ A moment to remember: 'When we eventually arrived in Texas in 1983 for the International Country and Western Music Association Gala, we had been travelling for 24 hours so we were pretty tired. We had been booked into the top class hotel in Forth Worth and the next day discovered that there were several functions going on at the hotel including a beauty competition to find Miss Texas and a Gay Convention! We don't see much of either up in Golspie so we must all have had our mouths open, glaikit. (for the benefit of Southern readers, 'glaikit' means . . . well, the way you look when your mouth's hanging open!)'.

GEMMA CRAVEN
'We're sending you the slipper to see if it fits . . .'
BORN: 1st June 1950 in Dublin, Eire. Father a Superintendent PTA for Ford Motor Company. EDUCATED: Loretta College, St Stephen's Green, Dublin. St Bernard's Convent, Westcliff. Bush Davies Dancing School, Romford, Essex. She studied piano from the age of five, passing all the Associated Board exams. FIRST JOB: Playing the part of the maid in *Let's Get a Divorce* at the Palace Theatre, Westcliff. After appearing in the provincial theatre in Westcliff, Blackpool and Watford, made her first appearance in London's West End, when she

played a minor role in *Fiddler on the Roof* at Her Majesty's. Subsequently appeared in two seasons at the Chichester Festival and with the Bristol Old Vic playing principal roles in both straight and musical productions. Back in the West End, she played the title role in *Trelawny* at the Prince of Wales in 1972; *Dandy Dick* at the Garrick, 1973; *Songbook* at the Globe, 1979; *They're Playing Our Song* at the Shaftesbury, 1980; *Song and Dance* at the Palace Theatre, 1983; *Loot* at the Ambassadors, 1984. It was her role in the 1976 Royal Performance film, *The Slipper and the Rose*, playing opposite Richard Chamberlain, which showed her to be a talented singer and dancer as well as an actress; a position she consolidated with her much praised performance in the 1978 television series, *Pennies From Heaven*. 1984 sees the release of the epic film *Wagner* in which she stars opposite Richard Burton. In 1976 she was named Most Promising New Actress in Films by the *Evening News* and won the Variety Club's Film Actress of the Year Award. In 1980 she won the Society of West End Theatre's Best Actress in a Musical Award for her performance in *They're Playing Our Song*.

■ Highspots of career: In television, *Pennies From Heaven*. Also winning the Best Actress in a Musical Award, and playing a highly dramtic role as Wagner's first wife opposite Richard Burton in *Wagner*. ■ A moment to remember: 'When director Bryan Forbes telephoned me to let me know that I'd won the role of Cinderella in *The Slipper and the Rose*, he didn't actually tell me that I had. He simply said, "We're sending you the slipper to see if it fits", and assumed I'd realize I'd got the part, only I didn't and I was too nervous to say I didn't quite understand! So I spent the whole of

Easter 1975 in a state of suspense until my agent heard officially after the holiday that I *had* got the part!' ■ Likes good friends, good food and good wine all together! ■ Dislikes people who telephone but won't leave a message on the answering machine. ■ Lives in London and Yorkshire.

CULTURE CLUB
'A brand of pop for young and old alike . . .'

Mikey Craig (Bass)
BORN: 15th February 1960 in London. At five years old was a fan of the Monkees. Was a good footballer at school and was offered trials with Fulham and Brentford, both of which he turned down because he wanted to be involved with music. Started to go to discos and clubs as soon as he looked old enough to be allowed in. Was a DJ at the Club Sept in London's Soho. Also worked on the roads and as a studio tape operator. Taught himself to play bass guitar. Following the birth of his two children, moved to Bristol for two years where he played with various semi-pro groups. On his return to London, having spotted a photo of George O'Dowd with Bow Wow Wow in a music paper, he caught up with him in a club and told him, 'I wanna be in a band with you, I'm a bass player.' 'At first he didn't know where we were going. It was a learning as we go type of thing and I remember feeling very excited.'

■ Likes dancing and football. ■ Has one son, Kito, one daughter, Amber.

Roy Hay
(Guitar, keyboards)
BORN: 12th August 1961 in Southend, Essex. Father a docker. **EDUCATED:** School in Corringham near Basildon, Essex. Taught himself to play guitar. **FIRST JOB:** Insurance clerk for three years. Worked as a hairdresser in Stamford while looking around for other musicians to form a band. In 1981 joined Russian Bouquet, a band run by the brother of his girl friend Alison Green whom he married in 1982. Auditioned for Culture Club, after a former insurance colleague, Keith Giddons, put him in touch with George O'Dowd. 'It's a good songwriting outfit. We're not just dummies for George, we're a band and we collectively write and produce music.'

■ Likes writing songs. 'I'm totally absorbed in music, that's always been the main thing in my life.' Dislikes all kinds of publicity that interfere with his music. ■ Married to Alison.

Jon Moss (Drums)
BORN: 11th September 1957 in London. Adopted by a Jewish family at birth. Father Managing Director of a clothing store. **EDUCATED:** Highgate School, London, where he obtained four 'O' levels, and three 'A' levels in English, Politics and History. Started playing drums at school. **FIRST JOB:** In his father's store. After two months, left to work as a tape operator at the Marquee Studios. Also worked as a cake salesman ('I didn't

sell any'), an apprentice printer, a van driver and errand boy for a music company.

First attempt to form his own band Phone Bone met with little success. He then auditioned for and joined The Clash. Other bands followed, London, The Damned, The Edge, none of them what he was looking for. He did some sessions with Adam Ant before the 'phone call from George O'Dowd, asking him to join Culture Club. 'At last I was allowed to do what I wanted and I was appreciated.'

Boy George (George O'Dowd)

BORN: 14th June 1961 in London. Father a builder. **EDUCATED:** Eltham Green Comprehensive School, London. He didn't like school and tried to avoid it as often as he could. His headmaster is quoted as saying: 'He wouldn't come to school and he wouldn't work when we got him here. He was more skilful than any pupil I have ever known at playing hookey. He knew what he wanted—no school.' Finally he was expelled. **FIRST JOB:** One week in Tesco's. Also worked as a salesman in a clothes shop in the Kings Road, Chelsea and did some modelling but more often than not was on the dole and living rough in a series of squats—old crumbling houses that were used as meeting places for art students and fashion designers who had no money and no jobs. It was then that he started to adopt his way-out mode of dress. It didn't matter how you dressed but you had to have style. George had it. He became friendly with aspiring fashion designer Michael Eggleton and the two of them would tour the junk shops and Oxfam shops buying the most outrageous clothes and jewellery they could find. Their outlandish gear made them a natural target for the Teddy Boys, as Michael recalls: 'Once we were on a bus going to Portobello Market and sitting next to us was a Teddy Boy and his girl friend. When they got up to leave the bus the Ted came over and punched George on the nose. But George didn't always get the bumps. When a crowd of us punks were walking over Waterloo Bridge and came up against a crowd of Teds, I looked round for George and he'd vanished. He was always good at that when there was trouble.' In 1977, disillusioned and out of work, George went to Birmingham, but the following year found him back in London living in a squat near Warren Street. When the Royal Shakespeare Company produced *Naked Robots* they wanted an authentic punk look and George was brought in to advise on the costumes. This led to a job window-dressing for Street Theatre, a clothes shop in Newburgh Street. 'But it was all so shallow. I wanted to do something more valuable, so I got involved with music and started writing lyrics to songs.' Malcolm McLaren, one time manager of the Sex Pistols, was holding auditions for singers at the Rainbow Theatre in Finsbury Park and George went along and got himself a job as joint singer with Annabella in McLaren's Bow Wow Wow. It didn't last. He fell out with McLaren and left. He had already met bassist Mikey Craig, and when he was introduced to drummer Jon Moss by a mutual friend, the foundation of Culture Club had been laid. Guitarist Roy Hay was the final member to be recruited and they got themselves set up with a few gigs. It was at one of these that they were seen by Danny Goodwin, talent spotter from Virgin Records. When he approached George and said he was interested, the reply was surprising: 'You're not serious?' 'Yeah, I think you're really good,' said Danny. 'Come off it, we're useless.' But in spite of the false modesty, Culture Club had got themselves a recording contract. Their

first two singles passed without notice, but the third, *Do You Really Want To Hurt Me*, was in the charts within two weeks and in October 1982 reached the No.1 spot. Within a year they were back at the top of the charts with *Karma Chameleon*. Whether it was the music or the image, Boy George and Culture Club scored an immediate hit across the Atlantic with their debut album *Kissing To Be Clever*, selling over a million copies and producing three Top 10 singles, the most to come from one album since the Beatles. Their next album, *Colour By Numbers*, sold more than two and a half million copies in the States and gave them two more Top 10 singles. From being penniless and unknown, Boy George, within the space of two years, was an international star and a multimillionaire. So, what's it all about, what makes him tick? 'I can't answer that one. I don't think you ever know yourself, that's why most psychiatrists or analysts are a waste of time. All I know is I'm not like David Bowie's Ziggy Stardust. I haven't created a stage persona, I am what you see.' Whether you like or don't like what you see, he is impossible to ignore and it came as no big surprise that he carried off the *Daily Mirror* Outstanding Personality of the Year Award in 1982. He did it again in 1983 when Culture Club also took the award for the Best Single with *Karma Chameleon*. Although Boy George is out front as singer and spokesman for the band, it has always been a very democratic affair. When he first met Jon Moss he told him, 'I don't want you to play drums *for* me, I want you to start a band *with* me.' And it's Jon who has been the steadying influence on the group, handling all business matters. Roy Hay is undoubtedly the strongest on the musical side. Together the three of them have come up with a brand of pop that is acceptable to both young and old alike.

■ **A MOMENT TO REMEMBER:** The scene, Nice Airport. Boy George and Culture Club are en route to the San Remo Music Festival. Immigration officials examine Boy George's passport. George O'Dowd. Sex: Male. they look at him, at the carefully made-up face and the full-length blue and silver kimono. They look back at the passport. Finally – 'Non' say the immigration men, he will not be allowed in unless he looks like a man. 'Shan't,' says George. The argument continues for three hours. Eventually after a telephone call from the British Consulate, the local police chief is called in and decides that Boy George and Culture Club are not worth a diplomatic incident. They are allowed in. George's comment: 'The French managed to stop our lamb, but they couldn't stop me.' ■ Likes dressing up, and all kinds of music. ■ Dislikes snobs.

NICK CURTIS
'Just one Cornetto . . .'

BORN: 9th June 1942 in St Austell, Cornwall. Father was Steward at King's School, Canterbury, which had been evacuated to Carlyon Bay. **EDUCATED:** Canterbury Cathedral Choir School; King's School, Canterbury; Royal College of Music, London. Studied singing and the French horn at the Royal College but gave up the horn when he was told it was bad for his singing. In its place took up classical guitar and dutifully called his professor 'Sir' even though he was only six months older than Nick himself, his name – John Williams.

Studied singing under Heddle Nash, Gerald English and Ruth Packering. **FIRST JOB:** Singing tenor in the *Messiah* while at the Royal College. 'We had to have the Director's permission to do any outside work and there was no problem regarding such works as the *Messiah*, but then Nigel Brookes asked me to do a summer show for him and the Director of the College said, "No, you could do your voice irreparable harm by singing in the chorus." The following week Nigel rang and asked him to do a TV show, and this time Nick didn't ask permission, and appeared on *Saturday Night Out* with Ted Ray, David Hughes and Yana. Nobody noticed, but when he accepted a series of *Stars and Garters* somebody spotted him in vision, shopped him to the RCM and he was asked to leave. But when the series came to an end after the summer holidays, he rang up and asked the Royal College to take him back again, and they did. He has sung with every vocal group and every choral director in the country. Has made numbereous commericals including the famous 'Just One Cornetto' which, rumour has it, the Princess of Wales hummed on her way to her wedding! He specializes in foreign languages, having done a world-wide campaign for MacDonald's singing in Dutch, French, German and Italian. Has also made a jingle for Kiwi shoe polish in Arabic.

■ Highspots of career: 'Certainly one of them was when I took a solo part in the opera *Il Tabarro* on a Tito Gobbi television series featuring him in his various roles. But the greatest delight for me is the pure variety of the work I do; for instance backing a heavy metal group on the *Old Grey Whistle Test* and the next day backing Placido Domingo at the Royal Festival Hall.' ■ A moment to remember: 'While I was still at the Royal College of Music, but during the holidays, I was booked by Peter Knight to do my very first pop session at a studio in Baker Street at 2.30 pm. I caught the 11am train from Canterbury which stopped at every station along the line and then made an unscheduled stop half way across London Bridge. And there we sat for an hour. 2.30 came and went. "I might as well go straight home", I thought, "this is the end of my career." I eventually got to the studio at 4pm apologizing profusely to Peter who said, "Not to worry, I sang your part on the first half of the session. We're just about to start the main title." It turned out to be *Venus in Blue Jeans* which became a big hit for Mark Wynter and it was the very first pop record I ever did the backing for.' ■ Likes fast cars and drives a Mercedes. ■ Dislikes people who sing out of tune. ■ Married to Glenda, has two daughters and lives in Hertfordshire.

LORNA DALLAS
'Commended by the Queen Mother . . .'
BORN: Illinois, USA. Father a lumber dealer. **EDUCATED:** Voice and Opera Major at Indiana University School of Music, Honours Graduate Advanced Degree. Also plays piano, violin, percussion. **FIRST JOB:** Singing ambassadress for Coca-Cola after winning their national talent contest, 'Talentsville USA'. Has been a campaign worker in the election of the Governor of Indiana and was the principal artiste with Metropolitan Opera National Company singing at Lyndon Johnson's inauguration ball in Washington DC. Her first broadcast in the USA was on *The Baptist Hour*; in the UK it was for the BBC World Service in June 1972. Has sung with the Stanley Black Quartet, BBC Radio Orchestra, BBC Concert Orchestra, Stan Kenton, Peter Knight Orchestra, Iain Sutherland Orchestra, Norrie Paramor, NBC TV Orchestra and John Dankworth. Broadcasts regularly on such programmes as Festival of Light Music, *Friday Night is Music Night, Among Your Souvenirs, Charlie Chester Show, Round Midnight, Weekend Early Show*. Television credits include BBC2's *Star Brass* and BBC1's the *Good Old Days*. 1984 saw her co-starring with Danny La Rue in *Hello Dolly* at the Prince of Wales Theatre.

■ Highspot of career: 'Being commended by the Queen Mother after singing for her in the 1982 Royal Variety Performance.' ■ A moment to remember: 'Minutes before I was to make my debut at the Royal Festival Hall, I found one false eyelash hanging precariously and my adhesive dried out. In a mad panic I accepted the only substitute to be found – UHU glue. Needless to say the standing ovation was not the only lasting impression of that eventful evening. That slang expression "give me some skin!" took on a new meaning!' ■ Likes photography, shopping for clothes in New York, and reading 'Time' and 'Newsweek' from cover to cover. Dislikes early mornings, the colour green, tasteless lyrics, self service petrol stations, cooking eggs and bacon first thing in the morning, white linen, Renaissance Art, liver, kidneys, kippers and/or sardines (not separately and most definitely not together!) [Sure there's nothing else Lorna?] ■ Married to Garry Brown, has two step-children and lives in Surrey.

DANA (Rosemary Brown)
'Always wanted to be a teacher . . .'
BORN: 1952 in Londonderry, N. Ireland. Father a hairdresser who played trumpet in the local brass band. **EDUCATED:** Thornhill Convent of Mercy, Londonderry. She took piano and ballet lessons at school, and sang for fun. When she was 15 entered a local talent competition with a friend, and when the friend became ill was persuaded to sing a solo and came second. She also came second when, at 17, she auditioned for the Irish song for the Eurovision Song Contest. The following spring while studying hard for her 'A' levels, she had a surprise telephone call asking her to sing 'All Kinds of Everything', Ireland's entry in the 1970 Eurovision Song Contest. 'I'd always wanted to be a teacher, and I was hoping to be accepted for teacher training college.' But that is one ambition she was not destined to achieve. She sang Ireland's entry, and became one of the youngest winners ever. Her old schoolmates suggested she changed her name to Dana. 'I wonder if I would have made it as Rosemary Brown?' she once said in an interview. *All Kinds of Everything* went to No.1 not only in Britain but also in several European countries. Her next record was a flop, and it looked as if she could be a one-hit wonder. Then came *Who Put The Lights Out* which made it to No.14. It was to be four years before she had another hit but during that time she was learning something about the business into which she had been so unexpectedly thrown.
She appeared in pantomime at Wimbledon in 1971, and the family moved to London. In 1974 she was given her first television series, and just as it looked as if she was really on her way disaster struck. A growth on her vocal chords resulted in two operations, and it was the best part of three years before she made a full recovery. But back she came and some good came out of her enforced rest as she said afterwards, 'Without it, I don't think I would have got married because before my illness I was so tied up with my career.I just wanted to work at it non-stop. And as a result of the operations I had to take singing lessons right from scratch. So in a funny way my voice is better now than it was.'

Throughout the remainder of the 70s and into the 80s her career went from strength to strength with several chart entries – *It's Gonna be a Cold Cold Christmas, Never Gonna Fall in Love Again, Everything is Beautiful.* Made her film debut in 1978 in *The Flight of Doves*, and in 1979 was voted Britain's Top Female Vocalist of the Year. A 1981 summer season at Torquay was followed in '82 by one at Blackpool. And that Christmas found her starring in her first pantomime since 1975 at the New Theatre, Hull, in *Snow White and the Seven Dwarves*, a role she repeated with great success in London's West End at the Phoenix Theatre, the following year.

■ A Moment To Remember: The occasion she appeared in three different countries all in one day. A TV in Germany followed by a TV in Holland followed by a concert in Birmingham. ■ Likes: Music, ballet and reading, and would one day like to become a teacher as originally planned. 'I want to teach music to mentally handicapped children. But meanwhile I'm content to go with the tide and find my happiness where I may.' ■ Dislikes: Second-hand books. 'They have an old musty smell that bothers me. So any book I read has to be new.' ■ Married to Damien Scallon, has two daughters, Grace and Susanna, and lives in County Down.

ELAINE DELMAR
'A memorable midnight stroll down Bond Street . . .'
BORN: 13th September 1939 in Harpenden, Hertfordshire. Father jazz trumpeter Leslie 'Jiver' Hutchinson. **EDUCATED:** Rhodes Avenue, Wood Green; Trinity Grammar, Wood Green. Studied piano from the age of six for eleven years reaching Grade VII of the Assoicated Board exams. 'I was very talented but very lazy.' Made her first broadcast at the age of 13 playing the piano on *Children's Hour*. 'The piece chosen for me to play by my teacher was *'Le Petit Negre'*, it sounds better in French! My father was furious!' Pianist/MD

Colin Beaton, who was a friend of Elaine's father, had a big influence on her musical career. 'He used to come along to our house and play Gershwin and I would chirp along. It was Colin who got together a song repertoire for me and he did the arrangements for my very first television.' **FIRST JOB:** Singing with her father's band at American bases, while she was still at school. In 1952/53 appeared in *Finian's Rainbow* in Liverpool. She sang with a group, the Dominoes, for a short while before going solo, playing the clubs— 'Three shows a night in different clubs, I don't know how I did it.' She also did many overseas tours. Has appeared in Several West End musicals: *No Strings* at Her Majesty's 1961; *Cowardy Custard* at the Mermaid, 1972; *Bubbling Brown Sugar* at the Royalty, 1977. Has made one film, Ken Russells' *Mahler*, and in 1983 appeared in a straight play *Map of the World* at the National Theatre.

■ Highspots of career: 'Playing at the National, as it was so far removed from anything I had done before'. ■ A moment to remember: ' I was living in Los Angeles in 1969 to get my Green Card, and although I wasn't working, people knew I was a singer. I got to know guitarist Herb Ellis and his family very well and soon after I got back to London, Herb came over to make an album with Oscar Peterson and he and his wife took me to dinner one night. Afterwards they suggested we walk down Bond Street and look in the shop windows as they'd heard so much about this famous street. As we were walking along at midnight someone came running up to us, tapped me on the shoulder and said "Are you Elaine Delmar, I think you're the greatest singer I've every heard." Herb and his wife just stood there, open mouthed, before Herb said, "The lengths some people will go to impress people!' I tried to explain that it had never happened before!' ■ Likes good restaurants and Mahler. ■ Dislikes bad intonation, cigarette smoke and usually the people who are holding the cigarettes. ■ Is divorced, has one daughter, Sarah, and lives in London.

BARBARA DICKSON
'I almost became a sex symbol over night . . .'
BORN: 27th September 1947 in Dunfermline, Scotland. Father a dockyard worker. **EDUCATED:** Obtained three 'O' Levels and took piano lessons at school. **FIRST JOB:** Civil Servant working for the Ministry of Defence. At this time she was also singing for £15 a night in Scottish folk clubs and it was there that she was discovered by Bernie Theobald who is now her manager. Got her first big break in 1973 when she was asked by Willy Russell whom she knew, to play piano and sing in his new musical about the Beatles, *John, Paul, George, Ringo and Bert*, which he was putting on at Liverpool's Everyman Theatre. The show transferred to London's West End, but Barbara was still not sure she was on her way. 'Even during the London run, I still needed to be assured I wouldn't be left with nothing when the show ended so I was careful to keep up my contacts in the folk clubs.'
Her first hit record, *Answer Me*, brought about a change of image. From being on the plump side with long straight hair and glasses, she switched to contact lenses and had her hair permed, saying, 'A perm is the greatest gift that God has ever sent me, and I got contact lenses because my glasses kept sliding down my nose when I was playing the piano. But it was really when a new French make-up artist called Regis did my face for an album cover photograph that I realized what

a fantastic difference hair and make-up can make to anybody. I almost became a sex symbol overnight!' The release in 1976 of the album of *Evita*, before the stage production, gave her career another boost. Her only contribution to the record was *Another Suitcase in Another Hall*; released as a single it got to No.18 in the charts in February 1977. In December of that year she made her debut at the London Palladium with David Essex. She was already a familiar face on television, having had a regular spot on *The Two Ronnies*, and an engagement at London's top jazz venue, Ronnie Scott's, proved that she had more to offer than the average pop singer. 'I have tried to corner the market in really good ballad singing. I do only good stuff and I only put out records that I'm not ashamed of. I can't sing awful lyrics. My tongue gets tied. The words must be able to reach every single person in the audience.' In December 1980 she took on her most challenging engagement yet, a one-woman show at the Royal Albert Hall in London which, if the critics didn't rave about, they certainly didn't condemn. In 1981 and 1982 she undertook some gruelling tours, playing in many out-of-the-way places, 'Lots of people don't want to travel 35 miles to a concert in a city. But they will go round the corner to a local theatre.' She doesn't play piano in her stage act anymore; 'It's all right if you're Elton John and stand on your piano, but if I tried that I'd end up breaking a leg!' She had always said she wanted to act, looking for something that combined her love of music with acting. In 1983, her wish was granted by none other than Willy Russell who had given her her first break in Liverpool 10 years earlier. He offered her the lead in his new musical *Blood Brothers* which opened at the Liverpool Playhouse in January 1983. Three months later it transferred to the Lyric Theatre, Shaftesbury Avenue and Barbara Dickson was back in the West End. It was to be her greatest triumph yet with the Society of West End Theatre Award for the Actress of the Year in a Musical in what was named as Musical of the Year. With typical modesty she commented, 'I had to be persuaded and cajoled into taking part in *Blood Brothers*, and I'm glad I listened to Willy Russell. It's fantastic for me to win, because really I'm only a singer and a musician, not an actress.' Telling words. She is a musician as well as a singer and therein lies the secret of her success.

■ Highspot of career: Winning the Society of West End Theatre Award for Best Actress in a Musical. ■ A moment to remember: 'The night I filled the Albert Hall. It was like playing inside a wedding cake!' ■ Likes animals, children, champagne and pink shoes. ■ Dislikes cruelty to animals and to children. ■ Is single. 'I've never married but I haven't given up. Maybe the right chap will turn up one of these days. Mr Right. There's a cliché for you, but it's true.' Lives in Middlesex.

BONNIE DOBSON
'One's career becomes a compromise when one is married . . .'
BORN: 13th November 1940 in Toronto, Canada. Father a union organizer. EDUCATED: Parkdale Collegiate, Toronto. University of Toronto. 'My one claim to educational fame is that I was the Valedictorian of my class at Parkdale and my name's in gold leaf on the board! I left University after one year to concentrate on my singing.' FIRST JOB: Appearing at the Exodus Club, Denver, Colorado with the legendary Blues duo, Brownie McGee and Sonny Terry. This was followed by an engagement at the Ash Grove in Los Angeles. She emigrated to the UK in 1969 having married an Englishman. 'I had always wanted to come to Britain and getting married seemed to be a very good reason.' Made her first broadcast in the UK in 1969 on Radio 2's *Country Meets Folk* and that same year made her London concert debut at the Queen Elizabeth Hall. Has broadcast regularly ever since appearing on most of Radio 2's music programmes. Has recorded for the Prestiege International, Mercury and RCA labels. In 1983 a single *Absence of Romance* was released on the Ritz label.

■ Highspot of career: 'The concert at the Queen Elizabeth Hall in 1969, which was a fabulous year for me. When I was in Canada I was totally devoted to my singing and consequently enjoyed more success than I've had here. But I

feel when one is married with children, one's career becomes a compromise. I love living in Britain and I love being close to Europe, I don't think I could ever go back to Canada to live.' ■ A moment to remember: 'When I was singing on the club circuit in Canada and America, my path often crossed that of a singer called Peter Yarrow and once when I followed him into a club in St Louis, he left a message for me with the club owner to contact him when I got to New York as he was thinking of forming a group. I never did, but Peter Yarrow formed his group. Their names were Peter, Paul and Mary!' ■ Likes cooking, reading, skiing, riding horses and Exmoor. ■ Dislikes soggy vegetables and people who say 'She sounds like . . .' ■ Married to Christopher Beaver, has a son, a daughter and a step-daughter and lives in London and Somerset.

VAL DOONICAN
'Just be yourself and you'll be a star . . .'
BORN: 3rd February 1928, in Waterford, Eire. Father a structural steel worker. EDUCATED: St Declan's National School for Boys and De La Salle College, Waterford. Found school work heavy going, especially Latin, and was told by Brother Patrick who taught him. 'I don't know what you intend to do

for a living, but you will not do it very well.' 'I've seen him since,' said Val, 'and at least he saw the funny side of it.' While still at school, teamed up with a friend from his Scout troop, Mickey Brennan, singing duets. They sang at many village concerts, but their proudest moment was, when billed as Doonican and Brennan at a show in New Ross, they were paid the princely sum of 10s. **FIRST JOB:** Knocking nails into boxes at which he became very adept. He got paid 22s. 6d. a week and while at the factory became friendly with a pattern maker called Bruce Clarke, who played piano and guitar. They decided to work up an act and applied for an audition to appear on a Radio Eireann show, *Beginners Please*. This led to their first broadcast. His first professional engagement came in the summer of 1947, when he was booked to play in a quartet led by Bruce Clarke at a ballroom in Courtown Harbour on the south-east coast of Ireland. It was at that time he paid £20 for his first guitar: up to then he had borrowed one. After a return booking in 1948, Bruce Clarke saw an advert for pianist and drummer in a touring band. They applied and got the job. Val had never played drums in his life, apart from the kettle drum in the Scout's band, so practised night and day for the last few weeks of the summer season. On his first night with the band, it took him a very long time to assemble the drum kit which was supplied, and after a couple of hours playing, his right foot, which was working the bass drum pedal, had become completely paralysed! For the next six months he played one-night stands seven nights a week over the length and breadth of Ireland. After more touring as guitarist and vocalist with a trio, he was asked to join the Irish vocal group *The Four Ramblers* and in 1952 came to London for the first time where they were appearing on a BBC radio series, *Riders of the Range*. The next eight years were spent working in variety, cabaret and on radio. It was during a concert tour with Anthony Newley that he did a short solo spot, sitting on a stool, with his Spanish guitar, singing an Irish folk song. Newley suggested he was on to something good and why didn't he try going it alone. An audition with television producer Richard Afton led to him being given a regular spot on *Beauty Box*. A radio series followed, *Dreamy Afternoon*, on which he was the resident singer and the producer suggested he might like to do his own introductions to his songs. It was so successful that when he was offered a new series, the title of the programme was changed to *A Date With Val*. The series ran for 120 shows and changed his life. He became a household name, although he was often referred to as 'that Val bloke on the radio'. Cabaret engagements, shows at American bases and the Northern Club circuit kept him busy. In 1963, David Jacobs, who was organizing a big charity concert, asked him to appear along with such stars as Vera Lynn, Frankie Vaughan and Dickie Henderson. Dickie Henderson was so impressed with Val's performance that he mentioned him to Val Parnell who, in turn, having caught his act at the Jack of Clubs in Brewer Street, booked him for *Sunday Night at the London Palladium*. Parnell's last words to him before he went on that night were, 'Just be yourself and tomorrow, I think you'll be a star.' How right he was. Recording contracts and television offers followed; Val Doonican had arrived. His first hit record came in 1964 with *Walk Tall*. In 1966 he was voted BBC Personality of the Year and Cabaret Artiste of the Year. He has starred in his own show at the London Palladium and has appeared in three Variety shows to date. His popular television series is one of the few that go out 'live' and his final song in the rocking chair has become his trade mark. A little bit of chat, a few chords strummed on a guitar and a simple folk song have made him one of the best loved entertainers in the country.

■ A moment to remember: The night he got fired as a drummer in the middle of a tango. Suffering from a bad cold and feeling very sorry for himself, he'd just got out the parts when without warning, the band leader counted them in. Having been taken completely by surprise with no time to blow his nose, he was soon in desperate need of a hankie which he tried to get out of his pocket with one hand while playing with the other. 'Stop' shouted the band leader and everyone staggered to a halt, including the dancers. 'What do you mean by blowing your nose in the middle of a tango? You're fired.' Without more ado, Val picked up his sticks and brushes, his only possessions as a drummer, and left the stage. One of the sax players who doubled on drums was told to take over which he would have done had there been any sticks to play with. Realizing that no sticks meant no drumer, the leader gave Val a dirty look; 'Get back on those drums'. He did and the subject was never mentioned again! ■ Likes playing golf and sketching. ■ Married to Lynette Rae, has two daughters, Sarah and Fiona, and lives in Buckinghamshire.

DURAN DURAN
'The road ahead paved with gold . . .'
Nick Rhodes (Synthesizer)

BORN: 8th June 1962 in Birmingham. **EDUCATED:** School appears to have been an irrelevant episode for him! 'On my very first day, there was this classroom full of kids and I had to sit down and listen to this rather tall, skinny and almost ugly screaming dragon teach a bunch of idiots and me how to read and write. I swore when I left school that I was never gonna use any of my 'O' levels. I knew they were going to be useless to me.'

■ A moment to remember: 'When we were in Sri Lanka, strolling down the street was quite something; suddenly you turn round and there's an elephant behind you. At first it's a bit of a shock, I can tell you. I was sitting down in a restaurant when we were filming the final scene for *Hungry Like a Wolf*, and there's this snake charmer sitting down with a little pipe, turban on, basket in front of him, and I thought he's not going to . . . So I went up to him and said; "Watcha got in there eh?" He taps the basket and these two cobras come wriggling out. I think I nearly got rigor mortis!' ■ Likes art, strawberries, animals and legs. Dislikes dishonesty, heavy metal and cats eating birds. ■ Married to Julie Anne Friedman.

John Taylor (Bass guitar)

BORN: 20th June 1960 in Birmingham. Father worked in a car components factory. **EDUCATED:** Roman Catholic primary school. County high school. Art college. At 14 became interested in music and wanted to learn the guitar at school, only to be told that only proper orchestral instruments were taught! Having teamed up with Nick Rhodes, spent his year at art college designing posters for Duran Duran and gained top marks for his display at the end of his first term. But he left after one year to concentrate on music.

■ A moment to remember: During their tour of Japan they were followed by hordes of Japanese girls wherever they

went. One day John and Roger thought they would be clever and tried to sneak out of their hotel to do some shopping, but they were recognized with the result that the police had to close the store in order to get them out and escort them back to the hotel. ■ Likes sun, sea and sand. ■ Dislikes dishonesty, megalomania and arrogance. ■ Is single and lives in West Midlands.

Andy Taylor (Guitar)

BORN: 16th February 1961 in Tynemouth. Father a fisherman. **EDUCATED:** Grammar and then a comprehensive school where the syllabus was so far behind what he'd been working on in his grammar school, that he lost interest. I became a real bum and drop-out; never used to go at all. Then I became the black sheep kid at school because I had long hair and

played in groups, while all the rest of the lads were going camping or something . . . I wasn't into that. I also became the black sheep of the family— "Ooh, can you make a living doing that?" **FIRST JOB:** Playing guitar for a gig when he was 13. He played with many local groups when he was in his teens, and simply stopped going to school. By the time he answered the ad in *Melody Maker* he was an experienced guitarist, having travelled Europe with bands and having spent over a year working in Germany. His first reaction on meeting the others at his audition: 'they were like the biggest bunch of weirdos I'd ever seen. Which turned us on straight away, cos I'd always felt like being weird, but I had no one to be weird with in Newcastle.'

■ Highspots of career: The world tour in 1982. 'I'm thankful

29

that I could even just go out there, go right round the other side of the world and see all that, which I'd never ever have done had I not been in the band.' ■ Likes Bourbon, Guinness and lots of loud guitars. ■ Dislikes hangovers, bad organization and losing his temper. ■ Married to Tracey Wilson.

Roger Taylor: 26th April 1960 in Castle Bromwich, West Midlands. Became interested in music when he was 10 years old and went to see the Jackson Five. Listened to his elder brother's collection of Tamla Motown records, but at 15 started collected Genesis records. Learnt to play the drums and while still at school organized several different bands. FIRST JOB: Playing with a punk band in a Birmingham club when he was 17.

■ Likes the 40s, 50s, and 60s, and black and white films. ■ Dislikes science fiction, cats and flying. ■ Married to Giovanna and lives in West Midlands.

Simon Le Bon (Vocals)
BORN: 27th October 1958 in Bushey, Hertfordshire. EDUCATED: Sixth form college. Birmingham University, (one year drama course). His family is descended from the French Huguenots. Attended acting classes from the age of five and sang in the choir of Pinner Parish Church, singing solos and making his first record. While in his teens he fronted a band called Dog Days. FIRST JOB: Working in a hospital, while taking an 'A' level evening course, having failed his 'A' levels at sixth form college. He was accepted for a drama course at Birmingham University but, during the summer term of his first year, heard from a girl friend who worked at the Rum Runner in Birmingham, that Duran Duran were looking for a new singer. He thought it might be a fun thing to do for the summer, so he put on his sunglasses and a pair of pink-spotted leopardskin trousers and went for an audition! As well as his trousers, they liked his singing and his lyric writing, so he got the job. He said sometime afterwards, 'They seemed to have some sense. They weren't interested in doing it as a hobby, they were thinking in professional terms and what I really wanted to do was to get up on a stage and perform, not train for it but actually do it.'

An early version of the group was formed in 1978 in Birmingham by Nick Rhodes and John Taylor. They got the idea for the name from a film about a 40th-Century astronaut, based on a highly censorable comic strip, *Barbarella*, starring Jane Fonda. John originally played guitar, with Simon Colley on bass and Steve Duffy on vocals. When Colley and Duffy left, they were replaced by vocalist Andy Wickett and Roger Taylor who came in on drums. They advertised for a guitarist in the *Melody Maker* which resulted in Andy Taylor joining the group, allowing John Taylor to move on to bass. There was to be one more change before their final line-up was complete. Andy Wickett left and drama student Simon Le Bon joined them on vocals. In 1980 Duran Duran were given a try-out at the Birmingham night spot, Rum Runner, owned by Paul and Michael Berrow. The Berrows were quick to realize the potential of the band and putting his money where his mouth was, Michael Berrow sold his house in order to finance them as a supporting act on a national tour headlining Hazel O'Connor. To save money, they lived in a camping bus and they each made about £10 a week. By the end of that tour, the record

companies were clamouring to sign up the newcomers. EMI won the bid, and the boys were put on a retainer of £50 a week.
Their debut single in the spring of 1981, *Planet Earth* went to No.12 in the UK, and No.1 in Australia. They were being described as 'The New Romantics', bringing something bright and new to an otherwise drab music scene, although a certain musical paper did describe them as frivolous. Andy Taylor's reply at the time was, 'Musicians are about playing music to people, and the imagery and all the fancy of it.' Their hit record led to their first headlining tour of the UK which turned out to be a triumph. Two more hit singles followed, *Girls on Film* and *My Own Way*, and their debut album *Duran Duran* was also a big success. April 1982 found the group filming a video in Sri Lanka at the start of a world tour taking in Australia, Japan, USA, Canada, Europe and the UK. Their first No.1 in the UK came in March 1983 with *Is There Something I Should Know*, and three months later all of them retreated to a secret address in the South of France, to play tennis, visit the Cannes Film Festival and take a well earned rest. It was the first break they had had in two and a half years of what had been a punishing schedule of recording, filming and touring the world. The crowning moment of their career to date came in July 1983 when, on a flying four-day visit home, they appeared at the Dominion, Tottenham Court Road, in a concert attended by the Prince and Princess of Wales. The press went overboard with such headlines as Duran Crazy, Durantastic etc, and three days later, Duran Fever Rocks Brum, when, back where it had all started five years previously, they appeared in concert at Aston Villa football ground. 1983 also brought them the British Rock and Pop Award of Best Group and in 1984 they won the title for the second year running adding to it the award for the Year's Best Album for *Seven and the Ragged Tiger*. With both looks and talent going for them, the road ahead is undoubtedly paved with gold.

DAVID ESSEX
'If at first you don't succeed, try something else . . .'
BORN: 23rd July 1947 in Plaistow, London. Father a docker. EDUCATED: Star Lane Primary School, Canning Town. Shipman Custom House School (has now been demolished). In 1983 he paid a surprise visit to Star Lane Primary School, which was a big thrill for pupils and staff alike! He deliberately failed his 11 plus exam because he didn't want to go to a school that played rugby as he was so crazy about soccer. FIRST JOB: Apprentice engineer. At 14, after a visit to London's Flamingo Club, he fell in love with the Blues and knew he wanted to be part of that musical scene. Drumming seemed to be the easiest way in. 'You just whack it and it makes a sound!' So he persuaded his father to buy him a drum kit and it wasn't long before he joined a semi-pro Blues band as a drummer. At 17, he was spotted singing and playing drums in The Eagle, Chobham Road, Leystone, by theatre writer Derek Bowman, who persuaded him to forget about the drums and concentrate on his singing.
But it was to be no overnight success story. After several unremarkable records and with the realization that his young protégé was getting nowhere in the pop world, Bowman, who had become David's manager, suggested he should turn to acting and join a repertory company. It paid off. Roles started to come his way. He played a sultan in *The Magic*

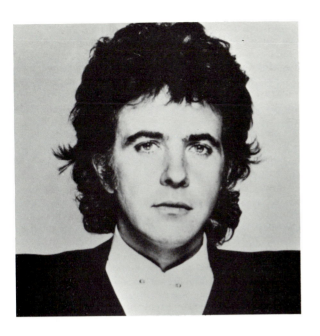

stage as Che Guevara in the Tim Rice/Andrew Lloyd Webber musical *Evita*. His performance once more attracted rave notices and he was joint winner with Elaine Paige (qv) of the Variety Club's Show Business Personality of the Year Award. He left the cast after five months to appear in the Great British Musical Festival at Wembley arena followed by another UK tour. In 1980 he returned to the screen in *Silver Dream Racer* a film for which he wrote the entire score including *Silver Dream Machine* which, released as a single, gave him another Top 10 entry.

A chance to undertake his first major straight acting role came in 1981 when he played the poet Lord Byron in Frank Dunlop's production of *Childe Byron*, at the Young Vic. BBC television gave him his own series of programmes showcasing new talent in 1982, a year that also brought him two more chart entries, *Me and My Girl* (Nightclubbing) and *A Winter's Tale*. His latest project is a stage musical of *Mutiny on The Bounty* with book and lyrics by National Theatre dramatist Richard Crane. The concept album *Mutiny* released in 1983, features the Royal Philharmonic and New London Orchestras, with Frank Finlay as Captain Bligh and David himself as Fletcher Christian. It also gave him another Top 10 entry with *Tahiti*.

Carpet at the Yvonne Arnaud Theatre, Guildford in 1968 and two years later had his first taste of the West End when he appeared with Michael Flanders in a revue, *Ten Years Hard*, at the Mayfair Theatre. The break through came in November 1971 when he landed the role of Jesus in the rock musical *Godspell*. During its three-year run at Wyndham's Theatre, in London's West End, he was given time off to make his film debut in *That'll be the Day* in which he co-starred with Ringo Starr. His performance won him the Variety Club of Great Britain's Most Promising Newcomer Award and a nomination by the Society of Film and Television Arts.

His success as an actor also brought him the success he'd been striving for for so long in the pop field. His recording of *Rock On*, which he'd written for *That'll Be The Day*, hit the No.3 spot in the UK charts and a few months later made it to No.5 in America, where it was nominated for a Grammy Award and won him a Gold Disc. The career of David Essex, singer/actor/composer, was assured.

His first two albums, *Rock On* and *David Essex* went Gold; the second providing him with two more hit singles, *Gonna Make You a Star*, which gave him his first UK No.1 and *Stardust*. His second film, of which *Stardust* was the title song, starred him with Larry Hagman (of J.R. fame), and Adam Faith. One of those strange coincidences occurred on the set one day. Larry Hagman had the line, 'Jim, you've got to get an album out by Christmas . . .' David, (playing Jim), back in his dressing room a few minutes later, got a telephone call from his record producer who used exactly the same words, 'David, you've got to get an album out by Christmas'. Although *Stardust* didn't win him as much acclaim as his first film, it gave him a cult following and his tour of Britain at the end of 1974 was a sell-out. His third album, *All The Fun of the Fair*, gave him three more hit singles, *Rolling Stone*, *Hold me Close*, his second No.1, and *If I Could*. In 1975 he toured America, appearing on 26 coast-to-coast TV shows. Tours of Europe and Australia followed in 1976, then it was back to the UK for a 50-concert tour culminating in a week at the London Palladium. June 1978 saw him back on the West End

■ Highspot of career: Playing the role of Jesus in *Godspell* in 1971. Not only did the Archbishop of Canterbury come around to bless him and the rest of the cast, but the production and his performance in particular drew praise from all quarters. The late Lord Butler said it had given a whole new meaning to the story of Christ and Harold Hobson, of *The Sunday Times*, described his performance as 'the best in London'. ■ A moment to remember: Arriving in Adelaide and being met by a crowd of 3,000 at the airport with parked cars lining the route all the way into town and people waving and shouting. His manager Derek Bowman recalls, 'He was really shaken and I think that was the moment he realized he had really arrived on the recording scene.' ■ Likes soccer, horse riding, spicy food, red wine and children. ■ Dislikes arrogance, cruelty, beetroot and red meat, (he's almost a vegetarian). Golf. (Derek Bowman once bought him a set of golf clubs as a present and had to take them back and change them. David had taken one look and said, 'but I don't like golf!' ■ Married to Maureen, has one daughter and one son and lives in Essex.

GEORGIE FAME (Clive Powell)
'Always looking way beyond the charts . . .'
BORN: 26th June 1943 in Leigh, Lancashire. Father a cotton spinner. **EDUCATED:** Windermere Road Secondary Modern School. Entirely self-taught musician and he still can't read music! **FIRST JOB:** 'I worked in a cotton factory for one year. It was either that or going down the pit.' At the end of that first year he went on holiday to Butlins with some of the lads from the factory and one night was encouraged to get up and do his Jerry Lee Lewis/Fats Domino bit. One of the resident bands at the camp was led by Rory 'Shakes' Blackwell, who was so impressed with Clive Powell's performance that he offered him a job with the band. 'When I told my parents, they were dead against it. My step-mother threatened me with the law, so I went to the police station and asked if they could whip me back, if I left home and took the job. And they said that as long as I behaved myself,

there was nothing they could do as I was over 16. So, egged on by everyone at the factory, off I went.'

He was with the band at Butlins for three months and when the band returned to London at the end of the season, Clive went with them, but work was short and he found himself sleeping on the floor in Islington, so he got himself a job playing the piano at weekends in an East End pub, the Essex Arms in Canning Town, and by passing the box around, he got enough to live on. Meanwhile Rory Blackwell got him an audition with Larry Parnes at the Lewisham Gaumont where he was putting on the Marty Wilde Show. 'I walked back stage and Larry Parnes asked me my name; "Clive Powell doesn't sound quite right, we'll call you Clive Wells. What do you want to do?". "I play and sing," I replied. "OK, after the next number, you're on". So, I got the job as pianist with his backing group and when his Rock and Roll stars didn't turn up, I would get up and sing in their place. He must have liked what I was doing, because on the opening night of the Eddie Cochran tour, Larry Parnes said, "I've got a new name for you. You can open the show, I'll give you three numbers to sing and I'm going to call you Georgie Fame." His backing group became The Blue Flames and when, according to Georgie, they got the sack, they decided to go out on their own. They landed a residency at a London night spot, the Flamingo Club, where they developed quite a following, playing a mixture of Rhythm and Blues, jazz and soul and West Indian Reggae. American singer Mose Allison was, and still is a big influence on Fame. They made a couple of albums while at the Flamingo and then in 1965 their first single, Yeh, Yeh, shot to the top of the charts, knocking the Beatles off the No.1 spot.

Looking far beyond the hit parade, although two more No.1's and several chart entries were to follow, Georgie Fame used the profits from Yeh, Yeh to finance an album on which he sang backed by the Harry South Big Band with Harry doing all the arrangements. 'My fans thought I was forsaking Rhythm and Blues for jazz and the jazz people thought, "Who is this young whipper-snapper singing with our heroes", but the musicians were never like that and we sent the album to Count Basie. He was due to come over for a tour with Tony Bennett, but had a few dates on his own without Tony, so we asked him if he'd like to do a concert with me while he was here. The answer was "Yes", so I went over to Boston to rehearse with him, and we did the concert at the Albert Hall. The following year, 1968, I did a two-week tour of Europe with him.'

The Ballad of Bonnie and Clyde, which made No.1 in the UK, became his first US chart entry in 1968. In 1970 he teamed up with ex-Animals singer Alan Price (qv). 'I had reformed the Blue Flames and Alan had produced our new album and we found ourselves working the same club circuit and often playing the same venues on the same night so this inevitably led to a jam session at the end of the evening. Word got around and we found ourselves being booked together for a guest spot on Lulu's television show. Then we made a record, Rosetta, which was a hit.' The partnership lasted for about three years, when each went his own way once again.

In 1981, wanting to record an album of Hoagy Carmichael songs, he wrote to the great man, hoping he would agree to do the sleeve notes, and back came an invitation to visit him at his home in Palm Springs. He did so, just a few weeks before Hoagy Carmichael died, and the result was an historic album, In Hoagland, recorded with Annie Ross. It's historic, in so far as Hoagy Carmichael himself sings on it — his last performance, at the age of 82. And his parting words to Georgie were, 'Boy, it doesn't matter what you sound like, my songs will make you sound great.'

1984 sees the release of an album of Benny Goodman numbers, In Goodman's Land. With the Blue Flames one tour follows another; he appears regularly at jazz festivals all over Europe, and makes frequent appearances with the BBC Big Band on Radio 2's Big Band Special. His singing has changed since his chart topping days, much more jazz orientated, his repertoire now includes such offerings as Neil Hefti's Little Pony with Georgie's scat singing providing the vocal version of Wardell Gray's famous tenor solo. His rendering of Steve Gregory's Hot Stuff with lyrics by John Hendricks is precisely that. Maybe one day he'll be persuaded to commit some of them to record. He may not make the charts any more, but he's fast making a name for himself as a jazz singer of remarkable ability.

■ Highspot of career: 'Several really, I suppose seeing Yeh, Yeh climb the charts, was one of the biggest thrills.' ■ A moment to remember: 'When I was a piano player with Gene Vincent we were doing one of those Moss Empire tours and we had an American called Davy Jones on the bill with us. He was a real wild character and one night at the end of the show, he was shimmying away very near the front of the stage as the curtain started to come down and he fell into the orchestra pit. The National Anthem started over the PA system and there he was still down in the pit raving away!' ■ Likes good music 'there are only two kinds of music, good and bad', good food and travel. ■ Dislikes flippancy in the media. ■ Married to Nicolette, has two step-daughters and two sons and lives in Somerset.

■ Highspot of career: 'Appearing at the Grand Ole Opry in Nashville, performing one song and getting an encore. Since then I've made eight appearances there; plus recording three albums in Nashville and duetting with country star Jean Shephard on one of them.' ■ Likes researching country music, the movies and swimming. Dislikes insects and insincerity. ■ Married to Joan, has one son and lives in Edinburgh.

GERRY FORD
'The cop who became a Country singer/DJ . . .'
BORN: 25th May 1943, in Athlone, County Westmeath, Ireland. Father a motor mechanic. **EDUCATED:** St Mary's College, Athlone. He sang in his local church choir and at the age of 17 bought his first guitar for £14 and taught himself to play. **FIRST JOB:** Apprentice baker and confectioner. Continued his training in Edinburgh and then in London where he qualified. While working as a baker in London he took a part-time job as compère/DJ at the Majestic Ballroom, Finsbury Park where he introduced the Beatles on their first London appearance. In 1965 he returned to Edinburgh and joined the Edinburgh City Police. He was a policeman for 11 years. Made his first broadcast in the summer of 1974 as a guest on *Country Sounds* on Radio Clyde. The following year, when Radio Forth opened up in Edinburgh he sold them the idea of letting him present a country show, *Forth Country Special*. In 1976 he was nominated Top Country DJ by the Country Music Association and that same year he resigned from the police and turned professional as a singer. In 1977 and '78 he won the Top Country DJ Award from the CMA. He then joined BBC Radio Scotland and has been presenting their *Country Corner* ever since.

Has appeared in Country Festivals in Norway, Sweden and Holland and in 1981 appeared for the first time at the Grand Ole Opry in Nashville. Has made eight return visits since and recorded three albums there, the latest, *Memory Machine*, recorded in January 1984. Although he's Irish by birth, he has never performed in Eire, but could be making his Irish debut at the Cork Festival in 1985.

Apart from his DJ awards, he was voted Best Male Vocalist by Aberdeen Country Club four years in a row, 1980–'83 and Inverness Country Club named him Top Male Vocalist in 1980. He is the only country singer from Scotland to be nominated at the Wembley Awards, for three successive years, 1982, '83, '84. He was also nominated for the BCMA Top Male Vocalist award in 1981, '82, '83, '84. He writes many of his own songs and has recorded nine of them.

KEELEY FORD
'Fell asleep at rehearsal . . .'
BORN: 13th October 1948. **EDUCATED:** County High School, Redditch, Worcestershire. 'I took singing lessons at the age of nine, but didn't like it!' **FIRST JOB:** *For Teenagers Only* on ATV television at the age of 14 and under her real name, Mair Davies. At that time joined a group, The Mavericks, and later a Leicester based group called The Rockets. Made her first radio broadcast on the *Ken Dodd Show* from the BBC's Manchester studios in July 1973. Has sung in top venues all over the world and in 1973 was the first girl to win the International Song Festival in Almeria, Spain and later that year shared first place in the Yamaha World Song Contest in Japan. Sings regularly on Dutch and German Radio and in 1977, representing the BBC at the Nordring Radio Festival, she won the vocal prize. Took part in 1982 in Radio 2's tribute to Judy Garland.

■ Highspot of career: 'Winning the Song Festivals in Spain and Japan and the Nordring Festival in Denmark for the BBC.' ■ A moment to remember: 'I was appearing in a summer season in 1977 when I was released to go to Denmark for the Nordring Festival. I got so tired travelling to and fro between Denmark and London that I literally fell asleep whilst rehearsing with Peter Knight and Nick Curtis!' ■ Likes knitting (a fanatic), crochet, embroidering and dressmaking. ■ Dislikes creepy crawlies, liver and smoking. ■ Lives in Worcestershire.

LEE GIBSON
'Dancer turned singer . . .'

BORN: 5th March 1950, in Watford, Herts. Father a butcher.
EDUCATED: Watford Girl's Grammar School. Took piano and singing lessons at school. Now plays the piano for her own amazement! **FIRST JOB:** As a dancer in The Black and White Minstrel Show. Spent a year as the lead in a revue at London's Talk of the Town, where she sort of got pushed into singing.

She made her first broadcast with the Phil Phillips Quartet in 1971 and has been a backing singer for Barbra Streisand, David Essex, Gerrard Kenny and Marti Webb. Has sung with Skymasters and Metropole Orchestra (Holland) and had a continental top Ten hit with *Chorale*. Has also sung with Bob Miller, Pete Winslow, Peter Knight Orchestra and for MDs Ronnie Hazlehurst, Alyn Ainsworth, Ken Moule and Neil Richardson. Broadcasts regularly with the BBC Radio Orchestra/Radio Big Band. Radio programmes include *Tribute to Judy Garland*, *Tribute to Gershwin*, *Bing Crosby Tribute*, *Night Owls* and *Big Band Special*. She has also sung at the Nordring Radio Festival for the Dutch and the Monte Carlo Producers Prize and the Knokke Competition which the BBC won. She is heard on most of Radio 2's music programmes.

■ Highspot of career: 'I'm not sure whether it was working in Los Angeles or meeting Terry Wogan or taking part in *Ring a Song!*' ■ A moment to remember: 'In 1981 I was asked to represent the Dutch team in the Nordring Festival which was being hosted by the British. At the rehearsals in London with the BBC Radio Orchestra, one of the brass section was off sick and a "dep" unknown to me was in his place. During the inevitable exodus to the pub at lunchtime, I was talking to several members of the orchestra, when the "dep", thinking I was Dutch, complimented me on my "incredibly good English", and couldn't understand the hilarity which greeted this remark! Since then I've been known to the orchestra as Lee Van Der Gibson.' ■ Likes swimming, reading, good food and wine. ■ Dislikes doing the accounts. ■ Married to drummer/arranger Gerry Boyce, qv, has one daughter and lives in Hertfordshire.

TONY GOODACRE
'I sang while she stripped . . .'

BORN: 3rd February 1938 in Leeds, Yorkshire. Father Director of a furnishing company. **EDUCATED:** Roundhay School, Leeds. Played piano by ear for family sing-songs at home. 'I would sing Richard Tauber songs and thought I was the bees' knees. Both my mother and my father were once in a concert party.' Bought his first guitar at 17, a year before he joined the RAF. We'd been watching a television programme, *All Your Own*, introduced by Huw Weldon, in which there were two lads playing guitars, and my mother said, "You can't carry a piano around with you in the RAF, why don't you get yourself a guitar?".' **FIRST JOB:** Police Cadet at 16½. In 1956 joined the RAF for three years. While stationed at RAF Bawdsey in Suffolk, he got together a skiffle group, the *Tigers* and played some local clubs and also the US bases at Woodbridge and Bentwaters. The Americans lent them records and they were soon into Country music. 'As I was the only Northerner in the group, when the others went home at weekends, I sang solo around the pubs.'

After his demob in 1949, worked in the sales office of John Dickenson in Leeds, but in the evenings was singing around the Yorkshire club circuit. Formed his own line-up, Goodacre Country, in 1969, the year he did his first tour of the UK. Didn't turn fully professional until 1973.

His first album *Roaming Around in Nashville* was released in 1974 and was so successful it is still in the catalogues some 10 years later. The same is true of his second album *Grandma's Feather Bed*, released in 1975. Since then he has made a new album every twelve months. Fulfilled a lifetime's ambition in May 1977 when he appeared at the Grand Ole Opry in Nashville and also guested on Ernest Tubb's *Midnight Jamboree*.

1981 saw him celebrating 25 years of Country music with a special 25th Anniversary Album which was given a five Star rating by Country Music People Magazine. In 1982 made his debut at the Wembley Festival and was voted Top Male Vocalist by the British Country Music Association; an award he also won in 1983 when he was invited back to the

Wembley Festival. His 1983 album, *Red Roses*, was followed up in 1984 by the *Sylvatone Song Book LP* and a mini EP, *Guernsey*, inspired by his many visits to the island. In July 1984 represented Britain at the International Country & Western Association Awards Gala in Fort Worth, Texas.

■ Highspot of career: 'My first appearance at the Grand Ole Opry in 1977. You never forget that first time. And also going back to Nashville in 1978 to make an album.' ■ A moment to remember: 'Playing one of the Northern clubs where the evening show included Bingo and the lunchtime show a stripper, who stripped to music from a cassette player. On this particular day, her cassette wouldn't work, so I had to play and sing while she stripped!' ■ Likes travelling, golf and relaxing with a good meal and a bottle of wine. ■ Dislikes politics. ■ Married to Sylvia, has two daughters, one son, two step-daughters, one step-son and lives in West Yorkshire.

ANITA HARRIS *'Slick, sophisticated, stunning and a WOW!...'*

BORN: 3rd June in Mid Somer-Norton, Somerset. Father owned a chain of cinemas and opened the first roller skating rink in Bristol. **EDUCATED:** Convent of the Cross, Bournemouth. Hampshire School of Drama. Trained as a dancer for two years with Pauline Grant of the English National Opera and Glyndebourne. Learnt to skate when very young and won many trophies and medals. After leaving school, continued her skating at Queen's Ice Club in London where she was asked by a talent spotter to audition for a chorus line. She did and got the job – in Las Vegas along with another 16 year old, Aimi Macdonald. **FIRST JOB:** Dancer in the chorus at El Rancho, Las Vegas. 'Because I was only 16, my parents had to go to Bow Street Magistrate's Court to sign a document giving permission for me to travel to America and once in Las Vegas, Aimi Macdonald and I had to report to the British Consulate once a week. As three of us were under age we were always chaperoned, but the boss did provide us with a

car to share. Having passed my driving test, the first thing that happened was I was stopped by the police for going too slowly! There was also the time when with eight of us in the car, we got a puncture and two policemen came to our rescue as we were struggling to change the wheel. It turned into quite a comedy routine!'

At the end of her six-month contract she returned to the UK and within three weeks had joined the Cliff Adam Singers. During the next three years she also sang with the Granadiers who included Gerry Dorsey (Engelbert Humperdinck) and cut her first record. Four years of one-night stands, touring clubs and theatres followed before things started to happen for her. She represented Britain at the San Remo Song Festival and brought home the Gold Medal; then came her first hit record. *Just Loving You* hit the No.6 spot in the summer of 1967 and remained in the charts for 30 weeks. The album of the same name entered the album charts early in '68 and when it was re-released in 1976, sales reached the two-million mark, earning her a Double Gold Disc. She played her first season at the London Palladium and frequent guest appearances on television led to her being offered her first regular television series with Leslie Crowther in *The Saturday Crowd*. A series of *Magic Box* with David Nixon was followed by the highly successful *Jumbleland*, a new style television show for children devised by her husband, Mike Margolis, which topped the children's ratings. As well as her own BBC Television Spectacular and series of late night shows, *Anita*, she played Beatrice Lilley in STV's *Remember Jack Buchanan* in 1979 and in 1980 undertook a straight role in the BBC drama series *West Country Tales*. Her film credits include *Carry on Doctor* and *Follow That Camel*.

On stage she has become known as Britain's No.1 Christmas Box Office lady, playing Peter Pan in the National productions of 1972/3, 1973/4 and starring in pantomime every year since, apart from the 1981/82 season which saw her making her third appearance at London's Talk of the Town. She had made a spectacular debut there the previous year with a cabaret act described as 'slick, sophisticated, stunning and a WOW!'. So successful was that unveiling of *The Act*, as it became known in the business, she was booked for a further month in the same year, an unheard-of occurrence at that particular venue. 'It's never a solo act. It may be just me on the stage but it's very much a team effort.' Anita and the team, including director Mike Margolis, MD Kenny Clayton and choreographer Irving Davies, carried off 17 of the Lanson Theatre Awards in 1982 and the Variety Club of Great Britain named her Performer of the Year. A cabaret season at the Savoy Hotel followed and in 1983, *The Machine*, a television show on the creating of *The Act*, was entered for the Montreux Festival.

In 1984, headlining the cabaret at the Variety Club's Ball of the Year, she performed a song written especially for the occasion by herself, Mike Margolis and Kenny Clayton. It was greeted so enthusiastically that *Touch the Heart of a Child with Sunshine* was released as a single in July with all royalties donated to the Variety Club. As well as appearing in two Royal Variety Shows, she has performed her cabaret act on many royal occasions and at the Lord's Taverners' Ball in 1976 was partnered by Prince Charles for a rendering of *Burlington Bertie*. Her impersonation of Vesta Tilley singing that song has led to her latest venture, *Bertie*, a musical of the life of Vesta Tilley written by Mike Margolis and Kenny Clayton, scheduled to go into production in 1985.

■ Highspot of career: 'My first hit record, *Just Loving You*, because it opened so many doors for me. But also playing Peter Pan and appearing at the Talk of the Town.' ■ A moment to remember: 'Having been educated in a convent, when I went to Las Vegas at the age of 16, I was pretty naïve. There were 12 of us girls in the chorus with eight boy dancers, doing three shows a night, starting at 7.30pm and finishing at 5am, when a lot of the show business people would meet for breakfast. Across the road from El Rancho was the Flamingo where Mae West was topping the bill surrounded by 25 marvellous 'he' men who spent hours each day working out in the gym and looked quite fantastic. The morning we'd arranged to meet these gorgeous creatures for the first time, we all got dolled up and imagine my surprise when they ignored us completely and went off with our eight fellas!' ■ Likes summer days and afternoon tea with cucumber sandwiches and strawberries in the garden and tea on the lawn at Glyndebourne. ■ Dislikes hotel rooms that have a glass shelf over the wash basin so that you bang your head everytime you bend down to clean your teeth! ■ Married to producer/writer/painter Mike Margolis and lives in London.

VINCE HILL
'Palladium with Benny, QE2 with Burns . . .'
BORN: 16th April, nineteen hundred and frozen to death . . .' in Coventry. Father a shopkeeper. **EDUCATED:** Whitemore Secondary School, Coventry. **FIRST JOB:** Pastry cook. Between the ages of 15 and 18 he had a variety of jobs, selling soft drinks, wheelwright; working in a coal mine. It was while he was on holiday with his parents in Margate, just after leaving school, that he won a talent contest at the Prospect. Did his National Service in the Royal Signals and sang with the Regimental Band in the Far East and Europe. Determined to break into show business, after his demob he went to London and got a job in the chorus of the touring production of the musical *Floradora*. Then sang with the Teddy Foster Band before joining up with two other boys and

a girl to form *The Raindrops* in 1958. A popular vocal group on radio, they appeared regularly on *Parade of the Pops* for two years. Vince then went solo and continued to sing on the programme for another five years. His first big break came when in 1963 he was offered a regular spot on television's *Stars and Garters*. 'After years of working on radio, people wondered what the face looked like and happily they survived the shock when they saw *Stars and Garters*.' The show made him a household name and in 1966 he hit the charts for the first time with *Take Me to your Heart Again*. But the really big hit came the following year with his chart topping *Edelweiss*. Two more television series increased his popularity; *They Sold a Million* and *The Musical Time Machine*. In 1970 he represented Britain at the Rio Song Festival and won the Most Popular Singer Award. Also writes songs with his MD/pianist Ernie Dunstall, but surprisingly it's Ernie who writes the lyrics and Vince the music. Their efforts have won the Castlebar Song Festival two years in a row and brought them a No.1 in New Zealand. Has worked all over the world and 1984 saw him entertaining the passengers on the QE2's world cruise. 'I only did it because George Burns was doing it as well!'

■ Highspot of career: 'There have been several, but the one that turned the biggest corner for me was *Edelweiss*. And I shall never foget the thrill of working with Jack Benny on *Sunday Night at the London Palladium*. I did a sketch with him about a guy who had just had a hit record, which I had. He kept giving me advice and I kept saying "Yes Mr Benny, of course Mr Benny." Then I started asking him why he worked in such an old fashioned way and it finished up with me putting my arm around his shoulders and saying, "Now listen Jack . . ." to which the reply was "What happened to the Mr Benny all of a sudden." That was a wonderful thrill for me.' ■ A moment to remember: 'My very first job in show business was when I was in the chorus of the touring company of *Floradora*. There were 12 of us in the chorus, six boys and six girls. The big hit song was *Tell Me Pretty Maiden* when, dressed in Ascot grey, with toppers etc, and the girls in frilly dresses, we had to perambulate around the stage, ending down at the footlights on bended knee. As we are getting near to our walk downstage, my partner says to me out of the corner of her mouth, while still smiling, "My knickers are coming down." Out of the side of my mouth I say, "Don't be ridiculous, they can't be coming down." "They are," she said, "and my underskirt is coming down with them." By this time we were down on bended knee and I knew there was no way we were ever going to get up unless I could quickly salvage the situation. So you can imagine, with a theatre full of people, there I was putting my hand up her skirt to see if I could pull everything delicately down so we could leave it on the floor. It must have looked grotesque! Needless to say we got in a complete muddle as she wriggled to help me but only succeeded in knocking off my top hat which fell into the orchestra pit. The other five couples were carrying on as if nothing had happened and eventually left us on stage on our own with the audience howling with laughter. At this point, the conductor threw his baton in the air and collapsed on the podium and they had to drop the curtain. That was the most embarrassing moment of my career and it was right at the start!' ■ Likes photography, art, swimming and tennis, and following Coventry City FC. ■ Dislikes rigidity in anything. 'I hate rules and regulations. I abide by them but I think rules are made to be bent a little.' ■ Married to Anne, (who was secretary to his agent, Tito Burns, when he was with the Raindrops), has one son, Athol, and lives in Oxfordshire.

THE HILLSIDERS
'You're never going to make a living playing that stuff . . .'

Jo Butler (Bass guitar, vocals)
BORN: 12th January 1939 in Liverpool. Father a store department manager. **EDUCATED:** St Francis Xavier's College, Liverpool. 'I didn't show any interest in music until the skiffle craze started, then I bought a guitar and a tutor and tried to copy the records.' **FIRST JOB:** Chopping down trees for the Forestry Commission. 'I shall never forget my first day. When I chopped down my first tree I shouted "Timber" and they all said I'd been watching too many movies!' Writes many of the group's songs and also finds time to host a Country Music programme on Merseyside's ILR station, Radio City.

■ Likes brewing beer and wine and drinking it. Photography and football, (he's an Everton supporter). ■ Dislikes objectionable people and 'trying to force myself to get up to go jogging every morning.' ■ Married to Ann, has one daughter, Helen, two sons, John and Gary, and lives in Merseyside.

Kevin McGarry (Guitar, vocals)
BORN: 20th June 1949 in Liverpool. Father a bricklayer. **EDUCATED:** St Swithin's School, Croxteth where he sang in the school choir. **FIRST JOB:** Cook on the Belfast boats.

■ Likes all forms of music (he writes many of the group's songs), fishing and home brewing. ■ Dislikes pompous people. ■ Married to Lillian, has two sons, Kevin and Wayne, one daughter, Julie, and lives in Merseyside.

David Rowlands (Pedal steel guitar and Dobro)
BORN: 7th January 1952 in Rayby, Cheshire. Father a farm worker. **EDUCATED:** Grange Secondary Modern School,

Birkenhead. Got interested in music by listening to late 50s records belonging to his elder brother. **FIRST JOB:** Apprentice engineer.

■ Likes stripping down and rebuilding motor cycles, all forms of music and home brewing. ■ Dislikes red tape, bureaucracy, and getting up early. ■ Married to June, has one daughter, Tracy, one son, Lee, and lives in Merseyside.

Brian Hilton (Lead guitar, Dobro, mouth organ, vocals)
BORN: 2nd January, 1939 in Birkenhead. Father a labourer. **EDUCATED:** Prenton Secondary Modern School, Birkenhead. Got interested in music listening to Lonnie Donnegan records. **FIRST JOB:** Time clerk at Cammel Laird's shipbuilding yard.

■ Likes fishing, home brewing and music, (he writes songs for the band). ■ Dislikes guitar leads that don't work. ■ Married to Valerie, has two sons, Ian and Stuart, and lives in Merseyside.

Brian Redman (Drums)
(Noddy to his friends)
BORN: 21st June 1941 in Huyton, Merseyside. Father a warehouseman. **EDUCATED:** Dingle Vale Secondary Modern School.

■ Likes home brewing and listening to records. ■ Dislikes Bank Managers. ■ Married to Maureen, has one daughter Lee and lives in Merseyside.

The Hillsiders came together during the post Beatle era in Liverpool, when too many musicians were chasing too few gigs. They were spotted by the manager of the Blue Angel Club, who liked what he heard and booked them for three nights a week. Their Country sound influenced by the beat music of their home town was something new and proved popular with the customers. Ignoring the scoffing of their fellow musicians – 'You ain't never going to make a living playing that stuff' – they went from strength to strength with bookings from all over the UK and a tour of American bases in Europe.
Their big break came during a European tour with American Country star Bobby Bare. Impressed with the band, he arranged with Chet Atkins for them to appear in Nashville and join him on an album, *The English Countryside*, which became a big seller on both sides of the Atlantic. In 1967 they became the first British band to appear at the Grand Ole Opry. Back home, appearances at the London Palladium and the Wembley Country Music Festival established them as one of the leading bands on the Country music scene. 1982 found them entertaining the troops in the Falklands, shortly after the conflict ended.
Their awards have been numerous over the years. At the end of the 70s they won the British Country Music Association Best Band of the Year Award three years in succession; in 1982 the readers of the *Daily Mirror* voted them Best British Country Music Band; in 1983 they were named Most Entertaining Band of the Year.

■ Highspot of career: 'The first big thing that happened to us was when we realized our ambition to appear at the Grand Ole Opry in 1967.' ■ A moment to remember: 'Many years ago we had a small red transit van which had no proper seats, so we had benches fixed in the back and one of the guys installed a whicker armchair, thinking it would be more comfortable. We were driving to a gig one day when we were stopped by the police who were doing one of those routine checks. The policeman walked around the van, which had no windows, opened up the back door, saw the whicker chair and said, "What are you, some kind of antique dealers then?" Riotous laughter as we explained that we were a group on the way to a gig.'

EDMUND HOCKRIDGE
'Four consecutive West End musicals . . .'

BORN: 9th August in Vancouver, Canada. Father a rancher **EDUCATED:** King Edward High School and Cloverdale High School, Vancouver. **FIRST JOB:** Royal Canadian Airforce at 18. Came to Britain with the RCAF in 1941 and during his first leave in London was fooling around singing one evening at the Beaver Club, Trafalgar Square, rendezvous for Canadian servicemen, when he was heard by a BBC producer. 'The next thing I knew was I had this telephone call asking me if I would do a broadcast for them. It was a forces broadcast in the presence of the Duke and Duchess of Kent, just a few weeks before the Duke was killed in an air crash. I was scared stiff, but I managed to get through *Rose Marie*. As a boy I had seen them making the film of *Rose Marie* near where I lived. My brother, who was in the Mounties, was actually taking part in it as the film company borrowed some of them from the Government for certain scenes. I played hookie from school and I got caned for it, but when I saw Nelson Eddy singing I thought, imagine making your living doing that, that's what I would like to do.'

Commissioned as a PRO for the Canadian Airforce Press and Radio Unit preparing for D Day, he was pulled out in order to help set up the Allied Expeditionary Forces Network which supplied news and entertainment for the troops in Europe. Over the next year he produced and sang in hundreds of forces broadcasts, many of them with his fellow countryman Robert Farnon who was with the Canadian AEF Band. Recordings of some of the shows found their way back to Canada with the result the Canadian Broadcasting

Corporation offered him a one-year contract in Toronto to star in his own coast-to-coast radio show. The one year became four years, during which time he played leading baritone roles in all of Gilbert and Sullivan's operettas and leading roles in *Don Giovanni*, *La Bohème* and *Fidelio* for CBC. In 1951 he returned to the UK, auditioned for and got the leading role of Billy Bigelow in *Carousel* at the Theatre Royal, Drury Lane. From *Carousel* he went straight into the lead role of Sky Masterson in *Guys and Dolls* at the Coliseum which was to turn out to be his home for the best part of the next five years. *Guys and Dolls* was followed by Cole Porter's *Can Can* in which he played Judge Forestier; and after 18 months that was replaced by *The Pajama Game* in which he played Sid Siorkin. It was his biggest success of a long line of successes, and his recording of one of the show's songs, *Hey There*, went to the top of the charts. He had also set up something of a West End theatre record by playing the leading role in four consecutive musicals without a break. He also appeared at the London Palladium in a six month season and at the Talk of the Town. Over the years has starred in many summer shows and pantomimes. His television credits include *Sundy Night at the London Palladium*, *The Morecambe and Wise Show*, *Bruce Forsyth Show* and numerous Spectaculars. He has appeared in six Royal Command Performances and in 1953 was chosen to represent Canada in the Westminster Abbey Choir at the Queen's Coronation. He headlined the cabaret on the maiden voyage of the liner QE2, and has made frequent tours overseas to Denmark, Holland, West Germany and Canada. His one-man show in which he sings some 32 songs and tells a lot of stories, leaves audiences shouting for more. His appearance in *South Pacific* at Worthing in the summer of 1983 broke the theatre records and *The Sound of Music*, in which he co-stars with Isla St Clair, looks like doing likewise in 1984. He was back in the West End in pantomime, Christmas 1983, starring in *Aladdin* at the Shaftesbury Theatre, a performance he repeats in Manchester Christmas 1984. In the spring of 1984 he returned to his birthplace for a five-concert tour with Robert Farnon (qv) and the Vancouver Symphony Orchestra.

Apart from his hits in the mid 50s, such as *Hey There, Young and Foolish, No Other Love* and *By the Fountains of Rome*, he hasn't had a great deal of chart success, although his albums have sold consistently well over the years. But he is undoubtedly one of the finest musical comedy stars we've had in this country over the past three decades.

■ Highspot of career: 'When I went back to Canada for four years after the war, I was studying opera and hoped that one day I might get into the Metropolitan Opera Company in New York. It was while I was in New York on a visit that I saw *Brigadoon* and *Carousel* and I suddenly thought, what am I doing in opera, this is what I want to do. I knew *Carousel* was opening in London, so I took a chance. I sold up everything and went back to England. I auditioned for *Carousel* along with 500 other chaps, but had the advantage of having seen the show several times so I knew the songs well. Also, although I was Canadian, I sounded American and I didn't have to bother about a work permit. At the end of the auditions, Richard Rogers' boss man who was in charge, took me to the telephone, put a call through to Richard Rodgers and said, "We've got the right man". That for me was like a launching pad for a rocket.' ■ A moment to remember:

'During the run of *Guys and Dolls*, I was waiting in the wings when I suddenly became aware that my trouser zipper had broken and slid to the bottom. No way could I take step forward without all being revealed. My understudy wasn't there and Lizbeth Webb was waiting on stage for me to join her for a romantic duet. I frantically looked around for something to carry and the only thing available was the bass drum carried by one of the Salvation Army who was standing side stage. I grabbed it and went on stage holding this drum. The conductor didn't know what was going on and Lizabeth Webb almost had hysterics. Somehow we managed to get through the duet!' ■ Likes being the father of four sons, 'they keep me young and so does my wife'. ■ Dislikes mowing the lawn. ■ Married to Jackie (whom he met in *Carousel*), has four sons and lives in Cambridgeshire.

JEFF HOOPER
'Keep going kid, there's not many of us left . . .'
BORN: 25th February 1959 in Llantrissant, South Wales. Father an aircraft fitter for British Airways. **EDUCATED:** Various schools in South Wales including Llantrissant Primary School and Ypant Comprehensive School. **FIRST JOB:** Singing with a group he formed at school when he was 13, called Black Orange. 'When I was 15 I decided I wanted to be a fitter like my father so I tried for a job as a motor mechanic with a truck firm, and got it. Three weeks later I auditioned for television's *New Faces*, got on the show and won it.' So instead of becoming a motor mechanic he became a singer. A record contract followed and he made two singles, *Ways of the World* and *Don't Let it Get Around*.
Made his first broadcast with the Northern Radio Orchestra in Manchester in 1978. 'Dave Blakely had put in a good word for me with producer John Wilcox, so I've got a lot to thank Dave for.' Radio shows include *Big Band Special* on Radio 2. He spent three years as singer/compère at the Double Diamond Club in Caerphilly where he was heard by Syd Lawrence. 'Syd was looking for a male vocalist at this time and asked me if I would be interested. By way of an audition he took out his trumpet and played a few bars of a song I'd never heard of, called *At Last*, and asked if I could sing it. I did and he liked what he heard so in 1981 I joined his band. I travel around 38,000 to 40,000 miles a year as, living in South Wales, I always have to drive a couple of hundred miles wherever we're playing.'

■ Highspots of career: Appearing on and winning *New Faces*; making his first record and at the age of 17 broadcasting with a large orchestra. ■ A moment to remember: 'In 1982 I was with the Syd Lawrence Orchestra at the Drury Lane Theatre in London, appearing on the same bill as Mel Torme. After the show he came up to me and invited me to his dressing room for a chat saying how much he had enjoyed my singing. His parting words to me were "Keep going kid, there's not many of us left." ■ Likes real ale. ■ Dislikes miserable people and lunatic drivers. ■ Is single and lives in South Wales.

FRANK IFIELD
'His first record at 13 . . .'
BORN: 30th November 1937 in Coventry, of Australian parents. Father a design engineer and inventor. **EDUCATED:** Various schools in Australia. **FIRST JOB:** At 13 he was a 'spruker' – 'roll-up, roll-up' man whose job it was to 'spiel' and pull the crowds into Australian tent shows and circuses. 'I worked with a fantastic old fellow called Big Chief Little Wolf, who taught me all the intricacies of showbusiness in the old fashioned manner.'
First appeared as a singer at the Hornsby Pacific Theatre in Sydney in 1950, and that same year made his first broadcast on Australia's Amateur Hour on station 2UE in Sydney. He also made his first record at 13, *Did You See My Daddy Over There* and within six years had 44 to his credit, making him the number one recording star in Australia, New Zealand and Tasmania.
Decided to try his luck in Britain in 1959, and was helped a great deal by the late Norrie Paramor who persuaded him to broaden his repertoire which consisted almost entirely of Country & Western. His first record in the UK, *Lucky Devil*, got to No.15 in the charts. His next, *I Remember You,* – very much a country/pop mixture thanks to the influence of Paramor – shot to the No. 1 spot, and became the first single to sell a million copies in Britain alone. It also established him in both the country and pop charts in America. A string of

hits followed throughout 1962–63—*Wayward Wind, Lovesick Blues, Nobody's Darling But Mine*, and he chalked up another first by achieving three consecutive No.1's in the British charts. Has appeared on many Royal Command Performances, and headlined his own show at the London Palladium.

His awards have been numerous, apart from many Silver, Gold and Platinum Discs from all over the world, he has been named Top TV Singer of the Year, Top Male Vocalist of the Year, and Show Business Personality of the Year.

Having proved that he could make it on the pop scene, it was inevitable that he should return to his country roots. In recent years has become very much associated once again with country music, and in 1981 and '82 was voted Best British Male Vocalist of the Year in the International Country Music Awards at Wembley. Has tremendous Country following in America and has been made an Honorary Citizen of the States of Tennessee and Kansas.

■ Highspot of career: 'Playing the London Palladium and the Grand Ole Opry in Nashville; and appearing on the Ed Sullivan and Mike Douglas Shows in the USA.' ■ A moment to remember: 'Opening night at the London Palladium, playing Robin Hood, and I was so nervous that I closed the wrong eye and missed the target completely. Robin was beaten by his Merry Men!' ■ Likes Indian food, gardening, collecting plants, touring the world and audiences. ■ Dislikes travelling by train, rude people and peole who mistreat animals. ■ Married to Gillian, has one son, Mark, and one daughter, Sarah. Lives in Hertfordshire.

BARBARA JAY
'Featured with Benny Goodman . . .'
BORN: in Cardiff, Wales. Father played trumpet with Roy Fox, Billy Cotton and Joe Daniels' Hot Shots. **EDUCATED:** All Saints School, Streatham, London. **FIRST JOB:** Singing with Geoff Love's eight-piece band. She made her first broadcast with the Billy Ternent Band. Has also sung with Ronnie Scott, Tito

Burns, Harry Hayes, Bob Miller and in 1969 was chosen to sing with the Benny Goodman Orchestra on its tour of Europe. Radio programmes have included the *Arthur Askey Show* and the *Kenneth Williams Show*. She broadcasts with the BBC Radio Orchestra as well as with her husband's own group, The Tommy Whittle Quartet, and is heard on most of Radio 2's music programmes. She has done a fair amount of touring both in the UK and abroad with Tommy Whittle and in 1984 appeared with him and the Jazz Journal All Stars at the Nice Jazz Festival.

■ Highspot of career: 'Being offered the position as featured vocalist with the Benny Goodman Orchestra.' ■ A moment to remember: 'During a "live" New Year's Eve broadcast with the Billy Ternent Orchestra from the Paris Cinema, I was getting into my strapless evening dress in the upstairs dressing-room when unexpectedly I heard the announcer introducing me over the intercom. Unbeknown to me the programme had been altered bringing my spot forward. I just made a mad dash down the stairs, through the curtain onto the stage as they were playing the intro to my song. But I didn't have time to do up my zip properly so when I started to sing, the zip started to come down. The only thing I could do was to stand with my arms pinned against my side through the whole song!' ■ Likes badminton, gardening and swimming. Dislikes British winters. ■ Married to Tommy Whittle, qv, and lives in Hertfordshire.

ELTON JOHN (Reginald Kenneth Dwight)
'Prefers soccer to pop . . .'
BORN: 25th March 1947 in Pinner, Middlesex. Father a Squadron Leader in the RAF. **EDUCATED:** Pinner County Grammar School. Royal Academy of Music, London. He played piano by ear by the time he was four and at the age of 11 became a Junior Exhibitioner at the Royal Academy of Music, where he studied for five years. **FIRST JOB:** On leaving school in 1964 worked in the daytime as a messenger for a music publishers while playing piano in the evenings at the Northwood Hills Hotel. His father, according to Elton, was 'very snobbish and sort of stiff'; he disapproved of 'in' clothes, horsing around and pop music, so much of Elton's early influence in music came from his mother who would bring home Bill Haley and Elvis Presley records. In 1965, he joined Bluesology, a band that specialized in backing visiting US soul stars, and then became a permanent backing group for Long John Baldry. It was around this time that Reggie Dwight decided to change his name, combining the first names of John Baldry and saxophonist Elton Dean.

In 1967, he met lyricist Bernie Taupin. They started writing songs together and signed a contract with Dick James Music. For two years they wrote MOR material for other singers, but it was only when they concentrated on songs for John himself to sing that they met with success. In 1970 formed the Elton John Band and around that time managed to lose a lot of weight (he'd always tended to be on the plump side). This meant that at long last he was able to wear the kind of mod gear that up until then had been denied him first by his father and then by his size. When he went on stage at the Troubadour Club in Los Angeles in August of that year, to make his American debut, he created a sensation. His album, *Tumbleweed Connection* entered the US charts; he also had a hit single on both sides of the Atlantic with *Your Song* and

he was on his way to his first million. His first No.1 in American came in 1972 with *Crocodile Rock*. Four more US No.1's followed in the next three years, but although he was consistently featured in the British charts, the No.1 spot always eluded him. The only time he made it was in 1976, and then only with a little help from a friend, Kiki Dee, with their duet *Don't Go Breaking My Heart*.

In 1973 his ninth album, *Yellow Brick Road* sold two million copies in six months in America and according to *Time* magazine, in 1975 his income was around seven million dollars a year. And he was spending it as flamboyantly as he dressed. It was not unusual for him to drive up to Cartier's in his Rolls Royce and buy 7,000 dollars-worth of gifts. But in a television interview with David Frost in 1978, he admitted that he preferred soccer to pop music and that he would willingly trade the stage for playing soccer at Wembley,

which of course, explains why he puts so much time and energy into being Chairman of Watford FC. He has been known to fly all the way from Los Angeles to see Watford play in the FA Cup, and then take the next plane back. One of the saddest moments of his life must have been when his team were beaten by Everton in the 1984 FA Cup final.

In 1978 his partnership with Bernie Taupin came to an end and many critics predicted that his career would suffer, but his new collaboration with Gary Osborne has continued to turn out the hits. 1984 found him down-under on a tour of Australia, a tour that was destined to hit the headlines for quite a different reason. The man who once said, 'I won't let anybody get close to me. I live alone in a 36-room house and I can't go into the kitchen because the alarms are on', had decided to drop the barrier. Much to everyone's surprise, he got married!

■ A moment to remember: 25th August 1970. 'I went to the Troubadour Club in Los Angeles dressed in the most outrageous gear I could find. No one believed I would actually go on stage and play like that. But I did, for the first time, and was so overjoyed I just leaped on the piano in clebration and that was it. I was free at last.' ■ Likes football and tennis. ■ Married Renate Blauel (his recording engineer) on Valentine's Day 1984.

SALENA JONES
'Two albums a year in Japan . . .'
BORN: 29th January 1946 in Newport News, Virginia, USA. (She lived just a block away from Ella Fitzgerald.) Father a guitarist and folk singer. **EDUCATED:** High school and college in USA. Studied to be a teacher. **FIRST JOB:** Cinema usherette. At 14, she had sung briefly in a local night club, but her parents found out and put a stop to it, although they allowed her to sing at weddings and private functions. Her first big break came when she won a talent contest at Harlem's famous Apollo Theatre, which resulted in her being offered a recording contract. She made her first broadcast on station WNEW in New York and appeared at several of the Greenwich Village nightspots. In 1965, wanting to see the world, she left the States to go to Spain where she spent six months singing in Madrid night clubs. She then came to the UK and in 1968 was booked to appear at Ronnie Scott's for two weeks. She stayed for seven! Throughout the 70s she appeared in major venues around the UK including three appearances at London's Talk of the Town. Has sung with Jack Parnell, Maynard Ferguson, Syd Lawrence, the Dutch Skymasters Big Band, the Australian Radio Orchestra and broadcasts regularly with the BBC Radio Orchestra/Big Band. In 1973 her albums *Alone Together* and *This and That* were released in Japan which marked the start of her love affair with that country. She made her first visit in 1978 and has been back every year since. She makes two albums a year in Japan and won a Gold Disc for *My Love*. She has also released many albums in Britain but has yet to achieve the tremendous popularity that has come her way in Japan.

■ Highspot of career: 'Several – winning a talent competition at the Apollo Theatre, New York; winning the Knocke Song Festival, Belgium; winning Gmunden Song Festival, Austria and being awarded a Gold Album in Japan in 1982.' ■ A moment to remember: 'One Christmas I was invited to sing on a lunchtime radio show on Radio Hilversum in Holland. Having already been booked to do an evening show at the Café Royal in London, I was reluctant to accept, but was assured that I would be able to catch a plane by three o'clock to be back in England by four o'clock. I travelled to Holland on the evening of December 30th, with my husband, and was booked into a beautiful small country hotel where we had a superb meal and a quiet drink. We remarked what a pleasant way it was to end the old year. The next morning when we awoke we found about two feet of snow and learnt that most Dutch and English airports were closed. All major airlines had cancelled their flights, but we managed to book a private jet that had to come from Rotterdam to Amsterdam to collect us. The weather at Rotterdam closed in and at seven o'clock in the evening a British Caledonian pilot decided to try for Gatwick although our luggage had already left for Heathrow. We landed at Gatwick at eight o'clock, caught the last transfer helicopter to Heathrow to collect our luggage and arrived at the Café Royal at 10 o'clock to be on stage at 11. The booking agent greeted me with "Well done Salena, you are the one artist I never have to worry about because you always give yourself plenty of time."!' ■ Likes cooking and gardening. ■ Dislikes liars. ■ Married to P.J. Rogers and lives in Hampshire.

TOM JONES (Thomas Jones Woodward)
'Tiger Tom of Pontypridd . . .'
BORN: 7th June 1940 in Pontypridd, Wales.
Was singing in public before he went to school! When he was only three his mother took him along to a local store to sing for a few shillings, and it wasn't long before he was performing regularly at weddings and at ladies clubs in the Pontypridd area. Two of his favourite party pieces were *Mule Train* and *Ghost Riders in the Sky*.
The Teddy Boy craze was at its height as he entered his teens, so it's hardly surprising that he became one. **FIRST JOB:** Determined not to become a miner, he went into the building trade, but his evenings were spent singing at working men's clubs where he was billed as 'Tiger Tom'. At 16 he got married and at 17 became a father, and for the next six years made a comfortable living while building up his reputation in the Welsh mining valleys where they take their singing seriously.
In 1963, another local boy, Gordon Mills, home from London where he was making a name for himself as a song writer, saw Tom performing, realized his potential and persuaded him to return to London with him. Mills became his manager, dropped the Woodward, hence capitalizing on the film Tom Jones, which had just been released, and set about getting him a recording contract. Up and coming young song writer Les Reed was brought in to collaborate with Gordon Mills in writing a suitable song. They came up with *It's Not Unusual*, Tom recorded it and the rest is history. Not only did it win the Ivor Novello Award for that year, it hit the No.1 spot in the charts within a couple of weeks of its release and sold three million copies.
But super stardom was still some way off for Tom. Offstage

he was quiet and shy, with not too much to say for himself and at a time when it was fashionable for young men to be thin and weedy with long hair, the brawny baritone from Wales, who looked more like a truck driver, wasn't the type that sent teenage rock audiences overboard. Watching his act in a club one night, Gordon Mills realized that it was the middle-aged matrons in the audience who were most affected by the bared chest and the swivelling hips. Here, was a ready-made market for the Jones boy, and Mills exploited it to the full. But it wasn't until 1969, when his hour-long television special, *This is Tom Jones*, was shown in America, that anyone realized just how big that particular pot of gold was to be. The American tour that followed was a sell-out with mobs of middle-aged women throwing their underwear onto the stage and causing him to be rushed from one place to another under cover of darkness in order not to be recognized. The hits continued to roll throughout the 60s and into the 70s, although he only had one other No.1 after *It's Not Unusual—The Green, Green Grass of Home* in November 1966 which turned out to be something of a prophetic song, because in the mid 70s he forsook the Welsh valleys to join the super-stars who reside in Bel Air,

California. It was the obvious thing to do, not only for tax reasons, but because he had become a regular attraction at Caesar's Palace, Las Vegas, which was to become almost his second home over the next decade.

His awards over the years, which have been numerous, include being voted World's Number One Vocalist in the US Disc Jockey Poll; America's Friars Club Entertainer of the Year; Variety Club of Great Britain's Show Business Personality of the Year and he's been voted World's Sexiest Male by readers of women's magazines.

In September 1983, he returned to Wales for the first time in 10 years and received a tremendous reception for his first concert at St David's Hall in Cardiff. They'd kept a welcome in the hillsides for the boy from Pontypridd, one he's never likely to forget.

■ A moment to remember: The day that Les Reed, Gordon Mills and Tom went to Sandie Shaw's agent with a demo disc of *It's Not Unusual*. After they had been kept waiting in the outer office for half an hour, Les got impatient and knocked on the door. 'What, do you want? I'm very busy with an important client.' (Des Lane, the Penny Whistle man was in the office at the time). 'We've got a demo of a new song and a new singer, but if you don't like the singer, maybe the song would suit Sandie', said Les. 'I'll give you just three minutes' said the agent. On went the record and after four seconds the reaction was brief and to the point. 'That'll never be a hit.' Les Reed takes up the story: 'Tom was a good demo singer, but we would have been quite happy for someone like Sandie Shaw to record our song. As we trekked back into town (we couldn't afford a taxi), Tom said, "If you don't let me do that song, I'm going to jump under a train." So we tried Decca and that was it! But when I think of what Sandie Shaw's agent missed! Because we were all free at the time – Tom, Gordon and I—she could have had the lot; and a £52 million empire, MAM, was built on the strength of that one song.' ■ Likes jogging, boxing and weight lifting.

■ Married to Melinda, has one son and one grandson and lives in California, USA.

KAREN KAY

'A hundred different voices . . .'

BORN: 18th July 1947 in Blackburn, Lancashire. EDUCATED: Penwitham County Secondary School, Nr. Preston. Southlands School, Chorley.

Took singing lessons at 12, which she liked and piano lessons at 14 which she didn't! Used to take off her teachers at school, although she didn't at first include impressions in her cabaret act. Made her first appearance on television at 14 in *Search for a Star*. She also made a pilot programme for Granada TV along with a young Jimmy Tarbuck! That same year was featured on BBC Radio's *Music Spot* from Manchester. 'While I was still at school I was entering talent contests and would often come home and change and then go off to sing in a club, earning a fiver here and a fiver there.'

FIRST JOB: 1962 summer season at a small theatre on the North Pier Blackpool. The following year she had to have her tonsils removed and had to stop singing for a while so took a job in an office. 'I had done a commercial course at school, so I thought this would be a good time to find out what it was like working in an office. It was dreadful. I was soon back in show business!' For the next few years worked in theatres

and clubs introducing more impressions into her act.

Her first big break in television came in 1975 with the LWT series *Who Do You Do*. This led to her appearing with Dickie Henderson in *I'm Dickie That's Show Biz* and guesting on the *Des O'Connor Show*. 'When I was 14 I entered a national talent contest in Manchester for which the prize was a trip to London to appear in the final at the Victoria Palace. The compère on that occasion was Des O'Connor and he was ever so nice to me. (I didn't win, I came 4th.) I reminded him of it when I first went on his show!'

The end of the 70s saw her appearing with Paul Daniels in summer shows at the Pavilion, Bournemouth and the Britannia Pier, Great Yarmouth, which were followed in 1980 by a 14-month run at the Palace Theatre in London. Meanwhile she was becoming a familiar face on the box with guest appearances on such shows as *Blankety Blank* and *Punch Lines*. Her half-hour show in the BBC series, *The Vocal Touch*, led to her being offered her own series of six shows on BBC 2 in the autumn of 1983. A second series followed in the autumn of 1984.

■ Highspot of career: 'Being given my own television series by the BBC in 1983.' ■ A moment to remember: 'Basically I'm a disaster area! There's the time I went to Malta and fell off the roof. I went running across this roof and jumped onto a wall, only I didn't, I just took off and went flying over the edge. I fell flat on my front, cracked a rib but still did the show that night—the show must go on and all that! The strange thing was, I went back to Malta again the following year and as I arrived a man fell off the same roof!' ■ Likes walking, driving, the countryside. 'I would have loved to have gone in for rally driving and flying but I've never got around to it.' ■ Dislikes litter and dozy drivers. ■ Has one son and lives in London.

ELEANOR KEENAN
'Fainted in the middle of a broadcast . . .'

BORN: January long ago in Belfast. Father was a British Army Captain. **EDUCATED:** In Africa and Northern Ireland. **FIRST JOB:** Appearing in a musical *Fancy Free* by Sam Cree at the Arts Theatre, Belfast. Made her first broadcast with the Johnny Joseph Five at the Playhouse in 1969. Has also sung with Ray McVay, Bob Miller, Johnny Howard, Christine Leer Set (all girls), Joe Loss and the Syd Lawrence Orchestra. has travelled half-way round the world backing Roger Whittaker (qv) and cruised to the Bahamas for a month singing on the QE2, (fabulous!) She broadcasts and tours with the Syd Lawrence Orchestra and is often heard on radio singing with the BBC Radio Orchestra/Radio Big Band.

■ Highspot of career: 'It hasn't happened yet!' ■ A moment to remember: 'I fainted during a "live" broadcast from the Royal Albert Hall, a concert given by the Syd Lawrence Orchestra and compèred by Alan Dell. I was singing *Don't Sit Under the Apple Tree*, with the group when I fell back into the middle of the sax section. Ug! The roadie carried me off and Syd said to the rest of the group, "keep singing" . . . I had the lead line . . . can you imagine!' ■ Likes reading biographies, cooking and the theatre. Dislikes cold weather.

GRACE KENNEDY
'Her first break at 18 . . .'

BORN: 2nd March, 1958 in Montego Bay, Jamaica. Father a motor mechanic. **EDUCATED:** Comprehensive School in Woolwich, London having come to live in the UK with her family. She took singing lessons from the age of 10. **FIRST JOB:** Clerk in office.
Got her first big break in show business when she sang on the *Frankie Vaughan Show* on television at 18. This resulted in her being given a half-hour spectacular with Southern Television. The 80s started well for her with frequent guest appearances on television followed by a series of her own for BBC Television. Has also appeared in two Royal Command Performances and her cabaret act has won acclaim not only in this country but also in such venues as the Palm Beach Casino in Cannes.

■ Highspot of career: 'Appearing in two Royal Command Performances.' ■ A moment to remember: 'Meeting Margaret Thatcher.' ■ Likes shopping for clothes, and Spaghetti Vongoli. ■ Dislikes heights. ■ Married to Robert Winsor, has one daughter and lives in London.

CAROL KIDD
'Likes laughing and sleeping—when she's not singing . . .'

BORN: 19th October 1947. **EDUCATED:** 'Not very!' **FIRST JOB:**
Singing with a Trad Band in Glasgow at the age of 15. Made
her first broadcast a year later on a show called *Come
Thursday.* Had her own record and chat programme *Jazz 'n'
That* for two years on Radio Scotland. Made many broadcasts
with the BBC Scottish Radio Orchestra before it was
disbanded. Now broadcasts with her own trio and the BBC
Radio Orchestra/Big Band. Recent television credits include a
series of *Hear, Hear* for STV.
Made her first appearnace at Ronnie Scott's club in London
in 1979 and has been back every year since. Works the jazz
club circuit with her own trio and in 1984 was joined by
Stephane Grappelli's guitarist, Martin Taylor. 1984 also saw
the release in the UK and France of her very first album,
Carol Kidd.

■ Highspots of career: 'Working at Ronnie Scott's and
making my very first broadcast with a whole orchestra
backing me.' ■ A moment to remember: 'Being hi-jacked
from a taxi en route to a recording session by a bunch of
musicians because the producer had given them a break at
10.45 and the pubs didn't open until 11 and if the "turn" isn't
there, they can't start without her. Mind you, it was
Christmas!' ■ Likes laughing and sleeping. ■ Dislikes
getting up in the morning. ■ Married to trombonist George
Kidd, has two sons and one daughter and lives in Glasgow.

SANDRA KING
'. . . that distinctive deep brown voice.'

BORN: 12th October 1953, in London. Father a postman.
EDUCATED: Leiton Grammar School, London. The Peggy
O'Farrell Stage School where she studied singing and
dancing. **FIRST JOB:** 1966, a modern Easter play on BBC
Television. At 17, she toured Bulgaria with the National Youth
Jazz Orchestra and at $17\frac{1}{2}$ did an audition for Ronnie Scott's,
sang there for three weeks and has made many return
engagements. She makes many concert appearances on the

Continent and has recently worked in the USA. Made her first broadcast on *Jazz Club* in 1968 with Pat Smythe Jazz Quartet. Has sung with Coe, Wheeler & Co., Danish Symphony Orchestra, Danish Big Band, The Metropole Orchestra of Holland, The Norwegian Symphony Orchestra, The BBC Radio Orchestra/Radio Big Band. Radio programmes include *Kaleidoscope* and *Midweek* for Radio 4 and all of Radio 2's music programmes at one time or another. Is heard regularly on *Big Band Special*, *Night Owls* and on BBC Radio Scotland, the *Gerry Davis Show* and the Radio Scotland *Road Show*.

■ Highspots of career: 'Giving a concert in Washington DC in April 1982, a performance which was recorded as an LP. Before that, it was singing to a thousand people in Bulgaria when I was 17 with the National Youth Jazz Orchestra.'
■ A moment to remember: 'Arriving in the tiny *Midweek* studio at Broadcasting House, complete with shopping bags at eight o'clock in the morning to sing two songs and having Desmond Wilcox, who was practically sitting on top of the piano (there were four other guests) describing me singing with my shopping at my feet. Kenneth Robinson even described my shopping in his article in the *Listener* that week!' ■ Likes listening to music, collecting Victorian cards, yoga, reading anything from Eastern philosophy to thrillers. ■ Dislikes ringing telephones in the early hours and cigarettes. ■ Is single and lives in London.

CLEO LAINE (Clemintina Campbell)
'A singer like no other singer . . .'
BORN: 28th October in Southall, Middlesex. Father came to Britain with the West Indian Expeditionary Force during the First World War and married a Wiltshire girl.
EDUCATED: Featherstone Road School, Southall.
Her first interest in music came with listening to the Salvation Army Band playing on the street corner; her first taste of show business was when, at the age of 12, she worked as an extra in the Sabu film, *The Thief of Baghdad*. **FIRST JOB:** Hairdresser's assistant. Her first week's wages came to the

princely sum of 7s. Also worked in a library, a hat shop, and a shoe menders, where she heeled and soled shoes, progressed to making up the books and eventually became the manageress. It was at a social evening at the British Legion Hall in Southall, that she was persuaded to sing and she was heard on that occasion by a musician who mentioned to Johnny Dankworth (qv) that he'd heard a singer like no other singer he had ever heard before. An introduction was arranged and so began what was to become a world famous musical partnership. The first thing that Johnny Dankworth did was to change her name, explaining that Clemintina Campbell would never fit on the bills. Some suitable names were put in a hat and out came Laine.

Her first professional singing job was in a cellar club in Great Newport Street, London in 1951. In 1952 she joined the John Dankworth Seven which the following year was expanded to a 20-piece band. In 1958 she became Mrs John Dankworth. Her first acting role came that year in a play at the Royal Court Theatre which brought rave reviews from the critics. She also played the lead in the Sandy Wilson musical *Valmouth* in 1958. In 1971 she scored a hit in the London revival of *Show Boat* at the Adelphi which became the longest running production ever of the Jerome Kern/Oscar Hammerstein musical. Her other theatre credits include *A Time To Laugh* with Robert Morley; the Weil-Brecht opera *The Seven Deadly Sins*; *The Women of Troy*; *Colette*, a musical written for her by her husband.

But first and foremost, she is a jazz singer and has taken her place alongside Ella Fitzgerald and Sarah Vaughan on the international jazz scene. Accompanied by the John Dankworth Quintet in 1972 she toured Australia and America playing to packed houses. In 1973 *Cleo Laine Live at Carnegie Hall*, recorded by RCA was nominated for a Grammy Award and in 1975 the *Los Angeles Times* presented her with the Woman of the Year Golden Feather Award. In 1975, with John fronting the Los Angeles Philharmonic Orchestra, she became the first British female vocalist to star in her own concert at the famous Hollywood Bowl. 1977 was a good year too; she made her Broadway debut with *Cleo on Broadway* and appeared in the Jubilee Royal Variety Show at the London Palladium, where she had just completed a sell-out season. Was also named Show Business Personality of the Year by the Variety Club of Great Britain, and Most Exciting Female on Television by TV Times.

As well as Gold Discs for *Fell Warm*, *I'm a Song* and *Live at Melbourne*, she achieved Platinum for *Best Friends* with guitarist John Williams and *Sometimes We Touch* with flautist James Galway. Her album *Smilin' Through* with pianist/actor Dudley Moore was nominated for a Grammy Award in the Female Jazz Vocal category.

In 1982 she was awarded an honorary Doctorate of Music by the Berklee College of Music, Boston, Massachussets, and in 1983 returned to Carnegie Hall for a special concert to celebrate the 10th anniversary of her first appearance there.

■ Highspot of career: 'Getting my first break joining the John Dankworth Seven.' ■ A moment to remember: 'John and I were appearing in cabaret at the big charity event in Los Angeles in April 1984, to raise money for the Olympics, which was attended by Prince Andrew. Just prior to the big night, Michael Caine gave a party to which we were invited. John had gone to the loo and I was standing talking to our

American road manager who is five foot nothing, very round and very bald. Ryan O'Neal, whom I'd never met before, accompanied by Farah Fawcett, came up to us and said, "Cleo, how are you? Farah, meet Cleo and John." At that moment John, tall, thin and with hair, returned and I explained, no, this is John. "Oh my God," said Ryan O'Neal, "that was a big mistake".' ■ Likes perfume. ■ Dislikes motor bikes, guns and smoking; 'they all kill'. ■ Married to John Dankworth, has a son, Alec, and a daughter, Jackie, and a son by a previous marriage. Lives in Buckinghamshire.

JEANIE LAMBE
'One broadcast changed her life . . .'
BORN: December 23rd, 1940 in Glasgow. Father a Music Hall artist. **EDUCATED:** In Inverness. **FIRST JOB:** Appearing with her mother and father on stage in their act at the Empire Theatre, Inverness at the age of 11. She went out on her own as a solo singer at the age of 15. Made her first broadcast for producer Ben Lyon on BBC Radio Scotland in 1957. Has sung with Clyde Valley Stompers, Kenny Ball, Acker Bilk, Chris Barber, Alex Welsh, Danny Moss Quartet, Eddie Thompson Trio, Dutch Swing College Band, Mike Cotton's Band, Pizza Express All Star Jazz Band, and most of the BBC Orchestras. Radio programmes include *Jazz Club*, *Workers Playtime*, the *Spike Milligan Show* and the *Rolf Harris Show*. Made many appearances with George Chisholm on the *Black and White Minstrel Show* on BBC Television during the 60s. Is heard regularly with the Danny Moss Quartet on most of Radio 2's music shows including *Sounds of Jazz*, *Night Owls*, *Big Band Special* and *String Sound*. 1984 saw her touring Australia with Danny Moss and in May of that year she appeared with him at New York's famous Rainbow Room, making her American debut. Two weeks at the Rainbow Room was followed by an appearance at Eddie Condon's Jazz Club in New York. An album with Danny Moss Quartet, *The Midnight Sun*, was released in the spring of '84.

■ Highspots of career: 'Meeting Ella Fitzgerald and Duke

Ellington; singing for the first time in America at the Rainbow Room in New York. ■ A moment to remember: 'I had been working in London and touring with jazz bands all over Britain. I needed time to think about my next move, professionally and personally, so I went back home to Inverness. One week later, my agent, Jack Fallon, called me to say he had one broadcast, BBC *Jazz Club*, for me. I said "You've got to be joking, all the way from Inverness for one broadcast! Anyway who is it with?" – "Danny Moss" he said – "I'll do it," I said. Can you imagine, I came all the way down from the Highlands of Scotland for that one broadcast but it changed my life. Danny proposed to me that week, I accepted and we have lived happily ever since. We now have two fine sons, Danny Junior and Robert.' ■ Likes golf and travelling the world. ■ Dislikes injustice and bad manners.

■ Married to Danny Moss, qv, has two sons and lives in Sussex.

LOIS LANE
'Formed the Caravelles, a hit on both sides of the Atlantic . . .'
BORN: 3rd April 1944, in Sleaford, Lincolnshire. Father a salesman. **EDUCATED:** St Martha's Convent, Barnet. Clarks College. Plays the guitar. **FIRST JOB:** Secretary/shorthand typist/receptionist. In 1963 formed The Caravelles and that same year their record *You Don't Have to be a Baby to Cry* reached No.5 in the UK charts and No.3 in the US charts. They toured the USA in 1964 appearing on the very first concert given by the Beatles in America. Lois made her first broadcast with the Caravelles in *Mark Time* with Mark Wynter and the Les Reed Band. As a solo vocalist her first broadcast was on *Music Thru Midnight* with the Tony Osborne Four in 1967. She has sung with the Ted Heath band, Don Lusher Quartet, the Tony Kinsey Quartet and all the BBC popular music orchestras over the years. She broadcasts regularly with the BBC Radio Orchestra/Radio Big Band and the Tony Kinsey Quartet and is heard on most of

Radio 2's music programmes including *Big Band Special* and all the daily shows known as the 'Strip' programmes (if you'll pardon the expression!). She is also a talented song writer and has written and broadcast many songs written in collaboration with Tony Kinsey, qv.

■ Highspots of career: 'Hearing that the Caravelles' first record had entered the charts: and the very first time I sang at Ronnie Scott's with Coleman Hawkins topping the bill. I had broken my leg and it was in plaster and Ronnie Scott introduced me as the best one-legged singer in the business!' ■ A moment to remember: 'During a "take" at a recording session, at the end of my song, the entire trumpet section stood up and played as their trousers dropped to their knees (they were all wearing red underpants) and I was wearing a red face – (print that if you dare!)' ■ Likes 'our narrowboat Melanie Anne'. ■ Dislikes cigarette ends in saucers, toilets or anywhere. ■ Married to 'Superman' of course! (better known as BBC producer Roger Pusey), has two children and lives in Surrey.

STEPHANIE LAWRENCE
'Her singing not appreciated by the nuns . . .'
BORN: in Hayling Island, Hampshire. Father musical director George Lawrence. Mother a classical ballet dancer who ran a dance troupe called The Kent Babes. **EDUCATED:** A convent, followed by the Arts Educational School, Tring, Hertfordshire. Her natural exuberance at the convent often led to her being chased by the nuns in order to be given a spanking and she used to hide in a room where all the nuns' habits were hung. They didn't think it was very funny. 'I used to sing and dance at all the wrong times and eventually the nuns had had enough and they suggested to my parents that perhaps they should send me to a school where my singing would be more appreciated! It was when I went to the Arts Educational School at Tring that I really started to learn. After that there was no stopping me.'
Her first professional appearance on stage was in pantomime at Watford when she was nine. At 12, she danced with the Royal Festival Ballet at London's Royal Festival Hall in Tchaikovsky's *The Nutcracker*.
'Coming from a theatrical family, I suppose it was only natural that I should go into showbusiness. When I was small and my mother was teaching ballet, I used to sneak into class and mimic the older pupils. I wasn't supposed to be there, but it was so exciting that I couldn't resist it.'
On leaving school, became a professional dancer and for the next few years worked with choreograhers all over the world. In 1971 made her West End debut in Peter Nicholls' *Forget-Me-Not Lane* at the Apollo Theatre. In 1978 she starred in *Bubbling Brown Sugar* at the Royalty Theatre and during the run of the show recorded a duet with Johnny Mathis, *You Saved My Life*, which was released as a single. They later recorded an album together. Her really big break came in 1980 when she was chosen to take over the role of Eva Peron in the hit musical *Evita*, a part she played for three years. In 1981 appeared in the Royal Variety Show and the following year played Mary Magdalen in the musical television play *Doubting Thomas*. In 1983 she left the cast of *Evita* to play Marilyn Monroe in the new musical *Marilyn* at the Adelphi. Although the show was a long way from being a hit, it was a personal success for Stephanie and gained her The Variety Club Award for Best Stage Actress of The Year. It also established her as leading musical comedy actress. 1984 saw her starring in the new Andrew Lloyd Webber musical, *Starlight Express* at the Apollo Victoria which provided her with her first solo single record, *Only He has the Power to Move Me*.
Her television appearances throughout the 80s have been numerous. Not only has she guested on such shows as *The Two Ronnies*, *Des O'Connor Tonight*, *The Les Dawson Show* and *Wogan*, she has also headlined her own shows for BBC Television.
Ambition: To make a lot more records and do a 'straight' play.

■ A moment to remember: Opening her dressing-room door after a matinee performance of *Evita*, to find Elizabeth Taylor standing there. Having seen many productions of *Evita* around the world, she had come backstage to congratulate Stephanie on what she said was the best portrayal of Eva Peron she had seen! ■ Is single and lives in London.

DENNIS LOTIS
'Ten shillings for his first broadcast . . .'
BORN: 8th March 1925, in Johannesburg, South Africa. Father a restaurateur. **EDUCATED:** In South Africa. As a boy soprano took singing lessons for four years. Plays the piano. **FIRST JOB:** Singing at the Metro Cinema in Johannesburg. Has also worked as a bus conductor and an electrician. He made his first broadcast in South Africa at the age of nine. On arriving in the UK in the early 50s he joined the Ted Heath Band and made numerous broadcasts with them. A hit record, *Cuddle Me* prompted him to go solo. He was voted the country's Top Vocalist by *Melody Maker* and in 1957 appeared in his first Royal Command Performance. He rejoined the Ted Heath Band for their tour of the USA and an appearance at Carnegie Hall. He has appeared in many films, musicals and straight plays including John Neville's Playhouse production of Shakespeare's *Measure for Measure*. Has had his own radio show, worked as a DJ and made literally thousands of

broadcasts. Is the star vocalist with the Ted Heath Band fronted by Don Lusher.

■ Highspot of career: 'Playing Lucio in Shakespeare's *Measure for Measure*.' ■ A moment to remember: 'Receiving the princely sum of 10s. for my first broadcast.' ■ Likes tennis and renovating old buildings. ■ Dislikes philistines who rip down ancient buildings. ■ Married to Rena, has three children and lives in Norfolk.

LULU (Marie McDonald McLaughlin Lawrie)
'Always in trouble for singing during lessons . . .'

BORN: 3rd November 1948 in Lennoxtown, Glasgow, Scotland, Father a butcher. **EDUCATED:** Whitehill School, Glasgow.
'I wasn't interested in school. I really didn't need things like science and geometry. School was good until I was 13, then I really hated it. I couldn't wait to leave and start full time in show business. My headmaster used to say; "You're an intelligent girl, why can't you do better?" I simply had no concentration whatsoever, and I was always in trouble for singing during lessons.'
Made her first public appearance as a singer at the age of four at a Coronation party. 'I've always been able to sing. My mother said I could sing before I could talk. I just loved to sing and I couldn't stop. At nine, I was Ruby Murray, at 10, Brenda Lee, then Kay Starr, Theresa Brewer and of course, Connie Francis. I used to listen to old 78s my father bought and would sit right up against the gramophone until he swore I'd go deaf.' When she was eight and on holiday in Blackpool, she pushed her way into a children's talent show and was so small she had to stand on a chair to reach the microphone. If the judges expected her to sing *Baa Baa Black Sheep*, they were in for a shock. She belted out Frankie Vaughan's *Garden of Eden* and carried off the first prize.
FIRST JOB: 1958, singing with the Caledonian Accordion Band at Bridgeton Public Hall, Dennistoun, for 10s. While still at school, sang with a local band called the Bellrocks, then at 14, started playing club engagements around Glasgow and Edinburgh with another local band, the Gleneagles. 'But Dad

made me be home by 11 o'clock every night!' It was while she was watching another group perform that she heard the song *Shout*, and liked it so much she included it in her act. It was at the Lindella Club in Glasgow, one cold winter's night, wearing three cardigans and singing in spite of a terrible cold, that Lulu was seen by Marion Massey, who was to become her manager. 'When I was 14, I was very lucky. I was discovered, to use that terrible term, by a person who was absolutely sincere. Since I was five, people had been coming up to me saying; "Stick with me baby, and I'll make you a star". In fact nobody ever did anything for me, then Marion came along.' The first thing Marion Massey did was to change her protégée's name. Having described her to some friends as 'a lulu of a kid', the name stuck and the Gleneagles became the Luvvers. The first record company they approached turned them down, but within weeks they were signed up by Decca and had cut their first single, Lulu's favourite song, *Shout*. Because of not being allowed by law to make personal appearances or work on television until after her 15th birthday, the record wasn't released until the spring of 1964. By mid-summer it had climbed to No.7 in the charts. Lulu was on her way. In 1965 she was voted Britain's Most Promising Newcomer in Showbusiness by the *Melody Maker*. 1966 saw her parting company with her backing group the Luvvers and joining forces with record producer Mickie Most. She also made her acting debut in the film *To Sir with Love* with Sidney Poitier, and on stage, in the pantomime *Babes in the Wood* at the Wimbledon Theatre. 'It was a funny thing about the film. The producer James Clavell came round to see me *sing* and when I heard I'd been chosen and he asked me to do it, I nearly fainted. I said, "You want me to *act*?" I couldn't believe it. When I started shooting I was so nervous. I walked on to the set the first day and all the other kids had been to drama school and I thought, Oh dear! But the cast were marvellous and when I got into it, it felt great.'
The film proved to be another big turning point in her career, because when it was released in 1967, it broke box office records all over American and her recording of the title song went to the No.1 spot in the American charts. She toured the States that summer, appearing on most of the top television shows coast to coast. In November of that year she was chosen to appear in her first Royal Variety Show at the London Palladium. Meanwhile her chart entries in Britain had continued with *Leave a Little Love*, *The Boat that I Row*, *Let's Pretend*, *Boys* and *I'm a Tiger*. As well as hosting her own BBC Television series in 1968, she also returned to the States for a series of cabaret engagements including the Cocoanut Grove in Hollywood and was voted The Most Promising Vocalist of the Year. Back home, more awards were waiting—Britain's Top Girl Singer, Top TV Artiste—and she was named The World's Top Female Singer of the Year by *New Musical Express*.
In 1969 she sang Britain's entry in the Eurovision Song Contest, *Boom Bang a Bang* and shared first prize. The 70s continued to be as successful for her as the 60s had been, with Eamonn Andrews uttering those immortal words 'This is your life' when she was just 23! She starred in *Peter Pan* in Manchester in 1972 and again at the London Palladium in 1975. Her chart entries became fewer, but after an absence of four years from the hit parade, a chance meeting with David Bowie (qv) provided her with *The Man who Sold the World*, which reached the No.3 spot in 1974.
She tried her hand at being a DJ with *Sunday Best* on

London's Capital Radio in 1982 and the following year starred in Andrew Lloyd Webber's hit West End musical, *Song and Dance*. Since that recording of *Shout* 20 years ago, acknowledged by many as probably the best rock 'n' roll performance by a woman in the history of pop, she has established herself as a star on both sides of the Atlantic and it would be hard to imagine the popular music scene without her.

■ A moment to remember: 'When I was appearing in cabaret in Sheffield, I was sitting in my dressing-room discussing plans with my television producer when David Bowie walked in. He invited me to dinner, but I had to refuse because I had a business meeting. Anyway, he went off to play his gig and when he returned, he offered to write me a song. I agreed and no more was said. A few days later he telephoned me and said that if he wrote me a song, he'd like to produce it as well. So we got together to find the right song and came up with *The Man who Sold the World*, which quite honestly, when it was finished, I never thought of as being a hit. When it reached the charts, I was absolutely thrilled.' ■ Married to hairdresser, John Frieda, and has one son, Jordan.

VERA LYNN (Vera Welch)
'The Forces' Sweetheart . . .'
BORN: 20th March 1917 in London. Father a plumber's mate.
EDUCATED: Central Park Road Junior School. Brampton Road School, East Ham. From the age of seven was singing in working men's clubs around the East End of London. At 11,

joined Madam Harris's Kracker Kabaret Kids and changed her name, choosing her grandmother's maiden name, Lynn. 'I always wanted to be a singer, and didn't think Vera Welch would look good on a bill.' Was with the juvenile troupe for four years and even took it over for a year when Madame

Harris retired. **FIRST JOB:** Sewing on buttons in an East Ham factory for 6s.6d. per week. She stood it for just one day and was sent a postal order for 1s.1d. She soon realized that one concert at 7s.6d. was worth more than a whole week in the factory. Got her first break while appearing in cabaret at the Poplar Baths where she was heard by local band leader Howard Baker. After two years with Howard Baker was booked to sing with the Billy Cotton Band for a two-week engagement in Manchester and Sheffield. Half way through the second week she was sent home and was never sure of the reason why, although many years later Billy Cotton admitted it was the worst day's work he'd ever done! She also auditioned for and was turned down by Henry Hall around the same time. But in August 1935 she auditioned successfully for her first broadcast with Joe Loss, qv. This was followed by a series of broadcasts with Charlie Kunz, then resident at the Casani Club, with whom she made her first commercial record, *I'm in the Mood for Love*.

A big step up the ladder came in 1937 when she joined Ambrose and made her first television appearance with him from Alexandra Palace in 1938. Her decision to go solo in 1940 resulted in a six-week variety tour followed by her West End debut in *Apple Sauce* at the Empire. That same year she married clarinettist Harry Lewis from the Ambrose Band. Meanwhile the girl from East Ham was becoming a firm favourite with the troops, topping the BEF singing popularity poll, beating Deanna Durbin, Judy Garland and Bing Crosby. Vera Lynn had become the Forces' Sweetheart. Her tremendous popularity throughout the next few years was to prompt one comic to crack the gag: 'the Second World War was started by Vera Lynn's agent'. Her hugely popular radio series, *Sincerely Yours—Vera Lynn*, in 1941, resulted in an avalanche of mail. For the boys overseas she was their link with home. Their wives and girl friends loved her too, although there was one memorable occasion when a distraught wife telephoned the stage door at the London Coliseum, where Vera was appearing, saying her husband had left her and she'd found a photograph of Vera Lynn among his possessions. She was somewhat placated when she learned that at least a thousand similar photos were dispatched every week!

1942 brought her first Royal Command Performance at Windsor Castle and her first film, named after one of her biggest hits, *We'll Meet Again*. She was to make two more films *Rhythm Serenade* and *One Exciting Night*.

In March 1944 she joined ENSA for a three-month tour of Burma, a tour that was to fix her even more in the hearts and minds of the men of that hard fought campaign. This affection is demonstrated to this day at her appearances at the Burma Star Association reunions at London's Royal Albert Hall. She was back on the West End stage in 1952 for a two-year run in *London Laughs* at the Adelphi Theatre, having made a series of appearances on Tallulah Bankhead's *Big Show* on American radio. Her popularity in the States was assured when *Auf Wiedersehn* became the first British record to top the hit parade on both sides of the Atlantic simultaneously. With the opening up of Independent Television in 1955 she was given her own 17-week series and the following year signed a two-year contract with the BBC. The 60s saw her undertaking a series of overseas tours: Australia and New Zealand with an astonishing 48 concerts in 40 days; South Africa and Canada, plus frequent concert tours in Holland and Scandinavia. And in 1969 came what

many people remember as her best television series for the BBC in which she was partnered by the Young Generation, her repertoire now including many of the current popular songs. This in turn led to her making an album *Hits of the 60s*. 'In terms of sheer enjoyment it was one of the best things I've ever done.'

In 1968 she was awarded the OBE and in 1975 received the ultimate accolade when she was made a Dame of the British Empire. Three years later the Dutch added their own tribute when they made her Commander of the Order of Orange-Nassau. At the time she said that she didn't believe in dramatic retirements followed by endless come backs, and that she would gently phase herself out by doing less and less. But 1983 saw her touring Australia once again, and 1984 turned out to be a particularly busy year with a TV Special in Holland to celebrate the 75th birthday of Queen Juliana, a concert in Toronto, a Liberation Day concert in Arnhem and the 40th anniversary celebration of D-Day in June.

Today Dame Vera is as popular as she ever was, and her voice still sends shivers down your spine. She once said, 'Most of my life I've been lucky enough to be in the right place at the right time.' But it's her ability to make even the most trite lyrics sound utterly sincere that has given her an unassailable position in the history of British popular music. Her autobiography, *Vocal Refrain*, was published in 1975.

■ Highspot of career: Being made a DBE. ■ A moment to remember: At the height of the blitz, a recording session which was due to begin at 9am in a studio in West Hampstead, a long journey from Barking at the best of times, and the morning after a heavy air raid was certainly not that. After several unsuccessful attempts to drive through the West End, she was told to divert and drive around the outside of London which resulted in her arriving at the studio with just 10 minutes of the recording session left. She sang both songs through once and that was it. The record was released, although she can't recall which songs she sang that day! ■ Likes gardening, sewing, painting and cooking. ■ Dislikes 'People smoking cigars in my face' and people who drink to excess. ■ Married to Harry Lewis, has one daughter, Virginia, and lives in Sussex.

MADNESS
'Nutty but nice . . .'

It all started in North London in 1976 when Mike Barson, Lee Thompson and Chris Foreman tried to play along with an old Fats Domino LP which, rumour has it, they nicked from a record shop in Camden Town. Mike was the only one who could actually play anything as he had had some piano lessons and had carried on from there. Chris will try anything, so he had a go at a one-string guitar and the drums. Lee fancied playing the saxophone and proceeded to teach himself. Anyone listening would have been hard put to imagine this as the nucleus of what was to be one of the most successful pop groups of the 80s. But it was to be a couple of years before some sort of sound began to develop, a mixture of Jamaican ska, Motown and Presley which they nicknamed the Nutty Sound.

In 1979, the Invaders, as they were known, became very briefly Morris and the Minors, before Chris Foreman came up with the perfect name for the nutty sound, Madness. That same year, The Specials launched their own record label,

Two Tone, and on it Madness released their first single, *The Prince*. It reached No.16 in the charts and the group signed with Stiff Records for their second single, *One Step Beyond* and their first album of the same name. The album entered the charts at No.16 and the single reached No.7. It was the start of the Madness era.

In 1980, having had 46 weeks in the singles charts and 56 weeks in the album charts, they were named Singles Artists of the year by *New Musical Express*. With their crazy visual presentation on stage, they were a guaranteed sell-out wherever they appeared. In March of that year they played a Saturday morning gig at Hammersmith Odeon especially for the under-16s: it was so successful that in December on their Twelve Days of Madness tour around the UK, each regular evening performance was preceded by an under-16 matinee.

In 1981, the Madness story, from its very beginnings in 1976 to 'take off' year, 1979, was immortalized on film financed by the boys themselves and their record company. Suggs said at the time, 'We want the film to be about us as people and how the band Madness came to be. Also we think someone should do a proper film about starting a group.' With several European tours and a brief visit to America in '79, behind them, April 1981 saw the start of their most ambitious tour aptly called, Absolutely Madness One Step Beyond Far East Tour, taking in New Zealand, Australia, Japan and the USA. In May 1982 all their previous promo videos were released as *Complete Madness* which shot to the top of the video charts and by the end of that year they had clocked up 13 consecutive hits in the UK along with five Top 10 LPs. But they had yet to crack the American charts. They did it in the summer of '83 after signing to the American label, Geffen Records. With *Our House*, their first single on the new label, in the US charts, the band undertook a five-week tour of the States. They seemed set to make it big on both sides of Atlantic, but all was not well within their ranks and in January 1984 Mike Barson left the band he'd helped to form eight years previously. He'd once said, 'I hate the attitude that there's somethig special about music or musicians. I think that anyone should be able to have a go at it.' At least he, along with the six other members of the group, have proved that point. They had a go and they succeeded. The remaining six Nutty boys have been joined by Clive Langer on keyboards and will hopefully continue to entertain themselves and their fans with their own particular brand of madness.

Mike Barson (Keyboards)
BORN: 21st April 1958 in Edinburgh. EDUCATED: Cricklewood Secondary School. Hornsey Art College. (1 year). Taught himself to play piano. Had a few lessons but mostly picked it up playing along with records. Very much influenced by his elder brother, Ben, who is a professional musician. FIRST JOB: Window cleaner. Then became a gardener before forming a group called The Invaders along with Lee Thompson and Chris Foreman.

■ Married to Sandra Wilson and lives in Holland. (He didn't tell the rest of the band he was getting married, he just said 'I'll be a bit late for rehearsals on Saturday.')

Lee Thompson (Thommo) (Saxophone)
BORN: 5th October 1957 in Kentish Town, London. FIRST JOB: Gardener. He liked the look of the saxophone so taught himself to play one. He's a natural showman and enjoys his music, saying, 'Music should be fun and above all, loving. I was never a punk for that reason. I wouldn't give it an inch because of the way they looked, the aggressiveness and everything.'

■ A moment to remember: During their first tour of Australia, while swimming off Bondi Beach, he was caught by a freak wave and rescued by two burly Aussie lifeguards, who then sheepishly asked for his autograph. A fair exchange. ■ Likes cycling and Gary Glitter. ■ Married to Debbie, has one daughter, Tuesday, and lives in London.

Chris Foreman (Chrissy Boy) (Guitar)
BORN: 8th August 1955 in University College Hospital, London. Father a folk singer. EDUCATED: Owen's Grammar School, The Angel, London. FIRST JOB: Gardener. He changed the name of the band from The Invaders to Madness, after the title of a Prince Buster song. Christened King of the Sydney Mods, by his fans down-under, he's very much the hard headed businessman, dealing with the tour schedules and keeping the books. Is a self-taught guitarist, who could barely strum a chord when he helped form the Invaders. Writes a lot of the group's material. 'I've written so many songs and bits of songs that it'll take years to get round to recording them all, by which time, no doubt, there'll be hundreds more! I feel like recording them all now!'

■ A moment to remember: Christmas 1983 when Madness held a party in Covent Garden. Feeling in festive mood he gave away his tickets to some fans waiting outside and was then refused admission himself, on the grounds he didn't have an invitation. His pleas of 'But I'm in the band', were of no avail; the man at the door was adamant, no ticket, no entry. He eventually made it with someone who had a spare invitation.

Mark Bedford (Bedders) (Bass)
BORN: 24th August 1961 in Islington, London. **EDUCATED:** William Ellis School, Islington. Formed his first band while still at school, which played mostly Beatles music. A classmate, Gary Dovey, who was playing drums for the Invaders, introduced him to the group, but left soon after, leaving Mark feeling somewhat stranded, as he admitted later 'it was a bit unnerving to suddenly find myself in a band with older blokes who I had no connection with.'

■ Likes the Motown sound.

Daniel Woodgate (Woody) (Drums)
BORN: 19th October 1960 in Maida Vale, London.
played drums, with his brother on guitar in a line-up called Steel Erection, with whom his friend, Mark Bedford, also occasionally jammed along on bass. But when Mark started playing regularly with the Invaders, Woody auditioned for them when Gary Dovey walked out. Since joining the band he has tried his hand at song writing. *Sunday Morning* was his first song-writing credit and he also wrote the music to Carl Smyth's words for *Michael Caine*. 'Really, the most rewarding aspect of the group for me is knowing that thousands of people are happy listening to a song that I play drums on!'

■ Married to ex Modettes' bass player, Jane.

Carl Smyth (Chas Smash) (Vocals, compère, dancer, 'most recent addition the trumpet.')
BORN: 14th January 1958 in the Middlesex Hospital, London. His parents were competitive Irish dancers. **EDUCATED:** Finchley High School, although by his own admission, his attendances were infrequent and he spent most of his youth 'on the razzle'. **FIRST JOB:** Window cleaner. But it was by almost following in his parents' footsteps that was to get him off one kind of ladder and on to another. 'I never went near a dance floor until I was 17 and I was always scared and nervous. I still find it really hard to dance, but when you've had a few bevvies, you have to move about, don't you?' It was his 'moving about' at the Dublin Castle in Camden Town one night that prompted Lee Thompson to ask him up on stage to introduce the Invaders. Carl got carried away and a new dimension of nuttiness was added to the band. The Chas Smash character came about by accident, literally, as, when a friend of Carl's had to have his head shaved because of a bad cut he got in a fight, Lee Thompson bet him he wouldn't dare have the same crop. Carl won the bet. But since those early days, he's developed a certain vocal style, become proficient at playing the trumpet and written the lyrics for *Michael Caine*.

VALERIE MASTERS
'Radio has an amazing advantage over television . . .'
BORN: 24th April 1940, in London. **EDUCATED:** in London. Has studied the technique of singing and has learned to sight

read music. **FIRST JOB:** Singing with the Ray Ellington Quartet in 1957. Made her first broadcast in 1958 on *In Town Tonight*. Has sung with many different bands throughout her career and has had her own television and radio programmes. She broadcasts regularly with the BBC Radio Orchestra. Recent television credits include *Come Sunday*, Yorkshire Television; *Sunday at Winchester*, Southern Television; *Seaside Special*, BBC 1; *Secret Army*, BBC 1; *P.S It's Paul Squires* series, Central Television. She represented the BBC at the 1982 Nordring Radio Festival where she won the soloist's prize which resulted in her being given her own show on Belgian radio. Was chosen by Barbara Streisand to sing counterpoint harmony with her on one of the songs in the film *Yentl*, released in 1984. Michel Legrand who was Musical Director for the film was sufficiently impressed to ask her to send a tape to him in France. Her voice is heard frequently on both television and radio commercials.

■ Highspot of career: 'When I had my hit record with *Banjo Boy* in 1959 and singing at the London Palladium.' ■ 'I have the greatest love for the BBC because through them, I have been able to keep singing and therefore keep in touch with all sorts of people, especially since the death of my husband. An amazing advantage radio has over television is that the artist can paint a picture of any type and try to get the listener to use his imagination, when in fact you are probably just sitting on a stool in a studio in front of a microphone.'
■ Likes painting, sewing and collecting. Dislikes smoking and arguing. Is the widow of pianist Dick Katz, has two daughters, one of whom, Debbie Katz, has made a name for herself as a singer. Lives in Buckinghamshire.

PAUL McCARTNEY
'Not bad for a scruff from Liverpool . . .'
BORN: 18th June 1942 in Liverpool. **EDUCATED:** Liverpool Institute. 'When I was 13 or 14, trumpeters were the big heroes, guitars hadn't come in yet, but I couldn't sing with a trumpet and I wanted to sing. The first time I really ever felt a tingle up my spine was when I saw Bill Haley and the Comets

on the telly.' He saved up his pocket money for weeks, so that he could go and see Bill Haley on his first British tour. 'The ticket was 24s. and I was the only one of my mates who could go as no one else had been able to save that amount. But I was single-minded about it, having got that tingle up my spine I knew there was something going here.' **FIRST JOB:** In 1956, while still at school, joined a group called the Quarrymen which had been formed by John Lennon. He had been invited to the Walton Garden Fete where the Quarrymen were playing. 'I noticed this fella singing with his guitar and he was playing bum chords and he was singing *Come Go With Me* and I realized he was changing the words into folk song and chain gang words, a clever bit of ingenuity, and that was Johnny Lennon. My mate Ivan knew them, so we went backstage and after a couple of drinks we were around the piano singing songs to each other. Later they sort of approached me on a bike somewhere and said, "You wanna join?". We used to go round the record shops, listen to the record in the booth and then not buy it. They used to get very annoyed with us, but we had the words by then.'

Another school friend, George Harrison, also joined the Quarrymen and after playing locally, they got an audition with impresario Larry Parnes who sent them off on a tour of Scotland as backing group to Johnny Gentle. They changed their name to the Beatles and accepted an engagement in Hamburg. It was on their second visit to Hamburg that they made their first records as a backing group for Tony Sheridan under the direction of Bert Kaempfert. Back in Liverpool, appearing at the Cavern, the Beatles were taken in hand by record shop owner Brian Epstein who arranged an audition with Decca records. Nothing came of it, but George Martin at EMI liked their demo tapes and offered them a recording contract in September 1962. Their first single *Love Me Do*, reached No.17 in the charts and a couple of months later, their second, *Please Please Me* shot to No.2 and the Beatle bandwagon had begun to roll. 'It was a fabulous band to play with, the Beatles, and we played together long enough to get very comfortable with each other on the music side.'

McCartney had started writing songs with John Lennon while they were still at school. His way with a melody coupled with a certain romantic charm in his writing made a perfect foil to the aggressiveness and satiric bite of John Lennon's work. Together they made a formidable team and their output over the next seven years was to rank them with the Gershwins. With the break-up of the Beatles in 1970, he made his debut solo album called simply *McCartney* and the following year formed Wings with his wife Linda, whom he'd married in 1969. It became one of the most successful groups of the 70s with *Mull of Kintyre* in 1977 breaking all records as Britain's biggest-ever selling single. With the break-up of Wings in 1980, he continued to turn out the hits, duetting with Stevie Wonder on *Ebony and Ivory*, and with Michael Jackson on *The Girl is Mine*. In January 1984, the title track from his album *Pipes of Peace* topped the charts 21 years after his first chart topper with the Beatles. In 1979 he received the Triple Superlative Award and a Rhodium Disc from the Guinness Book of Records to commemorate his achievement as a composer with 43 songs with sales of over one million copies each, as well as sales of over 200 million singles and albums. Those totals have long since been exceeded and they are unlikely to be equalled by anyone in the forseeable future. As he once said, 'Not bad for a scruff from Liverpool!'

■ Highspot of career: 'I think one of the big highspots of what we did with the Beatles, was opening up the American market for Britain. At that age we were so cocky and confident in our own ability that we said to our manager that we wouldn't go to America until we'd got a No.1. And that was the crux of the whole thing. That American tour took off from the fact that we were No.1 and that's why they still remember it as a big show business event.' ■ A moment to remember: 'In the early days in talent spotting contests, we kept getting beaten by this woman who played the spoons. We reckoned we were never going to beat this little old lady as she wiped the floor with us every time. That's when we decided to knock talent contests on the head!' ■ Likes drawing, painting, making pottery and playing his guitar.
■ Married to Linda, has one son and three daughters.

GEORGY MELLY
'Good time George . . .'
BORN: 17th August 1926. Father a wool-broker. **EDUCATED:** Stowe School, Buckingham. He served in the Royal Navy 1944–47. **FIRST JOB:** Art Gallery Assistant at the London Gallery for three years. Sang with Mick Mulligan's Jazz Band 1951–62 and made his first broadcast sometime in the early 50s. In 1956 he started to draw the Flook strip cartoon and continued to do so until 1971. Left the Mulligan Band in order to concentrate on journalism, joining *The Observer* first as TV critic and later as film critic. he won the IPC Critic of the Year Award in 1967. Returned to music with John Chilton's Feetwarmers in 1973. Has been voted *Melody Maker* Male Vocalist of the Year many times, has made numerous recordings and his BBC 2 television series *Good Time George* has won much acclaim. He also makes regular appearances on Radio 2's *Jazz Score* and as well as being rated as a very fine Blues singer has become a larger than life personality in the jazz world. Has written many books including *I Flook* (1962); *Rum, Bum and Concertina* (1977); *Mellymobile* (1982).

■ Highspots of career: 'Singing a duet with (a) Bette Midler and (b) Eartha Kitt, two of my goddesses and both as warm and friendly as could be. The former turned up at a jazz club in Camberley before she was well known in the UK. Also going back on the road with John Chilton, visiting Australia and getting a rave review in the *New York Times*.' ■ A moment to remember: 'I went up to the Newcastle area to do a local television commerical for a home improvements supermarket. I sang a little song and jumped about the supermarket – all in the day's work. Not long afterwards I was appearing at Ronnie Scott's in London, when a young Geordie boy came up to me in the club and said, "You are the man that did that supermarket telly commercial aren't you?" So, yes I admitted this, and he said, "That's why I've come to see you." And I thought, God, I've been at it since 1948, singing Blues, flogging up and down the roads of Great Britain, travelling the world and finally someone is prepared to pay to come to see me at Ronnie Scott's because I've done an advertisement for a supermarket! A sign of the times I suppose.' ■ Likes Bessie Smith, Rene Magritte and fly fishing. ■ Dislikes politicians (with very few exceptions), authority figures and moog synthesizers. ■ Married to Diana, has one son, one daughter and a step-daughter and lives in London and Powys.

World of Music. Radio 3 programmes include the Strauss opera *Wiener Blutt* and the operetta *les Cloches de Cornville*.

■ Highspot of career: 'Isn't our business one long high spot? ■ A moment to remember: 'It didn't actually happen, as it was a dream, but a very vivid one. I arrived at a broadcasting studio to meet everyone coming out. The show was over and worst of all, nobody had missed me!' ■ Likes driving, embroidery, horseriding and gardening. ■ Dislikes packing and unpacking . . .ugh! Oh yes, and spiders! ■ Is the sister of tenor Vernon Midgley (qv) and lives in Surrey.

MARYETTA MIDGLEY
'Our business is one long highspot . . .'
BORN: 27th May, in Edinburgh, Scotland. Father the international tenor, Walter Midgley. **EDUCATED:** Holy Cross Convent, New Malden, Surrey. She won a music scholarship to the Trinity College of Music, London where she studied singing and the piano. **FIRST JOB:** Soloist with the George Mitchell Singers. Made her first broadcast as a child in *Round the Horn*. Has appeared in the *Fol-De-Rols* at the Congress Theatre, Eastbourne and in *Camelot* at Drury Lane. She broadcasts regularly on Radio 2 on such programmes as *Friday Night is Music Night*, *Melodies for You*, *Among Your Souvenirs*, *Saturday Night is Gala Night* and *Robert Farnon's*

VERNON MIDGLEY
'On stage alone, singing a duet . . .'
BORN: 28th May in Worcester Park, Surrey. Father, the international tenor, Walter Midgley. **EDUCATED:** Bishop's Stortford College. Royal Academy of Music where he studied singing and the piano. (Sisselle Wray Scholar). **FIRST JOB:** Entomologist with the Ministry of Agriculture, Fisheries and Food, Pest infestation Headquarters at Tolworth, Surrey. 'At one time I was offered the job of Assistant Pro to Vic Saunders at Coombe Wood Golf Club, but I turned it down.' Made his first broadcast in *Lights of London* in 1971. Has sung with the Ambrosian Opera Chorus and with most of the military and brass bands in the country. Has sung in many full-length operas and operettas on Radio 3. Radio 2 programmes include *Grand Hotel*, *Ring Up the Curtain*, *Among Your Souvenirs*, *Your Hundred Best Tunes*, *Bakers Dozen*, *Glamorous Nights*, and *Walter Midgley Remembers*; and on Radio 4, *Music to Remember*. Broadcasts regularly on Radio 2's *Friday Night is Music Night* and *Melodies for You*.

■ Highspots of career: 'Whenever I have been privileged to be presented to a member of the Royal Family. In broadcasting, it took place in Israel on Good Friday, 1981 when I sang in a Bach concert relayed by the Israel Broadcasting Authority. The Old City was *the* exciting place to be on a Good Friday and I shall never forget the smell of orange blossom in the evening. The Swedish conductor, Eric Ericson, and I were the only non-Israelis taking part.' ■ A moment to remember: 'During a "live" public performance of *Friday Night is Music Night*, at the Free Trade Hall, Manchester in September 1978, I found myself alone on stage, singing a duet! The soprano was locked in the toilet of her dressing-room. Happily I knew her lines, but the conductor slowed the performance to a snail's pace in a vain attempt to enable the unfortunate girl to join us, which she eventually did as I was singing the line, "Tell me that where e'er you go . . ."'! ■ Likes golf, cricket, painting and drawing. ■ Dislikes tripe, bagpipes played too near and discos. ■ Married to New Zealand soprano Alexandra Gordon, has a son and a daughter and lives in Surrey.

'Nothing funny ever happens to me – disastrous, yes; tragic, yes; hysterical, yes; horrendous, yes; funny? never, but I'm open to offers!' ■ Likes dancing, gardening, swimming and cooking. ■ Dislikes the cold, noisy people, accountancy and bank managers. ■ Lives in Surrey.

TRACY MILLER
'Nothing funny ever happens to me . . .'
BORN: in County Durham. Father a brick maker. **EDUCATED:** Fence Houses Secondary Modern School. Durham Technical College. Studied singing at the Guildhall School of Music London. **FIRST JOB:** Singing at the Continental Hotel, St Helier, Jersey. Made her first broadcast as a backing singer with Clodagh Rogers in 1968. As a soloist in 1979. She has sung with many vocal groups – Sounds Bob Rogers, Polka Dots, Skylarks, Coffee Set, Neil Richardson Singers, Ladybirds, Breakaways, Ambrosian Singers, Charles Young Chorale, Cliff Adam Singers, Ray Charles Singers, Anita Kerr Singers. Has sung with the bands of Syd Lawrence and Jack Parnell. As a soloist she sang on the Monte Carlo Radio Prize entry in 1982 and the 1979 Nordring Radio Prize. She broadcasts regularly with the BBC Radio Orchestra and is heard on most of Radio 2's music programmes including *Night Ride* and *String Sound*. Television credits include the Val Doonican series *Helen McCarthy Show* for Scottish Television and *World of . . .* on BBC 2.

■ Highspot of career: 'Appearing with Perry Como on the Royal Variety Show in 1976. ■ A moment to remember:

MATT MONROE (Terry Parsons)
'Headlining at The Sands, Las Vegas . . .'
BORN: 1st December 1930 in London. Father a chemical worker. **EDUCATED:** Various schools in the East End of London. When his father died in 1934, and his mother became ill, he spent a year in an orphanage. At school sang in the choir but was never allowed to sing a solo as they said he sang out of tune! **FIRST JOB:** Offal boy at the Imperial Tobacco factory in City Road, where he nearly smoked himself to death! Numerous jobs followed – an apprenticeship in the building trade and a fireman on the railway – but he wanted to see the world, so enlisted in the army at 17 and was posted to Hong Kong. He entered and won six talent contests and was banned from entering any more! Made his first broadcast on Hong Kong Radio, introduced thus. 'And now Terry Parsons sings.'
Demobbed and back in the UK, he took a job as a long-distance lorry driver and on a trip to Glasgow, cut a demo record which a friend sent to Winifred Atwell. He switched to driving buses and while driving a No.27 bus in London was told that Winifred Atwell had got him an audition with a recording company. So he turned up at his first professional recording session wearing his bus driver's uniform. At the end of that session, the musicians applauded. His new career had started and he changed his name: Matt after the first Fleet Street journalist to write about him and Monroe after Winifred Atwell's father. His first break on radio came when he became the regular singer with Cyril Stapleton's Show Band. People thought he sounded like Sinatra, so much so that in 1959 he was asked to appear as the mystery singer on

a Peter Sellers album, *Songs for Swinging Sellers*. He was billed as Fred Flange, the inference being it was Ol' Blue Eyes himself.

The following year brought the hit record Matt had waited so long for. 'I recorded *Portrait of my Love* which I was convinced was the most uncommercial song I had ever heard. But within about two weeks of release, it was in the charts and stayed there for months. 'Other hits followed, *My Kind of Girl, Softly as I Leave You* and the title track of the James Bond film *From Russia with Love*. Has had many successful albums over the years, including several in America where in November 1983 he topped the bill at The Sands, Las Vegas, with a return booking in January 1984. The hits may no longer be forthcoming, but Matt has joined that élite band of international cabaret performers whose talent is applauded the world over.

■ Highspots of career: 'Appearing at a Royal Command Performance, working at the London Palladium, and topping the bill at The Sands, Las Vegas.' ■ A moment to remember: 'I had been asked to appear at the opening night of the Greaseborough Working Men's Club. A little mining village in the middle of nowhere. We arrived in the afternoon of the rehearsal and everything was fine. They had bought a special mike for me to use and after we'd run through everything, I drove back to the hotel where I was staying, I think it was in Huddersfield. That night, when I drove back to the club for the performance, it was pitch dark, of course, and we got hopelessly lost. I had the Roller in those days and there we were, four of us in the car all dressed up to the nines, driving around this mining village and it was as black as coal! No street lights or street names, when we saw an old fellow shuffling along the side of the road, so I stopped the Roller, down with the electric window, and "Excuse me, can you direct us to the Working Men's Club?" He peered in and said, "Aye, you turn round, go back up road, turn to right and when you get to top of rise, look down and you'll see a lot of lights down bottom of hill, That's it, but you'll not get in, Matt Monroe's on tonight." I don't know who he expected to see driving around Greaseborough at 11 o'clock at night in a Rolls Royce!' ■ Likes desserts and television, preferably together! ■ Dislikes women who make up in public, especially at table. 'It really turns my stomach. Smoking doesn't bother me because I smoke, but I don't wear lipstick!' ■ Married to Mickie, has a daughter, Michelle, and a son, Matthew, and lives in London.

MARIAN MONTGOMERY
'A confirmed Anglophile . . .'

BORN: Natchez, Mississippi, USA. Father a hotelier. **EDUCATED:** Gainesville, Georgia High School. Virginia Intermont College. Brenau College. **FIRST JOB:** Singing on television in Atlanta, Georgia while still in her teens. Was an established cabaret performer in the States before coming to the UK in 1965 and has a thousand tales to tell . . . like driving along the Los Angeles freeway with Cy Coleman singing *You Are My Sunshine*, with the tears streaming down their faces from the smog and later, at Coleman's house rehearsing songs for an album, the doorbell rings and it's Doris Day, more than a little annoyed that she hadn't been asked to do the album; and the time she, Nancy Wilson and Peggy Lee used to vie for the same material . . . Peggy always won! Being in Miami

with Mel Torme, Jack Jones, Dave King, Joe Williams and Shirley and Gordon McCrea when they all used to wind up at an after-hours club and sit in with the band . . . the club became the most popular rendezvous in town! Since living in the UK, Marian has presented her one-woman show and had a very successful collaboration with classical pianist/composer Richard Rodney Bennett. She broadcasts regularly with the BBC Radio Orchestra/Radio Big Band and is heard on many of Radio 2's music programmes including *Night Ride* and *Big Band Special*. She has appeared at Ronnie Scott's, Quaglino's, the London Palladium and at top cabaret venues around the UK. 1983 Saw her touring with American guitarists Herb Ellis and Barney Kessel.

■ Highspot of career: 'Every time I go on stage.' ■ A moment to remember: 'I was working in Australia and on my return to the UK was due to sing at a Gershwin concert in London. My husband, Laurie Holloway, telephoned me and said we were one number short, how about doing *Why do I love You*. "Fine" I said. So I get back from Australia and the next day is the day of the concert. Laurie's done a super arrangement but I rang Chappells, the music publishers, just to check that I had remembered the lyrics as I hadn't got a song copy. Much to my surprise they said they hadn't got a copy and would have to telex New York. "Oh come off it", I said, "you must have a copy of *Why Do I Love You*. We have a copy of Jerome Kern's *Why Do I Love You*, but not Gershwin's.' Horror of horrors, we had made a dreadful mistake and how was I going to sing a Kern song in a Gershwin concert? No way could I drop it, because there was nothing else ready. So I came on stage and told the story of how George Gershwin and Jerome Kern were good friends and over dinner one night, they got to discussing who could write the best song and they both said they would write *Why Do I Love You*. "Ladies and gentlemen" I said, "I will leave it to you to decide whether this was the best song", without saying which it was! I thought I had got away with it until someone in the audience came up to me after the concert and said "That was a nice little story, I happen to know those two songs were written years apart. One day that's going to end up in a book."' [How right they were, it has!] ■ Likes reading and riding! ■ Dislikes big parties, phoney people and loud places. ■ Married to MD/pianist Laurie Holloway. (qv), has one daughter and lives in Berkshire.

THE NOLANS
'We'll pack it in as soon as people stop coming to see us . . .'

ANNE BORN: 12th November 1952 in Dublin.
MAUREEN BORN: 14th June 1954 in Dublin.
BERNADETTE BORN: 17th October 1961 in Dublin.
COLEEN BORN: 12th March 1965 in Blackpool.

Parents, Tommy and Maureen Nolan, were stars in Ireland before the girls were born. Tommy was the first singer to broadcast on Radio Telefís Eireann while Maureen was dubbed the Irish Forces' Sweetheart and when they teamed up as a singing duo they became known as the Sweetheart Singers.

In the early 60s, just after Bernadette was born, the family moved to Blackpool and it wasn't long before the children were being included in the act. Maureen recalls; 'My parents used to take us along to their shows and before long, we'd be up on stage singing with them. As we all became more and more interested in showbusiness, the entire family was worked into the stage act as each new arrival came along.' At one time there were nine members of the family taking part; Tommy and Maureen with daughters Anne, Denise, Maureen, Linda and Bernadette, and sons Tommy and Brian. The Sweetheart Singers worked in clubs and hotels throughout Britain during the remainder of the 60s and into the 70s. But the five girls were fast becoming the mainstay of the act and in 1974, Mum, Dad and the boys decided to bow out and leave the stage free for the Nolan Sisters.

One of their first major engagements on their own was in cabaret at the London Room in Drury Lane, London. But the big break came when they landed a BBC Television series, *The Cliff Richard Show.* Suddenly the Nolans became household names. The following year, 1975, they were the supporting act to Frank Sinatra for his European Concert Tour including an appearance at London's Royal Albert Hall. It was still very much a family business with Tommy acting as the group's business manager, paying each of the girls a weekly wage. In 1976 he decided to move the family to the London area. Bernadette: 'When we first came to London we were really naïve. I think it was coming from a big family. We were all very close, and all brought up to help others, but when we came to London we found out that life wasn't as simple as that.' The girls had had a strict Roman Catholic upbringing – no dating before 18, no lipstick before 16 and no stockings or tights before 14. Bernadette: 'With Mum, her bark was worse than her bite, but Dad just had to say one word and that was it. I never argued with him, his word was final. They wouldn't let me go out on my own when I was younger, and it did get on my nerves. Looking back, it must have been difficult raising six daughters, but I don't think I would be as strict as that with my children.'

Coleen at 13, was still too young to join the act in 1978 when Denise decided to leave in order to go solo. So the five Nolans became four and went on to conquer new heights. Later that year they appeared in the Royal Variety Show at the London Palladium. 1979 saw their first Top 10 entry with *Spirit, Body and Soul,* but they were already top recording

stars in Japan and made their first tour of that country in 1980. They've sold an astonishing nine million records in Japan to date. Bernadette: 'It's amazing there, the fans are all teenagers. Young kids who follow us around, throwing presents up on stage, like we're The Police or something!' The summer of 1980 saw them headlining with Mike Yarwood at the Blackpool Opera House and during the season, Anne, who had married footballer Brian Wilson the previous summer, announced she was going to have a baby. Coleen was still too young to work full time, but once Anne left in October, she made several appearances with the group, although she didn't join officially until her 16th birthday in March 1981.

Shortly afterwards, on another tour of Japan, the Nolans won the Grand Prix Award at the Tokyo Music Festival with their entry *Sexy Music.* But 'sexy' was the one adjective that was not being used by the Press to describe the homegrown act from Ireland. 'A singing sisterhood of set smiles and musical syrup' was how one journalist described them. The girls have their say: Bernadette, 'Linda, Maureen and I were called the three wise virgins when we went to a night-club in 1976; Coleen, 'When I went out with friends before I started singing in the act, they didn't like the Nolans and because they didn't, I pretended I wasn't a Nolan and didn't like them either.'; Linda, 'If I wasn't in showbusiness, I would be envious of the Nolan Sisters, and that's half the trouble with most people. I went to a concert one night with my boy-friend and someone at the bar pointed to me and asked; 'What's IT doing here.''; Maureen; 'Even though we have hit records, people still think of us as being puppyish and twee and all smiles. Our jaws ache from smiling. We get very close to tears at night when we are alone together. The slagging and the rubbishing we get does make us cry deep down. We are not hardened to it and we don't want to be. The exterior may be brave but if you get hard inside, you dry up. We'd like to appear sexier but without being a sort of Hot Gossip.' They tried changing their image to publicize their new single in 1983. *Dressed to Kill* was the title and the girls wore black punklike skimpies for the occasion, but it didn't work, their fans didn't like it and the record didn't do too well either after there had been rumours of chart rigging.

The four Nolans had become five again with the return of Anne late in 1982, but not for long. Towards the end of 1983, Linda announced she wanted to go solo. 'I'm leaving the group, but not the family. When I first talked about leaving, they said, "Please don't go, but you've got our blessing".' One of the most popular acts on British television, with regular entries in the charts, the Nolans are back to four once again, Anne, Maureen, Bernadette and Coleen – until the next one goes. Perhaps they should record their own version of the old nursery rhyme, starting with the words: 'Five little Irish girls . . .!'

■ Moments to remember: Anne, 'The day I went to see Torquay United play Bristol City. Torquay won 1–0 and when I went to move my car after the match it was surrounded by dozens of Bristol supporters. I thought they were going to turn the car over. It was the most frightening experience of my life.'
Maureen, 'The day a man hit Bernadette in a hamburger joint and I walloped him with my handbag. Next time something like that happens, I'll black somebody's eye. We do have Irish tempers you know!'

■ Dislike being asked to parties because they're the Nolans, and then being asked to sing. 'Well that's it, we're the first out of the door, because anyway you can't possibly sound as good as you do on stage with everything organized.'

Anne, married to Brian Wilson, has one daughter, Amy, and lives in Torquay.
Maureen, single.
Bernadette is single but has a boy-friend, Bob, who is a car salesman.
Coleen is single but has a boy-friend, Robin Smith, the group's Musical Director.

Bernadette, who is the lead singer, writes the odd lyric and does the choreography for the group, has the last say! 'Being a family protects us from the worst side of the business. You can be sucked into that way of life and I sometimes get sick of washing my hair, wearing make-up and dressing in smart clothes. In fact I'm not sure I like the business at all. I just love the singing, but even that won't last for ever and we've all agreed we'll pack it in as soon as people stop coming to see us.'

regularly as the 'star singer' on Radio 2's *Friday Night is Music Night*.

■ Highspots of career: 'I have had several . . . appearing at the Persian Room in the Plaza Hotel, New York, only the second British girl to do so at that time; singing at the Royal Albert Hall; and in 1982, singing *Land of Hope and Glory* with the Band of the Scots Guards after the Falklands war had ended.' ■ A moment to remember: 'I was doing a "live" broadcast of *Grand Hotel* from the Aeolian Hall some years ago, and although children under the age of 10 weren't usually allowed into the studio, the producer had given permission for my young daughter to be there. As I walked on and started to sing she had a fit of coughing from nerves for me! It was so loud in the silence of the Concert Hall, that a very irate producer crept in and pulled her from her seat — I don't know how I carried on. I was warned afterwards to leave my family at home in future. Surprisingly the producer did book me again!' ■ Likes cooking, crochet and writing. ■ Dislikes cruelty to children and animals.
■ Married to hairdresser, Colin Curtis, has two daughters and lives in London.

LEONI PAGE
'Discovered by Barney Colehan . . .'
BORN: 7th November 1936, in London. Father a salesman.
EDUCATED: Aida Foster Stage School. **FIRST JOB:** 'On leaving school, I worked in a dress shop and then sold gramophone records, but my first big professional job, at the age of 17, was in the original *King and I* at the Theatre Royal, Drury Lane when I played one of the King's wives, opposite Herbert Lom. Made her first broadcast on 23rd December 1957 with Morecambe and Wise and the Alyn Ainsworth Orchestra in a programme produced by Geoff Lawrence. That same year was 'discovered' by Barney Colehan and appeared in one of the first *Good Old Days* shows from the City of Varieties, Leeds. Many other television appearances followed. Has sung with the Royal Philharmonic Orchestra, Mantovani, Max Jaffa, Geoff Love, Frank Chacksfield, Kenneth Alwyn, the BBC Concert Orchestra, the Band of the Welsh Guards and the Scots Guards. Radio programmes include *Charlie Katz Music Box, Workers Playtime, Mid-day Music Hall, Strings by Starlight, Those Were the Days,* the *Sam Costa Show,* the *Charlie Chester Show, Round Midnight, Salute to Noël Coward, Music for Your Pleasure,* and *Among Your Souvenirs.* Is heard

ELAINE PAIGE (Elaine Bickerstaff)
'It would be a lie to say I wasn't enjoying success . . .'
BORN: 5th March 1951 in Barnet, Hertfordshire. Father an estate agent. **EDUCATED:** Southaw Girl's School, East Barnet, Aida Foster School of Dance and Drama. 'I wasn't over fond of the academic side of my schooling, the one exam I passed was CSE English. When I went to Aida Foster's at 15, everyone seemed so confident. I was quite shy but I loved the dancing and discovered I had a natural ability for it. I thoroughly enjoyed my time there.' **FIRST JOB:** Her first successful audition after joining Aida Foster's was the Anthony Newley/Leslie Bricusse muscial, *The Roar of The Greasepaint, The Smell of The Crowd.* After leaving stage school she joined the cast of *Hair* at the Shaftesbury Theatre, and yes, she did eventually strip off along with everyone else. 'A guy called Gary said he'd hold my hand for support. He was 6ft 4in. tall and it wasn't his hand I grabbed!' She then appeared in several productions at *The Roundhouse* including *Rock Carmen,* but in 1973 was back in the West End with *Jesus Christ Superstar.* The following year provided

her with her first leading role in a West End Production, when she took over the part of Sandy from Stacey Gregg in *Grease*. Her next musical was *Billy* with Michael Crawford and after 18 months in the West End she decided to leave the cast of *Billy* to look for some non-musical roles, a move that led to 'one of the longest spells out of work I've ever had. I had an overdraft and was desperate. It was horrendous and I was really thinking of giving it all up. I always seemed to get through to the last two or three at auditions but never got the part! My father, who has always been very supportive, used to say, "Stick with it, you must be getting close."' She was. March 1978 was the turning point in her career when she won the coveted role of Eva Peron in the Tim Rice/Andrew Lloyd Webber musical *Evita*. The show and its star collected rave notices and the awards; the Society of West End Theatre's *Best Actress in a Musical*; the Variety Club's *Show Business Personality of the Year*, shared with her co-star David Essex (qv), and Gold and Platinum Albums for the London cast recording of the show. She left the cast after 20 months, but this time there was plenty of work on offer. She made her concert debut at the Royal Festival Hall in 1981 and later that year was back starring in the West End in another hit musical, *Cats*. Her recording of one of the songs from the show, *Memory*, got to No.5 in the charts. She also appeared in her first Royal Command Performance and recorded an album, *Elaine Paige*, which entered the album charts. She left the cast of *Cats* early in 1982, starring in her own BBC TV Special and joining Tony Bennett, George Burns and Mike Yarwood for the Royal Gala opening concert of

London's new Barbican Centre. In 1983 she released *Stages*, an album of songs from the musicals of the last 20 years and was awarded a Double Platinum Album for sales exceeding 600,000 in the UK alone. 1984 saw her appearing on the London stage as Carabosse in *Abbacadbra* and also recording an album of film songs and working with Tim Rice, Bjorn Ulvaeus and Benny Andersson on the recordings of their new musical *Chess*.

■ Highspot of career: 'Playing Eva Peron in *Evita*. My whole life suddenly changed. Everyone wanted a bit of me. It was a mass media avalanche. I got carried away with it all and nearly lost sight of who I was. At times it was very frightening, but if I said I wasn't enjoying the success it would be a lie.'   ■ A moment to remember: 'In *Cats*, my final exit was on a giant rubber tyre which carried me way, way above the stage and from there I had to walk up a flight of stairs to disappear from view. That was the worst part of the whole thing. It was about 50ft up, I was in high heels, the treads weren't a full foot's width and there was nothing to hold on to. I used to take a deep breath, think of England and move fast!'   ■ Likes cheese, the sea, gardening, antiques, tennis and shopping for clothes.   ■ Dislikes flying in helicopters and going to the dentist.   ■ Is single and lives in West London.

LYNSEY de PAUL
'First woman to win an Ivor Novello Award . . .'
BORN: 11th June 1950 in London, Father a furrier who later

became a property developer. **EDUCATED:** South Hampstead High School for Girls. Hornsey College of Art. Studied piano from the age of 11, with a Professor from the Royal Academy of Music, and gained an 'O' Level in music. 'A' Levels in German and Art. **FIRST JOB:** While still at college worked as a cartoonist, designing backdrops for cartoon companies, and a whole range of children's posters. But it was when she started to design record-album sleeves that she became involved in song writing. 'When you illustrate album sleeves, you have to listen to the music and it gives you a very good idea of how a song is structured, and having had a lot of experience of piano playing, I just thought I'd try to write a song; and six months after I tried for the first time, I had a hit.' That was in January 1972 when *Storm in a Teacup* was recorded by the Fortunes and got to No.7 in the charts. In 1974 she wrote and recorded *Won't Somebody Dance with Me* and with it became the first woman ever to win the Ivor Novello Award. Two years later she won it again with the theme for the television series *No, Honestly*. In 1976, her song *Rock Bottom*, was the British entry, and came second, in the Eurovision Song Contest and that same year she was voted Woman of the Year for Music by the Variety Club. 1982 saw her starring in a thriller at the Churchill Theatre, Bromley and Christmas 1983 playing the Princess in *Aladdin* at London's Shaftesbury Theatre.

■ Likes animals. ■ Dislikes cruelty to animals. ■ Is single, has two cats and lives in London.

POACHER
'Always striving to be that little bit different . . .'

Peter Frampton (Lead guitar, keyboards, vocals)
BORN: 8th November 1948 in Guernsey, Channel Islands. Father a bus inspector. **EDUCATED:** Elizabeth College, Guernsey. Croydon Technical College. Leicester Polytechnic. Started playing guitar at seven, after finding his uncle's ukelele in the attic. **FIRST JOB:** Council work-study engineer. Turned professional in 1974 and came to England. Spent three years with David Parton before joining Poacher.

■ Likes French cooking (he has a French wife!), composing and producing in the group's studio. ■ Dislikes insincerity and insecurity. ■ Married to Mimy, has one daughter, Angelina, one son, Dean, and lives in Cheshire.

Tim Flaherty (Lead vocals)
BORN: 25th September 1950 in Warrington, Cheshire. Father a packer. **EDUCATED:** St Benedicts; St Stephens; English Martyrs Secondary Modern School, Warrington. Played harmonica from age of 10. **FIRST JOB:** Apprentice carpenter and joiner. Played with the Free Wheelers before forming Poacher.

■ Is a bachelor and lives in Cheshire.

Allan Crookes (Bass guitar, vocals)
BORN: 27th April 1952 in Warrington. Father a publican. **EDUCATED:** Boteler Grammar School, Warrington. Was given his first guitar for his 11th birthday.

■ Likes all kinds of music and working in their studio helping younger musicians. ■ Married to Carol, has a dog named Sam and lives in Cheshire.

Martin Duffy (Drums)
BORN: 10th April 1948 in Manchester. Father a tailor. **EDUCATED:** De La Salle College, Salford, Lancashire. Played in a local pipe band while at school. **FIRST JOB:** Apprentice medical technician. Played with American Echoes, which became Tammy Cline's backing group, before joining Poacher.

■ Likes 90 per cent of all music. ■ Dislikes injustice. ■ Married to Carol, has two daughters, Helen and Jane, one son, Martin, and lives in Cheshire.

After Tim Flaherty left the Free Wheelers in the early 70s he wanted to get together a band to play basic American country/rock music. He got to meeting other musicians at a pub, The Poacher in Winstanley, Wigan, where each week they would get together to play the kind of music they enjoyed. The personnel changed quite a lot over the first couple of years, but gradually settled into a regular line-up who named themselves after the pub, and so in 1977 Poacher launched themselves onto the country music scene, with considerable success. During their first year, they won television's *New Faces* which led to bookings all over the UK on the club and theatre circuits. They made their American debut at the International Music Festival, Tulsa, Oklahoma in 1978, which coincided with the release in America of their British single *Darlin'* and with it they became the first British Band to enter the American Billboard Country Singles Chart. The record also made it to No.21 in the French charts and they appeared on both the Sacha Distel and Demis Roussos shows recorded in Paris. Making their first appearance at the Wembley Country Music Festival in 1979, they were named Best British Group, a title they carried off four years in succession. That same year they were awarded second prize by the American magazine *Cashbox* as Best New Vocal Group in the USA for their single *Darlin'*. They have appeared in Holland, Sweden, Denmark and represented England at the Golden Orpheus Music Festival in Bulgaria, following it up with a two-week tour of that country. They've made two tours of the UK with Don Williams and in the spring of '84 toured with Foster and Allen.

Their television and radio credits are numerous but they are still looking for a British hit with a British song. 'We have no direct musical policy, but choose songs which will appeal to our audiences. We're not a "Western" band as such, as we aim to have a much wider appeal and we're always striving to be that little bit different.'

■ Highspot of career: 'Finding the song *Darlin'* in the record company archives, recording it and seeing it enter the American and French charts.' ■ A moment to remember: 'When we went to Bulgaria, we lived like kings for two weeks, because you're not allowed to take any money out of the country, so we had to try to spend everything we had been paid. Going out, we had split the baggage up evenly between us, but coming back we checked in separately and we had bought so much stuff that our excess baggage bill was horrendous. I [Peter Frampton] checked in two guitars and two suitcases and was charged £180 excess from Sofia to Manchester!'

THE POLICE
'A success on their own terms . . .'
The original Police line-up Stewart Copeland, Sting and Henri Padovani, recorded their first single, *Fall Out*, in February 1977 with £150 Stewart Copeland had borrowed from a friend. Released on Copeland's own label it sold a couple of thousand copies, enough to cover the cost of the recording studio and to leave the group with a small profit. It was all part of the overall plan to be self supporting. After the departure of Henri Padovani and the recruiting of Andy Summers, Sting began contributing more songs to the band's repertoire including one that was to change their fortunes. *Roxanne* was about a prostitute and when it was released as their next single in April 1979, the BBC refused to play it, but, nevertheless, released on the A&M label this time, it made

enough money to cover the cost of a Laker flight to America. Stewart's brother, Miles Copeland who had taken over the management of the group, booked them into clubs along the East Coast. They travelled in a van, stayed in the cheapest motels they could find and allowed themselves $20 a day expenses. At the end of the tour, they'd made a profit and *Roxanne* was being played on more and more of the American radio stations. Their debut album, *Outlandos D'Amour*, from which *Roxanne* had been lifted, was released in the UK and on their return from the States they discovered that people were at last beginning to take notice and, in spite of the BBC's ban, *Roxanne* had reached No.12 in the charts. Still refusing subsidies from their record company, they returned to America to promote their album and with *Roxanne* at No.32 in the American charts they were making it on both sides of the Atlantic simultaneously. 1979 was to be their year.

The summer found them headlining a British tour for the first time, followed by the Reading Festival where they topped the bill in front of 30,000 screaming fans. The charts reflected their growing popularity, three mammoth hits in quick succession: *Can't Stand Losing You* at No.2; *Message in a Bottle* and *Walking on the Moon*, both making the No.1 spot. And in December they made history by playing the Hammersmith Palais and the Hammersmith Odeon on the same night, hiring an army half-track personnel carrier to take them around Hammersmith Broadway. Needless to say thousands of fans filled the streets and the traffic was brought to a halt, but it was a great publicity stunt.

Having conquered the UK, in January 1980 The Police set out to conquer the world. In a few short weeks they played in 19 countries, 37 cities and 4 continents. It was a triumph in every way. In just three years The Police had proved that they could go it alone without help from anyone and with the world at their feet they could pick and choose exactly what they wanted to do from now on. Each member could do his own thing; Sting making movies, Andy Summers taking photographs and recording with other musicians; Stewart Copeland undertaking various musical and film projects, and pointing out; 'It's absolutely crucial that we continue to diversify. We must have other things going on. Playing with other musicians, movies. We've got to get out of the group so we can get into the group.' 'If we don't do that,' added Sting, 'we'll turn into a circus.'

Together they continued to turn out the hits. *Don't Stand so Close to Me* became their third No.1 in the UK in 1980. With *Every Little Thing She Does is Magic* making it four in 1981, and in 1983, came the double No.1 when *Every Breath you Take* topped the charts on both sides of the Atlantic. Their albums have all made Platinum or Gold, not only in the USA and the UK but also in virtually every other country in the world, and in 1983, *Synchronicity* became their third LP in a row to enter the UK album charts at No.1. Their talent and their ability to come up with fresh ideas should guarantee their position at the top for as long as they have the wish to remain there, although in April 1984 Stewart Copeland had this to say, 'We've abdicated the throne for a year, to let the other boys have a go. Call it a sabbatical if you like, but we'll be back.'

■ Highspot of career: 'There have been two pinnacles. Headlining at the Marquee Club in Wardour Street in 1978 and appearing in front of 60,000 people at Shea Stadium,

New York in 1983. An appearance there is symbolic of conquering America and only five or six bands, including the Beatles, have ever played there. We sold it out in just five hours.'

Stewart Copeland (Drums)
BORN: 16th July 1952 on an airplane landing at Washington's National Airport! Father worked for the CIA. **EDUCATED:** Millfield Public School, Somerset, UK. University of California, San Diego, USA. He spent most of his early childhood in Beirut where his father was based from the late 50s until 1966, when the family moved to the UK. He showed no interest in music until his elder brother, Ian, got hold of a set of drums, but from then on he wanted to study percussion and took lessons while living in Beirut. He left Millfield with 7 'O' levels, and 'A' levels in English History and English Language. **FIRST JOB:** Selling advertising for a college magazine. Also worked as a 'roadie' for his brother's rock management agency and was road manager for Joan Armatrading on her first American tour. Back in the UK once again, he joined Curved Air, a group that was being promoted by his brother, Miles, but that was not having a great deal of success. However it did provide him with a wife, Sonja Kristina, who was fronting the band, and it started him thinking on how to beat the system of bands being tied to and subsidized by record companies, who took the majority of their profits. 'It suddenly began to dawn on me that the whole thing was completely bogus. The advances were so high that every album we made had to be a 100,000 seller just to break even'. So he decided to form a band that would be beholden to no one; it would make its own records, play the kind of music it wanted to play and keep its overheads low.

First recruit for the new line-up was guitarist Henri Padovani: the next, Gordon Sumner, nicknamed Sting, who he'd seen at a gig in Newcastle. 'It was a terrible gig. Everybody was taking it all very seriously and it was awful, but they were going down a storm because of Sting who had this fantastic presence. It was obvious he had enormous potential.' The newly formed trio rehearsed in Stewart's Mayfair pad. He had written enough songs to make up a 15-minute set and in order to get the band seen and heard, brother Miles put them on the road as a backing group for punk Cherry Vanilla, whom he'd brought over from the States. They played their first date at the Stowaway in Newport, South Wales. The Police were on their way. But why 'The Police'? 'You know how it is when a teenager takes his parent's car without permission and he's not insured, and maybe he has a little marijuana in his pocket. He's driving along and in his rear mirror he sees a police car. It sets the adrenalin flowing, there's an enhanced alertness, a tingling behind the eyeballs. That's the reaction we set out to get when we go on stage; and that's why we chose the name The Police.'

■ A moment to remember: 'Years ago at a concert at the Round House in London, after the sound check in the afternoon, we all went to the nearest greasy chip to get a cup of tea and something to eat. Going back to the theatre, the others had gone ahead and I was by myself. When I got to the theatre, the doorman wouldn't let me in. I had to drag him round to the front-of-house posters which had these psychadelic impressions of us all and point to my supposed likeness and say; "That's me." That sort of thing happens quite frequently at concerts. There are always plenty of enthusiastic bully boys pushing people around and they invariably push aside one of the band, shouting; "Out of the way, the band's coming through!" Does he ever get frightened with thousands of screaming fans all eager to get as close as possible? 'No, that's like asking a millionaire businessman who goes to the office everyday if he gets nervous when he's juggling with his millions. No, for me the stage is a warm, comfortable spot, it's my home, it's where I like to be.' ■ Likes horses and playing polo. ■ Married to Sonja Kristina, has two sons and lives in Oxfordshire.

Sting (Gordon Sumner) (Vocals, bass guitar)

BORN: 2nd October 1951 in Wallsend, Northumberland. Father a milkman. **EDUCATED:** Obtained a 'few' 'A' levels. Teacher training college. At school he liked to be noticed and always wanted to be top of everything. Good at athletics, he became the Northern Counties 100 metres champion and was entered for the National Championships. He came third and never raced again. 'I realized when I came third, that there were two people in my age group who were better than I was and there was no possibility of me beating them, so I just stopped running. I didn't want to be part of the pyramid. I wanted to be top. I like to be the best and I enjoy it. I wouldn't get on stage and do what I do if I wasn't.' **FIRST JOB:** Worked on a building site and also for the Inland Revenue before going to teacher training college and becoming a teacher. Having taught himself to play guitar while at school, he joined a Newcastle group called Last Exit and it was while he was playing a gig in a draughty polytechnic classroom in 1976 that he was seen by Stewart Copeland who persuaded him to leave the security of his teaching job and join him in London to form a new band. Since joining The Police, he has appeared in five films: *Quadrophenia, Radio On, Brimstone Treacle* (which gave him a solo hit record with the 30s song *Spread a Little Happiness*), *Artemis '81* and *Dune*. Stewart Copeland thinks his success is due to the fact that he is a natural actor: 'He loves the camera as much as it obviously loves him.'

■ A moment to remember: August 1977. The Police are playing a punk festival somewhere in the South of France. They are way down the bill and hardly anyone notices them when they play a 20-minute set. Sting wonders whether there's any future for the band and a reporter covering the festival for *Melody Maker*, suggests he might be better off going back to his teaching job. July 1979. The Police are headlining at the Reading Festival before an audience of 30,000. Sting, well on his way to his first million, meets the same reporter. What price the teaching job now! ■ Was married to, and is now divorced from actress Frances Tomelty, has two daughters and one son.

Andy Summers (Guitar)

BORN: 31st December 1942 in Poulton-le-Fylde, Nr. Blackpool. Father a restaurateur. The family moved to Bournemouth when he was very young. **EDUCATED:** He left school after taking 'O' levels. San Francisco State College. Piano lessons were not a success, but when he was given a guitar at the age of 14, he began to take a fierce interest in music, listening to his elder brother's collection of jazz records and beginning to develop a technique of his own. **FIRST JOB:** Series of day jobs on leaving school, but the week revolved around Friday nights when he would go to the local jazz club, first to listen and then to play. It was there that he met George 'Zoot' Money who got him a job with Alexis Korner's backing

band and so he came to London. The 60s saw him playing with Soft Machine, The Animals, Dantalion's Chariot and Zoot Money's Big Roll Band. In 1969 he took off to the States, and enrolled for a classical guitar course at San Francisco State College. For the next four years he managed to keep himself by giving guitar lessons but he soon realized that the electric guitar and rock groups were where the money was and by playing in various bar bands, he gradually worked his way back into the music business increasing his bank balance at the same time. Returned to the UK towards the end of 1973, playing with the bands of Kevin Coyne and Kevin Ayers before joining Strontium 90 and meeting up with Stewart Copeland and Sting in Paris in May 1977. The three of them got on well swopping musical ideas. 'I'd always wanted to play in a three-piece band and at that point I'd just been backing people and was getting pretty frustrated with it. When I saw those two, I felt that the three of us would be very strong. They just needed another guitarist and I knew I was the one.' He joined The Police in July. They played a couple of gigs as a quartet before Henri Padovani left, his musical capabilities never being up to what Copeland, Sting and Summers had in mind.

■ Likes photography. His first volume of photographs *'Throb'* was published in October 1983. ■ He has one daughter.

ALAN PRICE
'Multi-talented Geordie . . .'

BORN: 19th April 1942 in Fatfield, Co. Durham. Father an acetylene filler for BOC. **EDUCATED:** Jarrow Grammar School. Self-taught pianist. **FIRST JOB:** Clerical officer with the Civil Service in Newcastle. He formed a skiffle group with his friends at school and from then on was always playing in semi-pro bands. When he left school and became a Civil Servant, he was playing in three bands at the same time which invariably meant he did more work between Friday and Monday than he did between Monday and Friday! In

1960 the Alan Price Combo was the resident band at Newcastle's Downbeat Club on Saturday nights, moving on to Club A Gogo in the city centre. When Eric Burdon joined the group on vocals in 1962, the name was changed to the Animals and they cut a demo disc which sold 500 copies to their fans up North and impressed record producer Mickie Most enough for him to travel to Newcastle to see the band in action. He brought them to London and in October 1963 Alan quit his job with the Civil Service and turned professional.

The following year the Animals hit the jackpot with *House of the Rising Sun*, making it to the No.1 spot on both sides of the Atlantic, which led to them making their debut in America that summer. Never too keen on flying, by 1965 Alan had left the Animals in order to form the Alan Price Set which concentrated on touring the UK. Within a year he'd made it into the charts wth *I Put a Spell on You*, following it up a few months later with *Hi Lili Hi Lo*. 1967 brought to more hits, *Simon Smith and his Amazing Dancing Bear* and his own composition, *The House that Jack Built*.

His brief, but highly successful partnership with Georgie Fame (qv) came in 1971 when their recording of *Rosetta* reached No.11 in the charts. By this time he had already composed the incidental music for the West End production of David Storey's *Home* and in 1973 his first film score, for Lindsay Anderson's *O Lucky Man*, brought him a string of awards: The British Society of Film and Television Arts Award for the Best Film Score; an Oscar nomination; New York Critics Award, Rolling Stone's Best Sound-track of the Year and Hollywood Press Association Golden Globe nomination. In 1974 he embarked on an album telling the story of a young man from the North-East making good in London. A sort of musical self portrait, it produced a most unusual hit, *Jarrow Song*. His next film score was for *Alfie Darling* in which he also made his acting debut. Hardly a memorable film but it earned him The Most Promising New Actor Award.

With a considerable reputation as a composer, from the end of the 70s his commissions for television themes have been numerous: *Turtle's Progress*, BBC 2's *Worlds' End*, BBC 1's *Fame is the Spur*, BBC's *Further Adventures of Lucky Jim*. The background music for another David Storey play, *Early Days*, and the score for another Lindsay Anderson film, *Britannia Hospital*, got the 80s off to a good start. 1982 saw him collaborating with Trevor Peacock on his first stage musical, *Andy Capp*, in which he also starred with Tom Courtenay. After an eight-week run in Manchester it transferred to the Aldwych Theatre and Alan made his debut on the West End stage.

The summer of 1983 was taken up with the much publicized world tour of the re-formed Animals, which included two concerts at London's Royal Albert Hall. But in 1984 Alan was back on the road in the UK with his own group and with plans for a new musical in the pipeline, the future for the multi-talented Geordie looks like being well taken care of.

■ A moment to remember: At four years old he was so keen to play the piano, that he turned up at the door of his brother's music teacher with his brother's music and when she wouldn't let him in, he threw a stone through her window. ■ Likes good food and wine. ■ Dislikes people who think he did the Maxwell House coffee advert on television! (It was Georgie Fame). ■ Has one daughter and lives in Buckinghamshire.

QUEEN
'Fan mail at the Palace!...'

In 1971 two students, Brian May who was reading physics and Roger Meadows Taylor who was reading biology, teamed up with Tim Staffell to form a group called *Smile* which played a few college gigs and even made a record. When Staffell decided to go solo, he persuaded his flatmate, art student Freddy Mercury, to take his place. Mercury with his theatrical flair brought a certain flamboyance to the line-up. He also suggested a change of name to Queen. Within a couple of months they had recruited electronics student John Deacon on bass, but unlike most new groups they had no wish to perform in public. For two years they worked on the sound they wanted to create and the act they wanted to stage. When the opportunity for some free studio time came their way, they recorded their first tracks, *Keep Yours Alive* and *Liar*. A record contract with EMI followed and in the summer of 1973 they released their first album, *Queen*. The two years of rehearsal had paid off, they were hailed as the most exciting rock group in decades and in March 1974 *Seven Seas of Rhye* hit the No.10 spot in the singles chart to be followed by their second album *Queen 2*, reaching No.5 in the album charts, which had the immediate effect of bringing their first album, *Queen*, into the charts some 20 places below. Named Band of the Year, they made their American debut, blazing a trail for the sell-out tours to come.

Their third album, *Sheer Heart Attack*, hit the No.2 spot and provided them with a No.2 single, *Killer Queen*, in the UK and a chart entry on the other side of the Atlantic. It was a record that almost didn't get made as Brian May was ill with hepatitis and an ulcer for most of 1974.

The headlining tours of Britain and America, following their chart success, established them as one of the most spectacular stage acts yet seen. Hardly surprising that it takes a 30-strong road crew to shift their 75 tons of gear! In January 1975 they were greeted by 3,000 screaming fans at Tokyo airport. 'It was just like I imagined Beatlemania had been,' said Roger Taylor. The tour of Japan was followed by months in the studio producing what was to be their biggest recording success to date. The album *A Night at the Opera*, which shot to No.2 in the album charts, gave them their first UK No.1 single that remained in that position for an amazing nine weeks. EMI had wanted to trim the six-minute-long *Bohemian Rhapsody* to a conventional three minutes, but the boys had refused saying 'We've always put our necks on the line. That is Queen.' They were right, the British Phonograph Industry voted it the best record of the last 25 years. Their first American No.1 wasn't to come until 1980 with *Another One Bites the Dust*, but from the mid 70s on, almost every new Queen release was guaranteed chart success. *A Day at the Races* (obviously fans of the Marx Brothers) and *The Game* both topped the album charts so it was hardly surprising that when their *Greatest Hits* was released in 1981, it spent a phenomenal 58 weeks in the charts, reaching the No.1 spot.

1976 saw the band staging a free concert for 150,000 fans in London's Hyde Park. 1977, Jubilee year, was the perfect excuse for adding a little something extra to their already elaborate stage setting – a 54ft by 26ft crown weighing 5,000 lbs. When they played the Lyceum in London, a hole had to be cut in the roof. It was the only way to get their gear onto the stage!

The 80s brought two new challenges; an invitation from film

producer Dino de Laurentiis to write the score for hs epic *Flash Gordon*, which earned them a BAFTA nomination for Best Film Soundtrack and gave them another Top 10 entry with *Flash*; and a South American tour playing the continent's massive outdoor stadiums. In Sao Paulo, Brazil, they drew a crowd of 131,000, the largest paying audience for one group anywhere in the world. Their five concerts in Argentina were a sell out which ironically insured that a British group was topping the Argentine hit parade at the height of the Falklands conflict, prompting John Deacon to say at the time, 'I don't suppose we'll get our royalties out now!' *Under Pressure* (an apt title in the circumstances) recorded with David Bowie also topped the UK charts.

The arrival of video on the pop scene chalked up another success for Queen with *Queen's Greatest Flix* dominating the video charts for some considerable time. 1983 saw the band taking time out from their punishing touring schedule of previous years, to work on their 13th album, recorded in Munich and Los Angeles and called, appropriately enough, *The Works*. As Brian May explained, 'That's exactly what it is, the definitive Queen album.' And in 1984 they were back in action topping the bill at the San Remo Festival in Italy which was televised across the world.

After more than 10 years at the top with record sales approaching the 80-million mark, John Deacon admits that money doesn't come into it any more. 'We're all financially secure for the rest of our lives. To stay on top is our aim.' But for how long? Perhaps Freddy Mercury gave a clue when he said: 'We won't be running around the stage at 45, that would be silly', which means *Queen* have got a few years yet to try to stay on top of the world of pop.

■ A moment to remember: An American fan wrote to them and addressed the letter to 'Queen, England'. Not surprisingly the letter was delivered to Buckingham Palace from where it was forwarded by a private secretary with a note saying, 'Opened in error'!

Freddie Mercury (Frederick Bulsara) (Vocals, piano)
BORN: 5th September 1946 in Zanzibar. Qualified graphic designer. Joined a group called Wreckage while at college before taking his flat mate's place in Smile with Brian May and Roger Taylor.
Has made a solo album but doesn't see it as any threat to Queen as a group, saying he has no intention of killing the goose that laid the golden egg. 'I'm still enjoying the whole business of singing in Queen. It's not a question of money any more. I spend money like it's nothing. If I was penniless tomorrow, I'd get back somehow.'

■ Likes the ballet, antiques and Chinese furniture, (he once bought up an entire exhibition of it at Harrods!)   ■ Is a bachelor and lives in London.

Brian May (Guitar)

BORN: 19th July 1947 in Hampton, Middlesex. BSc. in physics. Ph.D. in astronomy.

He also made a solo album which he describes as 'a certain artistic escape. Queen as a group is far more important than any individual. If you think being Brian May is glamorous, it's not, although I enjoy the touring and the excitement of being on the road, but basically I'm still like a little boy with the guitar, I just love the fat, loud sound of it.'

■ Married to Chrissie, has two children, and lives in London.

John Deacon (Bass)

BORN: 19th August 1951 in Leicester. First Class Honours degree in electronics.

With Roger Taylor is concerned with the business side of running the band. In 1979, after the band had formed their own company, Queen Productions Ltd, each member was estimated to have earned between £660,000 and £697,000 in director's fees!

■ Is married with three children and lives in London.

Roger Meadows Taylor (Drums)

BORN: 26th July 1949 in Norfolk, but was brought up in the West Country. Ph.D. in biology. **FIRST JOB:** Dentist. He also made a solo album *Fun In Space*. Although he's concerned with the running of the band he doesn't really know how much they earn. 'All I know is, we don't ever have to make another record.'

■ Married to Dominique, has one son and lives in Surrey.

ALAN RANDALL

'That's not George Formby, it's Alan Randall . . .'

BORN: 10th June 1939 in Bedworth, Leicestershire. Father a bus driver. **EDUCATED:** George Street Junior School; Leicester Secondary Modern School, Bedworth. Played piano from the age of six. 'As a teenager I saw Lionel Hampton playing the vibes in a Danny Kaye film and I thought: that's what I'd like to to do.' so at 18 taught himself to play the vibraphone. **FIRST JOB:** Aircraft engineer for three years. He played with several semi-pro bands during that time but his first professional job as a musician was with the Sonny Rose Band in 1959. Within three weeks of leaving his engineering job, he was playing

vibes with the Jerry Allen Trio on ATV's *Lunchbox* as a 'dep' and ended up doing 150 programmes. His ability to sing like George Formby, for which he has become famous, was discovered by accident. 'In 1968 I was recording some demo tapes on vibes and my wife suggested I should do one vocal. So, I recorded *Down by the Railroad Track* and when the demos were heard in London, the record company said they didn't know George Formby had ever recorded that song. Somebody explained that it wasn't George Formby it was Alan Randall. The upshot was they'd been looking for someone who sounded like George Formby and would I record some of his songs? I've been doing George Formby ever since!' He had always enjoyed watching George Formby but now his interest in the lad from Lancashire became much greater. He taught himself to play the ukelele/banjo and even managed to obtain some of Formby's instruments. He co-wrote with Ray Seaton the *George Formby Biography* and collaborated with Jim Cammell on a musical about Formby's life, *It's Turned Out Nice Again*. He has also written many tutors for ukelele and guitar.

As well as performing Formby songs he writes a lot of his own material for his cabaret act which he has taken all over the world, including Las Vegas, Australia, New Zealand and in May 1984 Swaziland for a four-week engagement at the Sun International. An unexpected highlight of the trip was a hole-in-one at the Royal Swazi Championship Golf Course. 1984 also saw him fronting the London Philharmonic Orchestra for a charity concert at the Royal Festival Hall and guesting on vibes with the Midlands Youth Jazz Orchestra.

The Alan Randall Quartet with Alan on vibes is heard on many of Radio 2's music programmes and his recent television appearances as a solo performer include BBC 1's *The Good Old Days*, the BBC series *Turns of the Century* and Tyne Tees *Super Troupers*.

In 1980 he won an award for writing the Radio Commerical Jingle of the Year.

■ Highspot of career: 'Appearing in Las Vegas in 1973. The George Formby routine went down very well.' ■ A moment to remember: 'Very early on in my career, when I was very "green", my trio was booked into the Windmill Theatre in London for eight weeks. It was our first variety engagement and following it we were booked to do a Moss Empire tour starting in Manchester. At the Windmill, the curtains opened sideways, and having no experience of theatres, we thought all curtains opened that way. When we got to Manchester, on opening night at the start of the show, the bass player walked forward as usual, expecting the curtains to part, but they went up instead, caught the top of his double bass and hoisted it up into the flies. There it was suspended in mid air. It got the best laugh of the evening!' ■ Likes most sport, including golf, and supports Coventry City. ■ Dislikes driving the car, and being away from home. ■ Married to Mary, has a son, Martyn, a daughter, Susan, a pet dog named Mr Wu and lives in Warwickshire.

MIKE REDWAY

'Likes the telephone to ring . . .'

BORN: 17th December 1939 in Leeds, Yorkshire. Father a baker. **EDUCATED:** All Saints School, Leeds. Plays piano and guitar as well as singing. **FIRST JOB:** Tailor. Has also worked as a baker, carpet salesman and song plugger. Made his first broadcast on the *Albert Modley Show* from BBC Manchester

in 1958. Has sung with Oscar Rabin, Mike Sammes Singers, Cliff Adam Singers and Maggie Stredder Singers. Is a talented song writer who has yet to hit the jackpot although his songs have had considerable success in America and on the Continent. *This House Runs on Sunshine* which he co-wrote with Brian Bennett of the Shadows reached No.10 in the American charts in the late 70s and his own recording of his *Good Morning* was also a chart entry in the US. *Suzanne Suzanne*, which hit the No.1 spot in the German charts around the same time, was written overnight and named after his daughter. 'I was doing a session the next day when I got a telephone call to say they were short of one song and if I could come up with something and it was good, it would be included. I did and it was, and what's more it became the "A" side of the record by Los Pop Tops.' His *Rock and Roll You're Beautiful*, which he wrote and recorded in 1982, has had seven cover versions to date, including one by B.J. Thomas. He has recorded numerous albums and singles and in 1978 moved into record production, producing Terry Wogan's *The Floral Dance*. He also has his own music publishing company, Red Rock Music. Is currently writing a series for children's stories and songs for television.

■ Highspot of career: 'Hearing one's own song recorded or just sung by another artist. I met a gig man once, who ran a small band and I happened to say to him, I don't suppose you know *Rock and Roll You're Beautiful*, and he replied "Of course I do, I play it every night"!' ■ A moment to remember: 'The day Burt Bacharach telephoned me and my wife took the call. She shouted to me, "It's Burt Bacharach for you." "Oh yeah," I replied, thinking it was someone like Danny Street playing the fool, I picked up the 'phone and in my broadest Yorkshire accent said "Hello Burt". Surprise, surprise!' ■ Likes breeding canaries, parrots and kestrels and having the telephone ring. ■ Dislikes not having the telephone ring. ■ Married to Marjorie, has one son, Mark, two daughters, Suzanne and Caroline, and lives in Middlesex.

CLIFF RICHARD (Harry Webb)
'The pop music scene would be the poorer without him . . .'
BORN : 14th October 1940 in Lucknow, India. Father worked for a catering company in India. With the granting of independence in 1948 the family returned to Cheshunt, Hertfordshire. **EDUCATED:** Cheshunt Secondary Modern School. He was demoted from being a prefect for attending a Bill Haley concert which had been deemed out of bounds. **FIRST JOB:** Growing up during the rock 'n' roll period, he played

local gigs with various skiffle groups but in 1958 formed the Drifters and they were soon playing small dates like the Regal at Ripley. But it was an appearance at the Gaumont, Shepherds Bush, which was to lead to the big time. They were heard by Norrie Paramor who got them a recording test and then suggested they cover an American hit, *Schoolboy Crush*, as their first disc. They backed it with a pulsating rock 'n' roll number, *Move it*, written by their bass guitarist, Ian Samwell, and within weeks it was in the charts capturing the No.2 spot in September 1958. That same month Cliff made his TV debut on *Oh Boy* produced by Jack Good, and he became an overnight sensation. His radio debut came the following month in *Saturday Club*, and the hits started to roll off the production line. Little did anyone envisage they would still be rolling over a quarter of a century later. *High Class Baby*, *Never Mind* and in 1959 his first No.1, *Livin' Doll*, which he sang in his very first film, the X-rated *Serious Charge*. The Drifters had now changed their name to the Shadows (qv) to avoid confusion with an American group, and with Cliff they starred in the film *Espresso Bongo* in 1960. With its release in the States, he made his American debut, although strangely enough, he was never to make it as big across the Atlantic as Tom Jones and Elton John.

1960 also saw him collect the first of hundreds of awards when he was voted by *New Musical Express* Top Male Artist in the UK. The following year the Variety Club of Great Britain made him Show Business Personality of the Year and he starred in what is probably his best film, *The Young Ones*. There were to be five more: *Summer Holiday*, 1962; *Wonderful Life*, 1964; *Finders Keepers*, 1966; *Two a Penny*, 1968 (sponsored and financed by the Billy Graham Evangelistic Organization); *Take Me High*, 1973. When *Summer Holiday* had its première in Leicester Square in 1963, he was unable to attend because of the huge crowds of fans waiting to see him. Beatlemania, then at its height, had not affected his tremendous popularity with young and old alike. Religion was beginning to play a big part in his life and in 1966 he appeared on stage at a Billy Graham meeting. His fans began to worry that he might be contemplating leaving showbusiness, but later that year he was starring in *Cinderella* at the London Palladium. In 1968 he sang the British entry for the Eurovision Song Contest, which almost lived up to its name, but not quite. *Congratulations* came second, but it made the No.1 spot in the charts, the eighth to do so in his first 10 years in the business, during which time he'd had an incredible 39 entries in the Top 20. But he still had one major ambition, to play a straight acting role, an ambition that was realized in 1970 when he appeared in *Five Finger Exercise* at the Bromley New Theatre. He was to have made a return visit the following year in *The Potting Shed* but a fire at the theatre led to the play opening at the Sadlers Wells Theatre in London.

The first of many appearances at the London Palladium had been in 1960 but in 1971 he topped the bill which featured his old backing group the Shadows who were now stars in their own right. The 70s weren't to be quite as prolific for him chartwise, with a mere 11 entries, but 1979 saw another No.1, exactly 20 years after his first – *We Don't Talk Anymore* – a song that also reached the American Top 10. A few months earlier, he had presented a series of special Gospel concerts at London's Royal Albert Hall. Not all of his fans took to his increasing involvement with religion. In reply to his critics he said, 'they attack me simply because they don't

like Christian ideas. They should get over their cynicism and catch up with my work. Faith in Jesus Christ is the most realistic thing that has ever happened to me. It's certainly not an illusion, it's opened my eyes to things I'd never seen before; made me face up to things I'd sooner not have thought about and do or say things where I'd sooner do nothing or keep silent.'

Of all the awards collected over the years, the ultimate came in 1980 when he was awarded the OBE, just a few months before his 40th birthday. For many people 40 is a traumatic age, but not for Cliff, he still had the same boyish good looks and his records were being bought by the children of his original fans. Wherever he goes in the world, and he undertakes many overseas tours, his concerts are sold out long before he arrives. Following his Silver Anniversary in 1983, one can't help wondering whether he'll still be going strong when the grandchildren of his very first fans are old enough to buy his records. One thing's for sure, the pop music scene would certainly be the poorer without him.

■ A moment to remember: The night a large box addressed to Cliff was delivered to the theatre where he was appearing. Out stepped a young lady from Leeds who had posted herself special delivery in order to meet her idol! ■ Likes walking, tennis and swimming. ■ Is a bachelor and lives in Surrey.

THE ROLLING STONES
'Their rebel image somewhat mellowed . . .'

The Rolling Stones had their beginnings in Alexis Korner's Blues Incorporated at Ealing Blues Club in 1962, when guitarist Brian Jones would occasionally sit in with the band that included drummer Charlie Watts and featured singer Mick Jagger. In June of that year, Jagger, Jones, Keith Richard and pianist Ian Stewart, who had been rehearsing together, 'depped' for Blues Incorporated at London's Marquee Club where they were billed as Brian Jones, Mick Jagger and the Rolling Stones. The following year, Charlie Watts joined them, as did Bill Wyman after being auditioned.

Early residency at the Crawdaddy Club in Richmond led to them being signed by PR man Andrew Oldham who negotiated a recording contract with Decca and also got rid of pianist, Ian Stewart, on the grounds he looked far too normal. Their first record, *Come On*, released in June 1963, was a minor hit and Oldham set out to mould the Stones into exactly the opposite image to that of the Beatles. He succeeded. Eleven boys were suspended from a Coventry school after the headmaster had ruled, 'Beatle your Rolling Stone hair'. Their hair seemed to command the most attention with one hairdresser saying they had the worst collection of hair cuts he'd ever seen and one of them looked as if he'd got a feather duster on his head. They were soon being dubbed 'the ugliest group in Britain', but 110,000 people forked out almost £200,000 for their first album *The Rolling Stones*, which was in the charts for 51 weeks and got to No.1. There was no looking back . . . everything they touched turned to gold.

It's all Over Now gave them their first No.1 single in July 1964 and it certainly wasn't all over, it was followed by four consecutive No.1's. January 1964 saw them topping the bill for the first time on a UK tour and later that year they made their American debut which resulted in their first entry into the US charts with *Time is on my Side*.

The summer of '65 saw them capturing the No.1 spot on both sides of the Atlantic with *I Can't Get No Satisfaction*, which had started out as a guitar riff Keith Richard thought just might be an idea for a track for their next LP. 'I'd woken up in the middle of the night, thought of this riff and put it straight down on tape. In the morning it still sounded pretty good but I never thought it was commercial enough to be a single.' The title, which was just a working title, stuck, and straight laced critics of the Stones immediately jumped to conclusions about its subject matter. They couldn't have been more wrong. *I Can't Get No Satisfaction* was a protest against life on tour moving from one hotel room to another. From then on all their singles were written by Mick Jagger and Keith Richard and as their fans increased, so too did their critics. Their behaviour in a German hotel prompted Olympic Gold medallist Lynn Davies to say, 'I felt sick and ashamed to be British as they poured out swear words at the breakfast table.'

They were famous but also notorious and nobody was really surprised when Mick Jagger, Keith Richard and Brian Jones were arrested on drugs charges in 1967. They spent the night of June 29th in Wormwood Scrubs before being granted bail of £7,000 each. Their sentences were quashed or set aside on appeal, but within 12 months Brian Jones, having left the group after a disagreement, was found dead in the swimming pool of his luxury home in Sussex. His epitaph, which he wrote himself, was read at his funeral. 'Please don't judge me too harshly.'

Brian Jones was replaced by Mick Taylor, who in turn was replaced in 1974 by Ron Wood. Throughout the 70s into the 80s the Stones kept the hits rolling and wherever they chose to appear, was a guaranteed sell-out. Now in their 40s, their rebel image somewhat mellowed, they live the lives of jet-set tax exiles. How long they can keep going is anybody's guess, although Bill Wyman in a recent interview, gave them three years.

■ A moment to remember: By the summer of 1964, the Stones were hot property, but they believed in honouring contracts. Twelve months previously, as unknowns, they had been booked to play at the 1964 summer ball at Magdalen College, Oxford for a fee of £100. In order to fulfil that engagement they had to fly back from the States. Their fares came to £1500 – an expensive gig!

Mick Jagger (Vocals)
BORN: 26th July 1943. Father a senior lecturer in physical eduction. **EDUCATED:** Maypole County Primary School. Wentworth County Primary School, Kent. Dartford Grammar School. London School of Economics. **FIRST JOB:** Physical education instructor at a US base when he was 18. His first stage work was with Alexis Korner. 'I always knew I'd be rich. I always thought I was special.' Having passed the 40 mark, 'The Mouth' still sounds off on a variety of subjects and is currently working on his autobiography for which the publishers are reputedly said to have given him a £1-million advance. His smile has that extra sparkle these days, not from using any particular brand of toothpaste, but from a diamond set in one of his front teeth. He tried an emerald but that looked like spinach and a ruby looked like blood, so a diamond was the final choice. 'I did it for fun.'
He still enjoys performing, and in a 1984 interview said, 'I feel that I can go on singing live for a long time, although obviously I can't do the high energy stuff for ever. But while I still can, I might as well carry on.'
Is reputed to be one of the richest rock stars in the world, worth well in excess of £10 million.

■ Likes cricket. ■ Has three daughters and has homes in London, New York, Mustique and France.

Charlie Watts (Drums)
BORN: 2nd June 1941. Father a British Rail lorry driver. **EDUCATED:** Tylers Croft Secondary Modern School. Harrow Art School. **FIRST JOB:** Worked for Charles Hobson & Gray, Advertising Agents. In the evenings was playing with a group called Blues By Five in the Troubadour Club, where he met Alexis Korner. He joined Alexis Korner's Blues Incorporated which played a regular gig at the Ealing Blues Club.

■ Likes horses and fine silver. ■ Married to Shirley, has one daughter, Serafina, and lives in Devon.

Keith Richard (Guitar, vocals)
BORN: 18th December 1943. Father an electrical engineer. **EDUCATED:** Westhill Infant's School. Wentworth County Primary School, Kent. Dartford Technical School. Sidcup Art School. Having been at the same primary school as Mick Jagger, the two met up again in 1960 when Keith was at Dartford Technical School and Mick at the London School of Economics. Played with a Country & Western Band while at Dartford but his musical tastes lay with Blues and R&B. Worked as a postman during the 1961 Christmas season. The

tearaway of the band, very much involved in the booze and drugs scene, he changed his lifestyle completely in 1977, and in an interview in 1984 said, 'Amazingly enough in the last few years I've become a happy and contented man. Before that I was too busy and then too strung out. Am I satisfied? Way and above my fantasies.'

■ Likes cooking. ■ Lives in Jamaica, France and England.

Bill Wyman (Bass)
BORN: 24th October 1941. Father a bricklayer. **EDUCATED:** Oakfield Junior School, Penge. Beckenham Grammar School, Kent. **FIRST JOB:** Bookmaker's clerk in London. After a spell in the RAF, he worked as an engineer with a firm in Streatham.

The Rolling Stone with the most interest outside the band. Has made three solo albums, taken the photographs for a book on artist Marc Chagall and is writing a book about the Rolling Stones. 'I love the band, but there are so many other things. Suddenly I'm past 40 and there's a lot I want to do before I get past 50.'

■ Likes modern art and photography. ■ Lives in Suffolk.

Ron Wood (Guitar, vocals)
BORN: 1948. He joined the band in 1974, replacing Mick Taylor, who had in turn replaced Brian Jones after his death in 1969.

■ Has three children and lives in New York.

with nothing to do and obviously peckish. I took a lunge at it, but noting the size of the beast, discretion took over and I'm afraid we found the next half chorus or so pretty hard to sing. Mercifully he'd chosen a piece we had already recorded, but the tears were streaming down our faces. To see this hulk cheerfully munching one bit of yer Best End of Irving Berlin was just hysterical. Then the lady in charge came round afterwards to collect the music. I told her it wasn't lost and I knew exactly where it was (give or take an elephant or two), but she was not amused and oddly enough we were never invited back again. This caused me no great grief, but I must confess it did put me off dialling trunk calls for quite a while afterwards.' ■ Likes pottering about in the garden and writing songs. ■ Lives in Surrey.

MIKE SAMMES
'On stage with Judy Garland . . .'

BORN: 19th February in Reigate, Surrey. Father a photographic dealer. EDUCATED: Reigate Grammar School. Plays the piano and cello (which he played in the school orchestra!) FIRST JOB: In the professional department of Chappells music publishing company under Teddy Holmes. His first professional performing job was with the top of the bill, on stage at the London Palladium! Has always fronted his own vocal group. The Mike Sammes Singers. Has had his own programme *Sammes Songs* on Radio 2 and has been heard on just about every musical programme going on the Light Programme followed by Radio 2. Is heard regularly on all Radio 2's music programmes and any 'Special' that requires a vocal group.

■ Highspots of career: 'Being on stage at the London Palladium with Judy Garland and to actually *feel* the electricity in the air and experience the tidal wave of emotion and affection that stopped her in her tracks when she made her first entrance. And the day I was talking to Bob Farnon on the 'phone about something we were shortly to be doing together, when he said "Have you heard from Gene Peurling?" (the genius behind and the founder member of both the Hi-Lo's and Singers Unlimited) "Er, no", I said. "Why?" "Oh he's a great fan of yours. We exchange letters a couple of times a year and he always says; 'What's Mike doing?' – I thought he was a friend of yours!" Astonished that he'd even heard of us, I remember commenting that if nothing else happened in the ensuing 364 days, it had been a pretty good year!' ■ A moment to remember: 'The night we tried to get a circus atmosphere into an Easter programme in the middle of Clapham Common. The bandstand was between where the animals go into and out of the ring, and we wound up just in front of it to one side on a little box about 4ft square. All went surprisingly well 'till about half way through the show, when I suddenly felt something like a king-size flexible hose probing about between my legs and looked around to see quite a large piece of my music about to disappear down the throat of a waiting elephant, bored

JOAN SAVAGE
'From the flying trapeze to Friday Night is Music Night . . .'

BORN: Blackpool. Father a comedian. FIRST JOB: Singing and dancing in Tower Children's Revue in Blackpool at the age of 12. Has also earned her living riding elephants and hanging upside-down on a trapeze. Made her first broadcast when she was 15 in a 'live' series of the *Ken Platt Show*. Has sung with the BBC Concert, BBC Radio and Northern Dance Orchestras, Max Harris, Gordon Langford, Max Jaffa, Geoff Love, Billy Ternent, Jack Parnell, Eric Robinson, Alyn Ainsworth, Dutch Metropole and Radio Orchestras, BRT Belgium, WDR Radio Orchestra, Bert Rhodes Band, Harry Rabinowitz and the Johnny Wiltshire Sound. Programmes include *Sweet and Savage*, Frankie Howard series, *Magic of the Musicals, The Pleasure of Your Company, Among Your Souvenirs.* She is heard regularly on *Friday Night is Music Night* on Radio 2.

Headlined *The Minstrel Stars* at the Wallington Theatre, Great Yarmouth for the 1983 summer season and at the Alexandra Theatre, Bognor Regis in 1984, which was a busy year for her with concerts celebrating the 40th Anniversary of D Day. She appeared in Southampton with the Bournemouth Symphony

Orchestra conducted by Carl Davis with narration by Ludovic Kennedy and in the Winter Gardens, Bournemouth, in a concert in which several changes of costume were called for to bring a touch of realism to such songs as *Bless 'em All, White Cliffs of Dover, Lili Marlene* and *Gonna get Lit Up*. 1984 also saw her starring in a Royal Variety Performance at Eastbourne in front of Princess Margaret.

■ Highspot of career: 'Appearing before members of the Royal Family and appearing in the BBC's winning entry in the 1974 Nordring Radio Prize, which won all the awards.' ■ A moment to remember: 'When I was appearing on a "live" television show, *High Summer*, for the BBC, I had to do quite a bit of chatting while they were changing the scenery for the next sketch. As I was coming to the end of one of my links I saw the Floor Manager signalling me to spread. Spread what, I thought, I've done it! But the scenery was falling down so I just had to go on. I still can't remember what I said, but I got a lot of laughs and I got a whole paragraph to myself the next day in the *Daily Express*. I was quite chuffed about that, but it's the sort of thing you don't want to happen too often.' ■ Likes watching old movies and watching other performers. ■ Dislikes learning words and script.
■ Married to Brian Offen, has one child and lives in Middlesex.

PETE SAYERS
'Four years of hosting Breakfast TV in America . . .'
BORN: 6th November 1942 in Bath, Somerset. Father a music teacher (piano, organ). **EDUCATED:** Newmarket Secondary Modern School, Suffolk. Sang in the church choir for six years. At the age of six, was given a half size violin by Gerard Hoffnung who was art master at the same school as his father was music master. 'I had some violin lessons, but I didn't get on very well.' At nine, was given a chromatic harmonica and learnt *Hymns Ancient & Modern*, working his way through the book. At 18 he bought his first guitar. He plays 5-string banjo, and 6- and 12-string guitars, dobro,

autoharp, mandolin and ukelele. **FIRST JOB:** French polisher.
At 18 joined Johnny Duncan and the Blue Grass Boys, touring Britain and Europe. A year later formed the first all British Blue Grass Band, playing the clubs and pubs. In 1966 he headed West to try his luck in Nashville where he not only became a regular at the Grand Ole Opry, but also hosted his own early morning TV show on station WSM for four years. During his five-year stay in America, he scored and appeared in a film for Walt Disney.
On his return to the UK in 1972, did three nationwide tours with George Hamilton IV and in 1973 appeared at the Wembley Country Music Festival. Made another appearance at Wembley in 1976 and in 1980 compèred the Festival as well as performing. His own series for Anglia Television in the mid-70s was followed by *Pete Sayers Entertains at the Maltings* on BBC2. 1978 brought his own series on BBC 1 and his *Electric Music Show* was a big hit on BBC 2 in 1982, '83 and '84. 'They gave me just two weeks' warning for the first two shows!'
In 1979 he starred in the first Country Music Summer show at Blackpool's Winter Garden Theatre in which he featured his now famous character of Dennis, Suffolk's vocal yokel and one-man band. Also hosts his own Grand Ole Opry England in his home town of Newmarket. Is an accomplished composer and his songs have appeared on many albums other than his own. His album, *Cyclone*, produced by Stuart Coleman who also produced so many of Shakin' Stevens' (qv) records, was a delightful mixture of well tried songs and Pete's own compositions. He admits he finds song writing hard work: 'I tend to find that when I'm very busy, working on the road, I'm not writing very much. Really I don't start writing songs until I'm on the point of boredom, then it's a matter of finding a story, and a direction to take it in. If you never have a hit record, and that's about as elusive as winning the pools, you may come up with some songs people will be listening to in 20 years time.'
Although basically a country singer, he's quite happy to sing other kinds of songs and his talent for comedy has led to him becoming an all-round entertainer in recent years and one who deserves a lot more recognition.
1975 was his year for awards when he was voted Best Male Vocalist, Best Song Writer and Best Group by the British Country Music Association. In 1978 he won the International Country Music Award for Best Solo or Duo.

■ Highspot of career: 'The first time I played the Grand Ole Opry in Nashville. I was one of the very first British solo artists to do so.' ■ A moment to remember: 'Porter Waggoner, the man who discovered Dolly Parton, had a series of television shows which were syndicated all over the USA. I guested on one of his shows and was waxing lyrical about the difficulty of getting the right instrument for playing country music. I happened to say if one could only get hold of a Martin D 28 guitar, but they were almost unobtainable. I never thought anymore about it, and that afternoon Porter beckoned me into his dressing room and there was a guitar case on the floor. He pointed to it and said, "Open it up". And there was this Martin D 28 guitar. "Go on, try it", he said. I did. "It's beautiful". "It's yours, said Porter Waggoner; "What do you mean it's mine?" I replied. "You play very well and I've enjoyed having you on my show and I want you to have it." I completely broke down. I don't see him very often now, but there's quite a bond between us and that was a marvellous moment.' ■ Likes gardening, carpentry, cycling, growing vegetables and cooking. ■ Dislikes the problem of finding food as a travelling musician. 'In other countries you can get a meal at any hour of the day or night. In Britain you can only eat at the same time as everyone else wants to eat!' ■ Married to Elizabeth, has a son, John, a daughter, Dinah, and lives in Suffolk.

SIR HARRY SECOMBE
'Alias Neddy Seagoon . . .'

BORN: 8th September 1921 in Swansea, Glamorgan, South Wales. Father a travelling salesman. **EDUCATED:** St Thomas Junior School and Dynevor School, Swansea, (where he once made history by achieving 0 per cent for a maths exam!) At eight was a choir boy at St Thomas Church, and he and his sister would perform a sketch, 'The Welsh Courtship', at church socials, with Carol as the comedienne and Harry as the 'feed'. Sundays would find the Secombe family having a sing-song in the parlour, but he was so painfully shy, that he would only sing solo from the outside lavatory. 'I don't know what the neighbours must have thought when they heard *Abide With Me* coming from the outside loo!' **FIRST JOB:** Junior pay clerk with a Swansea steel company. His 10s. a week wage was supplemented by selling tea and biscuits. 'I bought broken biscuits, which were reduced in price and by charging a penny a cup I made more money as tea boy than as pay clerk.' He served with the Royal Artillery in World War 2, seeing action in Sicily, Italy, Malta and North Africa. It was in the Army that he first met Spike Milligan who had managed to lose a huge 7·2 howitzer and Harry helped him look for it.

By the end of the war he and Spike Milligan, along with Norman Vaughan and Nigel Patrick, were performing with a semi-pro set-up called the Central Pool of Artistes. It was the start of his show business career and on being demobbed he auditioned for the Windmill Theatre. Vivian Van Damm took him on at £20 a week, six shows a day, six days a week. His contract was for three months and then it was back to the odd cabaret date. Sharing a flat with Spike Milligan, they used to frequent a pub in Victoria called Grafton's and the hysterical evenings spent there in company with Peter Sellers and Michael Bentine led to the birth of the Goons. In 1951 the first *Goon Show* took to the air and a new kind of humour burst upon a startled world; radio comedy would never be the same again. The *Goon Show* became a cult and still has its fans today, including the Royal Family. Although he'd rounded off his act at the Windmill with an impersonation of Nelson Eddy and Jeanette MacDonald, he'd never taken his singing seriously until, on a radio series called *Welsh Rarebit*, listeners kept asking for him to sing more. It was then he decided to have his voice trained and he studied with the Italian Manlio di Veroli for 10 years. A recording contract and hit records followed, with *This is my Song* giving him a No.1 in 1967. 'It was like Ben Hur winning the Grand Prix! I'm happy to be a middle of the road singer, presumably because there's no room for me on the pavement. Anyway, I like it in the middle of the road, you don't get jostled so much.'

Has appeared in two stage musicals: the title role in *Pickwick* in 1963, which played London and Broadway and won him a nomination for a Tony Award; and in 1968 *The Four Musketeers*. In 1975 he tackled his first 'straight' stage role in the West End theatre in *The Plumber's Progress* which won him acclaim from the critics. Has appeared in many films, notably as Mr Bumble, the Beadle in *Oliver*. His first Royal Command Performance was in 1951, his ninth in 1978. He has made regular CSE tours for the troops overseas and in 1983 was the first major star to visit the Falklands, where he gave 10 concerts in a week. With his numerous radio, television and theatre appearances over the years, he must qualify for the title 'all-round entertainer' more than most, although he's not as round as he was. Following a stern lecture from a blunt Australian doctor that he should diet or else . . ., he lost an unbelievable 5 st. 'From being a rallying point for fatties, I have gone into the waist disposal business.' Over the years the accolades for the man who loves to make people laugh, have been many and varied. In 1959 he won the Variety Club's Show Business Personality of the Year Award, in 1963 he was awarded the CBE for his services to the Army Benevolent Fund, in 1977 he received the Queen's Silver Jubilee Medal, and in 1981 he was knighted for services to entertainment and charity. For someone who, in his own words, has built a career on such tenuous foundations as a high-pitched giggle, a raspberry and a sprinkling of top Cs, he hasn't done too badly.

■ Highspot of career: Receiving his knighthood. At the time he said, 'I am delighted by the news and regard this as an honour for my profession, the illegitimate side of show business. At last comics have been made respectable. It won't make me any funnier and I won't sing any better, but it might get me a table a bit quicker when I eat out. Perhaps I should now be known as simply Sir Cumference.' ■ A moment to remember: 'Soon after I was demobbed in 1946, I went to a dance at the Mumbles Pier Hotel in Swansea. I had a few dances with an attractive dark-eyed girl, Myra Atherton, and arranged to meet her the next week at the Plaza Cinema. By the time the date came around I'd got cold feet. For the life of me, I didn't know what she really looked like, as I hadn't worn my spectacles at the dance. So I thought I would hide behind a pillar outside the cinema so I could have a peep and see what she was like, then if she wasn't too bright, I could fade away. Well, nobody turned up, so after waiting for half an hour, I came out from behind my pillar, just as Myra was coming out from behind hers. She'd had the same idea. We both saw the funny side of the situation and had a laugh. We've been laughing ever since because I married her.' ■ Likes weak tea. ■ Dislikes boiled rice. ■ Married to Myra, has two sons, two daughters, two granddaughters and one grandson and lives in Surrey.

THE SHADOWS
'Perfomers and Songwriters supreme . . .'

The Railroaders, with Hank Marvin, Bruce Welch, Eddie Silver (guitar) George Williams (bass) and a drummer named Jim, came third in a talent contest in London in 1958. With the departure of Eddie, George and Jim, Hank who had changed his name to Marvin (after Marvin Rainwater) for the contest, joined up with Pete Chester's Chesternuts. Made their first television appearance on 6-5 Special, but as the band did relatively few gigs, Messrs Marvin and Welch began playing in the 2 I's coffee bar where they met up with bassist Jet Harris and drummer Tony Meehan. Around the same time, Cliff Richard's manager, John Foster, was looking for a guitarist for the Drifters who included Terry Smart and Ian Samwell. Shortly after Marvin and Welch joined, Smart and Samwell were replaced by Jet Harris and Tony Meehan and the Drifters had become the Shadows. Although originally a backing band for Cliff, they began to record independently from 1959 onwards and were soon stars in their own right. During a 1960 UK tour they met up with singer/songwriter Jerry Lordan, who would while away the time on the coach picking out tunes on his ukelele. One of them was *Apache* which was to provide them with not only their first hit, but their first No.1. And what's more, to get there, they knocked Cliff Richard's *Please Don't Tease*, which had been written by Bruce Welch and Pete Chester, off the No.1 position. Nothing like keeping it in the family – which they continued to do for the next eight years, writing and recording songs with Cliff, writing and recording songs on their own. By 1968 Cliff had clocked up 43 hits including eight No.1's and the Shadows 24, including five No.1s.

There had been a couple of changes of personnel during that time, with Brian Bennett replacing Tony Meehan on drums and Brian Licorice Locking taking the place of Jet Harris on bass. He in turn made way for John Rostill. And for eight successive years they were named Top Instrumental Group by *New Musical Express*.

It was in December 1968 at the end of a season with Cliff Richard at the London Palladium, a theatre they had played on numerous occasions, that they decided to each go their separate ways; Hank to record a solo single, Bruce to spend more time with Olivia Newton John, to whom he'd become engaged, Brian to become Cliff's Musical Director for his season at the Talk of the Town, followed by a trip to Washington as MD for Tom Jones. But the split was far from

final, and when invited to tour Japan, they went, 'but only for the yen' as they said at the time! They continued to come together for the odd appearance and it was such an occasion, a charity show at the London Palladium in October 1974, that indirectly led to them getting back into the charts after a 10-year gap. BBC's Bill Cotton, who was in the audience that night, had the bright idea of persuading them to represent Britain at the Eurovision Song Contest. They didn't need much persuading. *Let Me Be the One* came second, but made it to No.12 in the charts. The Shadows were back in business, if not full time, at least part time. In 1977 their compilation album *20 Golden Greats* went to the top of the album charts. The following year *Don't Cry For Me Argentina*, featuring Hank, went to No.5 and in 1979 *Theme from the Deer Hunter* made No.9, with the album *String of Hits* reaching No.1.

In 1978 the famous three, Marvin, Welch and Bennett, took to the road again along with bassist Alan Jones and Cliff Hall on keyboards, and they have undertaken several tours since, both home and abroad and wherever they go it's a guaranteed sell-out. But they each still continue to do their own thing. Hank records solo and had his first vocal hit with *Don't Talk* in 1982. Brian has recorded his own compositions with the London Symphony Orchestra and Bruce has produced many of Cliff's records, most notably the *I'm Nearly Famous* album and his biggest selling single ever, *We Don't Talk Any More*. Late in 1982 the Shadows got together at the famous Abbey Road studios to record a 'live' album, *Life in the Jungle*, in front of an audience of their fans and the following year celebrated their 25 years of music with a world-wide tour.

The Shadows have the highest number of British hits of any British group and that includes the Beatles. They are also the only group to have No.1 LP, EP and single simultaneously. It's hardly surprising that in 1983 they received their second Ivor Novello Award for their outstanding contribution to music over the past 25 years, the first for the Best Contribution to Popular Music had come in 1961. July 1984 saw them teaming up with Cliff Richard again after a gap of six years to perform at a series of sell-out concerts starting at Wembley.

■ A few moments to remember: (or how to write songs quickly) (a) Hank Marvin and Ian Samwell acting as manager, on the return flight from their first US tour. While strumming guitars quietly the air stewardess asks them how they go about writing a song. 'We'll show you,' is the reply as they improvise a little ditty ending with the words *Gee Whiz It's You*. Time taken approximately 10 minutes. (b) Bruce Welch and Brian Bennett receive script of film *Summer Holiday*. Title song yet to be written. 'Let's have a go,' says Bruce and picking up his guitar sings, 'We're all going on a summer holiday . . .' Brian goes over to the piano, sits down and goes straight into the middle eight. Time taken approximately 20 minutes. (c) The film *Summer Holiday* completed but short. Bruce Welch gets a telephone call from Norrie Paramor. Panic stations, another song required quickly. Cliff happens to be there and together they set to work. By tea time they have a song, *Batchelor Boy*. Time taken approximately two hours. Obviously slipping!

Hank Marvin (Brian Rankin)
BORN: 28th October 1941 in Newcastle-on-Tyne. EDUCATED: Todd's Nook School; Snow Street School; Rutherford College, Newcastle-on-tyne. Taught himself banjo and guitar while at

school. Father gave him a Hofner guitar for his 16th birthday. Formed Crescent City Skiffle Group with his brother and some friends and in May 1957 won a talent contest at the South Shields Jazz Club. Was asked by schoolmate Bruce Welch to join the Railroaders playing working men's clubs, and they became well known in the Newcastle area. Auditioned for BBC Radio's *Skiffle Club* but were turned down by producer Dennis Main Wilson. **FIRST JOB:** Apart from gigs, on leaving school, was a delivery boy for four weeks. In the spring of 1958 went to London with the Railroaders to enter a talent contest. Became a Jehovah's Witness in 1973.

■ Likes tennis, being lazy and one-night stands.   ■ Dislikes impoliteness and rainy weather.   ■ Married to Carole, has one daughter, Tahlia, one son, Ben, twin sons by a previous marriage, Peter and Paul, and lives in Hertfordshire.

Bruce Welch
BORN: 2nd November 1941 in Bognor Regis, Sussex. **EDUCATED:** Red Rose School, Chester-le-Street. Rutherford College, Newcastle-on-Tyne. Was given a ukelele while at school. At 15 bought his first guitar for 19s. 6d. Formed a group at school and called them the Railroaders because they used to meet in a café at Newcastle Central Station.
His most embarrassing moment came the day he was being given an enema by an attractive young nurse, who leaned over and confided she had bought all of the Shadows' records and *Wonderful Land* was her favourite!

■ Likes punctuality and for things to be just right, travelling and tea.   ■ Dislikes going to bed and getting up in the morning.   ■ Married to Lynne, has one son, Dwayne, by a previous marriage, one step-son, Jason, and lives in Surrey.

Brian Bennett
BORN: 9th February in London. Father a printer. **EDUCATED:** Hazelwood Lane School, Palmers Green. Winchmore Hill School. After hearing the Glen Miller Orchestra on the radio one day in 1944, started to use his mother's saucepans as make-believe drums. Had some violin lessons at nine but was more interested in the drums and spent hours listening to Voice of America's *Jazz Hour* on the radio and the music of Count Basie and Stan Kenton. Managed to get himself a small drum kit and joined the school orchestra and the Hazelwood Lane Youth Band. Also played with the Esquires Dance Band while still at school. **FIRST JOB:** Left school at 14 and formed the Tony Brian Trio playing in working men's clubs, at weddings and parties. Supplemented his income by working in his father's printing works and delivering newspapers. A near neighbour, Frank Horrocks, who played piano for Ted Heath, took him to the Swing Sessions at the BBC's Aeolian Hall which confirmed his determination to become a big band drummer. In 1956 did a summer season at Ramsgate with a skiffle group and went cherry- and hop-picking by day plus the odd gig in a pub on his free evenings. Played with Ricky James for a while and during a week at Collins Music Hall invited his mother to see the show. The whole family turned up to see what turned out to be mostly a strip show! Was resident drummer at the 2 I's coffee bar in Soho 1957–59. Joined Marty Wilde's Wildcats in 1960 and in the summer of '61 was drummer for Tommy Steele at Great Yarmouth. Joined the Shadows, replacing Tony Meehan in October 1961.
As well as writing many of the hits for Cliff and the Shadows, he has also composed a considerable amount of library music over the years, some of which has found its way into *Dallas* and *Knots Landing*. He got his biggest surprise when he

sat down to watch the Royal Wedding on ITV in 1981 and discovered they were using one of his tunes, *Sound of Success*, as the theme music for the coverage. Has also written the theme music for BBC 2's golf programmes.

■ Likes golf, good music and friendly people. ■ Dislikes snobs. ■ Married to Margaret, has one daughter, Sarah, two sons, Warren and Jonathan, and lives in Hertfordshire.

SHAKATAK
'An instantly recognizable sound . . .'

Nigel Wright, who was a session musician and now produces Shakatak records, had the idea of getting a group together in 1980. Bill Sharpe had written a couple of songs with Roger Odell, so they hired a studio and cut a track, *Step In*, which was pressed up on a couple of hundred white labels and distributed around a few record shops including one called *The Record Shack*. 'We did it all ourselves, including distributing them.' Then Capital Radio got hold of the record and decided to play it, but the group hadn't been named at that point. When Capital rang up and asked who it was singing *Step In*, Nigel Wright had just been into *The Record Shack*, and it was that name that after a fair amount of juggling, produced Shakatak. A recording contract followed and their first single, *Easier Said Than Done* went to No.12. Their second, *Night Birds*, reached No.9, the title track of an album which went to No.4 in the album charts. *Invitations* was another album that made the charts and the single *Dark is the Night* went to No. 15. They produce a highly individual and instantly recognizable sound which has not only brought them success in the UK, but also in Japan, where after two visits in 1983, they were the country's top selling group with

four albums in the Top 50 at the same time, something nobody else had ever done before. Their fifth album, which could be called *Down on the Street*, depending on the success of that particular track when released as a single, is due out in the summer of 1984.

■ Highspot of career: '1982 was a great year with a concert at the Hammersmith Odeon, a concert at the Hammersmith Palais and the Capital Jazz Festival at Knebworth Park, where we played to our largest audience ever, 20,000. Then in Feburary 1983, came our first visit to Japan.' ■ A moment to remember: 'In Japan they always have a safety curtain which goes up at the start of every performance and on our very first concert in Osaka, we played our introduction, during which the curtain was scheduled to rise, and it got stuck half way, so all the audience could see was our feet. George did a little routine from the knees downwards for their benefit! Later that night we went to a disco where George continued his comedy routine by dropping his trousers in the middle of the dance floor! In Japanese discos, nobody dances together, they all dance facing large mirrors which line the walls, just looking at themselves. When we first went in, we thought we'd got into a "gay" disco! They have a sort of pecking order; if you're a good dancer you get to the front near the mirror, whereas if you're not so hot, you get relegated to the back.'

Bill Sharpe

BORN: 19th November 1952 in Bishops Stortford. Father a stockbroker. **EDUCATED:** O.B.H. School and Stortford College, Bishops Stortford. Birmingham University where he read Music, French and German and gained his Bachelor of Music. Took piano and flute lessons at school and taught himself to

play guitar. **FIRST JOB:** BBC Studio Manager (6 years). 'I was always playing in bands while I was at school and was with a couple of semi-pro groups, but when the BBC job came up, it seemed a good opportunity. We formed Shakatak in 1980, but it was two years before I gave up my BBC job, so I often found myself working a 24-hour day!' He plays keyboards and writes all the music for the group.

■ Likes MacDonalds and Herbie Hancock. ■ Dislikes cooked cheese, garlic, peppers and Country & Western music. ■ Married to Lisa and lives in Essex.

Roger Odell
BORN: 7th December 1951 in Epping. Father a train driver. **EDUCATED:** St John's, Epping. Buckhurst Hill County High School. Had private tuition on drums. **FIRST JOB:** Electronic engineer. Also worked as a semi-pro musician with a couple of groups, Tracks and CMU, a band which made a couple of albums and toured the University circuit. 'When I turned professional, I did a lot of session work with Nicky Worth, doing jingles and that sort of thing.' With Shakatak from its start in 1980, plays drums and writes all the lyrics to Bill Sharpe's music.

■ Likes fast cars and fast women. ■ Dislikes Guinness and sound checks before the start of a concert. ■ Married to Lorraine (she's fast!), has one son, Jamie, one daughter, Maxine, and lives in Essex.

Keith Winter
BORN: 5th July 1957. Father Personnel manager at Stanstead Airport. **EDUCATED:** Newport Grammar School. **FIRST JOB:** Civil Servant, working for the Inland Revenue.

■ Likes keeping fit. 'You might say I'm a fitness fanatic.' ■ Dislikes smoking.

George Adamson
BORN: 27th September 1958. Father a maintenance engineer. **EDUCATED:** West Greenwich Secondary School. **FIRST JOB:** Shipping clerk.

■ Likes the West Indian dish 'chicken and rice'. ■ Dislikes trad jazz.

Jill Saward
BORN: 9th December 1953. Father a bus driver. **EDUCATED:** Garrett Green Comprehensive School. **FIRST JOB:** Cleaner. As a singer did a lot of session work with Nigel Wright and Roger Odell before joining Shakatak at the start in 1980.

■ Likes brandy and curry. ■ Dislikes smoking.

ANNE SHELTON
'A golden bracelet from Glen Miller and a 2s. bet with Crosby . . .'
BORN: 10th November 1927 in Dulwich, South East London. **EDUCATED:** Sacred Heart Convent, Forest Hill. **FIRST JOB:** BBC Broadcast in 1940. 'I auditioned for a programme called *Monday Night at Eight*, and Ronnie Waldman was the first producer to put me on the air when I was 12.' Band leader Ambrose heard that broadcast and asked her along to the Mayfair Hotel to audition for him. 'I was wearing my school uniform when I met him and he took one look and said, "She really is a kid, can she look a bit different?" My mother assured him that I could and we went out and bought a plain

navy dress with a big white collar.' She did her first broadcast for Ambrose that very night and then she had to make a choice . . . to be evacuated from her convent school, or stay and sing with the band. She chose the band. From then on she was broadcasting regularly with Ambrose and his orchestra and in 1942 was offered a recording contract. She did many concerts for Lease Lend, entertaining the troops, although she was never with ENSA as Ambrose wouldn't release her for more than one or two weeks at a time. Her first series for the BBC was *Introducing Anne*, and the tune she hummed at the beginning became her signature tune. She only hummed it at first because the lyrics were in German. Tommy Connor wrote some English ones especially for her and she was the first to sing them . . . the song was *Lili Marlene*. Another of her wartime radio series was *Calling Malta*, the only link with that besieged island during the war. When Glen Miller arrived in Britain in 1944 with his AAF Band, he specifically asked for Anne to sing with him and she was with him on his first broadcast and for seven shows in all. Afterwards he presented me with the set of recordings we'd made together, in a box. I thought he was giving me a box of chocolates!' He also invited her to go to Paris with the band for their Christmas broadcast, but because she had six *Worker's Playtimes* lined up, Ambrose wouldn't allow her to go. Before he left on that fateful journey to Paris, Glen Miller gave her a heavy gold bracelet saying, 'There's more gold in your voice than in that bracelet and your voice matches my sound. After the war is over, we'll work together Stateside.' It was not to be. His plane never reached Paris. 'People said he was a hard man to work for, but he was always very kind to me.'

Another highlight of 1944 was an appearance with Bing Crosby at the Queensborough Club, (on the site of the old London Casino), before an audience of between two and three thousand. 'When I got a phone call saying that Bing had asked for me, I didn't believe it. Sorry, I'm having tea with the King, was my flippant reply! But then I got a call from Cecil Madden, who was Head of Overseas Broadcasting, so I had to believe it. It was the only time I ever worked with Bing, but he always sent little messages to me over the years and when we eventually met again when he was at the London Palladium in 1976, I asked him for a photograph and he wrote on it; To Anne, my dear friend, Bing Crosby. There were many special concerts during the war for various causes, one of which was organized by Mrs Churchill and the great man himself turned up. I met him afterwards and he told me I had a very warm and compelling voice.'

Many of her records throughout the 40s and 50s sold more than a million – *Lili Marlene*, *My Yiddishe Momme*, *I'll be Seeing You*, *Galway Bay*, *Village of St Bernadette*, *Lay Down Your Arms* – records that did well in the States as well as at home and she took her first trip Stateside in 1950 to appear on the Coca Cola Show with Percy Faith. She returned the following year and spent 11 months touring the country, headlining at the Flamingo in Las Vegas, Peacock Room in San Francisco, Shamrock in Houston and the world famous Copacabana in New York, where she was booked for two weeks and was such a hit that she stayed for four. She also managed to give over 2,000 radio interviews during those 11 months and appeared in Buffalo on the same bill as a young singer whose first record was in the process of propelling him to stardom: Johnny Ray. They've remained friends ever since and in March 1984 they appeared in concert together at London's Barbican Centre. She also worked on American television in the 50s with Sophie Tucker who was obviously very impressed with the visitor from England, telling her, 'If they ever film my life story, I'd want you to play me, but I'll tell you this, as long as you're alive, I'm sure never going to die!'

When the United Nations produced an LP in aid of UNICEF with such artists as Bing Crosby, Louis Armstrong and Caterina Valente, Anne was asked to represent Great Britain with the song *Greensleeves*. The album sold a million copies in one day and at a special Variety Club Luncheon to mark the occasion, she was presented with a Gold Disc by Yul Brynner. She also recalls the occasion when, a Royal Variety Performance, she shared a dressing room with Gracie Fields. 'We spent the whole afternoon swopping stories and singing songs and she said to me, "We should make an LP together and call it Our Anne and Our Gracie." She even gave me top billing!' In 1980, she appeared in the Royal Variety Show to celebrate the 80th birthday of the Queen Mother, whose favourite song she sang; *You'll Never Know*.

Also in 1980 she was invited to become Entertainments Officer for the Not Forgotten Association which looks after the wounded and disabled from 1914 up to the Falklands war of 1982. The oldest member is 103, the youngest 22. Anne organizes the two concerts which are held every year at Buckingham Palace: one in a marquee in the grounds and the other in the Riding School.

1984 was a very hectic year for her with the 40th anniversary of the D Day landings in June. Her many concerts included two with Syd Lawrence at Portsmouth, in memory of Glen Miller. 'I never stop, but I enjoy every minute.'

■ Highspot of career: 'Everything I do is a highspot, but in 1979 director John Schlesinger asked me to sing *I'll Be Seeing You* for his film *Yanks*. The recording studio was booked from 3pm to 7pm, but by 3.20pm I had finished. I just sang it the once and that was it. Not only did John Schlesinger invite me to the Royal Premiere in London in the presence of Princess

Anne and Captain Mark Phillips, but he also flew my husband David and sister Jo and myself over to the premiere in New York which was followed by a ball. The Tommy Dorsey Orchestra led by Buddy Morrow was there and I sang *I'll Be Seeing You* and also *God Bless America* and got a standing ovation. It was a marvellous moment.'   ■ A moment to remember: 'When I appeared with Bing Crosby at the Queensborough Club in 1944, we did a little routine which went something like this:

Bing: What kind of man do you like?
Me: Charles Boyer.
Bing: Why Charles Boyer?
Me: I like the way he flutters his eyelashes.
Bing: That's not love, that's air conditioning. I bet you 2s. I can give you a kiss without even touching you.
Me: OK you're on. [At which point he kissed me] But you touched me.
Bing: Sure I did. Here's your 2s.

And I kept that two-shilling piece as a souvenir. Over 30 years later I got a telephone call from Bing asking me if I would like to go and see his show at the London Palladium. He organized tickets for my husband, sister and myself and after the show we went backstage to his dressing room. His wife Kathy was there and he said to me, "Hey, do you remember that routine we used to do, let's do it again for Kathy." And we did it, but when he put his hand in the pocket of his dressing gown to find a coin, I said, "Would you like the original two-shilling piece you gave me?" and took it out of my bag. "You mean to say you've kept that all this time?" He couldn't believe it and was really touched emotionally. He was a marvellous person!'   ■ Likes perfume and jewellery.   ■ Dislikes unnecessary temperament and 'I can't stand rudeness.'   ■ Married to David Reid and lives in South-East London.

PETER SKELLERN
'There's no adventure in following the current pattern or trend . . .'
BORN: 14th March 1947 in Bury, Lancashire. Father a painter and decorator. **EDUCATED:** Derby School, Bury. Guildhall School of Music, London. He studied piano from the age of nine and at 11 learnt to play trombone, joining the school brass band. He always knew he was going to be a famous musician. 'At school concerts I would play pieces I knew were above average for a 12-year-old. Most importantly I was never afraid of the piano, it is simply a means of expression.' At 16 he was playing trombone with the National Youth Brass Band and was organist and choir master at St Paul's Church, Bury. **FIRST JOB:** Musical Director for a production of the *Caucasian Chalk Circle* at Crewe Rep. Six months after leaving the Guildhall School of Music, he joined a pop group, March Hare, because 'I didn't want to spend the next 40 or 50 years playing Chopin; however laudable, I felt there was more to life than that.' It was while he was with the group that he started writing songs. The band eventually split up and although he picked up the odd gig here and there, times were hard and he reckoned that in the two years since leaving college, he had earned just £100. Something had to be done, so in 1971 he moved to Dorset, got married and took a job as a hotel porter in Shaftesbury. It lasted six months and during that time he wrote the song that was to

change his life, *You're a Lady*. Not only did his own recording sell over a million copies, it was recorded by countless other artists.

Over the next few years he was to establish himself as one of the UK's leading singer/songwriters, but with a difference. He appeared on television in white tie and tails; he recorded and performed with brass bands with tremendous success, saying 'I like a challenge, I like doing things differently. There's no adventure in following the current pattern or trend.' With his white tie and tails image it was almost inevitable that he should record an album of songs made famous by Fred Astaire. Released in November 1979, the *Astaire* album earned him a Gold Disc and the Music Trades Association Award for the best MOR album of the year. His next album of songs from the 20s, 30s and 40s, *A String of Pearls*, was also a big seller.

Apart from numerous guest appearances on television, he wrote and performed a series of six autobiographical programmes, *Peter Skellern*, for BBC 2 and these were followed by a series of half-hour musical plays, *Happy Endings*. In 1983 he was the musical host for Maria Aitkin's BBC 2 chat show, *Private Lives*, for which he also wrote the theme music.

His appearance at the 1982 Salisbury Festival, with cellist Julian Lloyd Webber, led to the formation in 1984 of the group Oasis in which the two of them were joined by Mary Hopkin, and Mitch Dalton and Bill Lovelady on guitars. The aim of the group is to combine classical and pop music and their first album, *Oasis*, released in the spring of '84 entered the charts almost immediately.

■ Highspots of career: 'I don't think I've reached it yet, although there have been various peaks along the way.'
■ A moment to remember: 'Talking about highspots, this is the low spot! While I was working as a hotel porter in Shaftesbury, I was told one lunch time that the gent's toilet had become blocked and could I go and do something about it immediately. So there I was on my hands and knees with a wire coathanger trying to unblock the drain, when in came a businessman who was lunching at the hotel, and proceeded

to use the urinal almost above my head. I thought, this is about as low as I can get. Things have got to get better from now on!' ■ Likes peace and quiet and the countryside.
■ Dislikes traffic and the pace of modern life. 'The best time to have lived, for me, would have been the rural life in the South about 120 years ago.' ■ Married to Diana, has a son, Timothy, a daughter, Katharine, and lives in Kent.

THE SPINNERS
'Five thousand miles for a 45-minute show . . .'
It all started in 1958 when Tony Davis's Dad asked Tony and friends, who had formed themselves into a group in order to sing folk songs, to give a performance for a colleague of his. They were delighted but there was just one snag, they didn't have a name. One had to be found and found quickly. All sorts of suggestions were made – Song Spinners, Tobacco Spinners. Weavers . . . 'no, no one ever suggested the Weavers' . . . 'Yes they did' . . . 'no, they never did' . . . they enjoy arguing. But the upshot was that they became the Spinners although none of them remembers who actually chose it. Shortly afterwards they opened the Spinners Club in the basement of a restaurant in the heart of Liverpool which was a tiny little room in which the audience could hardly fail to become involved in their songs. This was to become their trade-mark and the secret of their enduring success over the years. They are able to communicate their sheer joy of singing to everyone else, whether it be in a club or somewhere like the Royal Albert Hall.

By 1962 they were making regular television appearances on BBC 1's *Barn Dance*, and apart from making guest appearances on just about everybody's show, from Morecambe and Wise to Jimmy Saville, they have starred in their own series *The Spinners* since 1966 and *The Spinners Christmas Special* since 1969. They gave up counting their radio shows after the total passed the 2,000 mark. The songs they sing come from all over the world and they have travelled the world with them. Their visit to Africa affected them all deeply as Cliff said, 'When I saw the poverty in West Africa, that really made me feel down'; and Hugh: 'War on Want is our favourite charity and we've been trying to help Mother Theresa of Calcutta and the Third World. When we went to Africa it was terrific to see just what effect charities like that have on the poverty there.'

Their concerts down-under are always a tremendous success. Tony recalls their tour of Australia in 1979: 'When we went on stage at the Perth Concert Hall it was like the Cup roar in Liverpool. It was quite unbelievable the roar that went up. We asked, "How many people here from England?" and there was a loud shout. We then asked "How many people here from Liverpool?" and there was an even louder shout!'

1983 saw them celebrating their 25th Anniversary. Twenty-five years together with never a cross word – well almost! They returned to the Liverpool Philharmonic Hall where they gave their first major concert in 1964, to record a double album, *Return to the Phil*, and were presented with the Gold Badge of the English Folk Dance and Song Society for their services to folk music. Their albums, which number at least 30 may never have been chart toppers, but they never go out of fashion. The Spinners today are as fashionable as they were when they started over a quarter of a century ago and will no doubt be still in fashion when they celebrate their 50th anniversary or for as long as they want to go on

enjoying themselves and bringing enjoyment to others.

■ A moment to remember: 'After 26 years in the business we're doing a one-night stand in San Diego, California, to entertain a group of English Central Heating Salesmen who are holding a five-day conference there. We fly out on Tuesday, perform on the Wednesday and fly home Thursday. Five thousand miles for a 45-minute one-nighter, it's crazy!'

Tony Davis

BORN: 24th August 1930 in Blackburn, Lancashire. Father a Life Inspector for the Prudential. **EDUCATED:** Wallasey Grammar School. Teacher training college. **FIRST JOB:** Working in a brick factory. He then became a clerk in a tobacco factory. Taught himself to play clarinet and for 10 years played with various New Orleans jazz bands. Also plays the banjo, tin whistle, guitar, kazoo, African thumb piano and the melodica! He formed a skiffle group with his future wife, Beryl, which was to form the basis for the Spinners.

■ Highspot of career: 'There are so many happening all the time, but if I have to choose, I think for me it has to be our first concert at the Royal Festival Hall in London. I love the Festival Hall and we were doing a three-part African song and we had the audience divided into three parts joining in. I suddenly realized that we had these 3,000 people all singing in a foreign language and it was magic. That was a tremendous experience.' ■ Likes New Orleans Jazz, golf, messing about in boats and good wine. ■ Dislikes being late. 'I hate being late but I am always late.' ■ Married to Beryl, has two daughters and lives in Merseyside.

Mick Groves

BORN: 29th September 1936 in Salford, Lancashire. Father a builder's labourer. **EDUCATED:** St Peter's Greegate, Salford. De La Salle College, Salford. **FIRST JOB:** Teacher.
Played in various skiffle groups and was at one time the only paid-up washboard-playing member of the Musicians' Union. He met his future wife, Margaret, while playing at the famous Cavern Club in Liverpool. It was while he was at teacher training college that he joined Tony Davis's skiffle group.
He plays 6- and 12-string guitars and also acts as the group's road manager, planning routes, booking hotels etc.

■ Highspot of career: 'Our 25th-Anniversary concert at the Royal Albert Hall. We had played there before with other people, but this was the first time we had been on our own and that was really fantastic! ■ Likes Mediterranean wines and Irish whiskey. ■ Dislikes hairy dogs and being sober! ■ Married to Margaret, has three sons, one daughter and lives in Merseyside.

Hugh Jones

BORN: 21st July 1936 in Liverpool. Father a builder, Mother a music teacher. **EDUCATED:** Highfield School, Liverpool. **FIRST JOB:** Clerk in a wholesale chemists. Coming from a musical family, he plays 6- and 12-string guitars, blues harmonica, and banjo. Has written many sea songs which have been performed not only by the group but also by many other folk singers.

■ Highspot of career: 'Meeting an old shanty man called Stan Hugill on a TV series we once did from Manchester. I used to take him home and he would spend the night with us and sit up until the early hours yarning away and smoking his half

twist. Terrific! And also being awarded the Gold Badge of the English Folk Dance and Song Society in our 25th year.'
■ Likes gardening and landscaping. ■ Dislikes rum.
■ Married to Chris, has one son, one daughter and lives in Merseyside.

Cliff Hall
BORN: 11th September 1925 in Oriente Province, Cuba. Father a farmer. His parents who were Jamaican, had emigrated to Cuba because of the lack of work in Jamaica, but eventually returned home. **EDUCATED:** English school in Cuba, ('Where we had to pay'). He grew up speaking both Spanish and English. **FIRST JOB:** Brickie in Jamaica; 'and I didn't get paid for the first week'. At 17 he joined the RAF, came to Britain, and decided to stay. Plays guitar and harmonica and also acts as the group's transport manager as he likes driving.

■ Highspot of career: 'Playing at the London Palladium where our concert was recorded for posterity on an album. The atmosphere was electric.' ■ Likes gardening, making super-8mm and video films and driving. ■ Dislikes unpunctuality.
■ Married to Janet, has one daughter, two sons and one granddaughter, ('I have a habit of predicting what the baby's going to be and I told my son that he'd have a daughter and she would be born in April and I was only two hours out in my prediction'). Lives in Cheshire.

ROSEMARY SQUIRES
'Singing with that delightful West Country burr . . .'
BORN: 7th December 1928, in Bristol. Father a Civil Servant. **EDUCATED:** St Edmund's Girls School, Salisbury, Wiltshire. Took piano and guitar lessons. Her mother's family were all musicians or singers and early training in correct breathing technique came from here. **FIRST JOB:** Made her first broadcast in *Children's Hour* from Bristol at the age of 12; singing and dancing at the age of 13 in a concert party after school that played army and airforce camps in the Salisbury area in 1941. Worked as an assistant in an antique bookshop at 14; in an office at 15. Sang with various American groups on army bases during the war and the Polish Military band 1946–48.

Has also sung with the Blue Rockets, Tommy Sampson, Ted Heath, Geraldo, Joe Loss, Cyril Stapleton, Eric Winstone, Eddie Thompson Trio, Alan Clare Trio, Max Harris and Kenny Baker. Broadcasts regularly with the BBC Radio Orchestra/Radio Big Band, and is heard on most of Radio 2's music programmes. Has been broadcasting regularly since the 40s, has had her own radio series on numerous occasions and has sung and worked with just about everybody who is anybody and is undoubtedly one of the most popular singers on radio, singing as she does with the delightful West Country burr which she has never lost.

■ Highspot of career: 'Singing at the BBC Festival of Jazz at the Royal Albert Hall with the Alan Clare Trio. A tingling atmosphere as I stepped from a blacked-out rostrum into a white spotlight and a hushed audience. Then the magical sound of applause afterwards. (Not terrifically exciting but it's as I felt at the time.)' ■ A moment to remember: '*Workers Playtime* often produced the unexpected, because the factories chosen often lay off the beaten track. One in particular was a secret rocket base in Yorkshire. So secret in fact that all the road signs had been removed within the last five miles of the base! We had to ask local passers-by the way. When we arrived the piano was out of tune, but the workers, who were so isolated, gave us a super reception!'
■ Likes old films, psychic matters, reading, dancing, walking, Tibetan culture (she was secretary of Tibet Society of UK from 1972–75). ■ Dislikes smoking, moral cowardice, over amplified pop noise, selfishness, rich foods and fog. ■ Lives in Kent.

TOMMY STEELE (Thomas Hicks)
'A talent to entertain . . .'
BORN: 17th December 1936 in Bermondsey, South London. Father a bookie's runner. **EDUCATED:** Bacon's School for Boys, Bermondsey. **FIRST JOB:** His mother wanted him to take a job as bellboy at London's Savoy Hotel, but he rebelled and joined a Cunard liner sailing to New York. During four years spent at sea he was a pantry boy, lift boy, assistant steward and finally assistant gym instructor. Part of the time he was

based in New York, cruising to Bermuda and the West Indies. Having taught himself to play the guitar, he joined forces while on the Mauretania with another crew member and put on a show for the passengers, with Tommy doing an impersonation of Norman Wisdom. Working abroad made him love 'home' even more and when he was 16 he wrote a letter to the *London Evening News* which they printed: 'It's all very well to knock Britain, but when you are in the Merchant Navy like me, and have stood on all the street corners of the world, you realize there is no place like it. Thomas Hicks (Merchant Seaman).'

The summer of 1956 saw Tommy back in London between ships and, wanting to make some money to buy a new guitar, he played a few gigs around the Soho coffee bars. It was at the 2 I's that he was seen by Hugh Mendl of Decca who offered to record him if he could find a song. He promptly teamed up with two skiffle-playing mates, namely Lionel Bart and Mike Pratt, and came up with *Rock with the Cavemen*. It got to No.13 in the charts. The following month, his cover version of a Guy Mitchell hit, *Singing the Blues*, made pop history by replacing the American version in the No.1 spot. The Merchant Navy had lost Thomas Hicks for good. He made his first stage appearance at the Sunderland Empire in November 1956 and Harold Fielding, who had booked him for the provincial variety tour, brought him into the Dominion, Tottenham Court Road. It was the beginning of four years of non-stop success in the pop world. He launched the BBC Television series, *Six-Five Special*, filmed the *Tommy Steele Story*, starred in *The Duke wore Jeans* and *Tommy the Toreador* in which he sang *The Little White Bull*. In 1958 he played Buttons in *Cinderella* at the London Coliseum. A change of direction came in 1960 when he played Tony Lumpkin in the Old Vic production of *She Stoops to Conquer*. The critics hailed it as a triumph. Three years later he starred in his first big West End musical, commissioned by Harold Fielding especially for him. *Half a Sixpence*, a musical version of H.G. Wells' classic novel, *Kipps*, was a smash hit and two years later opened on Broadway making Tommy an international star. A film version of *Half a Sixpence* was also a success and this led to him making two films in Hollywood, *The Happiest Millionaire* for Walt Disney and *Finian's Rainbow*, in which he co-starred with Fred Astaire and Petula Clark. More straight roles followed, including the part of Feste in a television production of *Twelfth Night* with Sir Alec Guinness and Sir Ralph Richardson. As an entertainer, he rationed his television appearances, concentrating on the occasional spectacular which he would work on for the best part of a year. Another successful stage musical in the mid 70s was *Hans Christian Andersen* at the London Palladium, and in October 1979 he opened in a one-man show at the Prince of Wales theatre in London for a 12-week season. It ran for 60 weeks, setting an all-time record for a one-man musical show in the West End and the Variety Club made him Entertainer of the Year. 1983 saw him back at the London Palladium in another lavish Harold Fielding production, *Singin' in the Rain*, this time as director as well as star.

Has written a children's book, *Quincy*, based on one of his television spectaculars and his first novel, *The Final Run*, entered the best-seller lists in 1983. Tommy Steele, OBE (he was awarded it in 1979) has come a long way from Thomas Hicks, Merchant Seaman and unlike so many of his pop contemporaries, proved he had the talent to entertain when

the hit records became a thing of the past.

■ Highspot of career: Starring in *Singin' in the Rain* at the *London Palladium*. ■ Likes squash and painting. ■ Dislikes being asked questions about what he dislikes! ■ Married to Ann and has one daughter, Emma.

SHAKIN' STEVENS (Michael Barratt)
'An uncanny ability to make old hits his very own . . .'
BORN: 4th March 1948 in Ely, Wales. **FIRST JOB:** Upholsterer. Formed his first band, The Sunsets, in 1969, working mainly on the college/university circuit. At what was a low point for rock 'n' roll, the band, with its leader almost a carbon copy of Elvis Presley was something of a rarity and worked continuously throughout the 70s. Their first album, *A Legend*, was released in 1970 and they made several records over the next six years without any spectacular success.

The big break came with Shaky, as he likes to be called, landing one of the three roles of Elvis Presley in the hit musical *Elvis*, which opened at the Astoria, Charing Cross Road in December 1977. For 19 months he portrayed his hero on stage in London's West End and people began to take notice. He was given a regular spot on the revived *Oh Boy* show on television and with the break up of the Sunsets after his long stint in *Elvis*, he was out on his own. In 1980, 11 years after starting in the business, he made it into the Top 30 with *Hot Dog*. Six months later *Marie, Marie* reached the Top 20. But it was the next one that was to be the big one. In January 1981 he went into the studio to record four songs, one of them done very much tongue in cheek, with nobody taking it too seriously, least of all producer Stuart Coleman. But *This Ole House* shot to No.1 and stayed in the charts for 17 weeks. Rosemary Clooney's version, 26 years previously, had only made it to No.10! And 25 years after Frankie Vaughan got *Green Door* to No.1, Shaky did the same hitting the No.1 spot for the second time in six months. His uncanny ability to pick out old hits and make them all his own was paying off. 1981 was a great year: four singles in the Top 10 with *You Drive me Crazy* at No.2 and *It's Raining* at No.10, and his *This Ole House* album at No.2 in the album charts followed by *Shaky* making it to the top.

Oh Julie, a song he'd written himself, gave him his third No.1 in 1982. Up until then he'd always written the songs for the 'B' sides of his records, but when producer Stuart Coleman heard *Oh Julie*, he realized they had a winner. He recalls, 'Shaky went all modest and said he didn't believe it, but not only did it make No.1, Barry Manilow recorded a "cover" version in the States, which was quite a compliment.'

The hits continued to roll throughout 1982: *Shirley, Give Me Your Heart Tonight*, both the single and the album charting, and the *Shakin' Stevens* EP which included *Blue Christmas*. 1983 saw him in the charts with *It's Late Come In* at No.11 and *Cry Just a Little Bit* at No.3. In 1984 *A Love Worth Waiting For* reached No.2.

Having conquered Europe – and he's as big on the Continent as he is in the UK – he has now set his sights on America. And with *Cry Just a Little Bit* entering the US charts in May 1984, it could be the break through he's looking for on the other side of the Atlantic.

■ Highspot of career: Getting to No.1 with *This Ole House* in 1981. ■ A moment to remember: Just after recording *This Ole House* in January 1981, he was invited to Nashville to take part in a National Jamboree hosted by Charlie Daniels and starring Billy Joel, Crystal Gayle, Ted Nugent plus many other top American acts. Record producer Stuart Coleman, who'd gone along not only as producer but also bass player and general factotum, takes up the story: 'Two days after that recording session in London, there we were, the two of us, walking around Nashville taking in the sights, when we came across this really ramshackle house. Thinking it would make a good publicity still to promote the new record, I took a photograph of Shaky in front of it. It was a good idea, but I was a bit late, by the time we got home *This Ole House* was well on its way to No.1! The Charlie Daniels Band were scheduled to back Shaky for two of his numbers at that concert, in front of an audience of 14,000, and much to my surprise I ended up joining them, after their bass player came up to me and said, "You seem to know more about this damn thing than I do so you'd better do the concert"! Shaky brought the house down!' ■ Likes Rock 'n' Roll and the history of the music hall along with acts like the Clark Brothers, which has had a good deal of influence on his style of performing; the comedy routines of Norman Wisdom; golf; horse riding and water skiing. ■ Dislikes 'being taken for a ride'. ■ Married to Carol, has two sons and one daughter and lives in Surrey.

STU STEVENS
'From mining to singing . . .'
BORN: 23rd September, in Kirkby-in-Ashfield, Nottinghamshire. Father a miner. **EDUCATED:** Annesley School, Kirkby-in-Ashfield. Plays piano, guitar and bass guitar but didn't become interested in music until he was in his 20s. **FIRST JOB:** Miner for nine years, during which time he saved up enough money to start his own business as an agricultural contractor. He had no thoughts of becoming a singer but one night in the early 60s, his brother entered him for a talent contest at the local Railway Club. 'I never went into pubs or clubs because I don't drink, and I still don't, but on this particular night it was raining and I agreed to go. I sang *Mexicali Rose* and when the

organist asked me what key I sang it in, I didn't know what he was talking about. I didn't know what a key was. I'll start and you follow me, I told him. Much to my surprise I won and got paid £10. After that, several people who had been in the audience asked me to go and sing at their clubs, so I did, for £10 a time. Then I realized that at £10 for a half hour's work, I was on to a good thing so I made a bee line for a guitar, learnt a few chords and became a guitarist/vocalist; and that's how it all started.'

His singing career gradually took over from his agricultural contracting business. He sent a tape to EMI and got himself a recording contract. 'Being a Northener I was always forward and I literally pushed my way into an audition for the Lonnie Donnegan Show at ATV and got it.' His first hit record was *The Man from Outer Space*, which he financed himself because the record companies didn't think it was hit material. He proved them wrong and having formed his own record company he used the profits from the record to build his own recording studio.

His first visit to America was in 1973, representing Britain at the International Fanfare in Nashville. He has made eight return visits to the States, playing at the Grand Ole Opry on three occasions. In 1983 he went to Forth Worth, Texas to receive the International Country & Western Music Association Award for the UK Male Entertainer of the Year. He won the British Country Music Association Award for Best Male Vocalist in 1981, '82 and '83, and the Silk Cut Award for Best Male Vocalist in 1983 and '84 at Wembley.

■ Highspot of career: 'When you've been in the business as long as I have it's impossible to name one as there have been so many.' ■ A moment to remember: 'When I was working down the pit, several of us got stuck one day in the lift half way down the shaft. We were carrying some girders which had tipped and jammed us into the side. The guy operating the motor couldn't do anything so I shinned 400 yards down the cable to the bottom and phoned for help. They lowered rescue equipment and we all got out. It doesn't matter who I meet in showbusiness or what they've done, for me the men who work down the pit are the salt of the earth.' ■ Likes

simple things – open spaces, the countryside, sunshine. Tinkering with cars, (he's an expert motor mechanic).
■ Dislikes people who say one thing and mean another.
■ Married to Daphne, has two sons, Stuart and Stephen, and lives in Nottinghamshire.

ROD STEWART
'An uncontrollable urge to go barnstorming from city to city . . .'

BORN: 10th January 1945 in London. Father owned a newsagent's in Holloway. **EDUCATED:** William Grimshaw Secondary Modern School where he was captain of the football team. **FIRST JOB:** A series of odd jobs on leaving school, erecting fences, digging graves etc. At 16 he signed with Brentford Football Club hoping to make soccer his

career, but soon became disillusioned with the wages and having to clean the first team's boots! When the coach told him he was unlikely to make it in the pro leagues, he thought he might try the music business instead. He became something of a beatnik, ending up in Spain from where he had to be repatriated because he ran out of money. He says he still owes British Airways the fare!

Having learnt to play guitar and banjo on his travels, on his return to the UK he joined a semi-pro outfit, Jimmy Powell and the Dimensions. His first record in 1964 didn't amount to much and the following year he joined Hoochie Coochie Men with John Baldry and stayed with him on his next line-up, Steampacket. After a personality clash, he left and joined Shotgun Express which wasn't a great success. 1968 saw Rod Stewart with the Jeff Beck Group which had quite a following in the States and for the first time, people started to take

notice of the singer with the hoarse sounding voice and the habit of strutting round the stage. When the Jeff Beck Group broke up, Stewart became lead singer with the Faces, an association that was to last for seven years, in which time he recorded seven albums with the group and built up a reputation for being an original stage performer. After an appearance with the Faces at Madison Square Garden, the *New York Times* said, 'Stewart doesn't need much help. He has the almost hypnotically appealing stage presence of a Mick Jagger; one watches his strutting cock-of-the-walk antics even when he isn't singing.'

While with the Faces, he had begun recording solo albums as early as 1970 and in '71, *Every Picture Tells a Story* included a song called *Maggie May* which was released as a single and captured the No.1 spot in the charts on both sides of the Atlantic. His status as a solo artist was assured although he continued to sing with the Faces for another four years. Today Rod Stewart is an international superstar with numerous Platinum and Gold Discs to his credit. His concerts at venues with audiences ranging from 10,000 to 50,000 are invariably sold out in the first 24 hours. The stamina needed to enable him to carry out his world-wide tours is considerable. He jogs three miles a day, plays soccer twice a week and also manages to do some weight lifting. New York music critic Robert Palmer once said, 'One suspects that this all but uncontrollable urge to go barnstorming from city to city, hitting stage after stage to the roar of thousands of fans and the clamour of superamplified drums and revved up electric guitars, is precisely what separates the rockers . . . performers for whom rock 'n' roll isn't just a medium but a calling . . . from the entertainers, who happen to be using an accessible pop idiom. Rod Stewart is a rocker.'

■ A moment to remember: The day he arrived on the set to film a video, wearing very tight yellow and red satin trousers. To make sure he'd remembered the words correctly, he did a run through of his song with his back to camera. Half way through, the familiar Stewart grind of the hips came into play and the red and yellow pants duly parted asunder giving the cameras a bird's eye view of the sexiest wriggle in show business.   ■ Likes soccer.   ■ Dislikes the thought of growing old.   ■ Has one son, one daughter and lives in California and Berkshire.

RICHARD STILGOE
'I've had this nice boring career . . .'
BORN: 28th March 1943 in Camberley, Surrey. Father a water engineer. Moved to Liverpool at the age of three. **EDUCATED:** Liverpool College. Monkton Combe School, Bath, Somerset. Clare College, Cambridge, where he became involved in the Cambridge Footlights around the same time as the Goodies and the Monty Python lot. Started playing the piano at seven. **FIRST JOB:** Selling football pools door to door in Liverpool. In 1958, while still at school, formed a skiffle group with Bernard Falk playing at the Cavern in Liverpool. They called themselves Tony Snow and the Blizzards. 'I was Tony Snow because we rehearsed at my house!'

After coming down from Cambridge, he appeared in cabaret at the Royal Court Theatre Club in London, followed by an engagement at the Blue Angel, where he worked for six months with the legendary Leslie Hutchinson (Hutch). 'He was 72 and I was 21 and I learnt a lot from him.' Almost all of

his work since the mid 60s has been in cabaret for which he writes his own material. 'I'm not good enough to sing other people's material and my material isn't good enough for other people to sing, so that leaves me singing my own songs. I class myself as an entertainer in the tradition of Flotsam and Jetsam and Noel Coward. I suppose you could describe me as a sort of neutered Tom Lehrer.' His first broadcasts were in *This Time of Day* with Lord Arran, but it was what he describes as 'singing silly songs' on the *Today* programme with Jack de Manio that first made people sit up and take notice. 'It was really an attempt to make the nation cut itself while shaving.' He gradually became more established both on radio and television and in 1983, his *Hamburger Weekend* for Radio 2 won the Monaco Radio Prize.

'I've had this nice boring career without any big jumps up the ladder which often means you end up sliding back a few rungs.' But his nice, boring career changed direction when he met Andrew Lloyd Webber (qv) on the Michael Parkinson show. 'Michael has his uses, I won't hear a word against him. Andrew needed an opening number for his show *Cats*, which was just about to go into rehearsal, so I wrote it for him. He then said he had this idea lying around for a musical about trains and would I be interested?' And so a £2 million musical was born, *Starlight Express*, and Andrew Lloyd Webber's new partner was Richard Stilgoe. 'I've got a musical in a drawer at home that I wrote when I was 17, all about horse racing which needed real live horses on stage! It was awful. Just because I've written a successful one now doesn't make the old one any better.'

■ Highspot of career: 'Appearing in cabaret at Windsor Castle for the Queen and her guests following a private dinner. I've never been so frightened in my life, but it was all right; I was neither knighted nor beheaded at the end.'
■ A moment to remember: 'The job that taught me more about music than anything else was when I played piano every weekend for a year in a pub in South London. I had to play for anyone who wanted to sing. They'd come up and

say, "I'm going to sing this", and I would have to play it in all 12 keys they meandered through in the space of a couple of minutes. The place was a bit of a thieves den and as I found out afterwards, I actually accompanied one of the Great Train Robbers after he'd committed the crime, but before he was caught. He sang *Buddy Can You Spare a Dime!'* ■ Likes children, Mozart and cheese. ■ Dislikes Barry Manilow! ■ Married to Annabel, has three sons and two daughters and lives in Surrey.

first broadcast on the Joe Henderson Show in October 1974. In 1975 won television's *New Faces* and was given a recording contract. Has toured the world in cabaret appearing in Australia, South Africa and many European countries. Has also done several troop tours for BFBS. Has sung with Nat Temple, Chris Allen and Ray Davies. Is heard regularly on many of Radio 2's music programmes.

■ Highspot of career: 'My first broadcast'. ■ Likes walking in the country. ■ Lives in Essex.

DANNY STREET
'One of the busiest singers . . .'
BORN: 22nd April 1941, in Stirling, Scotland. Father a master butcher. EDUCATED: Stirling High School. As a tenor sang in Logie Church Choir. Studied stage craft and singing for six years. FIRST JOB: Also his first broadcast, singing on *Come Thursday* on BBC Radio from Dundee. Sang with the Jack Carter Band in Castle Richmond for a year before moving to London in 1963. Spent the next seven years as vocalist with the Johnny Howard Band. Broadcasts regularly with the BBC Radio Orchestra/Radio Big Band and is one of the country's busiest session singers. Is heard on most of Radio 2's music programmes and seen on just about every television show that uses a backing group. Probably one of the most familiar faces on the screen if you know who to look for, although he has been known to wear various disguises!

■ Highspot of career: 'My own half-hour show with the Scottish Radio Orchestra on BBC Television in Scotland. Also representing the BBC at the Nordring Radio Festival in Jersey in 1981.' ■ Likes golf and good wine. ■ Dislikes beer. ■ Married to Helenor, has three children and three boxers and lives in London.

GEOFF TAYLOR
'New Faces winner . . .'
BORN: 2nd March 1948 in Ilford Essex. Father a maintenance manager. EDUCATED: William Morris Technical College. FIRST JOB: Lead singer with a vocal group at the age of 15. Made his

MARIE TOLAND
'£40 down the drain . . .'
BORN: Newcastle upon Tyne. EDUCATED: Kenton Comprehensive School. South East Northumberland Technical College. FIRST JOB: Singing with the Don Smith Band at the Oxford Galleries Newcastle upon Tyne. 'I had always wanted to be an actress and studied acting and drama from the age of eight. I also took a Drama Design course at college.' Has played at the People's Theatre Newcastle upon Tyne. Made her first broadcast on Metro Radio. Has fronted her own band Burlesque, and her own vocal groups, the Berkeley Squares and the Chickadees. Has sung with Tommy and Jack Hawkins, Ray McVay, Andy Ross, Ray Davies, Johnny Howard, The Greatest Swing Band in the World (on a Johnny Mathis tour), Stan Reynolds, Monty Babson and the Syd Lawrence Orchestra. Also spent 12 months as a backing vocalist with Freddie Starr ('what an experience!'). Is heard regularly on many of Radio 2's music programmes, singing with the Birmingham String Orchestra conducted by Ray Davies and also with the Art Walters Quintet.

■ Highspots of career: 'Touring with Johnny Mathis with my vocal group the Chickadees and ending up with a week at the London Palladium, and appearing at the Royal Festival Hall with Syd Lawrence. Also hearing for the first time the great voices of Sassy, Ella, Sinatra, Bennett and Mark Murphy.' ■ A moment to remember: 'When I went for my audition with Syd Lawrence (qv), I had spent £40 on having my hair permed. I was very nervous, but I thought I looked

nice and sang well. When Syd came out of the sound box, his face was white and had a look of horror. He told me I had the job, but my hair was, to put it mildly, awful and I should go and get it straightened! Well, £40 down the drain, but I had a great job with a wonderful band. I never did get it straightened, I waited until it grew out, so I had my £40 worth. As for Syd, I often thought of wearing a shocking pink wig to work, just to see the "little waster's face"!' ■ Likes cooking, the theatre, jazz, reading and travel. ■ Dislikes pretentious people, cold weather and greediness. ■ Lives in London.

TRACEY ULLMAN
'Mum, they won't stop laughing at me . . .'

BORN: 30th December 1959 in Burnham, Bucks. Father a company director. **EDUCATED:** Italia Conti Stage School. 'The only person connected with show business in our family was Uncle Sidney who played guitar with the Planet Set and when I found out I could sing, I used to go on these package tours with him.' **FIRST JOB:** A dancer. 'When I left stage school I just started dancing because it was a laugh and all my mates were doing it.' Her first acting role was as Frenchy in *Grease* at the New London Theatre. Also played Janet in *Rocky Horror* and was in *Elvis* at the Astoria. 'I did two and a half years in the West End and looking back on that period, all I can remember is jiving and singing 'shoo-wa-be-daddy daddy-shoo-wa".' Her agent then decided it was time she did some serious acting and sent her to the Liverpool Everyman where she appeared in *It's a Madhouse*. The following year, 1981, saw her playing the part of a club singer in *Four in a Million* at the Royal Court Theatre in London. 'I was taking the part very seriously but on the first night people were laughing so much I had to stop, I was very upset and said to my Mum, "They won't stop laughing at me".' They haven't stopped laughing since and she has found a whole new metier for her talents. BBC Television starred her in *McKenzie* and that was followed by the *Three of a Kind* series. Tracey Ullman, singer and dancer, was making a name for herself as a comedienne. Now was the time to cash in on her new

found fame and in 1983 her first single *Breakaway* made it to No.4 in the charts, to be followed by *They Don't Know* at No.2 and an up-to-date version of the Doris Day hit, *Move Over Darling*, which reached No.8. Released in the USA, *They Don't Know* made it to No.8 and led to her first visit Stateside early in 1984 where she appeared on the Johnny Carson show and was guest presenter for a week on the 24-hour Music/Video channel MTV. Her first album, *You Broke my Heart in 17 Places*, which had made it into the British Top 10, entered the Top 40 in America.

She set something of a precedent when she persuaded Neil Kinnock to appear on one of her promotional videos. She also persuaded Paul McCartney to do the same although no one believed it was actually him, but it was!

In 1983 she won the award for Best Light Entertainment Performance of the Year and was also named Best Female Singer and Best New Artist at the British Rock and Pop Awards.

■ Highspot of career: 'When *They Don't Know* got to No.2 in the charts.' ■ A moment to remember: Leaving the West End and going to the Everyman in Liverpool for a six-month stint. 'All the others would come in in sloppy sweaters talking about the Worker's Revolutionary Party while I sat there in my fur coat. They weren't used to a dancer in lip gloss and a fur coat, but we got to be really good friends after they accepted the fact that I didn't want to walk around in a torn sweater!' ■ Married to Allan McKeown and lives in London.

FRANKIE VAUGHAN (Frank Abelson)
'A dusty sheet of music bought for 1s. 6d. in Glasgow . . .'

BORN: 3rd February 1928 in Liverpool. Father an upholsterer. **EDUCATED:** Harrison Jones School and Granby Street School, Liverpool. In 1941 was evacuated to Endmoor, near Kendall, in the Lake District where he attended Preston Patrick School followed by Boys National School, Lancaster. Leeds College of Art.

He went to Leeds College of Art with a view to becoming an art master, but it wasn't to be. The annual College rag put on a revue at the Leeds Empire in which Frank sang a couple of

songs; the applause was thunderous. In the audience was BBC producer Barney Colehan who urged him to give up his art studies and go into showbusiness, but Frank had just won a National Design competition and his work was on display at an exhibition at Earls Court, so he was determined to go to London to see if he could sell some of his designs. However he took with him a letter of introduction from Barney Colehan to agent Billy Marsh, and after failing to sell any of his designs, and desperately short of money, he went along to the Delfont office. The result, a week's engagement at the bottom of the bill at the Kingston Empire and a loan of £10 so that he could hire a pianist. On the Monday night Frank Abelson stopped the show. Art had lost, show business had won. 'I decided I had to change my name but nobody had any bright ideas, then I remembered how my grandmother would always call me her Number Vaughan grandchild saying, "whatever he does, he will always be number vaughan." So Frankie Vaughan I became. One of the best bits of advice I was ever given in those early days came from that veteran of the Music Hall, Hetty King. She told me, "If you want to be a star, behave like one. Buy the best even if you can't afford it." So I did and it paid off.' His top hat and cane became his trademarks and a dusty sheet of music, *Give me the Moonlight*, he'd bought in a shop in Glasgow for 1s. 6d. became his signature tune. In 1953 he signed a recording contract and got his first hit, *My Sweetie Went Away*. For the next decade he was rarely out of the charts, with *Garden of Eden* and *Tower of Strength* providing him with two No.1's. In 1957 he got his first big film part in *These Dangerous Years* for Herbert Wilcox and went on to make three more. *Wonderful Things, The Lady is a Square* and *The Heart of a Man*. In 1960 Hollywood beckoned and Frank starred in *Let's Make Love* with Marilyn Monroe. But neither he nor his wife Stella took to life in Hollywood and as soon as the film was completed they returned home. He no longer features in the charts and he rations his television appearances, 'When I go on the box, I want it to be something special'. He works untiringly for The National Boys Clubs, of which he is the President, and in 1965 was awarded the OBE for his services to the welfare of young people.

■ A moment to remember: 'During one of my engagements in Liverpool, I was being driven back from an Everton/ Liverpool match by Norman Jones, well-known bouncer and minder of mine in Liverpool! Norman is a great mate of mine and a dead ringer for Jimmy Tarbuck, he looks like his twin. Well, we had a puncture and called a local garage for assistance. They sent a young lad out to deal with us, and being about 5.30pm on a Saturday, he wasn't very happy about being sent out on a cold evening just before knocking-off time! After a short while he suddenly seemed to recognize us, thinking Norman was Jimmy and seeing us together, his whole attitude changed! He took the tyre away, returned very quickly and had not only changed the tyre but washed the wheel, changed into a tie and jacket and had a young lady in the passenger seat of the car. While he was putting the tyre back on, he was chatting about being a great fan of mine and that he did a bit of singing himself. In fact it turned out that he had recently won first prize in a Mecca singing competition. "Yeh," he said, "I did *I Remember You* and won £5"! As we drove off we noticed his girl friend was giving him a right telling off!' ■ Likes 'Being Stella's husband and my children's father, the very private person called Frank

Abelson; and grandfather to a beautiful granddaughter called Natalie. I also like, and enjoy very much, being Frankie Vaughan.' ■ Dislikes phonies, and warm white wine. ■ Married to Stella, has two sons, one daughter and one granddaughter and lives in London.

to bathe in it. Swimming. ■ Dislikes jellied eels. ■ Married to Philip Sanderson. (Not only did Tommy Sanderson get me started in my career, he introduced me to his son!) Has one daughter, Molly (named after her hit song), and lives in London.

LOUISA JANE WHITE
'My backing band was led by Elton John . . .'
BORN: 10th October 1951 in Dudley, Worcestershire. Father an engineer. EDUCATION: Wellington Girl's High School, Shropshire. FIRST JOB: 'The very first time I was booked for a gig was when I was six years old. I sang with my 10-year-old brother at a concert at an old people's home.' She sang with various groups while still at school and left before taking her 'O' level in music, in order to continue her singing career full time. She was 'discovered' in Wolverhampton by pianist/MD/record producer Tommy Sanderson and his wife, Lily, who brought her to London at the age of 16 where she made her first record. Her first broadcast was on the Dave Lee Travis Show in 1968. She has made regular broadcasts ever since, singing with most of the BBC Orchestras. Has written several songs with Lily Sanderson, including *Milly Molly Mandy*, a chart entry in 1975. They also wrote the theme song for the film *Digby, The Biggest Dog in the World*, starring Spike Milligan.

■ Highspot of career: Representing the BBC at a song festival in Poland in 1972. ■ A moment to remember: 'My first television date was on *Disco 2*, the forerunner to the *Old Grey Whistle Test*, which was broadcast from the *Late Night Line Up* studio at Television Centre. The small studio had its permanent set of a low coffee table and several chairs. As there was some sort of labour dispute going on at the time, no one was allowed to move anything in the studio, so I ended up singing while standing on the coffee table. The whole thing had to be shot in close-up and afterwards everyone wanted to know what was wrong with me that I was only seen from the waist up! The backing band, by the way was led by Elton John.' ■ Likes the sun but rarely gets

PAT WHITMORE
'I hear a bird . . .'
BORN: Wolverhampton. Father a steelworker. EDUCATED: St Bartholomew's School, Penn. Municipal Grammar School, Wolverhampton. Took singing lessons in Wolverhampton and in London studied with Dorothy Robson. Also plays the piano. FIRST JOB: Dental nurse. Has also worked in accountancy. Made her first broadcast in February 1958 for BBC producer John Simmonds. Has sung with the Band of the Welsh Guards, BBC Concert Orchestra, The Royal Philharmonic Orchestra, Bill McGuffie Quartet, Cliff Adam Singers, Mike Sammes Singers, Ambrosian Singers and the Birmingham Symphony Orchestra. Programmes include literally hundreds of varying documentaries for Charles Chilton; *Roundabout, Sam Costa Show, A Year in Song, Grand Hotel, Joe Henderson Show.* Is heard regularly on Radio 2's *Friday Night is Music Night, Melodies for You, String Sound, Among Your Souvenirs.*

■ Highspots of career: 'Singing under the direction of Elmer Bernstein with the Royal Philharmonic Orchestra, closely followed by meeting Nat King Cole and also appearing in the Nordring Radio Festival in Norway in 1975.' ■ A moment to remember: 'On one occasion I was recording a programme for the Army at Colchester. I was singing *How are Things in Glocca Morra*, or at least I was supposed to sing it. The orchestra played the introduction and I started to sing the first line, "I hear a bird", but I had started in the wrong key. I stopped. Intro again, "I hear a bird" 'wrong key again. A third time the intro and "I hear a bird" and from somewhere in the hall a voice came, "Why don't you ask it to give you the note"!' ■ Likes dressmaking, Brownie/Guiding (as a Guider), my family. ■ Dislikes violence in any form. ■ Married to John Newman, has two children and lives in Middlesex.

ROGER WHITTAKER
'The best songs write themselves . . .'

BORN: 22nd March 1936 in Nairobi, Kenya. Father from a family of grocers in Staffordshire, emigrated to East Africa on medical advice in 1929. **EDUCATED:** Nursery school at age of four. 'Most of my days in nursery school consisted of my singing old George Formby songs to the rest of the class.' Boarding school in East Africa, where he sang in the school choir. University of Capetown, South Africa; University of Bangor, Wales where he obtained his B.Sc. Speaks Swahili and a little German.

At the age of seven was given his first guitar by an Italian prisoner of war working on a farm near his home. 'I can remember my arms were so short that I couldn't reach round it. However that was the start of my musical career and I sat down and learned how to master the instrument. By then, my sister Betty, who had been given a mandolin, and I were so stage struck that our poor neighbours used to be dragged over to watch us singing, dancing and telling terrible jokes!'

FIRST JOB: Two years' National Service in the Kenya Regiment. 'Stuck in bush camps for months on end meant we had to make our own entertainment. Before I knew it I was standing on a make-shift stage, guitar in hand, having enormous fun developing into a second Elvis Presley.' After being demobbed in 1956, he went to Capetown University to study medicine, but after 18 months of playing more rugby than studying, decided to leave and take up teaching. But he could only go so far without the proper qualifications, so he enrolled at the University of Bangor in Wales, close to his grandparents, who lived in Prestatyn. Came to Britain in 1959 and spent three years studying zoology, bio-chemistry and marine biology. He obtained his B.Sc. with the second highest marks of his year. But meanwhile had recorded a song in aid of the University's charity appeal, and on the strength of it had been given a recording contract. On the day he heard he had got his degree, he also learned that his second single, *Steel Man* had got into the hit parade. What to do? His professor gave him what was to turn out to be the best advice he'd ever had. 'Have a try in show business and if you

haven't made it in 10 years, come back here and teach.' He didn't need 10 years, but after a disastrous summer season in Northern Ireland, he realized he had a lot to learn. It took him five. The turning point came in 1967 when he was invited to represent Britain at the Knokke Festival in Belgium. Not only did Britain win, but Roger won the Press Prize for the Personality of the Festival. His competition entries, *Mexican Whistler*, which he wrote himself, and *If I Were a Rich Man*, went to No.1 and No.2 in three European countries. It was the start of an extremely successful career on the Continent, although back in the UK he was still virtually unknown. All that changed with the release of another of his own compositions, *Leavin'*, better known as *Durham Town*, in 1969. It got to No.12 in the charts and was the first of a whole string of hits, *I Don't Believe in If Any More*, *New World in the Morning*, *The Last Farewell*, which was the single that was to open up the American market for him. Suddenly Roger Whittaker was fashionable. He was writing most of his own material. 'Although I admire and record material by other songwriters, I feel it is very important for an artiste to write his own songs. I wrote my first one when I was in the army. It was called *Crinkle Face* and it was awful! At least three-quarters of all my new songs end up in the waste bin, and only about one per cent of the remainder is ever good enough and worth recording. The best songs write themselves. *Durham Town* was like that, conceived and written in a dressing-room at the BBC Television Centre. They came in and asked me in the morning at the start of rehearsals, if it was possible for me to write a song during the day and sing it on the show in the evening. I had recently been to Durham and had fallen in love with it; and I remember picking up my guitar and playing the song to my manager, straight off the top of my head, without having anything written down. It sounded virtually the same as the finished record and I sang it for the first time on the show that night.'

His American debut came about in 1976 because *The Last Farewell*, recorded five years previously, had been played on a station in Atlanta, Georgia, as a track from an album, the station director's wife had picked up on her travels in Canada! It became so popular that it was released as a single and within weeks was in the American Top 10. In 1980 he triumphed on a coast-to-coast tour of the States, appearing on many of the top television shows. Another US tour followed in 1981, and 1982 found him touring Canada, and visiting his native Kenya to make a television special and an album, *Roger Whittaker in Kenya*. 'It was a true eye opener. I thought I knew my own country, but for me, too, it was a journey of discovery, seeing places and people and hearing stories never told to me before.' That same year he was the subject of *This is your Life*, but it was back to America again in 1983 for yet another tour and his debut in cabaret at Lake Tahoe. A British tour, followed by concert dates in Germany and Austria and a major tour of Scandinavia, not forgetting a short cabaret season in Atlanta and a major tour of Canada, didn't leave him much spare time in 1984!

He is without doubt, one of the most travelled entertainers in the business, which explains why he pilots his own plane both in the UK and on overseas engagements.

■ Highspot of career: 'One of my proudest achievements was writing *I Don't Believe in If Any More*. I was in Helsinki at the time but was shortly due to go to West Africa. There were a multitude of visas to be obtained, together with a long list of innoculations which I had to have for the African visit. I had to go to 14 different embassies and medical centres. I really didn't know if I was coming or going. Then the Olympia Music Hall in Paris offered me a season providing I could get back from Africa on exactly the right day. It was chaos. I ended up talking to myself saying, *if* I can get visas, *if* I can get the innoculations, *if* I can get the right flight back to Paris, *if, if, if,* Oh, I don't believe in if any more – a song was born. I dashed back to my hotel and started writing. Fortunately I managed to get everything sorted out and a few weeks later, I recorded that song!'

■ A moment to remember: 'At one crazy time in my career, I found myself appearing on a television show in each of three European countries in one day! Not long afterwards came a week when I was recording a TV series every day in the west of England and appearing in cabaret in London at night. There was only one thing to do, hire a private plane, with pilot to ferry me back and forth. On one of those trips, the pilot asked if I would like to have a go at the controls. Well, as you can imagine, I was a little apprenhensive, but after that I was hooked. I took lessons, got my pilot's licence and then went on to obtain my Instrument Rating which enables you to fly in all weather conditions and in the airways controlled by Air Traffic. I started off flying Cessna 150 Aerobats and Beech Barons, but with an increasing number of overseas tours, I switched to my first turbo jet, the nine-seater Rockwell 690 Commander. Even my wife, who used to hate the thought of flying, now holds a pilot's licence. So you could call us the flying Whittakers!' ■ Likes food, wine, playing bridge and backgammon, all wildlife and beautiful cars. ■ Dislikes smoking, strong spirits and people who say they are bored. ■ Married to Natalie, has three daughters, two sons and lives in Essex.

IRIS WILLIAMS
'So excited she nearly crashed the car . . .'

BORN: April 1944 in Pontypridd, South Wales. **EDUCATED:** Secondary Modern School. Cardiff College of Music and Drama. **FIRST JOB:** On leaving school, worked in a glove factory for three years. Her first singing job was in a social club in Wales. 'As far back as I can remember, I've enjoyed singing and I always wanted to be a singer. I used to say to my mother, "I'm not working for a living, that's for sure." Little did I know what hard work singing could be!'
Made her first broadcast on *Disc A Dawn* for BBC Wales and since then has made numerous appearances on radio and television. Has also appeared at the London Palladium, starred in pantomime and entertained the passengers on several of the QE2 world cruises. 'I usually only go for 10 days at a time, which is ideal. Any longer than that on a boat and you begin to think that buildings and houses don't exist.' Her first record, *He Was Beautiful*, released in the summer of 1979, was a big hit, reaching the No.18 spot in the charts. 'When I made that record, people thought that was the only kind of song I could sing, but I won't devote myself to a particular style, because I like to sing everything from pop to jazz.'
Her recording of the Roger Webb/Glen Mason song, *The Gentle Touch*, in 1984, came about almost by accident. 'Glen Mason, who doesn't live very far away from me, was playing golf with a girl friend of mine and happened to say he had

written a song with Roger Webb and they couldn't think of a good person to record it. "Why not get Iris to do it", said my friend. And that's how it happened. When I heard the song, I fell in love with it immediately.' In 1981 she was named Vocalist of the Year.

■ Highspot of career: 'Appearing with Bob Hope in his 1982 Golf Classic cabaret and being presented to Princess Margaret who was in the audience that night.' ■ A moment to remember: 'After I recorded *He Was Beautiful*, I heard it on the radio for the first time on the Jimmy Young Show, when I was driving somewhere. I was so excited that I nearly crashed into the car in front of me!' ■ Likes driving, reading, music, animals, food and tennis. ■ Dislikes Heavy Metal music, housework and answering the telephone. ■ Married to Clive Brandy has one son, Blake, and lives in Berkshire.

NORMA WINSTONE
'In a class of her own . . .'

BORN: 23rd September 1941, in London. Father a labourer. **EDUCATED:** Dagenham County High School. Studied piano and organ at the Trinity College of Music, London. **FIRST JOB:** Clerk in an insurance office. Was also a temporary transport manager for a time when the transport manager dropped dead and his assistant walked out! Made her first broadcast on *Jazz Club* in April 1967. Has sung with the Michael Garrick Sextet, Mike Westbrook Band, John Dankworth Orchestra, Mike Gibbs, Kenny Wheeler Big Band, and Azimuth (with husband John Taylor and Kenny Wheeler). Has recorded one album with the Kenny Wheeler Big Band and three albums with Azimuth. Programmes include *Jazz in Britain* (Radio 3), various co-productions with Dutch and German Radio on Radio 2. Sang on the Dutch entry for the Nordring Radio Festival in 1981 when they won. Broadcasts regularly with the BBC Radio Orchestra/Radio Big Band and is heard on many of Radio 2's music programmes including *Big Band Special*. Has established herself as one of the country's top jazz singers. Has also written the lyrics to many songs.

■ A moment to remember: 'My very first broadcast went out at 1.30 on a Sunday morning, I remember I was singing Clifford Brown's *Joy Spring*. The next day my husband had to telephone Carmen McCrea who was in town for a few days, about a recording session. He just happened to mention that I admired her singing very much and wanted to meet her. "Did you say Norma Winstone?" said Carmen McCrea, "I want to meet her, I heard her on the radio last night." Quite a coincidence that she should have been listening to her radio at 1.30am! It was a great thrill.' ■ Likes reading and Indian food. ■ Dislikes meat but isn't a a strict vegetarian. ■ Married to pianist John Taylor (qv), has two sons and lives in London.

PAUL YOUNG

'Everything's working out just the way I want it to . . .'

BORN: 17th January 1956 in Luton, Bedfordshire. Father a Vauxhall car worker. 'My Dad always wanted to play a musical instrument, but never did, so he wanted to give me the chance to. When I was seven he bought me a piano. I can never thank him enough.' **FIRST JOB:** Apprentice at the Vauxhall car factory. In 1978 he decided he'd had enough of working in a factory and joined a group called Streetband. 'At first my parents were very concerend whether I would make any money from pop. They were worried that I had given up a proper career as a car worker, but they're really proud of me now. They've been to all kinds of gigs from the grottiest pubs to when the Q Tips supported The Who at Wembley.' He joined the Q Tips as lead singer after leaving Streetband and the next four years were a series of punishing tours around the UK. One of Britain's highest paid and most popular 'live' acts on stage, they packed something like 700 concert halls in three years, but in spite of it all had no success with their records.

The moment of decision came for Paul when a recording company showed an interest in signing him without the band. 'In the end I had to put myself first but I still feel sad about the split because the group were excellent, although we never fulfilled our potential. One of the saddest parts was that I'd known one of the guys in the band since I was two. When I decided to go solo, it was agony telling him, but everything's all right now and we're still friends.'

Within 12 months, his version of the Marvin Gaye classic

Wherever I Lay my Hat, That's my Home, was No.1 in the charts and he was being hailed as the best white soul voice in the country. 'It's a very strange feeling. I'm doing the same thing now as I always have been. It's just that more people are taking notice. Everything's working out just the way I want it to. I'm not saying I wouldn't have liked all this to happen years ago, but I'm better prepared now.' After a chart topping single and album, he was named Best Newcomer of 1983 by the British Record Industry and a few weeks later was voted Best Male Singer at the annual Rock and Pop Awards.

■ Highspot of career: Being voted Best Male Singer in the Rock and Pop Awards in February 1984. ■ A moment to remember: 'When I was younger and I saw somebody who was a star or something, I'd remember every single detail about them, every little move they made, what they said, what they were wearing, how they acted. And that makes me very conscious of everything I do because now I know how they must have felt. As soon as you become someone everyone wants to know you, and they are the same people who were ignoring you when you were a nobody. It's a very cruel business.' ■ Likes collecting records. 'I've got piles of them and I collect rare ones.' Indian food and afternoon tea. ■ Is a bachelor and lives in London.

SECOND SECTION

Instrumentalists/Musical Directors/
Composers

CLIFF ADAMS
'Sing Something Simple' . . .'
BORN: 1923 in Southwark. **EDUCATED:** Was a choirboy at St Mary-le-Bow, the city church of Bow Bells fame. Studied piano and organ. **FIRST JOB:** Dance band pianist and then joined the RAF for the duration of the Second World War. After the war he established himself as an arranger working for Ted Heath, Cyril Stapleton, Eric Winstone and Stanley Black among others. In 1949 he formed the Stargazers which became the top vocal group of the 50s. Record hits included *I See the Moon, Broken Wings, Twenty Tiny Fingers* and *Close the Door.* They appeared in three Royal Command performances. In 1954 he formed the Adam Singers for the BBC *Show Band.* Television credits include *The Val Doonican Show, Something Old Something New,* and *Singalong Saturday. Sing Something Simple* was first broadcast on BBC Radio in 1959 and has been running continuously ever since on Radio 2. The Cliff Adam Singers have had several albums in the charts and have won a gold record. Cliff himself writes for television commercials and has won many international awards.

■ Highspot of career: 'When I appeared with Duke Ellington and his Orchestra at Conventry Cathedral in 1966 and had the accolade of being invited by Ellington to a repeat performance in Oxford two years later.' ■ Is married with two daughters, one son and two grandsons, and lives in London.

ALYN AINSWORTH
'He put the Northern Variety Orchestra and himself on the map . . .'
BORN: 24th August in Bolton, Lancashire. Father a plumber. **EDUCATED:** Church Institute in Bolton. He studied the guitar from the age of seven. **FIRST JOB:** He left school at 14 to join Herman Darewski's Orchestra as a boy soprano, and appeared at the London Palladium. The outbreak of war and the breaking of his voice coincided, so he was sent home to Bolton, where he became Assistant Park Superintendent, designing flower beds around the Town Hall, the gardens of the Crematorium and a nine-hole golf course! This resulted in him changing direction once again with the desire to become a professional golfer, so he became the assistant pro at the Bolton Golf Club. But he also decided to concentrate on the guitar and started to do some arranging.

At the age of 18, took one of his arrangements to show Oscar Rabin who was playing at Belle Vue in Manchester and the following week got a telephone call from Leicester, the band's next venue, asking him to join as guitarist/arranger. After two years with the Rabin Band, he took a couple of arrangements along to show Geraldo, with the same result, he was offered a job, and found himself writing for Tip Top Tunes along with Bob Farnon, Bob Sharples and Wally Stott. It was during the 1950 summer season at Blackpool that he was approached by Hamilton Kennedy who said, 'What's a Northern boy like you doing down in London, you ought to come back here. We're starting a new orchestra, so why don't you come up here as our arranger?' May 1951 saw the birth of the Northern Variety Orchestra with Vilem Tausky as its first conductor, but within six weeks he had moved on to conduct the Northern Symphony Orchestra, and Alyn was offered the job as conductor of the Northern Variety Orchestra with the brief: 'At the moment it's like any other orchestra, we want you to put it on the map.' And he did. With such series as *Make Way For Music,* with Roger Moffatt and Sheila Buxton, the Northern Variety Orchestra became

one of the best known line-ups in the country. So much so that the original radio series transferred to television and Messrs Ainsworth, Moffat and Buxton found themselves starring on the *Billy Cotton Band Show*. It was around this time that he was offered the London Palladium by Val Parnell, but the answer was 'no'. That was still in the future. After nine years with the NVO, he decided it was time to move on and he joined Granada Television, working on such shows as *Spot The Tune*, on which his vocal talents, unused since his days as a boy soprano, were heard once again forming a trio with Billy Raymond and Marion Ryan.

1961 saw him as MD of his first West End musical, *Bye Bye Birdie* at Her Majesty's. It was to be the first of many. *Gentlemen Prefer Blondes* at the Princes Theatre, *Hello Dolly* with Mary Martin at Drury Lane; *Funny Thing Happened on the Way to the Forum* at the Strand Theatre; *She Loves Me* at the Lyric and *The Admirable Crichton* at the Shaftesbury. He orchestrated *The Roar of the Greasepaint* for Anthony Newley and was MD for Shirley Bassey for an eight-week season at the Pigalle. He also accompanied her to Las Vegas in the mid 60s and was her MD for her appearance at New York's Carnegie Hall. The 60s saw him accepting Val Parnell's offer to take over as MD of *Sunday Night at the London Palladium*. This was followed by International Cabaret from the Talk of the Town and a whole series of shows for BBC Television, such as the 'live' series of *Dee Time*, *The Rolf Harris Show*, *The David Nixon Show* and many more.

In 1976 he conducted the winning song of the Eurovision Song Contest, *Save All Your Kisses For Me*, sung by Brotherhood of Man (qv). He has MD'd 11 Royal Variety Shows to date and has written the theme music for many of television's top shows: *The Stanley Baxter* series, *Play Your Cards Right*, The BAFTA Awards, and *Live From Her Majesty's*, all of which he has been associated with as Musical Director, along with *Bruce's Big Night*, *Canon and Ball* (five series), *Search for a Star* and the Faith Brown series. At the time of going to press he is working on an album of television themes called *Ace of Themes*. His compositions include *Bedtime for Drums*, *If I Were a Buddy Rich Man*, *Italian Sunset*, *Mi Amor*, *Pete's Party*, and many, many more.

He is without doubt, one of the busiest and most popular MDs in the country and has been for more than three decades!

■ Highspot of career: 'There have been so many!' ■ A moment to remember: 'There was this incredible weekend in the mid 60s when I found myself in the studio on Saturday morning, recording a song from *Camelot* with Laurence Harvey; a session with Tony Newley in the afternoon working on the music for *The Roar of The Greasepaint*; I conducted the first house of *She Loves Me* at the Lyric and then dashed across to the Strand Theatre to conduct the evening performance of *A Funny Thing Happened On The Way To The Forum*. The next day there were rehearsals all day for *Sunday Night at the London Palladium*, with the "live" show in the evening. I survived to tell the tale!' ■ Likes cooking and good food. ■ Dislikes 'I don't really have any. I'm pretty level headed and if I don't like anything, I don't bother with it, but I don't like things going wrong that are my fault.' ■ Is single, although in the 50s he was engaged to Teddy Beverley. 'I decided I didn't want to become the fifth Beverley Sister; Billy Wright (who had married Joy Beverely) became the fourth!' Lives in London.

RONNIE ALDRICH
'And The Squadronaires . . . one of the finest bands this country ever produced'.
BORN: 15th February 1916 in Erith, Kent. Father a shop manager. **EDUCATED:** Harvey Grammar School, Folkestone. Guildhall School of Music. Studied piano, also violin, clarinet and saxophone. **FIRST JOB:** Playing violin in the Folkestone Municipal Orchestra and playing saxophone in Phil Cozzi's Jazz Club. During the war joined the RAF and became pianist and arranger for what has been described as the finest swing band ever to be heard outside America – The Squadronaires. After the war he took over the leadership of the band which became known as Ronnie Aldrich and the Squadronaires. Has conducted and played with most of the radio orchestras over the years and has recorded and broadcast with his own orchestra as well as his own Continental Sextet. Now works as a freelance conductor, solo pianist and arranger with the strings of the BBC Radio Orchestra and is heard on just about all of Radio 2's music programmes.

■ Highspot of career: 'For me, every time the red light goes on.' ■ Likes music, sailing, good food and wine. ■ Dislikes pretension. ■ Married to his business manager! Has one child and lives in the Isle of Man.

PETE ALLEN
'The Pete Allen Jazz Band, a family affair . . .'
BORN: 23rd November 1954 in Newbury, Berkshire. Father a musician. **EDUCATED:** Downs School, Compton, Nr. Newbury. He had music lessons at school but is also self taught. Plays the clarinet, alto and baritone saxophones. **FIRST JOB:** Selling musical instruments in a small music shop in Newbury. Then spent nearly three years as a Police Constable in the Thames Valley Force. In 1976 he left the police force to join the Rod Mason Jazz band and made his first broadcast with the band that year. Two years later he decided to take over the semi-pro jazz band that had been formed by his father Bernie Allen in 1971. Bernie remained with the band on banjo and vocals and since then they have appeared on numerous radio and television programmes, as well as working

extensively on the Continent. 'Peter Clayton once said of the band 'The Pete Allen band is totally useless if all you want to do is be miserable.' They were the first ever jazz band to broadcast on Radio 2's *Friday Night is Music Night* and are now heard regularly on that programme as well as such shows as *Music All The Way, Early Show, Weekend Early Show, Night Ride*. Recent television credits include *Jazz Cellar* for TSW and *Showcase* TVS.

In 1983 and '84 they appeared at the world's greatest Dixieland jazz festival, the Sacramento Dixieland Jubilee in California. 1984 also saw them undertaking the first of what is planned as an annual 30 concert tour of the UK with Tommy Burton and Beryl Bryden in *Jazzin Around*. As well as touring the UK, they topped the bill at the Enkhuisen Jazz Festival in Holland. The band also now have their own record label A.R.B. Records.

■ Highspot of career: 'Being invited to the Greatest Dixieland Jazz Festival in the World, the tenth anniversary of the Sacramento Dixieland Jubilee, California, USA in may 1983. Playing with over 90 other bands from around the world in front of an audience around the 200,000 mark. ■ Likes all types of sport, television and radio and Indian cooking. ■ Dislikes cooked cheese and warm beer. ■ Married to Trish and lives in Wiltshire.

KENNETH ALWYN
'Over 30 years of broadcasting . . '
BORN: 28th July 1927, in London. Father a Civil Servant.
EDUCATED: John Ruskin School, Croydon. Royal Academy of Music, London. He plays piano, organ and viola and trombone. **FIRST JOB:** Announcer and Conductor of the Radio Orchestra on Radio Malaya in Singapore. He made his first broadcast on BBC radio in 1952 and since then has conducted all the BBC Orchestras apart from the Symphony Orchestra. He was principal conductor for the Royal Ballet at Covent Garden for seven and a half years, and has also conducted such successful West End Musicals as *Camelot*, *Half a Sixpence* and *My Fair Lady*. Has conducted most of the major symphony orchestras in Britain and makes frequent

trips abroad working in both the concert hall and recording studio. He is probably best known for his frequent appearances on *Friday Night is Music Night* but contributes to many other radio programmes.

■ Highspot of career: 'My first pay cheque'. ■ A moment to remember: 'During a short spell in New Zealand as conductor of the New Zealand Choral Society, someone in New Zealand Broadcasting thought I was an actor! When I presented myself for an audition, he handed me a radio script of Anouilh's play *Point of Departure* (A modern Orpheus). I read 'Death', got the part and a few others as well! I must have been terrible but at least I was terribly "French"!' ■ Likes flying and jogging. ■ Dislikes people who say they're going to do something, and don't.
■ Married to actress Mary Law, has two children and lives in Sussex.

JOHNNY ARTHEY
'A collection of almost 50 Gold Discs. . .'
BORN: 24th September, in London. Father an engineer.
EDUCATED: Royal Liberty School, Essex. Is a self taught pianist.
FIRST JOB: Pianist with a Military Band Concert Orchestra during National Service. His first broadcast was with his own

orchestra on the BBC Light programme in 1962. Has worked for record companies as a musical director/arranger, and has provided the backing for many a hit record both in this country and on the Continent. For BBC he conducted The Soul Train Orchestra 1972–76; The Softly Sentimental Orchestra 1975–78 and since then has been a regular conductor of the BBC Radio Orchestra. He also broadcasts with the Johnny Arthey Orchestra and can be heard on just about every music programme on Radio 2.

■ Highspot of career: 'Conducting at the "Olympia" in Paris'. ■ Likes ufology. ■ Dislikes junk food. ■ Married to Sylvia, has two children and lives in Surrey.

VIC ASH
'Enjoys the late night broadcasts . . .'
BORN: 9th March 1930, in London. EDUCATED: London. Originally a self taught musician but then took private lessons. Plays all the saxes, clarinets and flutes. FIRST JOB: With the Kenny Baker Sextet 1950–53. During the '60s and '70s he toured with his own group on the modern jazz circuit. Made his first broadcast in 1951. He has played with Vic Lewis and Johnny Dankworth among others. Now does freelance session work and records with his own quartet for radio.

■ Highspot of career: 'Playing in the orchestras that have backed Frank Sinatra on all his UK, European and Middle East tours since 1970. 'I particularly enjoy late night broadcasts with my quartet as these are the rare times I can play the standard tunes of the great composers like Gershwin, Porter and Kern.' ■ Likes listening to records, seeing shows and watching TV. ■ Dislikes onions. ■ Married to Helen, has two step-children and lives in London.

KENNY BAKER
'Plays and sings at the same time . . . well almost!'
BORN: 1st March 1921, in Withernsea, East Yorkshire. Father a shoemaker. EDUCATED: Local primary school. Had music lessons from his mother who started him off on piano, then he tried piano accordion, violin and saxophone and hated the lot. 'One day I went around to see my uncle, who played in a brass band, and there was this E double bass stood in the corner. "Ooh, what's that, can I have a blow?" I said. I was only 11 at the time and I could hardly get my arms around it, but I wanted it, so my uncle took me along to band practise

the following week and they gave me a tenor horn to play, which was a bit disappointing as I wanted to play that bass. But I joined the band on tenor and then progressed to cornet and trumpet, which I found much easier to play than the fiddle, sax and accordion.' FIRST JOB: Playing at local gigs. In 1939 he joined the Lew Stone Orchestra, appeared at the Palace Theatre in Under Your Hat with Jack Hulbert and Cicely Courtneidge and on the Road Show with Sandy Powell. Made his first broadcast with Lew Stone in 1940. Has played with Ambrose, Jack Hylton, Geraldo, Syd Milward, Maurice Winnick, Ted Heath, Ken Johnson, George Shearing and Robert Farnon. 1951–58 had his own show on radio, Listen to My Music with Kenny Baker's Dozen. Can be heard with his own quartet on most of Radio 2's music programmes. Also plays with the Best of British Jazz and the Ted Heath band directed by Don Lusher. Has the astonishing ability to sing and play at the same time – well almost!

■ Highspot of career: 'All of it! But especially being demobbed at the end of the war after six years in the RAF and joining the newly formed Ted Heath Orchestra on lead trumpet.' ■ A moment to remember: 'In 1951, BBC producer Pat Dixon suggested I should get together 13 musicians, call them Baker's Dozen and do a "live" broadcast every week to be introduced by Wilfrid Thomas. The idea was to go into the studio, do some "head" arrangements, the red light would go on at 10.30pm and we'd have a programme. "Just point at people to take the next chorus", said Pat, "and then we can do as many choruses as we need." That was all very well in theory, in practice it wasn't quite so easy. The antics that went on were quite unbelievable especially as Pat always insisted we should end with 50 seconds of signature tune come what may. I evolved a sort of sign language in the studio which everyone became accustomed to after a while, but Pat would be in the box holding up cards saying Speed up, Slow down, Take another chorus, Repeat from letter L, Drop the next chorus. The series ran for over seven years and by the end, because the BBC had tightened up on money, Wilfrid Thomas had been dropped and I was doing all the announcing as well as contracting and paying the musicians and doing most of the arrangements. It was a marvellous time musically, but when people ask me if I'm thinking of getting together another Baker's Dozen, the answer is "NO"! ■ Likes gardening and DIY. ■ Dislikes bad cooking. ■ Married to Susan, has one daughter and lives in Hertfordshire.

KENNY BALL
'Played at the Royal Wedding . . .'
BORN: 22nd May 1930 in Ilford, Essex. Father an overseer bookbinder and all-in wrestler who played the piccolo. EDUCATED: Mayfield Central, Seven Kings, Essex. At school played the harmonica and bugle in a bugle band. Learnt the trumpet at 14. FIRST JOB: Office boy for the advertising company, J. Walter Thompson. In 1948 joined the REME for two years. After his demob played with Charlie Galbraith's Jazz Band. Also played with Freddy Randall and Eric Delaney. In 1954 joined Sid Phillips. 'Sid was like a father to me, he not only gave me a job he also paid for trumpet lessons and kept me on the straight and narrow!' Four years later he formed his own line-up, the Kenny Ball Jazzmen, and they've been together ever since.

Their first hit came in 1961 with *Samantha*, followed by three other chart entries that year, including *Midnight in Moscow* which reached No.2 Their next single *March of the Siamese Children* went to No.4 and the hits continued to roll throughout the 60s. While riding high in the hit parade in 1961, they topped the bill at the Cavern Club in Liverpool, supported by a group calling themselves the Beatles!
The band made its American debut in Chicago in 1962 and was back again the following year when Kenny was presented with the key to New Orleans. Since then they have toured the world, appearing in Japan, Hong Kong, the Fiji Islands, Hawaii and Australia. Back in the UK they shared the bill with Louis Armstrong in 1968 on his final European tour, and in the 70s spent five years as resident band on BBC 1's *Saturday Night At The Mill*.

They won the Carl Alan Award three years in succession, 1962–64, for Most Outstanding Traditional Jazz Band, and after celebrating their 25th anniversary in 1983, are still one of the most popular jazz bands in the country.

■ Highspot of career: 'Playing with Louis Armstrong in 1968 and more recently I was ecstatic and honoured to be asked to play at Buckingham Palace for the wedding of Charles and Diana. That for me was a far greater honour than all my Gold Discs and other awards.' ■ A moment to remember: 'Several! Playing the Fire House Club in Los Angeles where the dressing room was upstairs and you had to slide down a pole to the stage; the pianist tried it one handed holding a pint of beer. Playing for a Police Ball when part of the drum kit was stolen. Topping the bill at Greaseborough where the compère asked for two minutes silence at the start of the floor show as a mark of respect to the committee member who had died the previous day. The comedian who followed also died . . . nobody would stop talking!' ■ Likes music, food, golf and working. ■ Dislikes bad manners and inactivity. ■ Has four daughters, one son and lives in Essex.

CHRIS BARBER
'1959 was a great year . . .'
BORN: 17th April 1930, in Welwyn, Hertfordshire. Father a statistician, and amateur violinist. EDUCATED: King Alfred School and St Paul's School, London. Guildhall School of Music. He plays double bass, trombone, trumpet and baritone horn. FIRST JOB: before becoming a musician, he worked as life assurance clerk. He thinks his first paid job as a professional musician was probably with Beryl Bryden. Has also played with George Webb and Ken Colyer, before forming the *Chris Barber Jazz Band*. Made his first broadcast in 1950 on a BBC Jazz Club. Has had several radio series – *Chris Barber's Bandbox* in 1958; *Trade Tavern* in 1961. Was the castaway on *Desert Island Discs* in 1959, the same year he had a hit record with *Petit Fleur*, a hit record that came about almost by accident. Making an LP, they decided to include a clarinet solo as one of the tracks, 'I told Monty Sunshine to go away and think of something to do, and he

came back the next day with Sidney Bechet's *Petit Fleur*, which we included on the album. That album was released in 1957. Two years later I hear that we are No.1 in the German charts. 'With what', I ask, 'we haven't got a single out?' They had released *Petit Fleur* as a single in Germany and in America. We went to the States in January 1959 and as I walked down Broadway every record shop was blasting out *Petit Fleur*. To my horror I discovered they'd put another clarinet solo on the 'B' side, but I managed to get that changed in Britain and had the band playing on the 'B' side when it was released here.' Made his American debut in New Orleans in 1959 and has been back six times, the most recent being in May 1984 when the band were the only European artists to appear at the International Jazz Festival at the Louisiana World Exposition in New Orleans where they shared a concert with the Duke Ellington Orchestra directed by Mercer Ellington. 1984 also saw him playing in Abu Dhabi and Dubai, Poland and the Toronto Jazz Festival, the band's first visit to Toronto in 20 years. The band gives around 240 concerts a year, half of which are in the UK. Is a partner in the company that owns the Marquee Club and recording studios in Soho and that runs the Reading Rock Festival.

■ Highspot of career: 'My first concert in New Orleans in 1959.' ■ A moment to remember: 'When we were in the States in 1959, we had a couple of days off in Chicago and I went to visit Muddy Waters, whom I'd brought over to the UK the previous year. His band was playing a gig in the steel town of Gary, Indiana and he asked me to go along. That night I got up on the stand with him to play a couple of numbers which went down very well with the audience, but as I came off the stage a large, handsome black lady came up to me. "Are you Chris Barber?" "Yes," "Did you make that record *Petit Fleur*?" "Yes," "Ah don't like it." End of conversation!' ■ Likes motor racing, record collecting and snooker. ■ Dislikes instant coffee and margarine presented as the 'real' thing. ■ Lives in London.

ACKER BILK

'Bowler hat and waistcoat still very much in evidence . . .'

BORN: 28th January 1929 in Pensford, Avon. (It was Somerset then!) Father a cabinet maker. **EDUCATED:** Local school in Pensford, where he had piano and recorder lessons. He had heard a visiting preacher (his family were Methodists) playing the recorder when he was four years old and from then on he pestered his mother until she bought him one. Later he taught himself to play the clarinet. **FIRST JOB:** Working in Wills Tobacco factory in Bristol for 24s. a week. Has also worked as a blacksmith and a builder's labourer. As a member of the village boxing team, he never lost a bout but did lose his two front teeth. This and the loss of a finger in a snow sledging accident accounts for his instantly recognizable style of clarinet playing according to Acker! It was in 1948, with the Royal Engineers in the Canal Zone, that he borrowed a clarinet and started copying the sounds he heard on records. A spell in the Glasshouse for sleeping on guard duty, gave him lots of time to practise. When he was demobbed he formed his first band in Bristol, and then joined Ken Colyer's Band in London, but hated London so much that he returned to Bristol and formed the Paramount Jazz Band. **FIRST BROADCAST:** In 1954 for producer Brian Patten in Bristol. Since

then has been heard on just about every music programme on the Light Programme and then Radio 2: His own show *Acker's 'Alf 'Our* has proved to be one of the most popular of the evening music programmes on Radio 2. His own original hit *Stranger on the Shore* which in 1961 was the first ever record to be No.1 simultaneously in the UK and the USA, wrote him a meal ticket for life. It remained in the charts for over a year. Other chart successes include *Summer Set*, No.5, and *Buona Sera*, No.7, in 1960; *That's My Home*, No.7, in 1961; and *Aria* No.5, in 1976 which featured his clarinet with strings. His albums have also provided him with many Gold and Silver Discs, not only in the UK but also in Australia, New Zealand and Canada. He has appeared in two Royal Command Performances, 1978 and 1981. In recent years has toured extensively all over the world. 'Acker', by the way, means 'Mate' or 'Friend' in the Somerset dialect which is a pretty good summing up of Mr Bernard Stanley Bilk!

■ Highspot of career: 'Certainly my most satisfying moment was when Duke Ellington recorded *Stranger on the Shore*.
■ Likes playing darts, fishing and snooker. ■ Dislikes pain!
■ Married to Jean Hawkins, has a son and a daughter, Peter and Jenny, and lives in Herefordshire.

STANLEY BLACK

'I deplore the musical bigotry that exists in some quarters . . .'

BORN: 14th June in London. Father in the boot and shoe industry. **EDUCATED:** Matthay School, London. (Run by Professor Raw Robertson and his wife Ethel Bartlett who were famous piano duettists. Myra Hess and Harriet Cohen also attended the Matthay School.) Started learning piano at the age of seven and at 12 had one of his compositions broadcast by the BBC Symphony Orchestra. **FIRST JOB:** His 16th summer was spent playing piano in a dixieland band at

would suggest that there is the same emotional intellectual depth in a popular movie score as there is in a Brahms symphony, but this doesn't mean that the movie score is valueless and shouldn't be enjoyed on its own level. Why not learn to appreciate and enjoy both?'

■ Highspot of career: 'I'm so deeply involved with anything I'm doing that that moment becomes a highspot'.   ■ A moment to remember: 'When I was on a visit to America I was flying from Washington to Boston and my "carry on" bag was sitting at my feet with the label which had my name on it, uppermost. One of those typical blue-rinsed American ladies came and sat beside me, noticed the name on the label and said: "Well how odd. You're British of course, I can tell by your accent, but do you know we have a famous pianist here in the States called Stanley Black and I have all his records". I simply couldn't bring myself to tell her who I was!'   ■ Married to Edna, has one son, one daughter, three grandchildren and lives in London.

the Dreamland Ballroom, Margate. Played with the bands of Ambrose, Lew Stone, Harry Roy, Maurice Winnick and with his own pick-up group broadcast on such programmes at *Palestine Half Hour* and *Here's Wishing you Well*. Joined the RAF in 1939 and was in charge of entertainment for Group 20 in the Wolverhampton area. On his demob in 1944 was appointed conductor of the BBC Dance Orchestra and over the next nine years notched up some 3,000 broadcasts as well as appearing in his first Royal Variety Show at the Victoria Palace. There have been many since. Has also conducted the orchestra for two Royal Film Performances and in 1984 was commissioned to write a special fanfare for that occasion. He is a regular guest conductor of the BBC Concert Orchestra and broadcasts frequently with his own Quartet featuring himself on piano. In a busy round of concert engagements in 1984, he conducted the Bournemouth Symphony, Royal Philharmonic, National Philharmonic, Halle, Liverpool Philharmonic and English Northern Philharmonia Orchestras.

Has worked extensively in films as composer and Musical Director for all of Mario Zampi's productions. Other credits include *Hell is a City*, *The Long and the Short and the Tall*, *The Young Ones*, *Summer Holiday* for which he was co-winner of the Ivor Novello Award for Best Score, *Wonderful Life*. Stanley Black albums have always sold well in America and he has several Gold Discs to his credit. The 60s saw him conquering the Japanese market with six concert tours of that country when he conducted the Tokyo Symphony and the Osaka Philharmonic Orchestras. This led to him being appointed Honorary Associate Conductor of the Osaka Philharmonic. In 1972 he was the conductor for a 19-concert Promenade Season in New Zealand and he returned for another Promenade Season in 1974.

He is one of those rare musicians who enjoy playing all kinds of music whether it be playing jazz piano, conducting a symphony orchestra or composing the scores of more than 95 films. 'It's all music, music to be studied and digested and made available for others to enjoy, and I deplore the closed minds and musical bigotry which exists in many quarters. Naturally, there are many different levels and only a fool

GERRY BOYCE
'The excitement of the next gig . . .'
BORN: 6th July 1933 in Peterborough. Father an engineer. **EDUCATED:** Kings College, Peterborough. Studied the piano from 10 to 15 and from then on was self taught, which included teaching himself to play the drums. **FIRST JOB:** 1959 at the American Club, Lancaster Gate having spent eight years as a semi-pro in Peterborough. At the local jazz club there, had backed all the well known British stars including Tubby Hayes, Don Rendell, Vic Ash, Joe Harriot etc. Made his first broadcast around 1966 as a Nigel Brooks Singer(!) in *Fanfare*, a 'live' show from the Camden Theatre. Has played drums with Ted Taylor, Bob Miller, Don Lang, Pete Winslow, Ian Cameron and Gordon Langford. Has contributed to most of Radio 2's music programmes over the years not only as a drummer and leader of his own group but also as an arranger.

■ Most exciting moment of career: 'The next gig'. ■ Likes reading, writing, boozing and collecting jazz tapes. ■ Dislikes synthesized theme tunes. ■ Married to singer Lee Gibson (qv), has one daughter Claire and lives in Hertfordshire.

ALAN BRADEN
'The moment you bring that baton down, that's the moment of truth . . .'

BORN: 5th February 1927 in Manchester. Father a professional violinist. **EDUCATED:** 'Various schools of no importance.' Born into a musical family, (his elder brother, Edwin Braden, was MD for such radio programmes as *Round the Horn*), he turned out to be something of a child prodigy, playing the piano and violin at five, the saxophone at nine and treading the boards at 12 as a boy soprano and multi instrumentalist. **FIRST JOB:** Playing alto sax on evening gigs. After two years in the army, he joined the Oscar Rabin Band playing alto and arranging. 'I had always been more interested in writing music, so after 10 years as a sideman, I sold my instrument so I wouldn't be tempted to go on playing. When I got home that night I thought, My God, what have I done.' He didn't remain out of work for long; after a spell as an arranger for Southern Music, he joined David Toff as a staff arranger and wrote for just about everybody, Geraldo, Ted Heath, even Troy and his Mandoliers. 'Those were the days when if a singer or band performed a new song on the air, the publishers would provide them with a free arrangement! It was after doing 230 different versions of *Que Sera Sera*, that I thought to hell with this as a way of earning my living, and left. But I was fortunate in that I had made a lot of contacts and Steve Race who was MD for Associated Rediffusion at the time, asked me to join him as his assistant, and when he went off to front more and more television shows, I took over from him.'

He has written several television themes, including *Wish You Were Here*, and also the incidental music for Eric Sykes' *The Plank* and *It's Your Move*. He also had a hand in the writing of the chart topper *Two Little Boys* in 1969, which an Australian had sung over the telephone to Rolf Harris. 'Nobody knew who had written the music originally, all Rolf had to go on was this Aussie singing down the telephone! So I helped him to put it together.'

Over the years has been associated with many of television's top shows and is probably best remembered for his eight years spent with Thames Television and the *Sooty/Braden*

Show Band, which only ended when Harry Corbett suffered a heart attack. Other programmes include the Mike Yarwood and Jim Davidson shows, *Stars and Garters* and *Name That Tune*.

■ Highspot of career: 'My next show! But it's a highspot every time you bring down the baton when you're hearing your arrangement for the first time. When you're writing at home, it's all in your head, no one knows what it's going to sound like. The moment you bring that baton down, that's the moment of truth.' ■ A moment to remember: 'I shall never forget when I was asked to organize an all-girl rock band and an all-girl swing band for an all-girl television spectacular starring Kathy Kirby, which took place in front of an all-male audience consisting mainly of policemen. We rehearsed for two weeks in a grotty rehearsal room with a girl drummer who couldn't keep time and I thought I was going to have to wear a frock. But they fixed it so I could conduct so the bands could see me, but the cameras couldn't. It was a nightmare and the show, which was meant to run for one hour, finished up as 40 minutes, because that was all they could salvage out of it. To cap it all my car was pinched that night.'
[Author's footnote: 'I was playing trombone in the band!']

■ Likes good Chinese food and making furniture. 'Now I don't play anymore, I like to work with my hands. As well as making furniture, I'm a good handyman.' ■ Dislikes synthesized music. 'In a few years time I can see the MD becoming redundant.' ■ Married to Margaret, has two sons and one grandson and lives in Middlesex.

BRIAN BROCKLEHURST
'Have bike, will travel . . .'

BORN: 16th August in Buxton Derbyshire. Father a musician. **EDUCATED:** 'Yes!' Born into a musical family, he learnt to play piano, guitar and drums. Now plays double bass. **FIRST JOB:** Playing guitar and piano in a dance band at the Pavilion Gardens, Buxton at the age of 12. Joined the Merchant Navy as a Radio Officer. Made his first broadcast playing guitar with his own group around 1947. Has played with Ken Mackintosh, Jack Parnell, Humphrey Lyttleton and Ted Heath. As a session musician has backed Marlene Dietrich on her last tour of the UK, Shirley Bassey, Tommy Steele, Petula Clark, Simon and Garfunkel. Has played with many of the jazz greats including Jack Teagarden, Willie 'the Lion' Smith, Pee Wee Russell, Kai Winding and Buck Clayton. Has appeared on literally hundreds of radio shows over the years such as *Country Meets Folk* (seven years), *Round the Horne* (all of them), *I'm Sorry I'll Read That Again*, *Jazz Club*. Fronts his own line-up, Brian Brocklehurst and Brocade, which is heard regularly on both BBC and Capital Radio. Has made something of a name for himself by cycling around London with his double bass slung on his back! Runs his own music company. Brock Music.

■ Highspot of career: 'Working with Mel Torme, Lena Horne, Josh White, José Feliciano, Marlene Dietrich and the Jazz Greats was extremely stimulating to say the least!' ■ A moment to remember: 'Programme . . . *Pebble Mill at One*, "live". My brief: to cycle down Pebble Mill Road with my bass and into the studio, dismount, unzip (the bass cover) and join

orchestra, playing second alto to his sister and doubling on violin for solos. His father had taught him to play the saxophone which he also played with Pop Brownlee's Circus. He came to Britain in 1942 and studied clarinet at the Royal College of Music, achieving his ARCM. He broadcast regularly in Canada, but first broadcast for the BBC was with the Royal Canadian Airforce Band in 1942. After the war he played with Ambrose, Ted Heath, Geraldo and George Melachrino as well as performing with the London Symphony Orchestra, the Royal Philharmonic Orchestra and Sinfonia of London. Plays with Benny Goodman on his continental Big Band tours and also does chamber music tours with John White and Gavin Bryars. He played on all the *Goon Shows* and many other light entertainment shows on radio including *Hancock's Half Hour*. Has also made many chamber music broadcasts.Has been leading his own quartet since 1951 appearing in jazz clubs around the country and making frequent broadcasts on Radio 2's music programmes.

■ Highspot of career: 'Walking onto the platform of the Royal Festival Hall and performing a concerto which had been written for me by Robert Farnon (qv) accompanied by 85 members of the Royal Philharmonic Orchestra.'   ■ A moment to remember: 'When a producer advanced to a band leader who had just played a solo on the rehearsal, "You are flat" which drew the reply . . ."OK, I'll stand back a little!"'
■ Likes his quartet.   ■ Dislikes snobs, bigots, hypocrites and anyone who doesn't like his quartet!   ■ Has one son and two daughters and lives in London.

the group already playing, then launch into the following dialogue . . ., Leader to me "Where have you been, we're 'live' you know". "Ah", I replied, "it was very foggy on the M1 this morning and then I got lost on the one-way system here in Birmingham, Bi-sically speaking, that's my explanation." And then we all finished the number together. Later that week, in a hostelry near Maida Vale Studios in London, a chap who had seen the show said to me "I've seen you charging around town on your bike with your bass, but I never realized you pedalled up to Birmingham with it." "Ah, yes." I replied; "but I always check with Michael Fish at the wet [Met.] office to see if there's a following wind before I go!" Which explanation seemed to satisfy him!'   ■ Likes photography, planes n' playing n' phood!   ■ Dislikes – 'don't like to mention them.'   ■ Married to music! and lives in London.

BOB BURNS
'I'm really serious about my quartet . . .'
BORN: 16th May 1923 in Toronto, Canada. Father a jeweller/musician. **EDUCATED:** P.C.I. Ontario. Royal Academy of Music and Royal College of Music. **FIRST JOB:** In his father's

LENNIE BUSH
'A never to be forgotten concert with Louis Armstrong . . .'
BORN: 6th June 1927 in London. Father a chef. **EDUCATED:** Hornchurch Junior School. He won a scholarship to Royal Liberty School, Romford, Essex. Studied the violin from the age of 7. 'I got rid of it as fast as possible but it took me 10 years!' At 16 he bought himself a double bass for £3 10s. and

was singing a medley of spirituals which had been arranged for him by Leonard Bernstein and which he'd already tried out in New York. We had two days of rehearsals, not with the orchestra but with the conductor, who shall be nameless, playing the orchestral parts on the piano. Louis insisted on calling him "Fats", which didn't go down too well. When it came to the concert itself, we launched into this spiritual medley and suddenly everything started to go wrong. The conductor was waving his hands about, but obviously the small group and the orchestra were in different places in the score with Louis singing "Nobody knows the trouble I'm in . . ." He got to that line the second time around – "Nobody knows the trouble I'm in . . . Jesus!" he sang! It was absolute chaos. We managed to stagger to the end of that medley, God knows how and the orchestra were then meant to play the final piece, *Hungarian Rhapsody*. But the audience wouldn't let Louis off the stage, so the conductor dismissed the orchestra and stalked off himself and that was the end of a never to be forgotten concert!' ■ Likes motor racing. 'I once took a course at Brands Hatch and did all right with 92 out of 100 which meant I did eight things wrong!' ■ Dislikes certain kinds of people . . 'but I'm pretty easy going really.' ■ Married to Anne, has one son Andrew who plays trumpet, and lives in Hertfordshire.

taught himself to play it. **FIRST JOB:** Working in a solicitors' office, which he hated, so he left and got himself a job as a projectionist at a cinema in Romford. At 17 became bass player for a variety act, Rolling Stones and Dawn. (Dawn being a ballet dancer). The act folded and he started to frequent Archer Street, meeting up with Ronnie Scott (qv), Tony Crombie and other musicians who gathered in the Fullado Club in New Compton Street at 3pm opening time, for jam sessions. 'That was my introduction to the jazz scene.' Joined Nat Gonella when he was 21 at the time when Phil Seaman was on drums. In the early 50s he played with Roy Fox on tour and 1953 found him with Ronnie Scott's nine-piece band which involved more touring. When Jack Parnell went to ATV in 1958, he stayed more or less put for the next 10 years playing on Jack's television sessions. He also did most of Robert Farnon's recording sessions, working with Frank Sinatra, Quincy Jones, Singers Unlimited and Henry Mancini among others. Has played with many of the American Jazz Greats while at Ronnie Scott's, including Ben Webster and Clark Terry, and was with Bing Crosby at the London Palladium in 1976. He did three European tours with Benny Goodman which included making the *Benny Goodman Today* album in Stockholm in 1978 and the following year was once again with Goodman and his American band on another tour of Europe. In 1983 was at the National Theatre for their production of *Guys and Dolls*. He always appears with the Ted Heath Band fronted by Don Lusher although he never worked with the band when Ted Heath was alive. For many years he came second in the Melody Maker Poll: 'Johnny Hawksworth always used to beat me into second place.

■ Highspot of career: 'The best band I've ever played in was Ronnie Scott's nine-piece and I enjoyed the tours with Benny Goodman; at least they get you out of the country!' ■ A moment to remember: 'The Hungarian Relief Concert at the Royal Festival Hall in 1958, brought together Louis Armstrong with a small group including myself, George Chisholm (qv) and Sid Phillips, and the London Symphony Orchestra. Louis

COLIN CAMPBELL
'A musical family . . .'

BORN: 3rd May 1940 in Birmingham. Father a foreman metalworker. **EDUCATED:** Moseley School of Art, Birmingham. He studied the piano privately from the age of 8 to 16 and studied the clarinet from 12 to 16 at the Birmingham School of Music. Plays the piano, synthesizer, organ, sax and clarinet. **FIRST JOB:** As part of a multi-instrumental group known as the Merry Macs, playing throughout the Midlands 1952–56. After leaving school he formed a double act with a girl called Christine (she later became his wife) and they toured in variety shows as Christine and Colin Campbell. Made his first broadcast on the Welsh Home Service in *Seaside Nights* in

1958. Spent four years as pianist/arranger for television's *New Faces*. Has made numerous broadcasts as the conductor of the Midland Radio Orchestra. Radio series include *Keep it Maclean* with his own group, The Colin Campbell Clan. Broadcasts with his own orchestra and was the Musical Director of the BBC's 1982 pantomime, *Dick Whittington*. As a freelance MD/arranger/pianist, backs many stars on the air in a wide variety of programmes.

■ Highspot of career: 'When I was MD for Vera Lynn at the Bluejays Baseball Ground in Toronto in 1980 and 18,000 people stood up at the end of her act and sang *Land of Hope and Glory!* ■ The Campbell family are all musical – wife Christine had a record in the charts in 1962 and son Kevin is a drummer. ■ Likes skiing, sea fishing and golf. ■ Dislikes punk music. ■ Married to Christine, has one son, Kevin.

GEORGE CHISHOLM
'Probably the best jazz trombonist this country has ever produced . . .'
BORN: 29th March 1915 Glasgow. Father an engineer.
EDUCATED: ? Glasgow! Plays trombone, euphonium, baritone, piano, vibes and xylophone etc; 'I'm mostly self taught, with some lessons from the local LRAM on piano, and trombone lessons from Jimmy Chalmers who was the solo trombonist with the SCWS Band in Glasgow.' **FIRST JOB:** 'Playing the piano in a Glasgow cinema at the age of 14, for silent films . . . fitting the appropriate music to the action on the screen.' He played in Greens Playhouse ballroom in Glasgow, West End Cafe, Edinburgh and the Tower Ballroom in Glasgow, from where he made his first broadcast, he thinks in 1932. Moved to London in 1936 getting a job playing in the Nest Club, (which he describes as naughty, West End). It was at that famous late night rendezvous in Kingly Street that visiting American jazzmen would congregate for jazz sessions lasting through the night. The resident Brits would step down off the stand in favour of such jazz greats as Benny Carter and Coleman Hawkins, but one night the young trombonist from Glasgow was asked to stay, a solitary white face among the black ones. Benny Carter was so impressed, that ĩe invited George to join him for some recording dates in Holland. Played with the bands of Lew Stone, Harry Roy, Jack Harris and in 1937 he joined Ambrose and remained with him until the outbreak of war in 1939. From 1939–50 was a member of the famous Squadronaires Dance Band in the RAF along with several other ex-Ambrose sidemen. It was in 1939, during a visit to the UK by Fats Waller, that George joined him for a recording session at Abbey Road studios. 'That was

FRANK CHACKSFIELD
'The most promising new orchestra of 1953 . . .'
BORN: 9th May 1914 in Battle, Sussex. Father an engineer.
EDUCATED: Battle and Langton Schools, Sussex. Studied organ under the late J.R. Sheehan-Dare. Plays both piano and organ. **FIRST JOB:** Gigs with various bands in Sussex and Kent. Has had a resident band at Hilden Manor Road House, Tonbridge, Kent and L'Etacq Hotel, Jersey. His first broadcast was *Original songs at the Piano* from Glasgow. He conducted both Henry Hall's Orchestra and the Geraldo Orchestra. When he formed his own line up in 1953 it won an award as the most promising new orchestra and that same year had two Top 10 entries with *Little Red Monkey* and *Limelight*. The following year *Ebb Tide* gave him another top 10 entry. He was awarded two Gold Discs for his recording of *Limelight* and a Gold Disc and Baton d'Honneur for *Ebb Tide*. Has recorded over 100 LPs and numerous singles. Has also conducted the music for several films and his orchestra can be heard regularly on radio.

■ Highspot of career: 'My first trip to America with *Limelight* and *Ebb Tide* in the Top 10.' ■ Likes music. ■ Dislikes curry and Chinese food. ■ Married to Jeanne Lehmann and lives in Kent.

tremendous fun because Fats always kept a bottle of John Haig handy on the piano and during one of the tracks you can hear him shouting? 'Go fetch me some John Haig, Man'. Great advert!'

Played with the BBC Showband 1950–55 and in 1958 appeared with Louis Armstrong in the Hungarian Relief Concert at the Royal Festival Hall. 'I'd never met him before and he'd flown himself over free of charge to appear that night with my small group and the London Symphony Orchestra. That was quite a night.' (qv Lennie Bush). Has made valuable contributions to many radio series, including *Band Wagon, It's That Man Again* (ITMA), *Much Binding in the Marsh, The Goon Show* and in the 1960's became a well known face on television with his comedy routines on *The Black and White Minstrel Show*. Unfortunately for jazz lovers, his great talent for comedy has somewhat overshadowed his even greater musical talent, because he is probably the best jazz trombonist this country has ever produced. Is heard regularly with his Gentlemen of Jazz on radio and makes frequent guest appearances as a soloist on television.

In recent years has toured with Keith Smith and Hefty Jazz and is often the featured soloist with some of the country's top brass bands, such as Yorkshire Imperial, Grimethorpe and Royal Doulton with whom he made an album. 1984 saw him appearing at the Edinburgh Festival with such stars as Doc Cheatham, Buddy Tate, Warren Vache and Jim Galloway after which he returned to America for his second Gibson Party in Denver, Colorado. 'Dick Gibson is an American who dotes on music, musicians and particularly trombone players. He organises these annual seminars which brings together musicians from different countries. I did my first one in 1980 and one does get a chance to wave the British flag, being the only one from Britain there.' Awarded the OBE in 1984.

■ Highspot of career: 'Playing and recording with Benny Carter and Coleman Hawkins in Holland; recording with Fats Waller; and playing with Louis Armstrong at the Royal Festival Hall in 1958. ■ A moment to remember: 'Doing a broadcast with the Squads from Aberdeen on New Year's Eve 1947 . . . much whisky flowing. We were "issued" with an OB announcer and balance engineer, both of whom passed out before the transmission. We took over the announcements as it was a "live" broadcast and afterwards went round to the side room to ask the balancer how it had gone, only to find him slumped over the controls fast asleep. We were told later that it was the best broadcast we'd ever done and that the balance was excellent! (He'd obviously switched the controls to "George"!)' ■ Likes arranging, orchestrating and has a vague leaning towards DIY. ■ Dislikes intolerance and impatience. ■ Married to Etta, has one son, one daughter, one son by a previous marriage, five grandchildren and lives in Bedfordshire.

ALAN CLARE
'Played in clubs around the world . . .'
BORN: Walthamstow, London. Father a clerk. **EDUCATED:** Roger Asham School and Eliot Wittingham School, Walthamstow. Plays piano, piano accordion and organ. Had piano lessons but is mostly self taught. **FIRST JOB:** Playing piano in the Orford Social Club at the age of 11. Has played in many clubs around the world including the Coconut Grove in Palm Beach, California, and the Cotton Club. While in the army

appeared in *Stars in Battledress*. Has also worked for Leeds Music Publishers. Made his first broadcast in *Piano Playtime* and has been heard on *Variety Bandbox, Ignorance is Bliss* and *Kings of the Keyboard*. Has played with Cab Calloway, Sid Millward and the Nitwits, Stephane Grappelli, Maurice Winnick, Jack Payne, Ted Heath, Harry Parry and Sid Phillips. Now has his own group The Alan Clare Trio.

■ Highspot of career: 'Getting to know Billy Strayhorn and hearing my own compositions sung and played on the radio by such stars as Eartha Kitt, Cleo Laine, John Williams and Peter Sellers.' ■ A moment to remember: 'Five minutes to go before a "live" broadcast when the pedal fell off the piano. The producer and the balancer pushed a piano from an adjoining studio and got it to me with 20 seconds to go!' ■ Likes music, fishing and reading. ■ Dislikes snobs, bigots, drunks, parsnips and getting old. ■ Married to Bloom, has a daughter and a son and lives in London.

TONY COE
'Featured soloist on the Pink Panther theme . . .'
BORN: 29th November 1934. Father a professional musician (Sax and clarinet). **EDUCATED:** Simon Langton Boys School, Canterbury, Kent. 'I was very much influenced by my father who was always playing records of Duke Ellington, Artie Shaw and Benny Goodman.' His father started him off on clarinet and he took lessons from the age of 13. Took up the alto at 16, but didn't switch to the tenor until his mid 20s. Studied composition under Alfred Nieman, Nicholas Maw and Richard Rodney Bennett. **FIRST JOB:** Cub reporter with the

Kentish Gazette. 'I only lasted two months!' He became a professional musician and joined the Army for three years, playing with the band of The East Kent Regiment under Bandmaster Trevor Sharpe. At 22 joined Humphrey Lyttelton (qv) on alto and toured the USA. After four years formed the Tony Coe Quintet, described at the time as the best mainstream jazz group in Britain.

The 60s was an exciting time for him with an offer to join Count Basie in 1965 and a couple of years later an invitation to join the Kenny Clarke–Francy Boland Band which he accepted, touring Europe and working alongside such great names as Stan Getz, Johnny Griffin, Herb Geller and Art Farmer. At the end of the 60s he teamed up with trumpeter Kenny Wheeler to form a quintet, Coe, Wheeler and Co. Other small groups followed; Martrix with clarinettist Alan Hacker; Axel which made its debut at the 1977 Camden Music Festival where, it was selected by the Arts Council for an extensive concert tour.

1982 saw him playing with the Thad Jones Big Band at the San Remo Festival, touring France and Switzerland with the English Symphony Orchestra and recording with Paul McCartney (qv). His ability to move across the various musical boundaries make him a much sought after musician. He has played on many film scores including *The Devils* and *The Boyfriend* and is the featured soloist in Henry Mancini's music for the *Pink Panther* films in which he plays the main theme.

His recordings over the years have been numerous, many of them with the Clarke–Boland Band. An album of jazz standards, *Coexistence* was released in 1979; *Tournee du Chat* on the Paris NATO label in 1983; *Nutty (on) Willisau*, recorded 'live' at the Willisau Jazz Festival in 1984. He was also featured on clarinet on Paul McCartney's *Take it Away* and on tenor on Brian Prothero's *Pinball*. Other scheduled 1984 releases are an album recorded in New York with Bob Moses and a single in France featuring the Melody Four on which he also handles the vocal.

As well as writing for his own groups, his compositions have been played by the Danish Radio Big Band, the Metropole Orchestra and Skymasters Band of Holland. In 1976 he was commissioned by the Arts Council to write an extended orchestral composition, *Zeitgeist* and in 1982 composed a 40-minute work for full orchestra and four soloists for the Chelsea and Kensington Festival. 'This involved working on trains and staying up all night in hotels and I just made it in time for the performance!'

Apart from his playing he also teaches at various courses throughout Britain and France and is a part-time professor at the Guildhall School of Music in London. His days as a cub reporter on the *Kentish Gazette* have stood him in good stead because he contributes regularly to the Paris publication *Jazz Ensuite* and is the author of the article on jazz in *Culture, Idealogy and Politics* published by Routledge & Kegan Paul.

He claims some responsibility for the formation in 1966 of the rock group *Soft Machine*, the members of which went to his old school, saw his name on one of the honours boards and were inspired by it to start a band!

■ Highspot of career: 'It has to be playing with the Clark–Boland Band for sheer excitement, although I get a great kick out of hearing my compositions being played for the first time, that's exciting too.' ■ A moment to

remember: 'When I was playing with Thad Jones in May 1982, the lead trumpet was an Argentine and this was just as things were brewing up in the Falklands. One day he said to me: 'Hey, what I doing playing with you? I should be killing you!' His name was Amerigo Bellatti.' ■ Likes good food and drink. ■ Dislikes aggressive macho-type males and mindless bureauocracy.

■ Married to Sue Stedman Jones, has two sons, Simon and Gideon, from a previous marriage and lives in London.

GRAHAM COLLIER
'Composer first, band leader second . . .'
BORN: 21st February 1937 in Tynemouth. Father a 'silent picture' drummer, who with the advent of the 'talkies' worked for Vauxhall Motor Company. **EDUCATED:** Luton Grammar School. Learnt the trumpet at 11 and played with local bands and the school orchestra. **FIRST JOB:** Band boy in the Army (The Green Howards) at $16\frac{1}{2}$. During his seven years in the Army took up string bass and dropped the trumpet. Also started to arrange and compose. Spent three years of his service in Hong Kong where he entered a composition competition in the American magazine *Downbeat* which had, as prizes, tuition at the Berklee School of Music in Boston. Won a small prize which paid some of the tuition costs. Spent two and a half years in Boston paying for his tuition by playing bass in local bands. Played with the Jimmy Dorsey Band before graduating at the Berklee School of Music in September 1963. Returned to the UK and formed the Graham Collier Septet early in 1964. The septet became a sextet and then Graham Collier Music.

In 1967 was the first jazz composer to be awarded a Bursary by the Arts Council, resulting in his compostion for 12-piece band, *Workpoints*. As well as writing for his own band was doing an increasing amount of work for radio bands and orchestras on the Continent, both writing and conducting. The mid 70s saw him making a conscious decision to be a composer first and band leader second. His composition *Day Of The Dead*, using the words of Malcolm Lowry's *Under The*

Volcano, for the Ilkley Literature Festival in 1977 led to a BBC commission to write the music for the Hi Fi Theatre production of that work.

He was back in front of the band for a tour of India in 1979 and following a cartilage operation, decided to give up the bass. Now plays keyboards or stands out front. In 1983 was commissioned by the Bracknell Festival to write a piece for the band of his choice which included American trumpeter Ted Curson, Kenny Wheeler and John Surman. As well as being performed at the festival, *Hoarded Dreams* was broadcast on Radio 3 and was the subject of a Channel 4 documentary. Although 1984 saw Graham Collier Music touring Greece, its leader, who has written the music for several documentaries and commericals, would like to get involved in writing more music for the theatre. He has written two musical to date: *A Kind of Game* which had its première at Manchester's Library Theatre and is currently awaiting a German production and *Silver Queen Saloon* a musical western on which he collaborated with playwright Paul Foster and which was performed in Antwerp and at London's Riverside Studios.

Publications include *Inside Jazz* (A guide for the layman), *Jazz* (a students and teachers guide) which has been translated into Norwegian and German, *Compositional Devices, Cleo and John.*

■ Highspot of career: 'Getting a standing ovation at the end of my 72-minute *Hoarded Dreams* at the Bracknell Festival in 1983.' ■ A moment to remember: 'In the days when I was still playing, one night I was struggling back from a gig which had been badly attended, badly paid and the band had played pretty badly as well. I was in a foul mood and as I came out of the underground station with my bass on my back, a young man passing by with his friends came up to me and said, "Mr Collier, I just want to thank you for some lovely moments in music", and away he walked. That made me feel a lot better!' ■ Likes good wine and good food. ■ Dislikes pomposity and attempts to merge jazz and classical music by people who don't understand jazz. ■ Is a bachelor and lives in London.

JOHN CRITCHENSON
'West country farmer to West End jazzman . . .'
BORN: 24th December 1934 in East End of London. Father worked for the Admiralty. The family moved to Bath, Somerset in 1939. **EDUCATED:** City of Bath Boys School. At the age of three, he was taught the rudiments of piano playing by his grandfather, but from then on was entirely self taught and has always played by ear. 'It was seeing the film *Rhapsody in Blue,* that inspired me to take the piano seriously.' **FIRST JOB:** Farmer. 'I stuck it for three months and it nearly drove me potty.' He then served a five-year electrical apprenticeship with Westinghouse. It was during this period that he met another Westinghouse employee, Jack Pennington, and discovered that he liked to play jazz. Together they formed a jazz club at the Chippenham Community Centre and one of the first artists booked, was Bill Le Sage. The club then moved to a room over a pub, the Spirit Vaults, where it became known as Jazz At The Ice Box. 'We ran a really good jazz club and I played with just about everyone who was anyone during those five years.'

At the end of his electrical apprenticeship he decided to turn professional and joined Ted Carter's Band at the Regency in

Bath. After three months it folded and in 1957 he moved to London, playing three nights a week with Rex Rutley at the Ritz Ballroom, Kingsbury. To keep body and soul together he took a daytime job with Boosey and Hawkes servicing Hammond organs. 'After six months I got totally fed up with the whole scene and went back to Bath, got married and became a semi-pro agan.' A whole series of jobs followed, including a three-year spell with the Gas Board where he progressed to middle management. He then moved further west, to Bridport and Torquay and for eight years tuned car engines. In 1977 he was offered a summer season playing at the Imperial Hotel Night Club in Torquay. He stayed for 18 months and, at the end of the second summer, was persuaded by Bill Le Sage to try his luck in London once again. His big break came in May 1979 when he was asked to join Ronnie Scott's Band; he's been with them ever since. In 1980 he joined up with Dick Morrissey and Jim Mullen (qv) for a three-year spell and also plays with Martin Drew and Ron Mathewson in a line-up they call CDM. Their first album, *Summer Afternoon* was released in 1982, their second, *New Night,* in 1984. 1984 also saw him touring India and Cuba with Ronnie Scott.

■ Highspot of career: 'Getting the telephone call asking me to play with Ronnie Scott's band in May 1979'. ■ A moment to remember: 'Ronnie Scott is not only a very witty man he is also very good at Gurning. (For the uninitiated, making your nose touch your chin). I shall never forget the first time I saw him gurn. We were playing a gig in Grantham in this lovely old house. The library was serving as a dressing room and there was a cap lying on one of the chairs. Ronnie put it on, made this gurn face and with his nose touching his mouthpiece played the most diabolical version you've ever heard of *All the Things You Are.* It was so funny, I collapsed and thought I was going to have a heart attack!' ■ Likes nice ladies, the countryside, the sea and fishing off the beach at Eypesmouth in Dorset. ■ Dislikes taking off in aeroplanes, traffic and posers. ■ Is divorced and lives in London.

Michigan Chamber Orchestra in Detroit and in May 1982 was awarded an honorary Doctorate of Music by the Berklee College of Music in Boston Massachussets.

As well as coping with a heavy international concert schedule, he still manages to find time to run the Wavenden Allmusic Plan which he and Cleo initiated in the converted stable block of their home at Wavenden, Buckinghamshire in Easter 1970. Courses are held for young people, from all over the world, which aim at breaking down the barriers between classical, jazz and pop music. It was here that the hit musical *Side by Side by Sondheim* was given its first performance before going on to become a smash hit on both sides of the Atlantic.

■ Highspot of career: Playing with Benny Goodman and playing opposite Duke Ellington at the 1959 Newport Jazz Festival. ■ A moment to remember: See Cleo Laine's entry! ■ Likes cricket, watching snooker and long-drawn-out shaggy dog stories. ■ Dislikes blue jeans and following fashion in anything. ■ Married to Cleo Laine, has one son, Alec, one daughter, Jackie, and lives in Buckinghamshire.

JOHN DANKWORTH
'Increasing acclaim over the years . . .'
BORN: 20th September 1927 on the outskirts of London.
EDUCATED: St George Monarch's, Woodford Green. Royal Academy of Music, London. Studied clarinet at the RAM and while there started to play alto saxophone. On leaving the RAM played with Tito Burns, Ambrose and Lew Stone among others and also made guest appearances with Ted Heath. In 1949 was named Musician of the Year in the *Melody Maker* Jazz Poll and the following year formed the Johnny Dankworth Seven. In 1953 the Seven became an integral part of a 20-piece band which was not long in proving that big band jazz could still have popular appeal. John's own compositions, *Experiments with Mice* in 1956 and *African Waltz* in 1960, both reached the Top 10 in the charts. Even though he established himself very early on in his career as one of the UK's leading altoists, his compositions have brought him increasing acclaim over the years. They include *Improvisations* for Jazz Band and Symphony Orchestra; the ballet *Lystrata* for the 1962 Bath Festival; *The Diamond and the Goose* for soloists, choir and symphony orchestra with libretto by Benny Green; a string quartet, a piano concerto as well as the incidental music for many plays, television series and commercials. He has written two musicals, the first in 1968, *Boots with Strawberry Jam* in collaboration with Benny Green, and *Colette*, which he wrote in 1979 for his wife Cleo Laine (qv). His film scores include *Saturday Night and Sunday Morning, The Servant, Darling, Accident, Morgan* and *Modesty Blaise.*

November 1982 saw the release of an album made in collaboration with the cellist Julian Lloyd Webber, *Fair Oak Fusions*, commissioned by Fair Oak for its open air theatre in Sussex. Another album featuring the John Dankworth Quintet was released earlier that same year. In recent years he has involved himself with his wife's climb to international stardom and Cleo Laine and the John Dankworth Quintet have become one of the leading attractions throughout the world of jazz. During their tour of North America in the autumn of 1981, John appeared as guest soloist with the

RAY DAVIES
'Has written the ident music for several ILR stations . . .'
BORN: 7th October 1927 in Wales. **EDUCATED:** Swansea. Royal College of Music, London, where he studied the trumpet.
FIRST JOB: The Teddy Foster Band in Birmingham. Has also played with Oscar Rabin, Geraldo, Melachrino, Henry Mancini, Quincy Jones, Ambrose, Carol Gibbons, Burt Bacharach, Billy Cotton and Frank Chacksfield. As an arranger/composer/conductor has worked with many star names including Frank Sinatra, Ella Fitzgerald, Bing Crosby, Judy Garland and Bob Hope. Has MD'd at many music festivals all over the world. Made his first broadcast with Teddy Foster in 1943 in *Saturday Night at the Palais*. Conducts and arranges for the various BBC Orchestras and also broadcasts with his own line-ups, The Button Down Brass

and The Ray Davies Orchestra. Has composed the ident music for several ILR stations; Radio City, Beacon Radio, Radio Orwell, Swansea Sound, Pennine Radio and Metro Radio.

■ Highspot of career: 'Just being part of the musical profession means every day something exciting happens!'
■ Likes skiing, golf, swimming, music and travel. ■ Married to Diane, has three children.

JIM DAVIS
'Lead violin and now conductor . . .'
BORN: 16th September 1920 in Birmingham. Father an engineer. EDUCATED: Sladefield Road School, Birmingham School of Music. 1934–38. Plays the violin also the oboe, flute clarinet and percussion. FIRST JOB: Violinist with the City of Birmingham Symphony Orchestra after six and a half years in the Army 1940–46. He then joined the BBC Northern Orchestra for a year and from there went to the Royal Opera House at Covent Garden. He returned to the BBC in 1969 as Leader of the BBC Midland Light Orchestra/Midland Radio Orchestra. Has also played with Herman Darewski, The Army Radio Orchestra, Geoff Love, Joe Loss, The Liverpool Philharmonic Orchestra, The London Symphony Orchestra, Ad Socem String Quartet, Palm Court Trio, London Festival Ballet and spent two years with the Band of the Royal Regiment. Made his first broadcast on a Carrol Levis programme in October 1937, and in over 45 years of broadcasting has been heard on radio in a wide range of music from chamber and symphonic to light and popular. Is lead violin for Stanley Black, Frank Chacksfield, John Fox, John Gregory Orchestras. Is also the leader of the Vivaldi Chamber Ensemble and the Hepplewhite String Quartet and he conducts his own orchestra.

■ Highspot of career: 'Turning up for a rehearsal of the Mid-Day Prom at Manchester Town Hall to find the leader of the BBC Northern Orchestra taken ill and having to take on *Scheherazade* for a "live" public broadcast.' ■ A moment to remember: 'The late Gordon Franks, composer, conductor and brilliant jazz pianist was instrumental in my performing one of Stephane Grappelli's own compositions. Imagine the shock when the great man himself walked into the studio during the recording session. I also remember the time during

the late 50s when immediately after the musicians strike, I organized the BBC Orchestra's committee and as secretary eventually succeeded in getting management, Musicians Union and players' representatives around one table, which resulted in over 20 years free from industrial trouble!'
■ Likes fly fishing, philately and gardening. ■ Dislikes carrots. ■ Married to Sylvia Knussen, has two step children and three grandchildren and lives in Herefordshire.

BRIAN DEE
'Broadcasting is the most enjoyable of all session work . . .'
BORN: 21st March 1936 in London. Father a professional musician (arranger and saxophonist). EDUCATED: Minchenden Grammar School, Southgate. At the age of 10 went to a local piano teacher but in five years, only reached Grade 4! It was while doing National Service in the RAF that he began to take his piano playing seriously. Plays piano and organ. FIRST JOB: Playing at a jazz club in Southall. Joined the Lennie Best Quartet and turned professional in 1960. Has played with Eric Winstone, Frank Weir, Ken Mackintosh, Vic Ash, Harry Klein and Barry Forgie's Thames Eight. His first broadcast was backing singer Danny Street ('I can't remember the year') Now broadcasts regularly with his own trio, The Brian Dee Trio.

■ Highspot of career: 'No one moment – just being lucky enough to enjoy 95 per cent of what I do and being healthy. Broadcasting is the most enjoyable of all session work because it is the nearest thing to a spontaneous "live" performance.' ■ Likes watching speedway and owning an old London bus. ■ Dislikes getting up early. Has two children and lives in Surrey.

ROBERT DOCKER
. . . at the piano'
BORN: 5th June 1918 in London. Father a gas worker. EDUCATED: North Paddington Central School. Had private musical tuition and then studied piano, viola and composition at the Royal Academy of Music in London. Also plays the organ, harpsichord and the violin. FIRST JOB:

'Accompanying a working men's club concert for 12s. 6d. at the age of 14. Very good experience!' Had his first arrangement broadcast in 1936 and made his debut on the air as a pianist some 10 years later. Formed a well known two-piano partnership with Edward Rubach which lasted for 15 years. Has been heard on numerous radio programmes both as a soloist and an accompanist over the years. Appears regularly on *Friday Night is Music Night, Melodies for You, Among Your Souvenirs* and *Grand Hotel*, all on Radio 2.

■ Highspot of career: 'Receiving the Gold Medal for the best pupil at school during the final five years. This was undoubtedly due to the fact that I was the first and only pupil ever to win a music scholarship in the history of the school.' ■ A moment to remember: 'Accompanying Pat Whitmore in a *Melodies for You* broadcast, we decided to improvise a piano part as the exisiting arrangement wasn't in the right key or suitable (I seem to remember the song was *Ye Banks and Ye Braes*). Unfortunately I thought Pat asked for it to be played in E Major and we performed it only to find that she had asked for A Major, a fourth higher! Needless to say she sang it beautifully, if in the lower key, somewhat sexily!' ■ Likes bowls, indoors and outdoors. ■ Dislikes unpunctuality, dirty shoes and bad music copying. ■ Married to Meryl Unsworth, has two children and lives in Suffolk.

JACK DORSEY
'I have the scars still . . .'
BORN: 1929 in Wrexham, North Wales. Father a musician. EDUCATED: Hammersmith Central School. The Song School, Westminster Abbey, Royal College of Music where he studied trumpet under Ernest Hall and composition and orchestration under Gordon Jacob. FIRST JOB: As a boy chorister at Westminster Abbey. On leaving school he

played trumpet in the Grenadier Guards. Spent five years playing, arranging and conducting for the Crazy Gang and was in the orchestra for the West End musicals, *Kismet* and the *King and I*. Has been MD for the Rank Organisation and A & R Manager for EMI and Pye. Played trumpet with Ambrose, but since then has worked as an MD. Made his first broadcast about 1961/62. Fronts his own line-up, The Jack Dorsey Orchestra, and is heard on many of Radio 2's music programmes 'Looking back over the years, *Music While You Work* immediately springs to mind, I have the scars still to prove it but there have been other programmes with lesser scars!'

■ Highspot of career: 'Is yet to come.' ■ A moment to remember: 'Some years ago BBC Radio commissioned a major audience research survey. It revealed the startling fact that the highest audience was achieved during the two minutes silence prior to the Remembrance Service at the Cenotaph on Armistice Sunday. My suggestion of extending the two minutes silence to 30 minutes, in order to achieve an even bigger audience was turned down. In my view it is still a good idea!' ■ Likes photography. ■ Married to Hazel (the light of my life), has one son Martin, and lives in Sussex.

ALAN DOWNEY
'In trouble with the BBC top brass who dared to watch ITV . . .'
BORN: 11th February 1944 in Liverpool. Father an insurance agent. EDUCATED: St Margaret's Commercial Grammar School, Anfield, Liverpool. Had trumpet lessons but learnt mostly from tutor books and locking himself up. He also half finished a postal arranging course! Plays trumpet, flugel horn, even worse drums and piano. FIRST JOB: Ivor Kirchin Band, Sale Locarno in Cheshire, Made his first broadcast with the Dennis Mann Seven in Bristol in 1964. ('I was scared to death'!) Has played with Maynard Ferguson, Louis Bellson, Ronnie Scott, John Dankworth, Peter Herbolzheimer, Norwegian Radio Orchestra, Finnish Radio Orchestra. Metropole Orchestra in

Holland, SFB, NDR, SWF and James Last in Germany. The London Symphony Orchestra, The Royal Philharmonic Orchestra, the Bournemouth Symphony Orchestra, Bob Sharples, the Midland Light Orchestra and also had a spell with the BBC Radio Orchestra on lead trumpet. Now composes and arranges for the BBC Radio Orchestra, both the strings and the BBC Big Band and is one of the orchestra's regular conductors.

■ Highspot of career: 'Working with Maynard Ferguson and Frank Sinatra . . .' oh, and "opening time"!' ■ A moment to remember: 'When I was on the BBC staff playing in the Radio Orchestra, I got into trouble for working on ITV playing with Maynard Ferguson on the *Simon Dee* Show. When confronted by a few BBC chiefs (they thought) in an office, I just couldn't resist asking them, "How dare you watch ITV!"'.' ■ Likes playing the trumpet. ■ Dislikes Hitler, scotch and gin. ■ Has two children (I've seen!) and lives in Surrey.

MARTIN DREW
'Around the world with Oscar Peterson . . .'
BORN: 11th February 1944 in Northampton. Father a cabinet maker. EDUCATED: Chingford Secondary Modern School, Essex. Was interested in the drums from a very early age. 'When I was about six, I would bang away on anything I could find and as I loved Latin American music, Dad bought me some bongoes.' He graduated to a drum kit and at 13 studied with George Fierstone for three and a half years. 'I wish now that I had learnt to play the piano as well. In fact I had a few

lessons from my daughter's piano teacher recently, but had to give it up because I had no time to practise.' FIRST JOB: General dogsbody in a warehouse in Whitechapel. He had been playing drums on gigs since the age of 14 and at 17 was offered his first full time job as a musician, playing at the La Paloma Club in Westbourne Grove. After two and a half years, George Fierstone fixed him an audition with Edmundo Ross. He was offered the job but turned it down. 'I thought maybe I was going to end up playing in a night club for the rest of my life and I didn't want that so I decided to go back to being a semi-pro.'

For the next nine years he worked as a sales rep. for the hairdressing firm, Wella, while still managing to keep up his semi-pro work as a musician. Then came the gig that was to change everything. He was booked to play at Ronnie's New Place with Frank Rosselino, John Taylor and Ron Mathewson. 'It was one of the finest gigs of my life. We finished at 3am and I had to be up at 7am for the day job, I went home tired but happy and remembered what my father had once said, "If you've got the talent don't waste it. When they put you away, at least you can say," I had a go, even if you don't succeed. I chatted it over with my wife and decided to have another go at turning professional. I wrote my letter of resignation to Wella and walked past the post box a dozen times before I plucked up courage to pop it in.'

For the next few months he played with Bill Lesage at Albert's Plum and The Hungry Years in Kensington. When that folded it wasn't long before he became house drummer at Ronnie Scott's where he played with such jazz greats as Zoot Sims, Milt Jackson, Eddie 'Lockjaw' Davis, and Anita O'Day. But it was Oscar Peterson who was to have the biggest influence on the future pattern of his career. Appearing at Ronnie Scott's in 1974, he invited Martin up on stage for the last set of the Friday evening and it was the start of a new partnership. From then on he played on all of Oscar Peterson's European tours and from 1980 has accompanied Peterson on his concert tours all over the world, including the USA. This means that he spends three or four months of every year abroad. When he's in the UK, he plays with Ronnie Scott's Band and also fronts his own Quintet playing jazz clubs around Britain.

One of the few British musicians who has won acclaim internationally, he says he's always surprised by the number of people who know who he is in America. 'I feel I'm sort of an ambassador. The more I travel, the happier I am to get home and the prouder I am to be British.'

■ Highspot of career: 'My association first with Ronnie Scott and then with Oscar Peterson.' ■ A moment to remember: 'When I first started playing gigs, I used to play at a lot of weddings and bar mitzvahs. There was a saxophone player called Jackie Chilkes who always thought I played too loudly and he would always be turning around and saying, "Sh,sh . . ." So on one occasion I didn't actually play, I mimed and believe it or not, he turned around and said: "Sh . . ."!' ■ Likes photography and tinkering with cars ('I'm pretty good at it.') Some pop music. 'I also find myself listening more to classical music which I find very refreshing and so totally different.' ■ Dislikes majority of recording engineers who always seem to be deaf. 'I don't suffer fools gladly and I'm becoming more intolerant as I get older.' ■ Married to Tessa, has one son, Jason, two daughters, Danielle and Michelle, and lives in Middlesex.

ADRIAN DROVER
'Worked his way down from cornet to bass trombone . . .'
BORN: 19th May 1940 in London. Father a professional
musician. EDUCATED: Duke of York's Royal Military School,
Dover. Is a 90 per cent self-taught musician although he
learnt the basics from his father. Started on cornet, then
trumpet, saxes, clarinet, oboe, vibraphone and finally bass
trombone and tuba. Made his first broadcast on Granada
Television round about 1955 playing solo clarinet. As a
professional musician, *Music While You Work* with the Colin
Hulme Orchestra in 1962. Has also played with the Maynard
Ferguson Orchestra 1969–73 including three tours of the
USA. Played bass trombone with Scottish Radio Orchestra
from 1974 to 1981 during which time he did a lot of writing
and arranging for the orchestra. Now fronts his own line-ups,
The Adrian Drover Orchestra and the Adrian Drover Big
Band which are heard regularly on the air. Is in to Big Bands,
light orchestral jazz and trombone choirs.

■ Highspot of career: 'Probably playing with Maynard
Ferguson.' ■ A moment to remember: 'While playing once
on a recording session that was going rather slowly, the
trombonist next to me leaned over and said "Why don't they
just start at take ten, the first nine takes are always
rotten".' ■ 'Likes music, cookery and computers.
■ Dislikes wallpaper music, cheap and shoddy work and
discotheques. ■ Married to Louise Tobias (daughter of band
leader Bert Tobias), has one child and lives in Scotland.

GEOFF EALES
(Dr.) B.Mus., M.Mus., Ph.D., LRAM and all that jazz . . .'
BORN: 13th March 1951 in Aberbargoed, Gwent, S. Wales.
Father a church organist. EDUCATED: Lewis School for Boys,
Dengam, Monmouth. University College, Cardiff. At
university studied composition under Professor Alun
Hoddinott and piano under the concert pianist Martin Jones.
Obtained his B.Mus., M.Mus., LRAM. In 1980 was awarded a
doctorate, Ph.D, for his work on a thesis on Aaron Copeland,
and for composition. Plays all the keyboards and French
Horn. FIRST JOB: Playing piano for variety shows in South
Wales social clubs at the age of 13. Made his first broadcast
in 1961 at the age of 10 accompanying a local choir
conducted by the tenor Stuart Burrows, on BBC Radio Wales.
After leaving University, he toured the world for a year on a
Greek liner as the only British member of an all Greek band
. . . a trip on which he met many famous film names, Rita
Hayworth, June Allyson, Glen Ford and Cornel Wilde. Has

played with Joe Loss, Chico Arnez and the BBC Radio
Orchestra/Radio Big Band. Since leaving the BBC Radio
Orchestra in 1983, where he was resident pianist for four
years, has worked as pianist/arranger for many television
programmes including the highly successful BBC TV series
The Hot Shoe Show. Fronts his own line-up Electric Eales,
which can be heard on most of Radio 2's music programmes
including *Night Ride*, *Music All the Way* and the *Early Show*.
Has conducted and arranged for the BBC Radio Orchestra
and presented his own series of programmes featuring the
Geoff Eales Trio for BBC Radio Wales.

■ Highspot of career: 'There have been many in the past
couple of years, but one that stands out is working with
Andy Williams and the Royal Philharmonic Orchestra on a
recording session for EMI.' ■ A moment to remember: 'In
June 1984, I was booked to play piano on the sound track of
an American television film *Ellis Island* starring Richard
Burton, Faye Dunaway, Stubby Kaye and Peter Reigart at
Shepperton Studios. When they cast Peter Reigart they
thought he could play the piano, but as it turned out, he
couldn't. So not only was I dubbing his piano playing for him
I also had to teach him enough for him to look as if he was
playing. And on top of all that, they gave me a part in the
film as an audition pianist. So what started out as a
straightforward recording session ended up as my film debut!'
■ Likes swimming and tennis. ■ Dislikes gardening and
decorating. ■ Is a bachelor and lives in Hertfordshire.

BERNARD EBBINGHOUSE
'Plays bass trombone as a hobby . . .'
BORN: 18th March 1927 in Dusseldorf, Germany. Father a
playwright/drama critic. EDUCATED: Kings Mill School, Cromer,
Norfolk. Gresham School, Holt, Norfolk. King Edward VI
Grammar School, Stratford-on-Avon. Taught himself to play
the trumpet, but at the age of 20 swtiched to trombone after
hearing Bill Harris of the Woody Herman Band playing *Bijou*.
Studied composition at Guildhall School of Music and with
Matyas Seiber. FIRST JOB: Trombonist with Joe Daniel's Hot
Shots, replacing Don Lusher. Was a Dixielander wtih Freddie
Randall, a bebopper with Ralph Sharon. He played with

occasionally bass and valve trombone. **FIRST JOB:** George Evans Band at the Oxford Galleries in Newcastle. Made his first broadcast with the George Evans Orchestra from the BBC's Newcastle studios in 1951. Has also played with the Squadronaires, Joe Loss, Jack Parnell, Cyril Stapleton, Geraldo, Ted Heath. Has been a freelance session musician since 1967 but fronts his own group called Slightly Latin which is heard on many of Radio 2's music programmes. Also appears with the Ted Heath Band fronted by Don Lusher.

■ Highspot of career: 'Many, over 30 years as a professional trombonist, but I would single out working with Judy Garland and Liza Minelli at the London Palladium; working with Frank Sinatra and of course with the great Ted Heath Band.'
■ Likes golf and DIY. ■ Dislikes mechanical musicians.
■ Married to Sylvia, has three children, Peter, Elaine and Martin, and lives in Surrey.

Teddy Foster (who didn't) and Oscar Rabin. Made his first broadcast with Teddy Foster in the early 50s. He did arrangements for all the bands he played with. Also arranged for Geraldo and Edmundo Ross. He arranges for and frequently conducts the BBC Radio Orchestra and also fronts his own line-up for many of Radio 2's music programmes. Has been MD for the BBC Festival of Light Music, Nordring Radio Prize and Top Tunes. Has composed and conducted scores for over 50 films.

■ Highspot of career: 'Probably scoring my first major film, although a six-month TV series with Mel Torme didn't hurt either.' ■ Likes music! and playing the bass trombone and tuba. ■ Dislikes bigotry, especially perhaps in music.
■ Lives in Surrey.

JOHNNY EDWARDS
'Slightly Latin . . .'
BORN: 16th September 1927 in Plymouth, Devon. Father a painter/signwriter and also keen semi-pro musician. **EDUCATED:** Public Central School, Plymouth. St George's Selective Central School, Ramsgate. Learnt to play drums in school band. Played string bass while doing National Service with the RAF in Singapore, where he was in a CSE unit band. Started to play the trombone in 1949 at the age of 22, what you might call a late starter! Mostly self taught, but spent 18 months studying with the principal trombone with the Royal Marines Band in Plymouth. Plays tenor trombone,

ALAN ELSDON
'I never had this trouble with Sid Phillips . . .'
BORN: 15th October 1934 in Chiswick, London. Father in the Royal Navy. **EDUCATED:** Acton Central School. Acton Technical College. Started playing trumpet at 16 and studied under Tommy McQuater, Freddy Staff and Phil Parker. Plays trumpet, flugel, cornet and 'I sing, if you can call it singing. I do obligatory trumpet player's vocals. The BBC are to blame because when they book you for broadcast sessions they ask for six instrumentals and four vocals and someone's got to sing them and it's usually me!' **FIRST JOB:** Apprentice engineer. At 19, joined Cy Laurie's Band although still continuing with his engineering job. Was called up for National Service in 1955 and played with Fighter Command Band for 18 months. On leaving the RAF, played with Graham Stewart's Seven before joining Terry Lightfoot. In 1959 toured with 'Red' Allen on the Kid Ory tour of the UK, an experience he describes as the greatest turning point of his career. Two years later he

formed his own line-up, the Alan Elsdon Band, playing everything from university balls to jazz clubs and backing such stars as Wingy Manone, Edmond Hall, Dionne Warwick and Cilla Black. The band has toured extensively on the Continent as well as visiting Bahrain and Hong Kong. It broadcasts regularly and is heard on most of Radio 2's music programmes. Alan is also a regular guest on the panel of that same network's *Jazz Score*.

As well as fronting his band, in recent years he has taken on more and more solo work, with the Midnite Follies Orchestra, commercial jingles where a jazz trumpet is called for and various jazz venues. 1983 saw him at the Nice Festival with the Jazz Journal All Stars and in 1984 at the Brekcon, Edinburgh, Chichester and Bath Jazz Festivals.

■ Highspot of career: 'Playing with the Jazz Journal All Stars at the Nice Festival in 1983, although I'm constantly finding new highs these days.' ■ A moment to remember: 'I've had several "run-ins" with toastmasters over the years. There always seems to be a certain amount of antagonism between them and band leaders. I was playing at a Lion's Club dinner one night and had launched into the opening number when the toastmaster came running across the floor shouting, "Stop, stop". We ground to a halt in mid number, which is never a good thing. "We always start these do's with a waltz and as the Guvnor's wife is Irish we'll have *When Irish Eyes Are Smiling*, one, two three." And he counted us in! To our everlasting credit we fumbled into it but half way through he came running across the floor again saying, "Stop, the Guvnor's wife has gone to the ladies room [only he didn't use that expression] we'll do it again later." I told him where he could go (which you can't print) to which he replied; "I never had this trouble with Sid Phillips."!' ■ Likes golf and cooking. ■ Dislikes discos and most electronic music. ■ Married to June, has two sons and lives in Middlesex.

JACK EMBLOW
'Sing Something Simple has made him a household name . . .'

BORN: 27th June 1930 in Lincoln. Father a railway worker. **EDUCATED:** Various schools around the country. 'We moved around a lot'. Taught himself to play the piano accordion when he was 11. **FIRST JOB:** He formed a double act with pianist Eddie Thompson and they toured the Granada circuit as Brian Mickey Discoveries for three months. At 15 joined Al Podesta's Accordion Band and spent the next three years on tour during which time he made his first broadcast. 'Every week the BBC would do an Outside Broadcast from a provincial theatre, and we happened to be at the Palace, Newcastle. The show went out "live" and was quite horrific. I can still see the expression on the BBC sound engineer's face when he asked for some level!'

He did summer seasons with two other accordion bands before he was 'dragged screaming and kicking' into the RAF for two years' national service.

After his demob, in 1951, his first London-based job was with the Melfi Trio at the Paramount, Tottenham Court Road. He then spent three years with Ian Stewart's band at the Berkeley Hotel, Piccadilly, and with them broadcast regularly on such programmeas as *Music While You Work*. 'That was a good band to work for. We had holidays with pay and a valet to look after us. He would brush our suits after every session.'

His first broadcast as a solo artist was on *Midday Music Hall*. That came about because at the end of a *Music While You Work* broadcast, he was running through a solo with Ian Stewart when producer John Browell happened to come into the studio and heard him and said he would like him to do a *Midday Music hall*. 'I had done auditions for the BBC, and after years of trying to batter my way through the front door, it happened like that!' In 1959 Cliff Adams booked him to accompany his singers on a new radio show *Sing Something Simple*. A quarter of a century later it's still running, and one of Radio 2's most popular programmes. Although *Sing Something Simple* has made him a well known name, he does a vast amount of session work and has established himself as the foremost jazz accordion player in the country. He often lines up with John McLevy, Bobby Orr, Lennie Bush and Brian Lemon for broadcasts on Radio 2's *Night Ride* and *Music All The Way*.

In 1983 was awarded the British Academy of Songwriters, Composers and Authors Gold Badge of Merit. 'I don't know why they gave it to me but it was very nice. I was presented with a gold tuning fork, and I shook hands with Vera Lynn! (qv)'

■ Highspot of career: 'Meeting the American accordion player Art van Damme in 1981 when he came over to play at the Pizza Express. He had been my idol for years and when I actually met him and he said that he had heard of me, that really meant a lot to me. Now he always telephones me when he comes to Europe.' ■ A moment to remember: 'A *Worker's Playtime* which was coming from a very smelly cellophane factory near Bridgewater, Somerset. Harry Dawson, the singer, was on the bill with me, and when we finished rehearsal at 11 (the broadcast was due to begin at 12.30) we decided to get away from the smell and go down the road to the nearest pub for a pint. We ordered our pints and were standing at the bar where the landlord had the radio on. Suddenly we heard the announcer's voice: "*Worker's Playtime* today comes from a factory in Somerset . . ." Both of us went cold all over – our faces must have been a picture before the annoucement continued . . . "that's in an hour's time at 12.30". Sighs of relief – a very nasty moment – especially as I was first on!' ■ Likes real ale. ■ Dislikes accordion bands! ■ Married to Pat, and lives in Buckinghamshire with three donkeys, one goat, one sheep, two dogs and a cat.

BRIAN FAHEY
'Organizing the entertainment in POW camps . . .'
BORN: 25th April 1919 in Margate, Kent. Father a professional musician. **EDUCATED:** Colfe's Grammar School, Lewisham. His father taught him to play the piano and cello. **FIRST JOB:** A clerk in a leather factory. He joined the Territorial Army in 1938, was called up in 1939 and joined The Royal Artillery. He was wounded and captured by the Germans during the retreat to Dunkirk. He spent the next five years as a prisoner of war organizing entertainment in POW camps. When he

was demobbed at the end of the war he was determined to make it as an arranger. First job as a musician was with Rudi Starita's Band on piano. Started to arrange for Geraldo, Harry Roy and Ken Mackintosh. In the early 50s joined Chappell's as a staff arranger. Was Musical Director for Shirley Bassey 1966–72. He made his first broadcast with his own orchestra on the BBC Light Programme around 1960. In 1971 he appeared in the Royal Variety Show. Was conductor of the Scottish Radio Orchestra from 1972 to 1981 when it was disbanded. He now fronts his own line-ups, The Brian Fahey Concert Orchestra, Big Band, Little Big Band and Little String Orchestra, which are heard daily on radio, and with which he performs in both the concert and the dance hall. His best known compositions are *At the Sign of the Swinging Cymbal* (Alan Freeman's signature tune), *Fanfare Boogie* for which he won an Ivor Novello Award, and *The Creep* which he wrote with Ken Mackintosh who had a big hit with it in 1954.

■ A moment to remember: 'When Ella Fitzgerald came to give a concert in Edinburgh, I was booked to do the first half of the concert with my 75 piece Concert Orchestra and they would also be used to back Ella. Three days before the concert I had a call asking me if I would be willing to conduct the orchestra for Ella as she didn't have her conductor with her. Of course I said yes and the concert was an enormous success. It was the only time she had been backed by an orchestra of symphonic proportions in Europe and she was full of praise. Maybe the reason we got on so well was because we share the same birthday!' ■ Likes golf, gardening and reading. ■ Dislikes wastage of food, and hypocrisy. ■ Married to Audrey Laurie (who sang with Rudy Starita's Band), has three sons and three daughters and lives in Ayrshire.

ROBERT FARNON
'Lethal with a baton . . .!'
BORN: 24th July 1917 in Toronto, Canada. Father a clothier. **EDUCATED:** Our Lady of Lourdes Private School. Humberside College. Studied composition with Louis Waizman and was a student at the Broadus Farmer School of Music, Toronto. Plays percussion, piano, trumpet and trombone. **FIRST JOB:** Brian Farnon Orchestra (percussion) in 1932. Was principal trumpet with the CBC Concert Orchestra; also played with

the Toronto Symphony Orchestra and played trumpet and arranged for the Percy Faith Orchestra. Made his first broadcast with the CBC Radio Orchestra in 1935. Came to Britain with the Canadian AEF Band during the Second World War. After the war established himself as one of our most popular composer/conductor/arrangers. Is a prolific composer, his first published composition being *Jumping Bean*. His most popular are probably *Portrait of a Flirt* and *Westminster Waltz*. He broadcasts regularly with his own orchestra and also conducts the BBC Radio Orchestra and the BBC Concert Orchestra on numerous occasions.

■ Highspot of career: 'The performance of my first symphony by Eugene Ormandy and the Philadelphia Symphony Orchestra in 1941.' ■ A moment to remember: 'During the Vera Lynn Radio series, we were rehearsing an arrangement by Bruce Campbell. While he was peering into the score at close range checking some doubtful notes I accidentally caught him full force under the chin with the back of my hand during a sweeping up-beat, knocking him unconscious. We remained the best of friends, but he never again came within five feet if I had a baton in my hand and frequently referred to me as ''Henry the Hammer of Harmony''.'
■ Likes photography, golf and the Sport of Kings. ■ Dislikes temperamental singers and drum solos. ■ Married to Patricia, has five children and lives in Guernsey, Channel Islands.

deputy pianist with Alyn Ainsworth and the Northern Dance Orchestra. Has played with Bob Sharples ABC TV Orchestra and the Northern Radio Orchestra which he also conducted. As a freelance musical director and pianist he contributes to most of Radio 2's music programmes as well as many Light Entertainment programmes on the network including *Listen to Les*, *Castle's On The Air*, *The Grumbleweeds*. On Radio 4 in the north he provides the incidental music to drama productions and Richard Stilgoe's *Traffic Jam Show*.

■ Likes compulsory gardening. ■ Dislikes presumptuousness and dirty ashtrays. ■ Married to Jean, has two sons and lives in Cheshire.

BARRY FORGIE
'Making oneself understood, an occupational hazard . . .'
BORN: 28th Mary 1939, in Peterborough, Northamptonshire. Father an engineer. **EDUCATED:** King's School, Peterborough. University of Wales, Cardiff (B.Mus.). Plays trombone and piano. **FIRST JOB:** Teaching music at a school in Croydon. Did his first arranging for Ken Thorne on the first Val Doonican television series. Spent a year playing trombone with Syd Lawrence. Made his first broadcast with his own 13-piece band in September 1969. As a freelance MD/arranger/composer he fronts his own line-ups under various names; Thames 8, Swing Machine, Peter Dennis Boogie Woogie Band. Was the Festival conductor for the 1981 Nordring Radio Festival in Jersey and the following year conducted his own work, *A Beatles Symphony* at the festival in Malmo. Was the conductor of the winning British entry for the 1983 festival in Belgium and in 1984, conducted the Danish Radio Concert Orchestra for Britain's contribution to the non-competitive Nordring Festival held in the Tivoli Gardens, Copenhagen. Has conducted the Norwegian Radio, Dutch Metropole, Helsinki Light, Hamburg Radio and Malmo Symphony Orchestras. He conducts the BBC Radio Orchestra and is the principal conductor of the BBC Radio Big Band. Is heard regularly on Radio 2's *Big Band Special*, *Round Midnight*. In July 1984 his *Beatles Symphony* was given its UK premier by the Royal Liverpool Philharmonic Orchestra conducted by Carl Davis.

BRIAN FITZGERALD
'Has accompanied many stars . . .'
BORN: 9th February 1932, in Manchester. Father a sports journalist. **EDUCATED:** Xaverian Catholic Grammar School, Manchester. Learnt elementary piano while at school. **FIRST JOB:** At the age of 15, playing the piano in a dance band at the Casino Ballroom, Warrington. Has toured the UK and abroad as accompanist to many stars including Malcolm Roberts (South America), Gladys Knight, Russ Abbot and Andy Williams. Made his first broadcast around 1955 as

■ Highspot of career: 'Conducting my own 50-minute work, *A Beatles Symphony*, written for the 1982 Nordring Festival held in Malmo, Sweden.' ■ A moment to remember: 'Making oneself understood is an occupational hazard when working with foreign orchestras despite the universality of the English language. One one occasion in Oslo, I had used a delicate 'water bell' effect and spent some time explaining to the percussionist the technique of hitting the tubular bell with a wooden mallet and dipping it up and down in a bucket of water, so changing the pitch of the sound. Imagine my consternation when on the rehearsal this moment of unparalleled subtlety arrived and amidst a texture of shimmering strings and undulating woodwind chords, the bell was struck and was immediately followed by a sickening "clunk" as it crunched into the bottom of the metal bucket. The orchestra collapsed with laughter. "No". I said resignedly. "You dip it in the water, can't you see, the part says Dip in Water." "Ah, so sorry," came the bemused reply, "I thought it said "Deep in Water"!' ■ Likes chess, squash and opening time. ■ Dislikes predictability in all things. ■ Married to Tesni, has two daughters and lives in Surrey.

■ Highspot of career: 'Driving to Poland to conduct the Krakow Symphony Orchestra recording my own symphonic composition; and the launching of my Gershwin album at a special reception where the special guest was my mother! Without a good deal of help throughout my career, perhaps my musical world might never have seen the light of day and many of my musical ideas have been thought up while walking my collie dog Taly. But the biggest thank you must go to my lovely wife Joy and my family who have put up with my artistic temperaments!' ■ Likes walking with his collie in the country, listening to and reading about medieval music and instruments. ■ Dislikes interruptions when working, commercial holidays, adverts, bad drivers, bad manners, exotic foods and music in restaurants. ■ Married to Joy Devon (singer), has two sons and one daughter and lives in Surrey.

JOHN FOX
'Musical ideas while walking the dog . . .'
BORN: 30th January 1926, in Sutton Surrey. **EDUCATED:** Sutton West. 'I took piano lessons at an early age at 2s. a time! After the war I studied very hard at the Royal College of Music (piano, which I loved, and violin, which I played rather badly) and gained my ARCM. I also studied at Fitzwells College where I won a composition scholarship.' **FIRST JOB:** At the age of 15 playing with a young drummer at the local hall for 15s. Taught music for a short while at Wandsworth School and also ran a local amateur choir.
Accompanied all sorts of talent competitions at local cinemas. Made his first broadcast in the early 50s playing piano with the Harold Turner Quartet. Conducted the BBC Radio Orchestra for the first time in the mid 60s. Has also played with Fred Hedley's Big Band, the Jack Newman Orchestra, Johnny Howard Band, Lennie Lewis Quintet and with Harold Turner's Quartet at the Grand Hotel, Eastbourne. Conducts the BBC Radio Orchestra regularly and records and broadcasts with his own orchestra, always with the accent on strings. The John Fox Singers are frequently heard on *Friday Night is Music Night*.

GEORGE FRENCH
'Played many times in the Palm Court . . .'
BORN: 13th July 1921, in Bentley, Yorkshire. Father a parks superintendent. **EDUCATED:** King Charles I Grammar School, Kidderminster. Midland Institute of Music, Birmingham where he studied violin. **FIRST JOB:** Joined the London Philharmonic Orchestra as rank and file and left it as sub-leader to join the BBC's London Studio Players. Has been leader for Barry Gray (Thunderbirds etc), Mike Batt (Wombles), Gordon Langford, Reg Leopold Orchestra (*Melodies for You*) and the John Fox Orchestra. He made his first broadcast at the age of 15 in *Young Artists* for the BBC Midland Region. Radio programmes include *Grand Hotel* with Tom Jenkins, Jean Pougnet, Reg Leopold and Max Jaffa, and *Among Your Souvenirs*. He has lead and directed The Spa Orchestra for the BBC. Now conducts the London Studio Players.

■ Dislikes 'Bossy Boots' women, flying, and animal experiments. ■ Married to Marion, has three sons and lives in Middlesex.

JAMES GALWAY
'I'm a great fan of Elton John . . .'
BORN: 8th December 1939 in Belfast. Father a rivetter who also played the flute, as did his grandfather. **EDUCATED:** Mount Collyer Secondary Modern School, Belfast. Royal College of Music and Guildhall School of Music, London. Paris Conservatoire. At five, his father bought him a mouth organ.

He then progressed to the penny whistle and a very brief spell on the violin before playing the instrument he had wanted to play from as young as he can remember, the flute. 'The flute seemed easy and natural to me from the very start.' As a small boy he remembers the time a gypsy called at the house and told him that one day he would become a great musician. At nine he was playing with the Onward Flute Band and progressed from there to the Belfast Military Band and then the 39th Old Boys. At 10 he entered all three classes in the Irish Flute Championships, the 10 to 13 year olds, 13 to 16 and the open class. He won all three! **FIRST JOB:** apprentice piano tuner. He had applied for a job with a bookbinding firm, but had been turned down. He was at this time playing with the Youth Orchestra in Belfast and also made his first broadcasts with the Studio Orchestra run by BBC producer Havelock Nelson. His flute teacher Muriel Dawn arranged for him to be heard by both John Francis who taught at the Royal College of Music and Geoffrey Gilbert of the Guildhall School of Music which resulted in him gaining a scholarship to the Royal College. He studied later under Geoffrey Gilbert, and then went on to the Paris Conservatoire.

His first job on leaving the Conservatoire was with Sadlers Wells Opera. He also played at the Royal Opera House Covent Garden before joining the BBC Symphony Orchestra. Following that he was Principal Flute with the London Symphony Orchestra and the Royal Philharmonic. In 1969 he was appointed Principal Solo Flute with the Berlin Philharmonic.

After six years in Berlin, on the advice of his manager, Michael Emerson, he left the Berlin Philharmonic to go solo although few flautists had ever succeeded in this field. Within a year he had played 120 concerts in Britain and Europe and had launched his most finanacially rewarding venture yet, his recording career. His recordings of the Mozart Concertos won him the Grand Prix du Disque, but it was *Annie's Song*, released as a single in 1978, that made him a household name. James Galway was in the Top 10 at No.3 and that record stayed in the charts for 13 weeks. His first golden flute which he had bought while with the Berlin Philharmonic was now matched by Gold Discs. Having discovered his pot of gold, he recorded an album with Cleo Laine (qv), *Sometimes We Touch* and his venture into the so called 'cross over' field brought him Record of the Year awards from bcth Billboard and Cash Box as well as a Platinum and several Gold Discs. Not that he has neglected his classical recording career, the six concertos opus 10 by Vivaldi being released in 1984. 1983 saw him circling the world twice, with concerts in Japan, Australasia, Europe and America and the round of concert appearances continued in 1984.

He is President of the British Flute Society. His autobiography, *James Galway* was published in 1978.

■ Highspot of career: 'Being managed by Michael Emerson,

because together we really got it going. He's a very clever guy and morally very correct and that's very important in a manager.' ■ A moment to remember: While studying at the Paris Conservatoire, he was one of the first students to try earning some money by busking in the Paris Metro. Playing an aria from the *Magic Flute* one day, a woman stopped to listen and said, 'You ought to take up music professionally.' ■ Likes hanging around with his friends, going to the cinema and all kinds of music. 'I'm a great fan of Elton John and Pink Floyd. I like pop music.' ■ Dislikes people who smoke at the next table in restaurants. ■ Has two sons, Stephen and Paddy, twin daughters, Charlotte and Jennifer, and lives in Switzerland.

the first time.' ■ A moment to remember: 'I did a "dep" for Ronnie Verrall on a Bob Farnon broadcast and one of the numbers featured the drums (and during the solo catching the brass accents, not easy). I thought I did a good job. I listened to the show only to hear Radio 2 announcer Colin Berry say," . . . and some pretty good drumming there from Ronnie Verrall."UGH!' ■ Likes tennis. ■ Dislikes musicians who can't keep time. ■ Married to June, has one daughter, Allison, and lives in Berkshire.

ALLAN GANLEY
'Some pretty good drumming from Ronnie Verrall . . .!'
BORN: 11th March 1931, in Tolworth, Surrey. Father a bookmaker. **EDUCATED:** 'Not really!' Tolworth Secondary School. Plays the drums and enough piano to arrange and compose. Mostly self-taught, but in 1970 he studied arranging and composition at the Berklee School of Music in Boston, USA. **FIRST JOB:** Drummer with the Jimmy Walker Quintet, also made his first broadcast with them from the Aeolian Hall in Bond Street in 1952. Has recorded with Jim Hall, Ron Carter and Art Farmer. Has played with Jack Parnell, the first Johnny Dankworth Orchestra, Stan Getz, Dizzy Gillespies, Al Cohn, Stephane Grapelli . . .' Perhaps I should list who I haven't played for . . .' I had my own jazz group for many years then with Ronnie Ross formed the Jazzmakers. I then spent two years with the Tubby Hayes Quintet and became resident drummer at Ronnie Scott's.' Broadcasts now with his own sextet and his own Big Band on *Jazz Club*. But his radio programmes have included ('going back, and I can!') *Breakfast with Braden, Guitar Club, Variety Bandbox* ('I think'), even an interview with Peter Clayton on *Sounds of Jazz*. Does a lot of arranging and writing and his arrangements can often be heard on Radio 2's *Big Band Special*.

■ Highspot of career: 'Hearing my Big Band arrangements for

BILL GELDARD
'An experience I wouldn't care to repeat . . .'
BORN: 27th September 1929, in Spennymoor, Co. Durham. Father a school keeper. **EDUCATED:** Spennymoor where he played in the local brass band. Studied trombone with Joe Armstrong, Tom Collinson and Geo. Maxted. Also plays violin and viola. **FIRST JOB:** Playing trombone at the Eden Theatre, Bishop Auckland, January 1945. Made his first broadcast on 9th October 1945 on *Children's Hour*. Has played with Charles Amer, George Evans, the Squadronaires, Ted Heath, Oscar Rabin, Johnny Dankworth and Jack Parnell. Has also freelanced with Geraldo, Cyril Stapleton, Eric Winstone and Johnny Howard. Formed his own line-ups, the Bill Geldard Tentette in 1972 and the Bill Geldard Big Band in 1978 and has been guest conductor of the BBC Radio Big Band since 1978. Has done a fair amount of work with brass bands in recent years, both conducting and writing. Composed an album of brass band music performed by the Yorkshire Imperial Band in 1983. Apart from his writing commitments, is a busy session trombonist, playing with the Ted Heath Band fronted by Don Lusher, Nelson's Column, and

numerous concerts at various venues. June 1984 saw him at the Barbican with Henry Mancini and James Galway, followed a couple of nights later by an appearance with the Ted Heath Band at the 'Stage Door Canteen' at London's Lyceum as part of the D Day anniversary celebrations.

■ Highspot of career: 'Being the featured bass trombonist with a specially written solo, *Nelson's Blues* on *Nelson Riddle conducts the 101 Strings*.'   ■ A moment to remember: 'In the days of "live" broadcasting, round about 1953, I was with the Rabin Band and we were doing a series of late night programmes going out about 11pm. Every week we played a tribute to a famous American band, and on this particular night I was to play *Getting Sentimental Over You*. We also played a Latin number and as usual the trombone section were the ones that played the LA toys. Anyway during the rehearsal, about 9pm, disaster struck. I'd put my trombone on my chair during the LA number and before I could retrieve it, one of my section colleagues sat down rather quickly and it didn't do my slide any good at all. With a lot of tugging and pulling and lots of water, I managed to get it working in a fashion. The night was saved for me, but it was an experience I wouldn't care to repeat.'   ■ Likes golf and swimming.

■ Married to trumpeter Gracie Cole, has two children and lives in Surrey.

RON GOODWIN
'Over 60 film scores...'

BORN: 17th February 1925 in Plymouth, Devon. Father a policeman. **EDUCATED:** Willesden County School. Pinner County School, Middlesex. Started piano lessons at five and learnt to play the trumpet at nine. He took music as one of his subjects in School Certificate. **FIRST JOB:** Junior clerk in an insurance office. His mother, who thought music was 'not very respectable', said he should get himself a proper job. It didn't last long. After his boss suggested he should try getting a job in music, he became a copyist at the music publishers Campbell, Connelly & Co., which led to him studying arranging with Harry Stafford. He also played trumpet with Harry Gold's Pieces of Eight and in his spare time studied conducting with Siegfried de Chabot at the Guildhall School of Music in London. He then became a staff arranger for Edward Kassner and arranged for Ted Heath, Geraldo and Stanley Black as well as many of the top vocalists of the day. In 1951 Ron Goodwin and his Concert Orchestra made their first broadcast on *Morning Music*. His early radio credits also include *Variety Playhouse*. When George Martin put him under contract to record his own arrangements, his second LP, *Skiffling Strings*, went into the American hit parade under the title *Swinging Sweethearts* which led to his first visit to the States in 1957.
After scoring a couple of documentary films, in 1958 he composed the music for the feature film *Whirlpool* starring Juliette Greco, the first of more than 60 film scores he would compose over the next 25 years; *633 Squadron*, *Those Magnificent Men in their Flying Machines*, *Where Eagles Dare*, *Monte Carlo or Bust*, *Battle of Britain*, Alfred Hitcock's *Frenzy* and *Force Ten from Navarone* to mention but a few. It's hardly surprising that he is one of the most sought after composers in the business. Although associated with many big sound scores, he doesn't believe in music wall to wall,

feeling that there are many occasions when silence is more dramatic than music.
Has been the guest conductor of the Royal Philharmonic Orchestra, Bournemouth Symphony, London Symphony, Royal Liverpool Philharmonic, Ulster Orchestra, Gothenburg Symphony, Toronto, New Zealand and Sydney Symphony, BBC Concert and BBC Radio Orchestras. Broadcasts regularly with the BBC Concert, City of Birmingham Symphony, Bournemouth Symphony, and the Ulster Orchestras on such programmes as *Friday Night is Music Night*, BBC's *Festival of Light Music*, *Gala Concerts* and Ron Goodwin's *World of Music*. He also conducted the orchestra for three Royal Film Performances. Ron Goodwin Concerts, a mixture of film and MOR music, played by a symphony orchestra, have proved a tremendous success both on the concert platform and on record.
His awards over the years have been numerous. He has won six Ivor Novello Awards and in 1972 was presented with the Ivor Novello Entertainment Music Award for his outstanding contribution to British music. Also in that year he was nominated for a Golden Globe Award in Hollywood for his score for Alfred Hitchcock's *Frenzy*. In 1975, a Gold Disc marked the sales of one million albums of his Concert Orchestra; and in New Zealand he won Best Entertainment Award on Radio as presenter/conductor of *Pops '78*.

■ Highspot of career: 'Working with Paul Whiteman on the Patti Page Show on American television in 1957; and scoring *Frenzy* for Alfred Hitchcock and meeting him in 1972.'
■ A moment to remember: By the time he left school and took his first job in an insurance office, he was running a semi-pro band, Ron Goodwin and his Woodchoppers. After being caught using the office telephone to fix gigs for his band, he was told by his boss: 'You're not very satisfactory here. Music acts like a drug on people. I suggest you get out of here and get yourself a job in music.' He did and says it's the best piece of advice he's ever been given.   ■ Likes reading and walking the dog.   ■ Dislikes yoghourt.
■ Married to Heather, has one son and lives in Berkshire.

ALEC GOULD
'Mad about railways . . .'
BORN: 21st January 1930 in Northampton. Father a driver. **EDUCATED:** 'Slightly'. Plays the trombone. 'Self taught at the expense of the bands I've worked with over the last 30 years.' **FIRST JOB:** Trombonist and arranger, with the Oscar Rabin Band in 1953. Also played with the Vic Lewis Band and spent four years as a BBC Staff arranger. Made his first broadcast with the Vic Lewis Band in 1954. He now frequently conducts and arranges for the BBC Radio Orchestra/Radio Big Band and also fronts his own line up.

■ Highspot of career: 'Being asked to be in this book!'
■ Likes model railways, collecting railway books, food, booze and good cigars.   ■ Dislikes people who think they are important.   ■ Is married, has one daughter and lives in Middlesex.

STEVE GRAY
'Exploring the fantastic world of music . . .'
BORN: 18th April 1944, in Billingham, Co. Durham. Father a steelworker. **EDUCATED:** Acklam Hall Grammar School, Middlesbrough. Took piano lessons from the age of 10 and obtained a GCE 'O' level in music. Plays piano plus electric keyboards plus synthesizer etc. **FIRST JOB:** 'I formed my own band while still at school playing gigs in working men's clubs around Teeside. We were eventually resident at a local Country Club.' In 1962 was pianist with The Phil Seaman Quintet; 1964 Eric Delaney; 1965 Mike Cotton. Eventually settled in London with the Johnny Howard Band and became full-time session musician in 1968. Made his first broadcast with Eric Delaney Band on 27th April 1964 in *Top Beat* on the

BBC Light Programme. 'As a session musician I've played with virtually everyone from Quincy Jones and Buddy Rich through to Neil Diamond and Paul McCartney (pretty big time, huh?).' Is currently the keyboard player with Sky and also fronts the Steve Gray Trio. 'Between 1968 and '77 I worked on nearly all of the non classical music programmes from *Jazz Club* to the *Jimmy Young Show* (I preferred *Jazz Club*).' His arrangements are heard frequently on Radio 2's *Big Band Special* and the Steve Gray Trio is heard on many Radio 2 programmes. Although he is still a working musician, he has become one of the country's foremost arrangers over the past few years.

■ Highspot of career: 'Pretentious answer: Discovering the chord of D 7th, on the piano. I had only been playing a few days and it marked the realization that I could explore the fantastic world of music by myself.'   ■ A moment to remember: 'When I formed my first band, it was a three piece. Eventually we added a couple more members, but for some reason never changed the name, so there used to be a quintet going around Teeside called The Steve Gray Trio. This anomaly has followed me to the BBC. The first broadcast I ever did as a leader was with a trio, and although I've since conducted 40-piece orchestras on the radio, whenever the Beeb writes to me it addresses me as "Mr Steve Gray Trio".'   ■ Likes cycling, beer-drinking and reading time-tables.   ■ Dislikes nothing in particular – cabbage maybe.
■ Married to Heather, has one daughter, Suzanne and lives in Somerset.

JOHN GREGORY
'Ivor Novello Award winner . . .'
BORN: 12 October in London. Father band leader Frank Gregori. **EDUCATED:** Various schools in North London. He learnt to play the violin at seven years old and studied under Alfredo Campolio. 'My father played the accordion but wanted me to play the violin and I wanted to be a composer.' **FIRST JOB:** Performing at a public concert at the age of nine. 'Somebody had talked my Dad into letting me

do it and I remember it so clearly. The noise of the clapping scared the hell out of me! The very first school concert I took part in, one of the kids came up to me afterwards and said "I could see you were nervous because your left hand was shaking." So much for my vibrato!'

His father fronted a band at Quaglinos for 10 years and then moved to the Normandy Hotel in Knightsbridge where John, then in his mid teens, used to dep on whatever instrument was needed. 'I can play anything after a fashion.' The early 1950s found him working as an arranger for Kassners along with Ron Goodwin and Geoff Love during the day, playing violin at Quaglinos in the evening and then playing guitar in an Oxford Street night-club until 3.30am. 'My last bus used to leave outside the club at 3.29 and they wouldn't let me leave early to catch it so I had to walk home to Willesden each night and be at the office by nine in the morning!'

His sessions as a violinist included both symphonic and jazz work but he turned more and more to arranging and, three years after doing his first arrangement for Lew Stone, he had three records in the charts. In 1956 his orchestration for a double sided Russ Hamilton single made musical history as the first British record to make it to No.2 in the USA. In 1976 his composition *Introduction and Air to a Stained Glass Window* won the Ivor Novello Award for the best instrumental music. His Chaquito orchestra which he formed in 1960 made over 20 LPs and had its own fan club. He has written 14 film scores and has participated in two Royal Film Performances. Has made countless broadcasts including in 1984 a series with the BBC Radio Orchestra.

■ Highspot of career: 'There have been many, but nothing will ever top winning the Ivor Novello Award in 1976 when there were 200 entries.' ■ A moment to remember: 'Early on in my career, I was very keen on motor bikes – I still am – and used to ride around London on one. I was commissioned to do a jingle and was very late arriving at the studios in Baker Street. Looking for the entrance I saw a ramp leading up to what looked like a scene dock and roared up it to come to an abrupt halt on stage behind a curtain. I switched

off the engine to be greeted by a man shouting "Do that again, start your engine up". Apparently the orchestra in the studio had just stopped and the sponsors were deciding what sounds they wanted for their particular product when my motor bike roared onto stage and they said, 'That's it, that's just the sound we want". I was so surprised by the whole thing that I forgot to ask for any money and I never got paid!' ■ Likes walking and meeting people. ■ Dislikes cold weather, and "those damned clamps they're putting on cars". ■ Married to Joan, has two sons, two daughters and lives in Buckinghamshire.

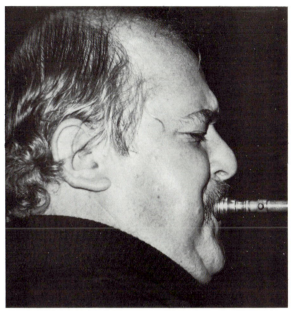

DAVE HANCOCK
'The best broadcast I nearly never did . . .'

BORN: 30th November 1937, in Wembley, Middlesex. Father a carpenter. **EDUCATED:** Acton Country Grammar School. Taught himself to play the trumpet, piano and vibraphone. **FIRST JOB:** Playing at a holiday camp on the Isle of Wight. Made his first broadcast with the Ronnie Pleydell Band on *Music While You Work*, but he can't remember when! Has also played with Ken Mackintosh, Teddy Foster, Ronnie Scott, Maynard Ferguson, Johnny Howard, BBC Radio Orchestra, Peter Knight, London Philharmonic and Royal Philharmonic Orchestras. Toured Europe 1960–61 as pianist/accompanist to the singer Myra de Groot. Was Musical Director for Anita Harris (qv) 1970–72. He now arranges for and conducts the BBC Radio Orchestra/Radio Big Band and also fronts his own line-up Hancock's Junk Band and is heard on most of Radio 2's music programmes.

■ Highspot of career: 'Hearing Segovia in person.' ■ A moment to remember: 'The best broadcast I nearly never did! Returning from the pub to perform "live" on BBC *Radio One O'clock* show in the late 60s, the BBC commissionaire didn't believe I was in the band and refused me entry. Standing there arguing I heard the signature tune being played with no melody (that was my part) . . . nobody noticed!' ■ Likes semi-pro football in which he is deeply involved! ■ Dislikes Scott Joplin's music! ■ Married to Marlene and lives in Kent.

■ Highspot of career: 'Writing and directing Yehudi Menuhin and Stephane Grappelli's joint LPs; Hearing my first *Art Tatum* record; the chart success of the *Gurney Slade* theme.'
■ A moment to remember: 'Having been introduced as a Pianist, Musical Director, Composer on a quiz programme,' was struck dumb on one particular question which prompted chairman Cardew Robinson to comment that I was obviously decomposing!' ■ Likes golf and wine. ■ Dislikes indifferent Chinese cooking. ■ Married to Nanette, has one son and one daughter and lives in Surrey.

MAX HARRIS
'Musicmaker for radio's top comedy shows . . .'
BORN: 15th September 1918, in Bournemouth. Father a master tailor. **EDUCATED:** Lylaph Central School. Private tuition on piano up to the final grade RAM. Plays piano and keyboards. **FIRST JOB:** Playing at the Paramount Dance Palais in London. He also gave piano lessons as a teenager. Made his first broadcast on *Jazz Club* in 1950. Has played with Tommy Whittle, George Chisholm, and Jack Parnell. Has arranged for the BBC Show Band, Ted Heath, Ella Fitzgerald, Stephane Grappelli and Yehudi Menuhin. The Max Harris Orchestra has provided the incidental music of many of Radio's top comedy shows over the years, including *Round the Horne*, *Stop Messing About, Sketch Book, Peter Goodwright Show, Frankie Howerd's One Man Show*, Windsor Davies and Arthur Askey. He has written numerous television themes including *Doomwatch, Mickey Dunne, The Spies, Poldark, Horseman Riding By, Porridge, Open All Hours* all for the BBC; and *Young at Heart, Mind Your Language, Father Charlie, Doctor's Daughters* for ITV. Three of his television themes have won awards; *Gurney Slade* won the Ivor Novello Award in 1960 and the *Kipling Series* won the same award in 1964. In 1980 *The Pink Medicine Show* won the Designer and Graphics Association Award. *Gurney Slade* was a hit for the Max Harris Orchestra, peaking at No.11 in the charts in December 1960. In the 70's he was the MD and arranger for the first collaboration on record of those two great violinsts Stephane Grapelli and Yehudi Menuhin. The highly successful album *Jealousy* was followed by three more, *Fascinatin' Rhythm, Tea for Two* and *Strictly for the Birds*. A fourth, *Men for all Seasons* was released in 1984. He has also made several albums with his own orchestra including *The Amazing Dancing Band* Volumes 1 and 2, and *Cradle in the Wind* on which he was featured on solo piano with his orchestra.

BOBBY HARRISON
'Over 2,000 broadcasts as soloist . . .'
BORN: 1st December 1933, in Brixton, London. Father an office worker. **EDUCATED:** Varndean Grammar School, Brighton. Played the trumpet in the RAF Fighter Command Band during National Service and then studied at the Trinity College of Music, London. Plays trumpet, flugel and drums. **FIRST JOB:** With Syd Dean at the Regent Ballroom, Brighton in 1954. Spent 15 years at the Talk of the Town in London and played solos on 'live' albums recorded there by Tom Jones and Shirley Bassey. Made his first broadcast with the Les Watson Orchestra in Jersey in 1954. Has played with Eric Winstone, Frank Weir, Phil Tate, Frank Chacksfield. On television has been the featured soloist on Miss World since 1965. And since 1973 has made over 2,000 broadcasts as a freelance soloist with the BBC Radio Orchestra, on such programmes as Radio 2's *String Sound*. The Bobby Harrison Quartet is heard on many of Radio 2's music programmes.

■ Highspot of career: 'Having my youngest son, Gavin, playing drums on my quartet broadcast.' ■ A moment to remember: 'Talk about the show must go on – I went up north to do a "live" broadcast with the Northern Dance Orchestra on sticks, due to a dislocated hip, only to find one of the other trumpet plays swathed in bandages after a firework accident. As we staggered on before the audience, we were announced as the Walking Wounded.' ■ Likes motoring and boating. ■ Dislikes loud bass players.
■ Married to Audrey, has three sons and lives in Hertfordshire.

RONNIE HAZLEHURST
'I thought about going home and not coming back . . .'
BORN: 13th March 1928 in Duckenfield, Cheshire. Father a railway worker. **EDUCATED:** St John's Church of England

School; Hyde County Grammar School. His mother taught piano and his father played the flute, piccolo and cello. 'My mother used to teach all the kids in the neighbourhood to play piano but she could never teach me. I had a few lessons when I was four, but that was it. My elder brother bought a trumpet just before he was called up in 1939, and I taught myself how to play it.' **FIRST JOB:** Clerk in a cotton mill office. 'I had to leave school when I was 14 in order to earn some money. But I remember playing in a small band at school and doing a gig for which we each got paid 5s.'

After leaving school, he played with several semi-pro bands, working two or three nights a week and learning how to read music. 'My jazz was pretty good, but the reading came a lot later, I would hang around the local palais in Ashton-under-Lyme where the George Chambers Band was resident. This for me was the big time and when they asked me to join them I was over the moon.' Shortly afterwards they won the All Britain Dance Band Championships and this led to his first broadcast. He was now earning £4 5s. a week and decided to pack in the day job and become a professional musician. 'I saw no point in knocking myself out from 8am to 5.30pm for 19s. 6d. a week!' He left George Chambers when they wouldn't give him a rise and played with various bands including Nat Allen, George Elrick and Harry Parry before doing his National Service which he spent playing cornet in the regimental band.

After his demob, he played with palais bands in the Manchester area and the odd session for Granada, where he met the MD of *Spot the Tune*, Peter Knight. In the late 50s an offer to join Woolf Phillips at the Pigalle, brought him to London and gave him his first taste of fronting a band when for an extra 10s. a week he conducted the cabaret and deputized for Woolf when he was ill or on holiday. He was also doing some arranging, something he had picked up in his days with the palais bands. 'In the early days, there seemed to be something morally wrong having all that time on my hands during the daytime, so I started taking down arrangements from records.' The period spent at the Pigalle allowed him to build up his arranging connections and when

Peter Knight invited him to join him as his assistant at Granada, he packed in the trumpet and took to writing full time. 'That was a mistake, because when Peter's contract came to an end after a year, there I was with no job and no lip. For nine months I sold records in a street market in Watford, but a 'phone call from BBC Radio saved me. They had noticed my name on some arrangements, they were looking for a staff arranger and would I like the job?' He spent four years with radio before moving across to television. In 1968 when Harry Rabinowitz (qv) moved to London Weekend, Ronnie became Head of Music for BBC Television Light Entertainment.

■ Highspot of career: Conducting the Royal Command Performance in 1982. ■ A moment to remember: 'Apart from one act I had to conduct the whole of the Royal Variety Show in 1982 and I lost a few pounds in weight that week. There was so much to do that during rehearsals, which were spread over four days, I never got out of the orchestra pit. On the final morning, we started the dress rehearsal which was meant to be a run through, but as none of the "play ons" and "play offs" had been organized, it was very much a stop and start situation all day. When I eventually hauled myself out of the pit a couple of hours before curtain-up, I went to the stage door to collect the key of my dressing room, to go and get changed. It was then that I discovered I hadn't got a dressing room as no one had allocated me one. So there I sat, on a chair, absolutely bombed, with my head reeling. I even thought of going home and not coming back again. I wonder what would have happened if I had! The fireman took pity on me and lent me his room to change in.' ■ Likes 'Laurel and Hardy, cricket, (I'm a member of Middlesex and Lancashire) Boddington's beer, good food, (I like basic Northern food like fish and chips, steak and kidney pie and tripe), and I'm totally in love with the music of Delius who I discovered very late in life.' ■ Dislikes pretentious people and 'I'm not too happy about the pop scene at the moment.' ■ Has two sons and lives in London.

LAURIE HOLLOWAY
"Strange happenings on Music While You Work . . ."
BORN: 31st March 1938 in Oldham, Lancashire. Father a french polisher. **EDUCATED:** Greenhill Grammar School. Was fascinated by the piano from the age of four and at seven took lessons. At 12 he was practising three or four hours a day and at 13 was organist and choir master at his local church. **FIRST JOB:** Playing piano at Billington's Dance Hall, Oldham on Saturday nights when he was 14. Two years later he was on the road and playing in summer season. He went on to play with Joe Daniels and his Hot Shots, Geraldo and Cunard, working on the boats, which took him to America for the first time. In 1959 joined Cyril Stapleton and from then on did an increasing amount of studio work. That same year he was Musical Director of the Rolf Harris radio series. Has also been MD for Cleo Laine, Liza Minnelli, Judy Garland, Tony Newley and Stephane Grappelli with whom he recorded 39 programmes for Radio Luxembourg. As MD for Englebert Humperdink from 1969 to '75, he worked on the Bob Hope, Dean Martin, Johnny Carson and Ed Sullivan television shows in America. Has been the MD for so many television shows, it would be impossible to list them all, but they include *3–2–1, Game For a Laugh* and the annual

Children in Need Telethon. He has recorded with just about everybody who is anybody and broadcasts regularly with his own Quartet, Quintet and 'Prism', a rock/jazz line-up he formed in the early 80's to play his own original compositions. Has composed around 30 television themes including *Russell Harty*, *Punchlines*, *TVS Sport*, *Game For A Laugh*, *Russ Abbot's Madhouse*. In 1981 was commissioned with his wife Marion Montgomery to write *A Dream of Alice* to commemorate the 150th anniversary of the birth of Lewis Carroll. Given its first performance at the Warrington Arts Festival it was subsequently shown on BBC Television.

■ Highspot of career: 'Playing for singer Marion Montgomery.' [The excitement proved too much, he married her!]
■ A moment to remember: 'I think my most amazed moment was during a "live" *Music While You Work*, when I saw a trumpet player strike a match on the microphone! On another "live" show, *Friday Night is Music Night*, I was accompanying a lady singer. I played the introduction and she started to sing the wrong song. It all finished well as we turned it into a medley.' ■ Likes golf, music and sport.
■ Dislikes cold soup. ■ Married to Marion Montgomery, qv, has two daughters and lives in Berkshire.

JOHNNY HOWARD
'Has always fronted his own band . . .'
BORN: 5th February 1931, in Croydon, Surrey. Father a dancing teacher. EDUCATED: John Ruskin Grammar School, Croydon. Learnt to play the saxophone at school and later studied with Leslie Evans. FIRST JOB: Semi-pro gigs around Croydon but turned professional at the Orchid Ballroom, Purley on 26 August 1959. In 1961 he took over from Lou Praeger as resident leader at the London Lyceum and between 1962 and 1967 played at most of the major London ballrooms on a resident basis. Made his first broadcast on the *Mid-Day Bandshow* in July 1960 and from 1962–67 was the resident band on BBC's *Easy Beat* every Sunday morning.

Other programmes during the 60s included *Jimmy Young Show*, *Saturday Club* and *Radio One O'clock*. He has always fronted his own band and is heard on most of Radio 2's music programmes. He also formed and fronts the Capital Radio Big Band.

■ Highspot of career: 'When my orchestra accompanied Miss Peggy Lee in concert, at the Royal Albert Hall, a memorable night.' ■ A moment to remember: 'Trying to conduct an interview with Tommy Trinder on a "live" outside broadcast from the Pavilion Ballroom, Weymouth, when the PA system went dead and both of us tried to continue above the noise of a very rowdy (and rather drunk) audience, mainly sailors! But the band played on!' ■ Likes music and spending time with his family. ■ Dislikes the gullibility of the British public as far as music is concerned. ■ Married to Carole, has a son and a daughter and lives in Surrey.

NEVILLE HUGHES
'31 years as sub-leader of the BBC Radio Orchestra . . .'
BORN: 24th Feburay 1918 in London. Father a tailor. EDUCATED: St. Dunstan's College, Catford. Trinity College of Music, London. Plays the violin and the saxophone. FIRST JOB: Playing at the Princes Restaurant, Piccadilly, London. Made his first broadcast playing a violin solo in the *Navy Mixture* in 1943. Has played with the BBC Revue Orchestra and was sub-leader of the BBC Radio Orchestra for 31 years. Was Musical Director of the Europa Hotel, London 1964–81. Has played with George Crow, Charlie Shadwell, Geoff Love, Frank Chacksfield, Malcolm Lockyer, Nat Temple, Bob Farnon, Neil Richardson, Dave Hancock, Roland Shaw and Peter Knight. Had his own twice weekly programme during the 60s with the Neville Hughes Septet, called *Just Seven*. Has fronted his own orchestra since 1978 and is heard on most of Radio 2's music programmes and was the first orchestra to broadcast *Music While You Work* when it was revived by the BBC on 4th January 1983. Has been seen in nine television plays as a 'Cafe' violinist!

Mancini, Nelson Riddle, Benny Goodman, Ronnie Aldrich, Cyril Stapleton, Bob Farnon, Harry Stoneham, National Philharmonic Orchestra, Bill McGuffie, Jack Parnell, Bob Sharples, George Chisholm, Phil Tate, Syd Lawrence, Ray Charles and Peter Knight to mention but a few! Also occasionally plays with the BBC Concert Orchestra and the BBC Radio Orchestra. Fronts his own line-up, The Peter Hughes Quintet, and is heard on many of Radio 2's music programmes.

■ Highspot of career: 'Working "live" with Lena Horne. I have worked with many "greats", but Lena, live, is the most exciting for me.' ■ A moment to remember: 'Two trumpet playing colleagues of mine were working with me on an out of town TV session, and each had identical trumpet cases. They also each had two pairs of false teeth, one for playing and one for everyday things like eating and smiling. After the session they decided to go for a blow at the local jazz club and try a glass or two of local beverage. After a splendid evening, they went their separate ways, one to continue the next day with the TV session and the other to London for a broadcast. Feeling a little the worse for wear, one duly opened his case in Maida Vale Studios at 10am ready for the broadcast and saw to his horror a strange trumpet and worse still, strange 'choppers', his colleague was doing the same thing 80 miles away!' ■ Likes cricket and finding good reeds. ■ Dislikes finding bad reeds. ■ Married to Mona, has one son Robert and lives in Middlesex.

■ Highspot of career: 'Getting demobbed in 1946.' ■ Likes table tennis and wine. ■ Dislikes unenthusiastic musicians. ■ Married to Joan, has two children and lives in Kent.

PETER HUGHES
'The case of the strange "choppers" . . .'
BORN: At an early age in Rochdale, Lancashire. Father a commerical traveller. EDUCATED: King Edward School, St Annes-on-Sea. Royal College of Music, Manchester and London's Archer Street! Plays all the saxophones, clarinets and flutes. FIRST JOB: Playing with the Bram Martin Orchestra in *On With the Show* at the North Pier, Blackpool. He also made his first broadcast from the North Pier, Blackpool in 1945. Has played with the RAF Band at Cranwell, Henry

MAX JAFFA
'Advice from Friz Kreisler . . .'
BORN: 28th December 1912, in London. Father a tailor. EDUCATED: St Marylebone Grammar School. Guildhall School of Music, London. Also studied violin under Sasha Lasserson. FIRST JOB: A concert appearance at the age of nine at the Palace Pier theatre, Brighton. At the age of 16, on leaving the Guildhall School of Music, he persuaded the Piccadilly Hotel in London to take him on a two week trial. He was given a contract and stayed five years. Made his first broadcast with

the Max Jaffa Salon Orchestra from the Piccadilly Hotel in August 1929. That same year, he was released from the Piccadilly for a season to become the leader of the Scottish Symphony Orchestra, the youngest ever to hold such a post. After the war, his meeting with cellist Reginald Kilbey and pianist Jack Byfield, led to the formation of the famous Max Jaffa Trio. Since 1959 has been Musical Director at Scarborough giving concerts with the Spa Orchestra for 17 weeks every year. He has made several series of broadcasts from Scarborough and other programmes include *Melody on Strings, Music for Your Pleasure* and of course the very popular *Grand Hotel*. For over 50 years the music of Max Jaffa has been heard on the radio, and on the concert platform, and in 1982 he was awarded the OBE for services to music.

■ Highspot of career: 'Going to Buckingham Palace in February 1982, to receive the OBE.' ■ A moment to remember: 'I was 17 years old and playing in the Piccadilly Hotel when the great Fritz Kreisler walked into the restaurant to have lunch. I was seized with panic, how could I go on playing with the great man only a few yards away. To my surprise I was asked to join Mr Kreisler for a drink and I started to apologize for the kind of music I was playing. He stopped me in my tracks saying "you must never apologize for playing music, whatever sort it may be. I, too have played in cafés. Remember this advice. No matter what you play or where you play it, if you give a good performance of that particular piece, then your own playing will never suffer and the value of the music itself will be enhanced by your performance." I have heeded that advice all my musical life.'
■ Likes golf and racing. ■ Married to Jean Grayston, the contralto, has three daughters, and lives in Middlesex.

PETER KING
'Attempted to make his first clarinet . . .'
BORN: 11th August 1940 in Kingston-upon-Thames, Surrey. Father an advertising manager. **EDUCATED:** Kingston Grammar School. He had a few piano lessons at prep school and a few violin lessons at grammar school, but could never get down to any serious practice, so soon gave up. But when he was 14 he fancied playing the clarinet, and being good at making models, tried to make his own clarinet! His parents, realizing that he was serious, bought him a second hand one which he taught himself to play. After listening to Charlie Parker records he switched to alto when he was 16. **FIRST JOB:** Trainee cartographer. He was also playing with a semi-pro Dixieland band and after a year his parents agreed to him leaving his job to concentrate on his music. It was at some of the modern jazz clubs in the London suburbs that he met up with Don Rendall, Tubby Hayes and Ronnie Scott. His first big break came in 1959 when Ronnie Scott asked him to play at the opening night of his club in Gerard Street, which led to him playing there on a regular basis with his own quartet. In 1961 he joined Johnny Dankworth for 11 months and shortly afterwards switched from alto to tenor. It was on tenor that he joined the Tony Kinsey Quintet for a couple of years at *Annie's Room*, Annie Ross' club in Covent Garden where he worked with some of the great American jazz singers such as Anita O'Day, Dakota Staton and John Hendricks. The late 60's found him playing with Stan Tracey's Big Band, the Tubby Hayes Big Band and Maynard Ferguson. Alternating between tenor and alto, he eventually decided in

favour of the alto, although when the Ray Charles Big Band was short of a tenor player towards the end of the 60's he produced his tenor at short notice and sight read a television show following it up with several concerts. Ray Charles offered him a job with the band for its scheduled tour of Europe. 'I had just eight hours to make up my mind, but I had just got married and we weren't allowed to take our wives with us, so I turned it down, and went back to playing the alto.'
Has played for several West End musicals, including *Applause* at Her Majesty's in 1972 and *Bubbling Brown Sugar* at the Royalty in 1977. 'In recent years, 90 per cent of my work has been jazz and I spend a fair amount of time working in France.' Has released two LP's with his quartet and quintet, *New Beginning*, and in October 1983 *East 34th Street* which was featured in the critics' choice of Best Jazz Album of '83. In 1959, while at Ronnie Scott's he won the *Melody Maker's* New Star Award. In 1983 he was beaten into second place by Phil Woods and Benny Carter in the Jazz Journal International alto poll, but in 1984 he beat Phil Woods, to come top. July 1984 saw him appearing at the Nice Jazz Festival.

■ Highspot of career: 'The 1983 tour of the UK with my quintet.' ■ Likes airplanes of all kinds, making models (although I don't have much time now), composing and classical music. ■ Dislikes Country and Western music.
■ Married to Linda and lives in London.

TONY KINSEY
'Studied in the USA . . .'
BORN: 11th October 1927, in Sutton Coldfield. Father a manufacturing jeweller. **EDUCATED:** Greenmore Collge, Birmingham. Studied percussion with Bill West and Cozy Cole in the USA. Studied composition and orchestration with Bill Russo. Plays percussion and piano. **FIRST JOB:** Playing in a dance band in Newquay, Cornwall. Made his first broadcast from Birmingham in 1949. Has played with John Dankworth,

Jack Nathan, Ronnie Aldrich, Oscar Peterson, Ella Fitzgerald, Lena Horne, Sarah Vaughan, Clark Terry. Fronts his own quartet, quintet and Big Band, and is heard regularly on Radio 2's *Night Ride*, *Night Owls* and *Jazz Club*. Has written several songs with singer Lois Lane.

■ Highspot of career: 'Conducting my first large orchestral compositions and playing my own music with a big band.' ■ Likes reading and swimming. ■ Married to Patricia, has one child and lives in Surrey.

PETER KNIGHT
'The Peter Knight Singers, pioneers of modern phrasing . . .'
BORN: 23rd June in Exmouth Devon. Father in the retail clothing trade. **EDUCATED:** Sutton High School, Plymouth. Studied piano, harmony and counterpoint privately. 'I was one of those little horrors who could play the piano by ear from about the age of three!' He made his first broadcast, playing the piano solo on *Children's Hour* in 1924 from a studio in Plymouth. 'It was one of those padded studios which was so dead that every word spoken dropped to the

ground 2 inches in front of you.' **FIRST JOB:** Civil Servant, working for the Inland Revenue in Torquay and then London. Before the war had been a very active semi-pro musician and after his demob in 1946, he joined Sidney Lipton at Grosvenor House in London. After four years with Lipton, he left to form the Peter Knight Singers, the first of the British vocal groups to pioneer modern phrasing. They were soon in demand in the recording studios providing the vocal backing for many of the hit records of the day. A founder member of the Peter Knight Singers was his wife Babs, who remained with them over the next three decades. As well as running the group he joined Geraldo for a year before becoming Musical Director for such West End shows as *Cockles and Champagne* and *Jazz Train*. The end of the 50s saw him as Musical Director for Granada Television and when he went freelance once again he continued to work in television and the recording studio, writing and conducting for such stars as Petula Clark, Edmund Hockridge and Sammy Davis Jnr. In 1964 he was MD for the tour of Anthony Newley's *The Roar of the Greasepaint*, and wife Babs was chorus master (or perhaps it should be Mistress!)

By 1977 his reputation had spread across the Atlantic and he was invited to visit Hollywood to work with the Carpenters. Several recording sessions and TV shows followed and from then on he was a regular visitor to the West Coast music scene. In 1979 he scored and conducted the music of Philippe Sarde for Roman Polanski's film *Tess* and since then has worked on 24 other films in both Hollywood and London.

■ Highspot of career: 'My first Hollywood visit and my first concert with the Carpenters when I conducted the Los Angeles Philharmonic Orchestra who were very, very good, although they weren't all that familiar with popular music.' ■ A moment to remember: 'The day I woke up to find a horse in the swimming pool. It was about 7am on a summer morning and when I looked out of the bedroom window, there was a horse's head sticking out of the pool. I woke up my wife saying "Where's my camera, there's a horse in the swimming pool." I won't tell you what her reply was! It took 12 people to get that horse out. The combined talents of the police, the fire brigade and the local farmer. Have you any idea how difficult it is to get a horse to put its two front legs on to the edge of a swimming pool when its standing in the water! What had happened was, that our pool was covered in those small plastic ping pong balls which are meant to conserve the heat and the poor horse had wandered into the garden and hadn't realized it was water underneath the floating balls. For the Mid Oxfordshire Gazette and the rest of the local papers, it was the story of the year!' ■ Likes Guinness and 'my family'. ■ Dislikes noise of any sort. 'I think the public playing of transistors should be punished by ten years imprisonment. We're far too tolerant of noise in this country.' Also dislikes prejudice. ■ Married to Babs, has two sons, two grandaughters and two grandsons, and lives in Hertfordshire.

BOBBY LAMB
'With Woody Herman's Third Herd . . .'
BORN: 11th February 1931 in Cork City, Eire. Father an electrician. **EDUCATED:** St. Peter's & Paul's School; Blarney Street School, Cork. Played euphonium at the age of nine with the Barrach Street Prize Silver and Reed Band in Cork. **FIRST JOB:** 1947 Apprentice engineer at the Harwell Atomic Energy

Research Station, which his father was helping to build. He had been working at Harwell for 12 months when he got food poisoning. 'I was covered from head to toe in the most hideous weeping boils you've ever seen. They had no drugs to clear things like that up quickly in those days, so the English doctors suggested I go home to Ireland, eat natural foods and wait for the poison to clear its way out of my system. As I couldn't leave the house, I had to have something to keep me occupied, and having recently seen a film with Tommy Dorsey, I thought I would like to make a sound like that on a trombone so I borrowed one from the Barrach Street Band.' From 17 to 18 he stayed at home teaching himself to play the trombone. With no television, no radio and no record player, there were no distractions. 'After practising eight hours a day, seven days a week for a year. I came out of that like a monster. I could play anything!'

His cure complete, he joined a touring circus band. He then worked his way through all the good bands in Cork and Dublin before coming to London in 1949 to join the Teddy Foster Band for a year. This was followed by a spell with Jack Parnell's Band before he decided in 1953 to emigrate to America. He studied with Charles Colin in New York before going to the West Coast to look for a job. 'I was in Portland, Oregon, when I got my first lucky break. Charlie Barnet's Band was on tour and he was missing some trombone players. I happened to be on the spot, so I got the job.' He completed a six week tour with Charlie Barnet, then flew to Las Vegas to audition for Woody Herman who was re-forming his Third Herd. There were 50 trombonists in for the one chair going – he got it and as the Third Herd was expanded, found himself sitting next to the great Bill Harris. Spent two years with the band 1956–58, during which time he met everybody who was anybody. Dizzy Gillespie, Duke Ellington, Harry James. 'It was a very exciting time for me.' After two years with Herman he got offers to join Billy May and Les Brown, but with a young family (Woody Herman is godfather to his second daughter) he decided for the good of the children's education to return to the UK. After six months'

holiday in Ireland, he walked into the BBC Showband with Cyril Stapleton. He had an offer from Ted Heath but 'I'd had enough of touring, and I wanted time to study composition and harmony'. So he joined the BBC Variety Orchestra under Paul Fenhoulet, and during the period 1958–68 studied with the French composer Eduard Michaels. He also found time to form the Bobby Lamb/Ray Premru Big Band.

His first composition to be recorded, in 1968, was a jazz version of *The Children of Lir* which won several awards, including the Blue Ribbon for the Outstanding Recording of the Year. In the early 70s he became the only jazz composer to win the Ivor Novello award, with his *The 17th March*. His film scores include *Flight Deck Story* for the BBC and *March Day For* Carl Foreman. He does a considerable amount of writing for continental orchestras with concerts commissioned from Norway, Denmark and Germany. 'The final culmination of my whole career took place on 21st July 1984, with the first British performance of my *First Symphony* for jazz band and symphony orchestra, when I conducted the Bobby Lamb/Ray Premru Big Band and the Wren Orchestra at Kenwood House.

In 1981 he was appointed Director of Jazz Studies at the Trinity College of Music, London. Is also the Musical Director of the European Community Jazz Orchestra.

■ Highspot of career: 'Conducting the first performance of my first symphony. ■ A moment to remember: 'When I auditioned for Woody Herman in Las Vegas, there were 50 of us hanging around the bar, listening as each one played a set with the band. One of the trombonists took me on one side before I went on and told me what tunes I would have to play and what keys they were in, so I ran round the corner into the toilet, got out my trombone and had a quick practice! Six hours I waited to see if I'd got the job. I was a nervous wreck. It was Woody's last night in Vegas, and he was so involved in saying goodbye to everyone he forgot to tell me! When I heard at 5 o'clock in the morning that I'd got it I went into the nearest telephone booth and was promptly sick!' ■ Likes red wine. 'There's no greater enjoyment in life than sitting down at a table with someone I enjoy talking to and drinking bottle after bottle. I love all kinds of good food, and my wife's an excellent cook.' ■ Dislikes apathy. ■ Married to Margaret, has three daughters, two grandsons and two granddaughters, and lives in Surrey.

DUNCAN LAMONT
'From trumpet to tenor . . .'
BORN: 4th July 1931 in Greenock, Scotland. Father a professional musician. EDUCATED: St Mary's High School, Greenock. Taught himself to play the trumpet while at school and was 21 years old when he switched to saxophone, clarinet and flute. FIRST JOB: Playing gigs around Scotland when he was 13 years old. His first professional engagement was with Kenny Graham and the Afro Cubists in 1951, on trumpet. Also made his first broadcast with the Kenny Graham Band in *Jazz Club* that same year.

Has played with the bands of Ted Heath, Geraldo, Jack Parnell, Malcolm Mitchell, Vic Lewis, Ken Mackintosh, Benny Goodman; and has recorded with Nelson Riddle, John Williams, Paul McCartney, Peggy Lee, Sarah Vaughan, Tony Bennett, Bing Crosby, Fred Astaire and Gene Kelly. Has had numerous *Jazz Club* broadcasts with his own small group and

by Peter Clayton. 'All my major works have been educational and are all aimed at capturing young people's imagination. In *The Carnival of the Animals*, which used completely different animals from the Saint Saëns composition, the trombone is the elephant. Rather than simply telling kids, this is the trombone, as soon as they think of the elephant as the trombone, they become interested. Peter Clayton did some marvellous rhymes similar to those of Ogden Nash.' *A Christmas Carol*, the story of Scrooge with Brian Matthew as the narrator was another musical portrait which had its first performance on Radio 2 in 1981. 1984 has prompted him to do something similar with George Orwell's *Animal Farm*, but at the time of going to press, he hadn't reached his two-week deadline! Apart from the specialized writing, a great deal of his time is taken up with composing 'library' music, which can be used to illustrate anything from a car chase to a murder. 'Some people write "library" music and make nothing, but for me it's probably the most lucrative part of my career. There's a certain knack attached to it and although it's strictly commercial, it can be very satisfying if it turns out well, and very depressing if it doesn't.'

He has also composed the music for several children's television series including *King Rollo and Mr Benn*, *Victor and Maria*, and *Towser*.

One of the top session players, he still manages to combine his playing with his composing, admitting: 'I think of all my work, I enjoy playing jazz the most.'

■ Highspot of career: Recording with Crosby and Astaire; touring with the Benny Goodman Orchestra and a trip to Israel with Sinatra. ■ A moment to remember: 'There are many stories about musicians, but this is my favourite. Musician to Conductor: "What a terrible arrangement." Conductor to Musician: "It's my arrangement." Musician to Conductor: "Well you can't do much with a tune like that." Conductor to Musician: "I wrote the tune." Musician (panicking) to Conductor: "Beautiful copying'!" ■ Likes music and travelling (with music). ■ Dislikes celery, a reminder of digs and days touring! ■ Married to Bridget, has two sons, Duncan and Ross, and lives in Surrey but manages to spend a few weeks each year at his house in Florida.

big band and his line-ups are often heard on Radio 2's music programmes.

In 1980 he was commissioned by Radio 3 to write a 'Young Person's guide to the jazz orchestra' which used the same Purcell theme and format as Benjamin Britten's Young Person's Guide to the Orchestra. 'We discussed a transmission date for the work over a period of months and eventually I said: "OK, let's make it four months from now." Well two weeks before the recording session was booked I hadn't written anything. So then I had to make a start. Luckily I write very fast. I always leave it to the last minute, always. It's not because I work better under pressure, it's because I've *got* to work under pressure. It isn't better really.' 1981 saw three more specially commissioned works for BBC Radio. 'It was quite a busy time. I think the BBC just happened to have more money to spend that year.' There was the *Suite on Charlie Parker's Life* for *Jazz Club* and also for the same programme, a jazz pantomime, *Cinderella* which the BBC used as their Euro-Jazz entry. Cinderella was the flute, Baron Stoneybroke the trombone, the Ugly Sisters were played by two saxophones, Prince Charming the trumpet, Buttons the flugel and the whole thing was narrated

GORDON LANGFORD
'A deep involvement in the world of brass bands . . .'
BORN: 1930 in Edgware, Middlesex. Father a precision toolmaker. **EDUCATED:** Bedford Modern School. Royal Academy of Music, London. Private tuition in piano from the age of five. He won a Middlesex Scholarship to the Royal Academy of Music where he studied piano, composition and trombone. Also plays the vibraphone. **FIRST JOB:** Playing trombone with a touring opera company. Made his first broadcast with the Royal Artillery Band in 1951, as a solo pianist. After National Service he played with Lew Stone, Billy Ternent, Henry Hall and countless radio and television orchestras. Programmes have included *A Man and his Music*, *Lines from Grandfather's Forehead*, *Music While You Work*, *Melodies for You*. He broadcasts as pianist/arranger/composer for *Friday Night is Music Night*, and as pianist/conductor/arranger with the BBC Radio Orchestra. He is also heard on many of Radio 2's music programmes fronting his own sextet. Accompanies Hubert Gregg for his song offering on *Thanks for the Memory*. He received the Ivor

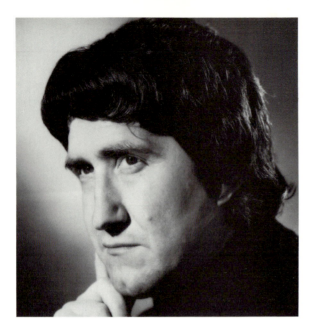

Novello Award in 1971 for his contribution to the world of Light Music. Composes a lot of music for brass bands and in 1980 was invited by the BBC to compose two pieces to represent its entry for the European Broadcasting Union's Competition for new music for bands. His march *Leviathan* and *A Foxtrot Between Friends* won first prize in both categories.

■ Highspot of career: 'Winning the Ivor Novello Award and the European Broadcasting Union prize' ■ A moment to remember: 'Adjudicating a brass band competition for the Grand Shield at Manchester's Belle Vue, being shut up in a box and having to listen to the same piece of music twenty times. What a way to earn a living, I thought!' ■ Likes tramways and railways. ■ Dislikes misuse of superlatives in radio programmes. ■ Lives in Devon and London (mostly Devon).

CHRIS LAURENCE
'Equally at home with both classics and jazz . . .'
BORN: 6th January 1949 in London. Father jazz pianist, Tony Laurence. **EDUCATED:** Catholic Primary School, Palmers Green Cardinal Allan School, Enfield. Ambrose Fleming School, Enfield. Royal College of Music. Guildhall School of Music. Studied piano from the age of seven and at 12 became a Junior Exhibitioner at the Royal College of Music, where they suggested he should take up the double bass as a second instrument. "I had to have a second instrument and as they didn't have any bass players for the Junior Exhibitioner's Orchestra on a Saturday morning, three of us were persuaded to take it up, and I've been playing it ever since.' At 17 went to the Guildhall School of Music for three years with bass as his first instrument and piano, his second. He was already playing with the National Youth Jazz Orchestra, and while at the Guildhall formed a quartet with Frank Ricotti. He had become interested in jazz at an early age through listening to his father's collection of George Shearing and Erroll Garner records, but having had a classical training,

he had the big advantage of being able to read anything. This led to him spending as much time playing classical music as jazz.
On leaving the Guildhall, spent some time with the BBC Symphony Orchestra as well as forming a quartet with Mike Westbrook, Jimmy Phillip and John Taylor.

He is Principal Bass with the London Bach Orchestra and also a member of the Academy of St Martin-in-the-Fields, and 1984 saw him undertaking an Arts Council tour as part of Brass Project, along with John Surman, Tony Coe and John Taylor. 'I've always liked doing both classical and jazz although I'm not one of those jazzmen who has all the chords of just about every known tune in his head. But as long as I have the chord sequences written down, I'm OK. I don't know of anyone else who divides their time equally between classical and jazz, but I've done it out of necessity. You're asked to do it, so you do it!'

■ Highspot of career: 'Most recently there have been two. A concert I gave in 1983 with Tony Coe and Tony Oxley at a weekend Jazz Festival at Willisau in Switzerland; and, in 1984, appearing with John Surman at the Camden Jazz Festival.' ■ A moment to remember: 'I was booked to appear at a school jazz concert in Farnborough, and, duly turned up at Farnborough in Kent looking for this school, only to realise that I had got the wrong Farnborough. I should have been in Surrey. I got there just in time to join the rest of the guys on their way to the pub at the end of the concert!' ■ Likes the A1 and decorating and DIY generally, provided it's nothing too strenuous. ■ Dislikes the M1 and driving back long distances on motorways at night. Hangovers. ■ Married to Pam, has one son, twin daughters and lives in London.

JIM LAWLESS
'The trumpet section were dying of thirst . . .'

BORN: 18th February 1935, in Woolwich. Father a Regimental Sergeant Major. **EDUCATED:** Isleworth Grammar School. Private piano lessons for three years, but apart from that, self taught. Plays vibraphone, xylophone, marimba, timpani, and all Latin American instruments. **FIRST JOB:** Touring with the Eric Delaney Band for three years. Before becoming a professional musician he studied electronics and obtained his Higher National Certificate. Made his first broadcast with Eric Delaney at the Playhouse in 1960. Has also played with Ted Heath, Jack Parnell, Joe Loss, Johnny Howard, Ken Macintosh, Eric Winstone, Denny Boyce, the Beatles, Brotherhood of Man, Blue Mink, The London Symphony Orchestra, the Philharmonic, The Royal Philharmonic Orchestra and the BBC Radio Orchestra/Radio Big Band. Has been broadcasting regularly since 1960. Everything from jazz to light music. He also fronts his own quintet and is heard on many of Radio 2's music programmes.

■ Highspot of career: 'Becoming a professional musician and also playing jazz at Ronnie Scott's with members of the Count Basie Band.' ■ A moment to remember: 'It was a "live" broadcast with an audience, on a very hot day at the Playhouse. I had two tacet numbers followed by a timpani roll into an announcement introducing the guest on the show. The trumpet section were dying of thirst, so I volunteered to nip out the back door, go up to the Ship and Shovel and bring back some lagers, thereby quenching their thirst and enabling them to perform more efficiently. I had plenty of time in two tacets, but unfortunately, while I was out, someone locked the back door. The audience was treated to the sight of a panic stricken band leader glaring at an equally panic stricken percussionist running (with clinking bottles) the length of the Playhouse and making the timp roll with two seconds to spare.' ■ Likes squash, eating curries and drinking cider. ■ Dislikes lack of professionalism, insincerity and undisciplined dogs and children. ■ Married to Carole, has three daughters and lives in Surrey.

SYD LAWRENCE
'A dab hand at repairing Hoovers . . .'

BORN: 26th June, 1923 in Shotton, Nr Chester, North Wales. Father a steelworker and semi-pro drummer. **EDUCATED:** Shotton Deeside Central School. Because his father played in a semi-pro band, there were often a variety of musical instruments in the house, which even as a tiny kid, he was

fascinated by. His father bought him a violin at which he excelled, passing his exams not only with distinction, but on one occasion, gaining the highest marks of anyone in the British Isles. 'My teacher thought she'd found another Jascha Heifitz!' But his career as a fiddle player came to an abrupt end at 13 when he broke his little finger trying to save a goal, while playing football. The finger refused to set straight, but not all that heart broken, he joined the local brass band, where they not only lent you an instrument, but also taught you to play it. He started on cornet. At 15 when his taste turned to dance music, he bought himself a trumpet on the never never, paying 3s.3d per week.

FIRST JOB: Steelworker in the Shotton Steelworks at 16, but by this time he was playing trumpet in local gigs in the evenings. He was then put on shift work. 'This meant that for two out of every three weeks I couldn't do my gigs, so I talked my Mum into allowing me to leave.' He then got a job as a van driver, which left him free to play in bands in the evenings. He turned professional in 1941, after being asked to join an ENSA band touring around the country. For 18 months he toured non-stop, often away from home for as much as three months at a time. He was called up in 1942 and was posted to the Middle East where he played with the RAF's Middle East Command Dance Orchestra along with Frank Cordell and Roland Shaw. For three years he gained valuable experience as a player and he also started to arrange and take down arrangements from records.

He was demobbed in 1946 and within 24 hours was on tour with the Teddy Foster Band. Over the next few years he played with Ken Mackintosh, Cyril Stapleton, Geraldo and with Sidney Lipton at the Grosvenor House. As a Northerner he wasn't happy living in London and in 1953 he packed it in and went home, to nothing. 'My colleagues thought I was mad, but I'd had enough. I hoped to get a job with the Northern Variety Orchestra, but there was nothing going at the time, so I took a job flogging and repairing Hoovers. I remember on one occasion sitting on this lady's floor with her Hoover in bits all around me, telling her that I used to play trumpet with Geraldo. After I left, I could just imagine what she must have said to her husband that evening. I had this crazy Hoover repair man here today saying he used to play with Geraldo! I think those 8 months will be embedded in my mind for ever.' But a telephone call from Alyn Ainsworth saved the day. Syd was invited to join the newly formed brass section of what was now to be known as the Northern Dance Orchestra. He was to remain with them for 15½ years.

During the mid 60's, the music policy of the NDO began to change. More and more pop was being played and one night, while playing at yet another pop orientated concert, he suddenly thought: 'What the hell am I doing here. This isn't the kind of music I want to play.' He decided to get together a rehearsal band which would meet every Tuesday night in a large room at the Mersey Hotel in Didsbury. Having been brought up on the Glen Miller sound, he transcribed several of Miller's arrangements off the records and in November 1967 the band held its first rehearsal. Word soon got around and it wasn't long before people started turning up on a Tuesday night in their hundreds to hear the band with the Glen Miller sound. At this time he was still playing with the NDO and was also running his own pub which he had taken on, thinking that the NDO might fold one day and no way was he going back to repairing Hoovers!

A telephone call from Granada Television, who had their scouts out and about, resulted in the band being filmed at the Mersey Hotel one Tuesday night. 'We got £12 each for what was intended to be a feature spot on local television, but we heard nothing more and I had almost forgotten about it, when I got another call from the same producer saying that they wanted to film the band again, using more cameras and that it was scheduled to be shown on network television at prime viewing time on a Saturday night!' The Syd Lawrence Orchestra duly took to the air and that was it. The reaction was tremendous and in the autumn of 1969 Syd left the NDO and took to the road with his own band playing the kind of music he enjoyed playing and millions of others enjoyed hearing. In 1970 The Syd Lawrence Orchestra played at the Royal Command Performance and in 1976 won the Carl Alan Award for the Most Popular Dance Orchestra. Fifteen years after the "off" the band still works anything from four to six nights a week. Syd doesn't run a band coach, like bands did in the 50's and 60's, his musicians live all over the country and make their own way to the various venues, which often involves them driving around a thousand miles in a single week. 'I toured as a young musician, but nothing like I've toured since! The dates keep coming in and the guys stay with me. We're all friends and there's a good atmosphre in the band.'

■ Highspot of career: 'The Royal Command Performance in 1970 and also our very first concert in London in 1969 when we appeared at the Royal Festival Hall and it was completely sold out in five days. The audience gave us a tremendous welcome.' ■ A moment to remember: 'During the 70's, at one of the Glen Miller Anniversary concerts at the Royal Albert Hall, we had several of the top brass from the American air base at Mildenhall sitting in the number one box. Alan Dell was compèring and it was all very dignified. The closing number was, as always Moonlight Serenade and we'd got about half a dozen bars into it when this fellow with a wild look in his eye leaps up onto the stage and starts to sing. The sound engineer, thinking it's all part of the show,

turned on the vocalist's microphone and it was awful. His voice was terrible. I managed to signal to the sound man to turn off the mike, and there the man with the staring eyes, stayed, singing to himself until the end when he jumped off the stage and disappeared. Afterwards he came up to me and apologized saying; 'I don't know what came over me. I've never done anything like that in my life before. I don't know what made me do it.' The whole thing took me completely by surprise, but we do have our funny moments. Wherever we play we invariably get a lot of requests handed up on pieces of paper and some of the titles you wouldn't believe! The Peanut Bender, Porky and Bess, Jumping at the Woodpile, Woodpecker's Ball, Murder on Tenth Avenue, Moonlight in Moscow, Star of India, Spanky and perhaps the best one of all, Catch the Hay Train!' (The Peanut Vendor, Porgy and Bess, Jumping at the Woodside, Woodchopper's Ball, Slaughter on Tenth Avenue, Midnight in Moscow, Song of India, Splanky, Take the A'Train.) ■ Likes curries, (they're the only places that are open when you've finished work!), chilli con carne, goulash and anything with a lot of spices in it. ■ Dislikes 'I can't really think of anything!' ■ Married to Catherine, has one son and one daughter and lives in Cheshire.

TONY LEE
'Kissed by Liza Minnelli . . .'
BORN: 23rd July 1934 in Whitechapel, London. Father a tailor.
EDUCATED: Local schools in Oxford and Bletchley where he was evacuated during the war. Learnt to play the piano from

his brother who was 14 years older than him. 'When he came home from the RAF after the war we started playing duets together and from then on I picked it up myself as I went along. I've never had a piano lesson as such.' **FIRST JOB:** electrician's mate. In 1952 signed on for five years in the RAF. After being demobbed in 1957 he went through a series of jobs, the most successful of which was two years spent as a sales representative when he became Area Manager. Was also playing in a local band in the Colchester area with his brother and eventually came to the conclusion that playing gigs at night didn't go too well with going to work first thing in the morning, so he packed in the day job in 1963 and became a professional musician.

He formed the Tony Lee Trio in 1963 with Martin Drew on drums and Tony Archer on bass. The current line-up has Terry Jenkins on drums. Also plays with The Best of British group along with Don Lusher, Kenny Baker, Betty Smith, Jack Parnell and Tony Archer, who've recently released an album on the Polyphonic label, *The Very Best of British*.

Over the past two decades has established himself as one of the country's leading jazz pianists and is invariably first choice to back visiting American jazzmen in Britain, having played with Sonny Stitt, Buddy Tate, Al Gray, Benny Walters, Eddie 'Lockjaw' Davis, Elvin Jones and Art Blakey to name but a few. 1984 saw tours with Turk Morrow and George Coleman. Well known as an exponent of the music of Erroll Garner, he has made four albums of the great man's music. And like Erroll Garner he still can't read the 'dots', only chord symbols! With actor/lyricist Tony Selby he writes songs. 'We've written one for Tony Bennett, but have yet to persuade him to record it.'

■ Highspot of career: 'I was playing at Ronnie Scott's and we were getting a fantastic reception from an audience consisting mainly of musicians, some of whom were from the Liza Minnelli Show which was playing in town. Liza Minnelli was also in the audience and she came up and asked me if I would back her for a couple of numbers. What's more she kissed me on the cheek, and I've still got the mark!'
■ A moment to remember: 'Phil Seaman worked with my trio for about 18 months and we were on our way to play at the Bull's Head in Barnes one day. We were very late and kept getting held up in heavy traffic. Eventually Phil got out his little bag and started to roll up his sleeve. "What the hell are you doing, surely you can wait until we get there," I said. But no he couldn't and he proceeded to try to inject his right arm which was perilously close to my left one. Moving in and out of the traffic, stopping and starting, the thought flashed through my head: 'If he misses and digs that needle into me instead, I'm going to arrive at this gig like a zombie!', he didn't , but it's something I shall never forget. Phil was in a bad way at that time, but he was a fantastic character.'
■ Likes cats, 'We've got seven', and steak; 'I'm mad about animals and I should really be a vegetarian, but I'm also a steak fanatic!'   ■ Dislikes *Coronation Street* and 'those women you see in TV commericals wth the helmet haircuts, the typical suburban housewife look.'   ■ Married to Olga, has one step-son and lives in Surrey.

BRIAN LEMON
'Frequent appearances at Ronnie Scott's . . .'
BORN: 11th February 1937, in Nottingham. **FIRST JOB:** Playing in local bands in Nottingham while in his early teens. Joined

Freddie Randall's Band in London 1956 and that year made his first broadcast with them. Has also recorded and broadcast with George Chisholm, Kenny Baker, Sandy Brown, Dave Shepherd, Danny Moss, Alex Welsh, Jack Emblow and John McLevy. Has worked at Ronnie Scott's many times playing with visiting jazz artists such as Ben Webster, Eddie Lockjaw Davis, Stephane Grappelli, Milt Jackson, Ray Brown, Ruby Braff and Benny Goodman. He did a broadcast with Benny Goodman on Radio 3. Broadcasts with the strings of the BBC Radio Orchestra playing his own arrangements and also fronts his own trio, quartet, quintet – Brian Lemon's Dixielanders who are heard on many of Radio 2's music programmes.

■ Likes golf.

REGINALD LEOPOLD
'The sound of Kreisler has stayed in my head . . .'
BORN: May 20th in London. Father an advertising contractor. **EDUCATED:** Trinity College of Music, London, where he won a scholarship at the age of 11, to study the violin. **FIRST JOB:** Leader of the orchestra at the Trocadero Restaurant, London. Played with Carroll Gibbon's Savoy Orpheans along with Hugo Rignold, George Melachrino and Eugene Pini. In the early 30s led the Fred Hartley Sextet. Fronted his own orchestra at the Dorchester Hotel in 1932. Was with the famous Palm Court Trio from 1957 for 17 years. Was a session musician for many years, 'Three sessions a day, seven

days a week. I don't know how I survived.' Made his first broadcast from Savoy Hill, 2LO, with Jack Payne around 1927. Fronts his own line-up, the Reginald Leopold Orchestra and is heard regularly on Radio 2's *Among Your Souvenirs* and *Melodies For You*.

■ Highspot of career: 'The first time I went to a Yascha Heifitz concert; and hearing Fritz Kreisler play the Max Bruch G Minor Concerto at the Royal Albert Hall, the sound has stayed in my head ever since.' ■ A moment to remember: 'During the war, we were living at Stanmore which was very much in the doodle bug area. We had a Chow dog at the time, and whenever I started to practise my violin he always went straight to the air raid shelter, whereas a record of Heifitz playing, never worried him!' ■ Likes any form of music if it's well played; and eating – 'my wife's a magnificent cook, but I got the habit of eating well as a kid with the Savoy Orpheans when George Melachrino taught me to eat oysters and I used to eat next door at Simpsons in the Strand every night.' ■ Dislikes driving ('but I do'). ■ Married to Jeanne (who comes from Monte Carlo – they met while he was resident at the Dorchester). Lives in Sussex.

TERRY LIGHTFOOT
'Almost a very original first broadcast . . .'
BORN: 21st May 1935, in Potters Bar Middlesex. Father a greyhound trainer at White City Stadium. **EDUCATED:** Endfield Grammar School. Self-taught musician. Plays clarinet, tenor, alto and soprano saxophones. **FIRST JOB:** Trainee newspaper reporter. Became a professional musician in 1956 when he formed his own band. Made his first broadcast that same year on BBC's *Jazz Club*. Has always led his own band apart from one year, 1967–68 when he played with Kenny Ball. His band is heard regularly on Radio 2's music programmes. He and his wife also run a pub, 'The Three Horseshoes' in Harpenden, Hertfordshire.

■ Highspot of career: 'Leading my own band at its debut

concert at the Royal Festival Hall in 1956, shortly after my 21st birthday.' ■ A moment to remember: Having passed a BBC audition in 1956 and feeling like a nervous wreck in the studio on my first broadcast, I discovered I still had the mouthpiece cover on, about five seconds prior to the red light! Highly original, but difficult to blow'. ■ Likes golf. ■ Dislikes extremely cold weather and vandalism. ■ Married to Iris, has three daughters and lives in Hertfordshire.

JAMES LOCKHART
'Conducted practically all the major orchestras in the UK . . .'
BORN: 16th October 1930, in Edinburgh, Scotland. Father a weights and measures inspector. **EDUCATED:** George Watson's Boys College. Edinburgh University. Royal College of Music, London. Plays the violin, piano, organ and harpsichord. **FIRST JOB:** Assistant conductor of the Yorkshire Symphony Orchestra in Leeds. Made his first broadcast as an accompanist with Margaret Price in 1962. Has conducted practically all the major orchestras in the UK. Musical Director, The Welsh National Opera; Generalmusikdirektor Staatstheater Kassel; Generalmusikdirektor Staatorchester Rheinische Philharmonie and Koblenz Oper. Since 1982 has been the principal guest conductor of the BBC Concert Orchestra.

■ Highspot of career: 'Conducting my first opera, *The Marriage of Figaro* with the Royal Opera House, Covent Garden. ■ Likes driving sports cars and hill walking. ■ Married to Sheila Grogan, has three children and lives in West Germany.

JOE LOSS
'Half a century of broadcasting and the first British Band to play in China . . .'

BORN: 22nd June, 1909 in London. Father a furniture maker. **EDUCATED:** Spitalfields. Trinity College of Music. London College of Music. Plays the violin. **FIRST JOB:** Playing the violin at the Tower Ballroom, Blackpool. Played with Oscar Rabin and when he formed his own band in 1930 became Britain's youngest bandleader at 21. His band has played such diverse engagements as Sandown Racecourse, the circus, the boxing ring and over the years has always been a firm favourite with the Royal Family, having played for private dances at many of the Royal residences. His band has travelled the world including a visit to China and every year since 1973 it has entertained the customers on the QE 2's annual world cruise. 'I've been fortunate enough to have taken my music around the world, and in doing so have made many friends.'
During the 60's he had many singles in the charts, *Wheels Cha Cha*, *The Maigret Theme* and *March of the Mods* being his biggest hits, but his records have sold in their millions around the globe. Has broadcast regularly since the 30's and remembers booking Vera Lynn for her first broadcast for which she got paid 30s. 1984 sees him celebrating 54 years as a bandleader which must be a record, beating the reigns of both Duke Ellington and Count Basie.
Was awarded the Queen's Silver Jubilee Medal in 1977, the OBE in 1978 and the MRVO in 1984.

■ Highspot of career: 'Being the first British musician to give a concert with my orchestra in China.'   ■ A moment to remember: 'It was just after the Second World War and I'd arrived home just before breakfast time from playing at a dance in the provinces. I grabbed a quick cup of tea and was dressed in my pyjamas and dressing gown when there was a

loud knock at the front door. It was the late Billy Cotton, who was always a cheerful character. He'd treated himself to a new car and brought it round to show me! I was very tired and wanted to go to bed, but Billy was insistent that I go with him for a trial run. Even though the snow was thick on the ground he managed to persuade me, and I went with him still in my pyjamas and dressing-gown.

Needless to say, he drove into the country and we ran out of petrol miles from anywhere! Petrol was rationed, but Billy was adamant that he could get some, and left me shivering in the car while he went to find a garage. I was sitting there with my teeth chattering when a local Bobby came along on his bike. I felt a proper fool when he asked me what I was doing there in my pyjamas. When I told him I was Joe Loss and that Billy Cotton had gone looking for petrol, I could see he was beginning to doubt my sanity! I was inwardly cursing Billy, but when he came back he did a much better job of explaining the circumstances than I did, and the young policeman went on his way with our autographs in his notebook. I doubt whether any of his colleagues believed how he got them, but I do know I've had many a chuckle thinking of that car ride with Billy.' ■ Likes motoring, walking and reading. ■ Dislikes insincere people. ■ Married to Mildred, has two children and four grandchildren and lives in London.

The Manchester College of Music and then came home and taught Geoff what he'd been taught! **FIRST JOB:** Playing trombone at the Carlton Ballroom, Rochdale. Made his first broadcast on Radio Normandy in 1937. Came to London with the Jan Ralfini Orchestra and then joined the Alan Green Band on Hastings Pier. Spent six years in the Army where he had his first 'go' at arranging. In 1946 joined Harry Gold's Pieces of Eight for one week and stayed until New Years Eve 1949. Formed his own line-up for *On the Town*, a Saturday night show for commercial television in 1955. A recording contract followed and a hit record, *Patricia*. 'Manuel of the Mountains' came into being in 1960 so that another record could be released without clashing with the previous hit. That also got into the Top 10 and for four years Geoff kept the identity of Manuel secret! Used another pseudonym in 1971 when he formed Billy's Banjo Band, now known as Geoff Love's Banjo Band. The Geoff Love Orchestra is heard on many of Radio 2's music shows.

■ Highspot of career: 'I've had so many and I've been so lucky, working with people like Judy Garland, Marlene Dietrich, Paul Robeson and Gracie Fields.' ■ A moment to remember: 'In 1981 I was conducting a concert at Golders Green Hippodrome which was being broadcast with an audience in the studio, when my trousers split up the back. I never sit down in my dress trousers as they're cut a bit on the snug side, but these were obviously just a little bit too snug! Have you ever tried conducting without moving your jacket!' ■ Likes water skiing or anything to do with water. ■ Dislikes dishonesty and people who don't keep their word. ■ Married to Joy, has two sons. Adrian and Nigel, and lives in Middlesex.

GEOFF LOVE
'Alias Manuel of the Mountains . . .'
BORN: 4th September in Todmorden, Yorkshire. Father Kid Love, who came to the UK from the USA, was World Champion sand dancer and met Geoff's mother whose family were all actors when they were playing the same town. **EDUCATED:** Roomfield Boy's School, Todmorden. Started to play the violin at the age of nine and hated it. The family doctor who was the President of the local amateur symphony orchestra and a trombone player, gave him a trombone and he learnt the rudiments of playing from the local brass band. The family doctor took trombone lessons at

DON LUSHER
'When I heard that band, I knew I had to be a professional musician . . .'
BORN: 6th November 1923 in Peterborough. Father a manager of an ironmongers and also deputy bandmaster of the Salvation Army Band in Peterborough. **EDUCATED:** Deacon's

School, Peterborough. Started to play the trombone at the age of six. 'In the front room there was always a selection of instruments and I started on the trombone, but then I played euphonium and cornet and I wanted to be a drummer very badly, but I went back to the trombone. Until I was called up at 18, I lived for the Salvation Army.'

Mostly self taught, but later on studied trombone with Will Bradley and Dick Nash. **FIRST JOB:** Driver/operator in the Royal Artillery. 'When I joined they asked me what I wanted to do and I said to be a musician, but it was a case of basic training first and then one thing followed another so I never did become a bandsman, although I did join a concert party just before I was demobbed. I shall never forget D-Day. We were sealed off in the compound at West Ham football stadium, thousands of troops and vehicles waiting to join the invasion and ENSA sent the Geraldo Band to give us a concert. They were appearing twice nightly at the London Palladium, and they came over to the football stadium between shows. I was becoming more and more keen on music, and I sat there and looked at that band in their uniforms . . . I remember Ted Heath was on lead trombone and there was Freddy Clayton, Alfie Noakes, Johnny Green and I watched them putting on their Crombie overcoats when they left and they looked like royalty to me. When I heard that band I knew that I had got to be a professional musician!'

After his demob in 1946 formed a co-operative band with four other musicians in Tenby. Within six weeks they were broke. Auditioned for Joe Daniels Hot Shots and got the job, but after a four week tour, the band folded and he went back home to Peterborough.' Mum and Dad weren't too keen on my becoming a professional musician; to them it meant drinking, women and smoking and my father said he thought I ought to get a proper job.' But when a telegram arrived – 'Come to Hammersmith Palais, audition immediately, Lou Praeger', – he went. He auditioned on a Saturday afternoon and that night made his first broadcast with the band on *Saturday Night at the Palais*. After 18 months, joined Maurice Winnick but it wasn't long before he got the sack, not because of his playing but because Eric Breeze trombonist with the Squadronnaires had had enough of touring, had been given the job. But it was an ill wind, Don auditioned for and was given a month's trial with the Squadronaires. 'When that month was over, nobody said anything, so I asked Tommy McQuater what I should do. "Nobody's said anything eh?" said Tommy, "Well, I'd stay if I were you".' And stay he did for three years. 'That was a marvellous band, they were all better than me. Come to think of it I've always been surrounded by better players than myself, until I joined the Ted Heath Band.' Following the Squads, he had a spell with Jack Parnell's Band in the show *Fancy Free* and then joined Geraldo which was where Ted Heath heard him for the first time. 'The two bands were doing a concert together and George Chisholm and I did a duet and I also had a short solo. On his way out afterwards Ted Heath nudged me as he passed: 'That was good, good Don. You want to come with my band one of these days?' He eventually joined the Heath Band in 1951, after a good deal of soul searching as he was happy with Geraldo. 'Ted made me a load of promises and he abided by every one of them and what's more he made my name.'

After ten years with Ted Heath, became well and truly established on the session scene. Does a lot of film work including the music for all the *Pink Panther* films, *Victor*

Victoria and the *Blue Max*; 'That was the biggest band I have ever seen, about 130 of us.' Has played with Henry Mancini, Nelson Riddle and backed many of the American singing stars on their visits to the UK. September 1984 saw him on lead trombone with the Buddy Rich Band and Frank Sinatra at the Royal Albert Hall.

He makes many solo appearances on television and fronts the Don Lusher Big Band, the Don Lusher Trombone Ensemble (a 10-trombone line-up) and the Ted Heath Band which he took over in the mid 70's at the invitation of Mrs Moira Heath. Holds clinics and master classes all over the UK; has been to Nashville twice for the International Trombone Association and attended a two week seminar in Australia for them in the spring of 1984. Is Editor in Chief of Boosey and Hawkes Popular Music Series and his compositions include *DL Blues* and *Lush Slide*. At the time of going to press he is working on a brass tutor which includes some of the stories he has to tell over the years. 'In my day the apprenticeship was enormous, we went from band to band learning all the time, never thinking about the money. And now when I do concerts with people like Mancini, one learns so much from watching guys like that, it makes me see how lucky I am to be in the position to do the work I do.'

■ Highspot of career: 'Playing at Carnegie Hall with Ted Heath.' ■ A moment to remember: 'There were a couple of things the late Ted Heath could not stand, one was being late for rehearsals, the other was any member of the band being off sick. His maxim was 'death is the only excuse'. Rehearsals for the Sunday concerts at the Palladium were at 2pm and we always started on time. On one occasion a certain well-known trombone player was quite late. When he did appear it was obvious he was more than worried as to what Ted's reaction would be and was searching desperately for an excuse. Ted turned on him with the words "Well, what happened?" whereupon the poor trombonist blurted out "I knocked a man over and killed him!" "Well, that's OK, now let's get on with the rehearsal" said Ted, and we did just that. You see "death" was the only acceptable excuse!' ■ Likes golf, tennis, swimming. ■ Dislikes poor quality in anything. ■ Married to Diana, has two sons and one step son and lives in Surrey.

HUMPHREY LYTTELTON
'The only way to avoid embarrassment is to own up . . .'
BORN: 23rd May 1921 in Eton College. Father a Housemaster at Eton. **EDUCATED:** Eton College. A self-taught musician. 'I taught myself to play the trumpet while at Eton and frequently had it confiscated.' **FIRST JOB:** Joined the Grenadier Guards straight from school, for the duration of the second world war. After the war spent two years at art school before getting a job in Fleet Street as a cartoonist, spending five years on the Daily Mail and a further two writing the story for Trog's Flook cartoon, (Trog being the nom de plume of clarinettist Wally Fawkes). He was also working as a musician playing with George Webb's Dixielanders in 1947 and forming his own band in 1948 with Wally Fawkes on clarinet which soon became the leading traditional jazz band in Britain. That same year, he was chosen to represent the UK at the First International Jazz Festival at Nice when he played alongside Louis Armstrong and Django Reinhardt. It was his appearance at the Nice Jazz Festival which led to his being interviewed by Joan Gilbert on television from Alexander

Palace. This in turn led to him being invited to take part in a Third Programme series, *Red Letter Day*. 'I talked about how I bought my first trumpet . . . very much a scripted affair.' And so, already adept at running two separate careers side by side, he now added a third; broadcaster. Various jazz quizzes followed and from 1963 he shared the presentation of *Jazz Scene* with Peter Clayton. Part of that programme was BBC *Jazz Club* which he compèred for 10 years. Was given his own jazz programme in 1969 and has been presenting the *Best of Jazz* on Radio 2 ever since. He has also been the Chairman of *I'm Sorry I Haven't a Clue* since it started.

From 1949, when he signed his first recording contract, the Humphrey Lyttelton Band went from strength to strength, recording with the great Sidney Bechet that same year. He renewed his acquaintance with Bechet on a nationwide tour of the UK in 1956, the year he played alongside Louis Armstrong's band at the Empress Hall, London. In the mid 50s, he moved away from the strict confines of New Orleans style jazz and, very much influenced by Louis Armstrong, Duke Ellington and Count Basie, the emphasis to this day has been on swing, entertainment and versatility.

His band has supported and accompanied many of the great American jazz stars on their European tours, including Eddie Condon's All Stars, Lionel Hampton and Jimmy Rushing. In 1959 the band toured America with George Shearing, Thelonius Monk, Anita O'Day, Lennie Tristano and Cannonball Adderley. Having accompanied Buck Clayton and the Essen Festival and on several tours of Britain during the 60s, in 1974 the band recorded an album of Clayton's compositions written specially for them, *Kansas City Woman*. In recent years he has concentrated on composing and has recorded over 100 of his own compositions, including of

course, *Bad Penny Blues*, which was the very first British jazz record to get into the Top 20 in 1956.

He has written three autobiographical books: *I play as I Please*, *Second Chorus*, *Take It from the Top* and two volumes of a three-volume set of books entitled *The Best of Jazz*, and at the time of going to press is working on the third and final volume. He contributes regularly to *Punch*, *High Life* and many leading jazz publications.

■ Highspot of career: 'Undoubtedly the Nice Jazz Festival in 1948, seeing and meeting Louis Armstrong for the first time. Not only Louis, but he had his All Stars, Earl Hines, Jack Teagarden and Barney Bigard. I sent a telegram home from Nice saying: "Have shaken hands with Louis Armstrong".
■ A moment to remember: 'Since the 1950s I've always considered Spike Milligan to be the patron saint of performers. He did a play and when he forgot his lines, he not only turned to the prompter but brought her on to the stage complete with book. He proved that the only way to avoid embarrassment, if you make a mistake, is to own up. One of my earliest broadcasts was introducing *Jazz Record Requests*. I laid all the cards face up on the table in front of me so I could read them easily without transferring them to a script. The red light went on and I promptly upset the water jug over everything, so I simply said, "I've upset the water jug all over your requests and I can't read any of them, so let's listen to some music." Nobody to my knowledge complained!
■ Likes bird watching as an alternative to playing golf or sitting watching wrestling on the television, and caligraphy.
■ Dislikes musical wallpaper and being 'sung at' in hotel lifts, supermarkets etc. ■ Married to Jill, has two sons, two daughters, two grandchildren and lives in Hertfordshire.

BILL McGUFFIE
'The nine fingered boy wonder . . '
BORN: 11th December 1927 in Glasgow. Father a physiotherapist and teacher of anatomy and pathology. **EDUCATED:** Mount Vernon, Coatbridge. Royal College of Music. Victoria College. Atheneum, Glasgow. Plays piano (awarded Victoria Medal aged 11). Accordian (2nd in British Championships aged 10), trombone, alto sax and violin. **FIRST JOB:** Playing piano at the Carmyle Welfare Hall at the age of 9, when he earned 5s. Lost one of his fingers in a childhood accident but he still managed to do, with nine, more than most kids of his age could do with ten! He studied to be a Naval architect before becoming a professional musician. Made his first broadcast on *Children's Hour* on BBC Radio Scotland in 1939 and was broadcasting regularly with the BBC Scottish Variety Orchestra at the age of 14. Has played with Joe Loss, Phil Green, Robert Farnon, Nat Temple, Sydney Lipton, Frank Weir, Ambrose, Teddy Foster and was featured soloist for 3 years with the BBC Showband when he became a household name. Also plays for Benny Goodman, British Band and American Sextet on his European tours. Has had his own Sunday radio programme alternating with Semprini. Other programmes include *King of the Keyboard, Piano Playtime, Baker's Dozen, Bedtime (and Breakfast) with Braden,* and *Round the Horne.* Fronts his own Big Band and the Bill McGuffie Quintet.

■ Highspot of career: (Three!) 'Meeting and marrying my wife through the profession. Being given my first break by Phil Green, from being a theatre rehearsal pianist to playing a concerto on a film he'd scored. Accompanying Sarah Vaughan singing *Polka Dots and Moonbeams* on the *Show Band Show.'* ■ A moment to remember: 'When one of the Show Band trumpet section goofed during a "live" broadcast and with the mike still open, one of his colleagues in the section turned to him and said "What will you have, a lady's handbag or a box of chocolates?" . . . it was heard by all the listeners in the UK.' N.B. Bill is the founder President of the Niner Club which raises money for autistic children. So called because of his missing finger. Ostensibly all members have something missing! ■ Likes golf, reading non-fiction, crosswords and the study of anatomy and psychology.
■ Dislikes self opinionated people who don't know anything and criticism of fellow musicians. ■ Married to Rosemary, has three children (by former marriage) and lives in Middlesex.

HENRY MACKENZIE
'An instantly recognizable sound . . .'
BORN: 15th February 1923, in Edinburgh. Father a college caretaker. **EDUCATED:** James Clark School. Edinburgh. Private tuition on the clarinet and saxophone for three years. Plays clarinet, saxophone and flute. **FIRST JOB:** Playing at the Havana Club in Edinburgh. Played in the R.A.S.C. Band for six months. Made his first broadcast with the Al Bertino Band in Edinburgh in 1942. Has played with Tommy Sampson, Paul Fenhoulet, Ted Heath, Eric Winstone, Billy Ternent, Henry Mancini, Nelson Riddle, Billy May, Don Lusher and Max Harris. Has many radio programmes to his credit including *Jazz Club, Radio 2 Ballroom, Friday Night is Music Night,* and the *Open House Variety Shows.* Fronts his own quintet which is heard on many of Radio 2's music programmes. As an ex Ted Heath sideman, plays with the Ted Heath band fronted by Don Lusher on all their concerts.

■ Most exciting moment of career: 'Playing with Ted Heath at Carnegie Hall.' ■ Likes watching sport, and music.
■ Dislikes gardening and DIY jobs! ■ Married to Barbara and lives in Surrey.

JOHN McLEVY
'A call from Benny Goodman in New York . . .'
BORN: 2nd January 1927, in Dundee. Father a shipyard engineer and semi-pro drummer. **EDUCATED:** Local schools in Dundee. Took trumpet lessons with the trumpet player in his father's band. **FIRST JOB:** Playing trumpet with the George Elrick Band in 1941. Made his first broadcast with George Elrick somewhere on the West coast of Britain, because of the bombing. Joined the army for the duration of the Second World War. After his demob, played with Les Ayling at the Lyceum Ballroom, London and was then with the resident band at London's Dorchester Hotel. Spent two and a half years with Cyril Stapleton and the BBC Showband and nine years with Francisco Cavez at the Savoy Hotel. Now fronts a small group with Jack Emblow and is heard regularly on many of Radio 2's music programmes.

■ Highspot of career: 'Being asked to play with Benny
Goodman. When he came over here in the early 70s I joined
his band for a tour of Europe. About a year after that the
telephone went one day, and it was Benny Goodman on the
line from New York saying "What are you doing in 10 days'
time – can you meet me in Helsinki?" "Yes," I replied,
"whatever I'm doing in 10 days' time I'll get rid of!" And so I
joined him in Helsinki and did another tour of Europe.'
■ Likes reading and golf.   ■ Dislikes nothing – 'I like
everything.'   ■ Has two daughters and lives in London.

RON MATHEWSON
'Learnt to play the double bass by accident . . .'
BORN: 19th February 1944 in Lerwick, Shetland Islands. Father
– Borough Treasurer. **EDUCATED:** Central School, Lerwick.
At three years old he could play Jingle Bells on the piano! He
took piano lessons from the age of eight and over the next
eight years walked away with most of the prizes at the local
music festivals. He learnt to play the double bass by accident
when he was 15. 'It was at the Shetlands traditional festival
UP-HELLI-AA where they build galleys and then burn them in
the parks, and everybody gets very drunk. There are about
twenty different halls with bands open all night until about 7
in the morning, and in one of them the bass player was
carried out unconscious at 1am. I was hanging around the
band and I asked the drummer if I could have a go. He
showed me where A and D was (they played everything in
the same two keys!) and I played bass for the rest of the
night. I ended up with blisters on all my fingers and was paid
£1 10s.'
FIRST JOB: Telephonist for MacFisheries. Also worked as a
paper boy (which he much preferred). He moved to
Edinburgh and worked in a photographic shop while building
up his musical connections. Having bought a double bass for
£30 he was doing regular semi-pro gigs at weddings and bar
mitzvahs until in 1962 he was offered his first professional job
as a bass player in Germany for five months. He never went
back to the photographic shop. In 1964 he joined Alex

Welsh. He also played with Tubby Hayes Quartet and in the
late 60's was a member of Ronnie Scott's 8 piece band.
In 1969 when the Kenny Clarke/Francy Boland Big Band
found themselves without bassist Jimmy Woods, Ron took
his place for the remainder of the tour followed by two weeks
at Ronnie Scott's. He also made two records with the band.
His first visit to America came in 1971 when he played with
altoist Phil Woods at the last of the Newport Jazz Festivals.
He also played with Woods at the Montreux Jazz Festival the
following year. He works regularly at Ronnie Scott's, and
plays jazz clubs all over the UK and Europe. 'I never get time
to play the piano now, not that I ever played jazz piano.
Maybe I should try it sometime!'

■ Highspot of career: 'There have been many but for sheer
excitement those few weeks I spent with the Kenny
Clarke/Francy Boland Big Band would take some beating.'
■ A moment to remember: 'The pay off to the famous story
already quoted in this book by John Taylor. When I
eventually got onto the train at Rome, with all the band's
luggage including the drum kit, I filled up one and a half
compartments. Along comes the ticket collector: "Which of
this luggage is yours?" "All of it" "I shall have to charge you
for being overweight." Then he saw the remainder of the
cases in the next compartment. "Those yours as well?" "Yep"
He got so fed up in the end he just went!'   ■ Likes
everything!   ■ Dislikes telephones and interviews.   ■ Is a
bachelor and lives in London.

PETE MOORE
'A unique album with Bing Crosby and Buddy Cole . . .'
BORN: 20th August 1924 in Lambeth, London. Father engineer
for an oil company. **EDUCATED:** Manor Road Elementary. Had
piano lessons at school. Trinity College of Music, London
where he studied orchestration with Henry Geehl. He also
studied Harmony/Counterpoint/Composition privately with
Prof. Nieman. **FIRST JOB:** Playing piano in a pub. In 1949 he
joined Teddy Foster and has also played with Ken

Mackintosh, Vic Lewis, Frank Cordell and Norrie Paramor. One of his first arrangements was of Leroy Anderson's *Plink, Plank, Plunk,* done for the Ken Mackintosh Band. Started to front his own line-ups towards the end of the 50's and during the 70's provided the backing for a number of albums featuring stars like Jimmy Rosselli, Johnny Mercer, Peggy Lee, Bing Crosby and Fred Astaire. In 1979, Pete Moore, along with record producer Ken Barnes, added orchestral tracks to the Bing Crosby/Buddy Cole Trio recordings made during the period 1956–60 resulting in a unique Crosby album, *Songs of a Lifetime.*

Has won numerous Gold Discs for his Bing Crosby recordings and was nominated for an award for his album, *Willie Wonka and the Chocolate Factory.*

■ Highspot of career: 'My most rewarding time to date was working with Johnny Mercer and Crosby and Astaire. Those studio recording sessions were a lot of fun and so professional.' ■ A moment to remember: 'On the recording session for the Fred Astaire album *They Can't Take These Away From Me,* there was one track, *I Wanna be a Dancing Man* that needed a couple of bars of tap dancing. Now Fred didn't want to do it but was finally talked into it by producer Ken Barnes who said: "No way can I get Lionel Blair along to tap dance on your record!" "Alright" said Astaire, "get me a tap mat and I'll do it as long as I don't have to think about it for too long". So we got the tap mat and were all ready to go, when Dick Lewzey, the sound engineer comes into the studio and says to Fred: "For heavens sake don't go dancing on the piano because I've got the mikes faded up". He really thought Fred was going to break into one of his dancing on the furniture routines! When we made the Crosby/Astaire album, *A Couple of Song and Dance Men,* the big problem was getting Bing to rehearse. After a lot of pressurising, he agreed to go into the studio half an hour before the session began, He'd run a song through once and say: "That ought to do it"!' ■ Likes Indian food. ■ Dislikes bagpipes and waste paper bins, (some of my arrangements have found their way into them, not with intent!) ■ Divorced, has two daughters and one son and lives in Middlesex.

DICK MORRISSEY
'Every other pop single seems to have a sax solo on it . . .'
BORN: 9th May, 1940 in Horley, Surrey. Father a bank clerk.
EDUCATED: John Fisher School, Purley. Sutton High School for Boys, Surrey. Taught himself to play clarinet at 15. 'Our Latin master at school played the clarinet and he got me

interested and lent me a lot of good jazz records.' **FIRST JOB:** Jeweller's apprentice at 17 for one and a half years. Then became a professional musician doing jazz gigs. Played at the Flamingo Club with Georgie Fame and at the Marquee Club in Oxford Street. Won the *Melody Maker* New Star Award in 1962. Formed the Dick Morrissey Quartet and in 1964 toured with Cannonball Adderley. Around the same time made a record with Jimmy Witherspoon at the Bulls Head at Barnes. The late 60's found him into Soul, working with Freddie Mack's Band and American soul singer J.J. Jackson. In 1969 formed a seven piece Jazz/Rock group, If, and the following year made his American debut. During the next four years made 10 visits to the States with If. The band folded in 1974 and he went back to playing jazz clubs and doing session work. In 1976 formed the Morrissey/Mullen Band with Jim Mullen (qv), but apart from that, finds himself doing a lot of recording sessions. 'Saxes are being used a lot on pop records these days. Every other pop single seems to have a sax solo on it.' 1984 saw him working with Paul McCartney on *The Long and Winding Road.* 'Paul was playing the piano and singing and it was recorded as a "live" performance. It was marvellous working with McCartney and George Martin.' Has also made several records with Vangelis including *Blade Runner.*

■ Highspot of career: 'When we were in New York to make a record with the *Average White Band,* we were doing quite a lot of our own gigs and played at Mikells where a lot of top musicians come to sit in after they've finished recording sessions. To have some of the best players in the world come and sit in with you is quite something.' ■ A moment to remember: 'When drummer Phil Seaman was with my

Quartet, I always remember his description of a really duff band he had been playing with one night; "Swinging that band is like pulling the Queen Elizabeth through a sea of Mars Bars."!' ■ Likes walking. ■ Dislikes American fast food.

■ Has two sons, Philip and Jasper, one daughter Johanna, two step-sons, Matthew and Patrick, and lives in Kent.

JIM MULLEN
'Trying to go beyond the different styles . . .'
BORN: 26 November 1945 in Glasgow. Father a carpenter.
EDUCATED: Whitehill School, Glasgow. He got hold of his first guitar when he was nine years old and taught himself to play it. At 14 he became interested in the double bass and when a friend introduced him to jazz, he switched from guitar to bass. **FIRST JOB:** Office boy in a contracts office. He then worked for a newspaper, first as a copy boy, but finishing up as sub-editor. Throughout this period he was also doing a fair amount of TV and session work as a bass player. When he was 20, becoming more and more absorbed with jazz, he reverted to playing the guitar. 'There were a lot of interesting things going on in the jazz world and figuring out what I

wanted to hear was a lot easier on the guitar. It was a process of learning through playing.'

He finally quit his newspaper job in 1969 to play guitar with a touring band. He came to London that same year and joined the Brian Auger Band. In the early 70s spent three years with Kokomo which took him on his first visit Stateside, where he met up with his fellow countrymen who were there with the Average White Band. It was through a mutual friend in the band that, on his return to the UK, he met Dick Morrissey (qv). Dick had been asked to go to New York for a recording session and it was suggested by their friend that Jim might like to join him. 'We did the recording session together and found that we had a lot in common musically. We'd both been through the rock band period and rock wasn't the most creative field to be in but one had to survive. And now we wanted to do something that was more a reflection of what we felt.' So in 1976 the Morrissey/Mullen Band was formed with a seven piece line-up. They spent a year in America playing the New York clubs, trying to get established and during that time worked on several occasions with jazz flautist Herbie Mann. Meanwhile the album entitled *Up* that they'd originally gone to New York to record, had run into difficulties and wasn't released, although several copies found their way back to the UK. When Herbie Mann returned to Europe for the 1977 Montreux Jazz Festival, the Morrissey/ Mullen Band accompanied him.

Back home they signed a recording contract with EMI. 'A lot of people didn't really understand what we were trying to do . . . jazz fusion instead of just straight ahead with elements of blues and soul. But basically we try to go beyond the different styles. It's because we enjoy experimenting that we formed the band.' Eventually things started to happen for them; regular appearances on Radio 1's *Jazz Club* and Radio 2's *Night Owls*; concert and club dates including Ronnie Scott's. 'We enjoy playing different kinds of venues and the contrast between the informality of a club with the more sombre setting of the concert hall where you can make the music more dramatic.' Their three most recent albums have been released on the Beggars Banquet label.

■ Highspot of career: 'Working in America with such great performers as the Brecker Brothers and Dave Sandorn, people who one really admires professionally.' ■ A moment to remember: 'Playing at one of the big Cambridge balls came as quite a cultural shock! One guy came up to Dick and said; "I say man, you play frightfully cool". There was also the occasion when someone came up to the band and asked; "Which one of you is Morris E. Mullen?".' ■ Likes football and although he doesn't support anyone in particular, admires teams like Liverpool. ■ Dislikes the phoniness of a lot of the pop scene, the reliance on 'the flavour of the month' attitude. Also London traffic.

■ Married to Lorna, has one daughter, Sian, and lives in London.

DANNY MOSS
'From Saturday Night at the Palais to Sounds of Jazz . . .'
BORN: 16 August 1927, in Earlswood, Surrey. Father an engineer. **EDUCATED:** Steyning Grammar School, Sussex. Is a self taught musician (still learning!). Plays tenor saxophone, clarinet, bass clarinet and flutes. **FIRST JOB:** Playing at Sherry's Ballroom, Brighton at the age of 16. Made his first broadcast

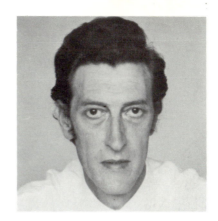

in September 1945 with the Wal Rodgers Quintet in *Saturday Night at the Palais*. Has played with Ted Heath, John Dankworth, Humphrey Lyttelton, Geraldo, Squadronaires, Oscar Rabin, Maynard Ferguson and Vic Lewis. Made his first visit to America in 1959, playing at the Newport Jazz Festival with John Dankworth. Has fronted his own Quartet since 1963. In around 40 years (well almost) of broadcasting has been heard on just about every dance band and jazz programme from *Music While You Work* onwards! The Danny Moss Quartet is heard regularly on Radio 2's music programmes including *String Sound*, *Night Owls* and Radio 1's *Sounds of Jazz*. Has done a considerable amount of touring abroad in recent years. A five week tour of Australia early in 1984, appearing at the Perth and Adelaide Jazz Festivals was followed by the Dresden International Jazz Festival which attracted a crowd of 10,000. In May of that year, with his wife Jeanie Lambe, he followed Woody Herman into New York's famous Rainbow Room for it's 50th anniversary celebrations. 'As British bandleader Ray Noble was the first to play there in 1934, they thought it would be a good idea to have a British line-up on the anniversary. What they didn't realize when they booked us is that Ray Noble came from Brighton and so do I!' Two weeks at the Rainbow Room was followed by an appearance at Eddie Condon's Jazz Club in New York.

■ Highspot of career: 'There have been so many, it's hard to select one, but flying into Rio de Janeiro for a Jazz Festival was one and appearing at the Rainbow Room in New York.' ■ A moment to remember: 'One broadcast that changed my life (see Jeanie Lambe)!' (qv) ■ Likes golf. ■ Dislikes bad music and cold climates. ■ Married to singer Jeanie Lambe, has two sons and lives in Sussex.

KEN MOULE
'Swinging Shepherd Blues in a couple of hours . . .'
BORN: 26th June 1925, in Barking, Essex. Father a factory manager **EDUCATED:** Chingford Boys School. Took piano lessons from local teachers at half a crown a time **FIRST JOB:** Playing piano with Oscar Rabin's Band in 1945. Made his first broadcast in May 1945 on a solo spot for promising young players. (Still promising!) Took a job as pianist on the *Queen Mary* in 1947 doing the Atlantic run and when in New York heard everyone – Charlie Parker, Dizzy Gillespie etc: Has played with Frank Weir, Ambrose, Ted Heath, John Dankworth and in the mid 50s led his own modern jazz band. Was also an arranger for Ted Heath during the 50s and arranged *Swinging Shepherd Blues* which became a big hit for

the band. 'My most successful arrangement ever and it took me a couple of hours.' He has also been Musical Director of several West End musicals – *Fings Ain't what They Used to Be*, *Cole* and *Oh Mr Porter*. Arranges for and conducts the BBC Radio Orchestra and is heard on many of Radio 2's music programmes.

■ Highspot of career: 'Listening to Kenny Wheeler's contribution to a Suite which I was invited to write for him by the Hanover Radio Orchestra in 1979.' ■ Likes proper music. ■ Dislikes exponents of the Three Chord Trick. ■ Married to Vera Baron, has two step children and lives in Surrey.

NIGEL OGDEN
'An entertaining organist . . .'
BORN: 21st November 1954 in Manchester. Father an accountant. **EDUCATED:** Burnage Grammar School, Manchester. West Midlands College, Walsall. Didsbury Teacher Training College, Manchester. **FIRST JOB:** Electronic organ demonstrator. He also worked as a demonstrator/representative for Boosey and Hawkes Electrosonics Ltd. First broadcast: December 1970 as a guest artist on BBC 1's *Screen Test*. Made his first radio broadcast the following May, on BBC Radio Manchester, while resident weekend organist at the Gaumont Theatre, Manchester. Following this Robin Richmond recorded a public concert at the Gaumont for Radio 2's *The Organist Entertains* and Nigel has been a regular contributor to the programme ever since. He now presents *The Organist Entertains* and also is one of several organists

featured on a rota basis on Charlie Chesters' *Sunday Soapbox.*

■ Highspot of career: 'Landing the job as presenter of *The Organist Entertains.*' ■ Likes keep fit/weight training, concert and theatre going. ■ Dislikes water, apart from for washing and drinking, and British summers. ■ Lives in Lancashire.

BOBBY ORR
'Might still have been playing trumpet but for that embrochure . . .!'

BORN: 15th August 1928 in Canbuslang, Lanarkshire. Father a steelworker and the drum major of the local pipe band. **EDUCATED:** Local school in Canbuslang which he left at 13½ His father taught him to play the drums and he was playing in the pipe band when he was nine years old. At 17 learnt to play the trumpet. **FIRST JOB:** Butcher boy and then at 15 became apprentice carpenter. Worked as a carpenter until he was 20 when he became a professional musician, joining the Bert Tobias Band at the Glasgow Locarno on trumpet. After five years, joined the Basil Kirchin Band in Edinburgh, but he was beginning to have embrochure problems and after a year, left the band in order to try and sort out the trouble he was having with his lip. Back home he heard that the Bobby Jones Band in Ayr needed a drummer. He auditioned and got the job. He never went back to playing the trumpet. After a stint with Malcolm Mitchell at Green's Playhouse in Glasgow, joined the Jack Parnell Band in 1956. Two years later he went to America with Vic Lewis, but prior to the start of the Lewis tour, played with the Johnny Gray Band in the States for two weeks. Back in the UK he played with Tubby Hayes at Ronnie Scott's and along with Tubby, Ronnie Scott, Harry Klein and Joe Muddell was booked as the regular group for BBC Television's *6–5 Special*. 'We all got the sack after three weeks because they thought we were too jazzy!'

Having got a foothold in the session scene, many tours followed with such stars as Shirley Bassey, Tommy Steele, Pat Boone, Carmen McCrae, Billy Eckstine and Sammy Davis. He also spent 18 months with the Ted Heath Band and six years with Joe Harriott's Quintet. In the 70s he did three European tours with Benny Goodman and made the *Benny Goodman Today* album in Stockholm. In 1977 he was in the London Palladium Orchestra for Bing Crosby's last appearance there and a few weeks later was on his very last recording session at Maida Vale 3, just a couple of weeks before Crosby died.

■ Highspot of career: 'The musical highspot has to be the three European tours I did with Benny Goodman within the space of 18 months.' ■ A moment to remember: 'It was while I was with Ted Heath on a concert where the stage was built up in two sections. My section started to wobble as I was playing and the vibration of the drums started to move it backwards. Unfortunately there was nothing to stop me falling off the back and it was in the middle of a drum solo that the whole lot tipped over taking me with it – end of drum solo. I got a tremendous round of applause!' ■ Likes golf (but I'm hopeless), DIY, pulling off and putting on roofs etc. ■ Dislikes crowds of any sort and driving in heavy traffic. ■ Married to Jan, has one daughter, one son and lives in Surrey.

JACK PARNELL
'Voted Best Drummer seven years running . . .'

BORN: 6th August 1923 in London. Father a music hall artist Russ Carr, who later became a theatrical agent. **EDUCATED:** Brighton and Hove Grammar School, Sussex. Studied the piano from five years old and 'was always banging on things . . . I can't remember not playing the drums but I suppose I started to take them seriously when I was about 13.' He studied drums for a year with Max Abrams. **FIRST JOB:** Playing drums for a concert party on the front at Scarborough in 1939. With the outbreak of war it closed down and he got a job at a ballroom in Cambridge. Three years in the RAF followed during which he played with a five-piece line-up led by Buddy Featherstonhaugh at Bomber Command Headquarters in High Wycombe. It was while he was in the RAF that he met Vic Lewis and together they formed the Vic Lewis/Jack Parnell Jazzmen. In 1944 he joined Ted Heath and remained with the band until 1951 when he left to form his own 12-piece line-up, which after four years became a 16-piece.

It was in 1956 that he became Musical Director for ATV, a post he was to hold for 25 years.

During the 40s and 50s was voted Best Drummer in the *Melody Maker* Poll seven years in succession. Has composed many television themes including *Family Fortunes*, *Golden Shot* and *Love Story*, for which he won the Harriet Cohen International Award. In 1973 became the first British musician to win an Academy Award, for the Barbara Streisand TV Special made by ATV. He went to Los Angeles to collect the award.

He currently plays with the Best of British with Don Lusher, Kenny Baker, Tony Lee, Betty Smith, and Tony Archer. Their album, *The Very Best of British Jazz* was released early in 1984.

■ Highspot of career: The success of the *Love Story* theme in the early 60s. ■ A moment to remember: 'There have been so many over the years. When I was at ATV I worked with just about everybody and I remember saying to Sammy Davis Jnr, "Can I get you a gin and tonic Sam?" To which he replied, "No thanks old boy I don't drink anymore. I don't drink any less either." There was the night the band was booked to play at East Kirkby, but nobody told us there were two places of that name. So half the band went to one and half went to the other and we ended up on the stand with half a band that night. Then there was the little argument that took place on the way to South Africa in 1953. There was plenty of fun going on in that airplane 35,000 feet up when a row broke out between some of the members of the band which ended with one of the trumpet players saying; "Perhaps you'd care to step outside?".' ■ Likes golf and the music of Bach. ■ Dislikes 'I can't think of a single one!'
■ Has three sons, two daughters and lives in Suffolk.

CHRIS PYNE
'You should be as good as you can be, whatever you're doing . . .'
BORN: 14th February 1939 in Bridlington, Yorkshire. Father a Local Government Officer and keen amateur pianist. **EDUCATED:** Bridlington Grammar School. Played piano from the age of three, being taught first by his father and then lessons at school. Got his first trombone at 14 and is entirely self taught. **FIRST JOB:** Working for a TV repair company but at the same time was playing trombone on a lot of gigs in the evenings. 'I knew exactly what I wanted to do, so when I joined up to do my two years' National Service, the RAF came as the break point. They wouldn't let me play trombone in the airforce without signing on, and I wasn't going to do that, but I did get to play with the occasional airforce band, mostly in Germany.'

After his demob he became a professional musician, working on a summer season in Yorkshire in order to save some money before moving South to London in September 1963. He spent a lot of time on the road during the 60s, playing with Alexis Korner, John Dankworth, Ronnie Scott's eight-piece band and Humphrey Lyttelton whom he joined in 1966 for four and a half years. The end of the 60s and the

beginning of the 70s found him playing with Maynard Ferguson's Band and becoming very active on the jazz scene generally. In 1969 was named Top Jazz Trombonist by *Melody Maker*.

■ Highspot of career: 'Many. I couldn't actually pin-point one.' ■ A moment to remember: 'I was playing at Ronnie Scott's in 1967 with John Dankworth's Band and John used to stand right next to me. I had quite a few features in the pad and one night I got a bit high. I can't remember the exact circumstances, but suddenly my slide shot across the table tops into the middle of the customers, one of whom dutifully handed it back to me, right under John's gaze. He didn't say anything, but the look was enough. I behaved myself for a whole week after that!' ■ Likes cooking. 'I cook for the family most of the time. My wife teaches and I have quite a lot of time off so it works very well. If I'm working I cook the meal the day before. I find cooking very relaxing after playing jazz.' Playing with the kids. ■ Dislikes '. . . a duff attitude to playing. You should be as good as you can be whatever you're doing.' ■ Married to Bridget, has two daughters and lives in London.

HARRY RABINOWTIZ
'Why don't you settle down and get a nice regular job . . .'
BORN: 26th March 1916 in Johannesburg, South Africa. Father a pharmeceutical chemist. **EDUCATED:** Athlone High School, Johannesburg. Witwatersrand University, South Africa. Guildhall School of Music, London. He came to the UK from South Africa in 1946 and while studying at the Guildhall School of Music started to do some sessions for the BBC as a pianist. **FIRST JOB:** Playing piano on such radio programmes as *Variety Bandbox*. Was also the house pianist at EMI Studios for a while. His first conducting job was a musical at the Adelphi Theatre, *Golden City*. He then went on to conduct four ice shows at the Empress Hall, and in 1953 was the Musical Director for *Paint Your Wagon* at Her Majesty's Theatre. 'Bobby Howes, who starred in the show had a very bad memory, and was always forgetting his lines and one night, in desperation, he threw out the line, 'Take him away

and hang him'. Unfortunately the character so addressed had a song in the next act, so the cast had to improvise some dialogue to explain why he couldn't be hanged just yet!'

In 1953 was appointed conductor of the BBC Revue Orchestra, a post he held until 1960 when he moved across to television as Head of Music for BBC TV Light Entertainment. During the next eight years he was responsible for the *Val Doonican Show*, *Billy Cotton Band Show*, *Michael Bentine Show*, Peter Cooke and Dudley Moore's *Not Only But Also*, the *Mikado* and *Kiss Me Kate*. Another move came in 1968 when he switched sides and joined London Weekend Television as Head of Music. His credits there over the next nine years included the David Frost series, *Black Beauty*, *Upstairs, Downstairs* and in 1976, *Love for Lydia*, the theme of which brought him a nomination for an Ivor Novello Award. Has written many other television themes, including the *Agatha Christie Hour*, 1982 and *Reilly Ace of Spies*, 1984, which not only got into the Top 20, but also was nominated for a BAFTA Award and won the Television and Radio Industries Council Celebrity Award for Best Television Theme Music of the Year.

Since leaving London Weekend Television in 1977 has worked freelance, dividing his time equally between films and television. His film credits as Musical Director include *The Greek Tycoon*; *Heat and Dust*; *Chariots of Fire*; *Time Bandits*; *Mon oncle D'Amerique*; *La Dentelliere*. He made his acting debut in *Electric Dreams*, in 1984 playing the part of a conductor who has to deal sharply with a lady cellist! He still finds time to return to the theatre occasionally, conducting the opening performances of *Cats* in 1981 and *Song and Dance* in 1982. 'I did six weeks on each of them, which was long enough. I believe in handing over to younger and prettier people. Just before my mother died, she said to me, 'All this dashing around working in television, films and the

theatre is putting lines on your face, why don't you settle down and get a nice regular job like your two brothers.' In 1977 he was awarded the MBE for services to music. It was at the investiture at Buckingham Palace, while talking to the Queen with the orchestra playing in the background, as it does on these occasions, that he said in passing, 'By the way there's an F sharp missing behind me Ma'am', as a violinist played a wrong note. 'I don't know how I didn't finish up in the Tower!'

In July 1983 he was invited to conduct the Los Angeles Philharmonic Orchestra in two concerts at the Hollywood Bowl which resulted in him being asked to conduct a further four concerts in July 1984. He frequently conducts the London Symphony, Royal Philharmonic and London Concert Orchestras at the Royal Festival Hall and the Barbican Centre in London.

■ Highspot of career: 'Conducting the Los Angeles Philharmonic at the Hollywood Bowl, and the opening night of *Cats*.' ■ A moment to remember: 'When I was conducting the orchestra for *Semprini Serenade*, the programmes were broadcast on the BBC's Transcription Service, consequently my mother was able to hear them in South Africa. After hearing the programme for the first time, she wrote to me saying, 'Your piano playing has improved dear, but why do you announce everything with an Italian accent?' ■ Likes looking for alpine plants in the Rockies. ■ Dislikes indifferent food and wine. 'When I'm hungry I go to the High Street in Calais for lunch; it happens about six times a year!' ■ Married to Lorna, has two daughters, one son and one granddaughter and lives in Surrey.

STEVE RACE
'My Music led to other things . . .'
BORN: 1st April 1921 in Lincoln. Father a solicitor. **EDUCATED:** Lincoln School. Royal Academy of Music. **FIRST JOB:** Pianist with Harry Leader's Band. He joined the RAF in 1941, the year he made his first broadcast. After being demobbed in 1946, worked as a freelance pianist/composer/arranger playing with such bands as Lew Stone and Cyril Stapleton and arranging for Ted Heath and Judy Garland. 1955–60 was Light Music Adviser to Associated Rediffusion during which time he was MD for many television series including the Tony Hancock and Peter Sellers shows.

Acknowledged as one of Britain's leading jazz authorities, he wrote a weekly page for the *Melody Maker* for 12 years and has contributed to most jazz magazines of note. A well respected musician, Steve has used his musical talent to provide himself with an extremely lucrative alternative string to his bow as Chairman and the compiler of questions of the very popular panel game *My Music* which Radio 4 pioneered and television has borrowed. This in turn led to him appearing on such programmes as *Any Questions* and *Many a Slip*. He also presents *Musician at Large* for the World Service. In 1983 wrote and presented the Radio 3 series *Jazz in Perspective* which was repeated in 1984.

'Piano playing was always a means to an end for me. I'm not in love with the piano, I'm in love with music. When one left the Royal Academy of Music one had to be a genius to get anywhere on the concert platform and I was never a genius in the performing sense. To hear music is to play it, to play it is to be able to write it down.' His numerous compositions include *Nicola*, which won the Ivor Novello Award in 1962;

Faraway Music; The Pied Piper: the incidental music for BBC Television's *Richard III*; *Cyrano do Bergerac* and *Twelfth Night*. Has also written many commercial jingles which brought him the Venice Award in 1962 and the Cannes Award in 1963. Film scores include *Calling Paul Temple; Three Roads to Rome; Against the Tide; Land of Three Rivers*. His autobiography, *Musician at Large* was published in 1979. He is also the author of *My Music* 1979; *Dear Music Lover* 1981, Steve Race's *Music Quiz* 1983.

■ A moment to remember: 'I was playing the Warsaw Concerto in a Birmingham radio studio when the leg fell off the grand piano. At the moment the keyboard descended firmly on to my right knee, I happened to have the sustaining pedal down. It stayed down until the end of the piece, when the studio manager thrust a chair under the treble end of the piano, and about time too. Two days later, I had a letter from a listener, which read: "Dear Mr Race I was sorry to note that you were guilty of over-pedalling. It is all the more to be regretted in an Academy-trained musician such as yourself, and sets a poor example to impressive students." (So did my language after reading the letter).' ■ Likes antiquarian pursuits, looking at paintings, the open air. ■ Dislikes cigarette smokers, cinemagoing and chatty taxi drivers. ■ Married to former BBC producer Lonny Mather, has one daughter, Nicola, and lives in Buckinghamshire.

LES REED
'Top of the Pops? . . . it's not unusual.'
BORN: 24th July 1935 in Woking, Surrey. Father a builder and part-time harmonica player who ran a semi-pro troupe called The Westfield Kids. **EDUCATED:** Various schools in Woking area. Royal College of Music which he left to join the Army. Piano lessons from the age of six, when his father gave him an accordion. He was then booked into the same clubs and halls as the troupe. His father also fixed for him to entertain the passengers on coach outings and as this entailed Les playing his accordion standing with his back to the driver, it's

hardly surprising that the coach always had to make an unscheduled stop to enable its entertainer to be sick! 'It put me off buses and coaches for life. I still can't ride in them even today!' On the way home from the coach outings, there would be the invariable stop at the pub and Les would find himself entertaining a considerably increased audience outside who were quite happy to throw some coins into his waiting hat. 'I used to pick up eight or nine pounds on a Sunday and that was big money in those days.' This revenue enabled his father to buy him his next musical instrument, a vibraphone. **FIRST JOB:** National Service in the Royal East Kent Regiment 1954–56. In the Malta Platoon, he was sent to Germany where Bandmaster Trevor Sharpe wanted him to play piano in the Regiment's dance band, but to do this, he had to play an instrument in the Military band, so Trevor Sharpe taught him to play clarinet. 'There I was, in my second year, in the band, probably the only National Service man ever to achieve that honour, as you had to sign on for three years to become a bandsman.' Also in the band at that time was tenorman Tony Coe, who many years later would make an album with Les and Robert Farnon, *Pop Makes Progress*.

Following National Service he became a session pianist and in 1958 joined the John Barry Seven. For the next three years he combined one night stands with daytime sessions in the recording studios as pianist and arranger for such stars as Adam Faith (Faith's first five hits had the magic Reed touch) and was starting to gain quite a reputation. As pianist/MD/ arranger, he hadn't thought seriously about song writing until, on an Adam Faith recording session, they were short of a song for the 'B' side. Les dashed off a little something and set himself on a road that to date has been paved with 93 Gold Discs, 8 Ivor Novello Awards, the 1982 British Academy Gold Badge of Merit and numerous other awards. It would be impossible in the amount of space available to list all his songs, but from 1964 with Applejack's recording of *Tell Me*

When, the charts nearly always included a Les Reed song. (Early in 1965 I interviewed Les, on a radio show, about a song of his that had just been recorded by Tom Jones. I remember introducing it as 'a possible hit of 1965'. I should have omitted the word 'possible'. The title of the song was *It's Not Unusual*!) Written with Gordon Mills, *It's Not Unusual* put Messrs Reed, Mills and Jones at the top of the proverbial tree. Shortly afterwards, Les teamed up with lyricist Barry Mason and in just one wet Sunday afternoon they penned five songs, including *The Last Waltz*, not a bad way to spend a rainy day. It was to be an extremely successful and lucrative partnership.

Apart from songwriting over the years, he records with his own orchestra; has conducted both Symphony and Light Orchestras all over the world; has won so many prizes at International song festivals, that in 1979 he was made Ambassador to the International Federation of Festivals Organisation. 1984 saw him writing four songs for, and producing, a new Tom Jones album; 12 new songs for the Lance Ellington/Janie Johnson album; a new single for the African group Umbumbulu, and working on the score for a new musical. He also finds time to play an active role on the board of the new ILR station County Sound, in Guildford, and is a Director of his daughter's music publishing company, Rebecca Music Ltd.

■ Highspot of career: 'I haven't reached it yet! If Richard Rogers kept going until he was 80, I reckon I've got another 30 odd years in which to prove myself! Up until now, I suppose the highspots have been my 61 major hits.' ■ A moment to remember: 'The day Barry Mason walked into a public loo and standing beside him was a chap whistling *The Last Waltz*. Barry couldn't resist saying, "I wrote that." "No you didn't", replied the man, "Les Reed did". "But I wrote the lyric", said Barry. "I'm not whistling the bloody lyric," came the reply!' ■ Likes 'My family and animals, we have two dogs, two cats, three horses and a budgie.' ■ Dislikes riding in coaches and buses. ■ Married to June, has one daughter, Donna, and lives in Surrey.

DON RENDELL

'Playing with the Kenton band was a real eye opener...'
BORN: 4th March 1926 in Plymouth, Devon. Father a musical director of D'Oyly Carte Opera Company and organist and choirmaster. **EDUCATED:** City of London School, which during the war was evacuated to Marlborough College. Had piano lessons from an early age but wasn't interested as all he wanted to be was a professional footballer. But at Marlborough College he saw and heard his first saxophone: 'it was like a switch going on in my head. I had to have one, so I asked my Dad and he bought me one, but a few months later he died, so he never knew that I was going to become a professional saxophonist.' **FIRST JOB:** Junior clerk in Barclays Bank for three months. By the time he left school he was playing tenor in a semi-pro band along with Stan Watson, Laurie Morgan and Denny Termer, whose uncle had a stage band that worked the variety theatres. He offered them a job, and at 16 Don turned professional.

After a spell in variety, he went on USO tours, entertaining the American troops in the UK. 'Jimmy Cagney appeared on one of the shows we did.' In 1946 joined Duncan White, the resident band at the Astoria, Charing Cross Road, with whom he made his first broadcast. He also played with the George

Evans 10 sax line-up and the Oscar Rabin Band. After appearing at Club Eleven, the first ever British Jazz club where Ronnie Scott and Johnny Dankworth both had bands, he joined the John Dankworth Seven and spent three years with them touring the UK and Europe. Formed his own band for the first time in 1953, it was to be the first of many which included the baritone of Ronnie Ross. But two years later he ran out of luck when a backer left him in the lurch with bills he couldn't pay, so both he and Ronnie joined the Tony Crombie Band. 'We went to Paris with Tony and stayed over for a recording session with Belgian tenorman Bobby Jasper and the guitarist on that session was Sacha Distel!' He joined Ted Heath for nine months in the mid 50s and left just before the band took off for the States in the first of the two way exchanges arranged by the Musicians Union. Travelling from West to East was Stan Kenton and within two weeks of leaving the Heath band Don had joined Kenton for a three month European tour.

1957 found him fronting and recording with his own band once again. This time the line-up included Phil Seaman on drums and Kenny Wheeler on trumpet. 'When you listen to the records we made, you realize how far ahead of his time Kenny Wheeler was.' The band spent a fair amount of time on the road, one tour being with the Gerry Mulligan/Bob Brookmeyer Quartet. In 1959 he played with Woody Herman's Anglo American Herd and the following year expanded his own band to record for an American label producing the album, *Roarin'* which attracted good reviews. Around this time he was guest presenter of BBC Radio's *Jazz Club* for six weeks. From 1964, his Quintet, co-led by Ian Carr, topped the *Melody Maker* poll three years in succession, and in 1968 appeared at the Antibes Jazz Festival. Throughout the 70s fronted his own small groups playing at jazz clubs and festivals throughout Europe. In 1983 his Quartet appeared at the Newcastle Jazz Festival and has since recorded four albums on the Spotlight label.

■ Highspot of career: 'I'm still getting them today, but looking back, accompanying Billie Holliday at the Flamingo

Club in the mid 50s, has to be one; and the three months I spent with the Stan Kenton Band. The attitude of the American musicians came as a total shock to me, their dedication was a real eye opener and very different to the British bands I had played with.' ■ A point to remember: 'I do quite a lot of teaching and I try to impress upon the youngsters I teach, the spiritual aspect of their music. How working at their instrument will keep them out of national and political squabbles. Music is an international language and music makes us all brothers provided you keep off National Anthems!' ■ Likes studying the Bible. 'My wife and I do a lot of voluntary Bible education work.' ■ Dislikes Radio 1.
■ Married to Joan, has one daughter, Sally, one grandson, Stephen, and lives in London.

HAROLD RICH
'Almost an impromptu performance . . .'
BORN: 24th January 1927, in Wolverhampton. EDUCATED: Wednesbury Boys High School. Royal College of Music, London where he studied piano and organ. FIRST JOB: Music master at a secondary modern school at Old Hill, West Midlands. Made his first broadcast in March 1946, a 15-minute solo spot *At the Piano* from Bristol (he was in the Royal Navy at the time). Has been accompanist to the George Mitchell Choir and the Continental Ballet. Has played with the Palm Court Trio, BBC Midland Light Orchestra 1960–73, the BBC Midland Radio Orchestra with Norrie Paramor 1973–80. In 1961 formed the Harold Rich Quartet, later to become known as the Easy Six, making numerous broadcasts. Also plays piano for the Stanley Black, Frank Chacksfield and John Gregory Orchestras. Has been MD on television for Tom Jones, Vic Damone and Eartha Kitt and is Musical Adviser to BBC 1's *Pebble Mill at One.*

■ Highspot of career: 'Receiving the Hopkinson Silver medal (1950) and the Hopkinson Gold Medal (1951) from Princess Elizabeth at the Royal College of Music. Also performing for the Queen Mother with the Palm Court Trio at an informal dinner party in Scotland.' ■ A moment to remember: 'Whilst giving a "live" afternoon recital of serious music from Birmingham, I was just about to begin Schubert's Impromptu in A flat (Op 90, No. 4) when I spotted a huge spider making its way across my foot and about to climb up my leg inside the trousers! The first few bars were spent in a vigorous shaking of same while trying to concentrate on the

music!' ■ Likes cats, 'My office walls are covered with pictures of cats and I have two Burmese and a Siamese'. Watching most kinds of sport and trying to play golf. ■ Dislikes cruelty in any form, especially to children and animals. ■ Married to Joyce, has one daughter Tanya and lives in Warwickshire.

GOFF RICHARDS
'Always exciting to work with top class performers . . .'
BORN: 18th August 1944, in St Miniver, Cornwall. Father a builder. EDUCATED: Bodmin Grammar School. Royal College of Music, London. Reading University. Plays piano and trombone. FIRST JOB: Music teacher at Fowey School, Cornwall. Made his first broadcast in 1968 on BBC's *Morning Southwest* from Plymouth. Formed his own band in 1970 and played at the Sinbad Hotel, Malindi, Kenya and the Beach Hotel, Seychelles. Now fronts a 23-piece line-up, the Goff Richards Orchestra and is heard on many of Radio 2's music programmes.

■ Highspot of career: 'Too many to pick one out. It's always exciting to work with top class performers.' ■ A moment to remember: 'In helping to co-ordinate a "live" Radio 1 broadcast from the Salford College of Technology, it was my task to select suitable students to be interviewed by the DJ Kid Jensen. The principal of the College was naturally keen that the students should give a good account of themselves. The programme was going rather well and the moment for the first interview arrived. After answering several of Kid's questions with great clarity and distinction, the student was finally asked if he wished to send a message to any of his friends. I waited with apprehension. "Yes" said the student, his face beginning to beam at the thought of the whole nation waiting in anticipation. "I'd like to say hello to Nigel Thomas and hope his piles clear up soon." The audience broke into uproar, Kid Jensen for once was speechless and I hastened to make a discreet exit!' ■ Likes cricket, golf, crosswords, collecting wines and travel. ■ Dislikes bad manners. ■ Married to Sue, has two sons, Matthew and Simon, and lives in Cheshire.

NEIL RICHARDSON
'A way with strings . . .'
BORN: 5th February 1930, in Stourport-on-Severn, Worcestershire. Father a clergyman. EDUCATED: Abberley Hall. Westminster Abbey Choir School. Lancing College. Royal

College of Music, London. Plays the piano, clarinet and saxophone. **FIRST JOB:** Playing with the Chris Curtis Band at the Trocadero Restaurant, London. During National Service played with the RAF Band, Cranwell. Worked as a staff arranger for Chappells, Peter Maurice and Keith Prowse music publishing companies. Is noted for his fine string writing. Is a regular conductor of the strings of the BBC Radio Orchestra, but also fronts his own line-up of strings, brass and singers and has been heard on just about every music programme on the Ligh Programme and Radio 2 since his first broadcast in 1957. His arrangements are played by all the BBC orchestras.

■ Highspot of career: 'When I was Musical Director for the Thames TV Telethon in 1980, also doing a radio series with Neil Diamond, and being invited to conduct the Baltimore Symphony Orchestra in April 1985.   ■ A moment to remember: 'Due to a mix-up of studios, we arrived very late for a morning *Music While You Work* being broadcast "live" from the Camden Theatre. The piano was facing down the raked stage. Several minutes into the broadcast, I realized that the piano was slowly rolling down the stage. Wild gestures to the "box" only elicited smiles and "thumbs up" signs from the producer for far, far too long and I was fascinated by watching the microphone rapidly approaching the frame of the piano! The situation was finally saved by three burly studio attendants holding on!'   ■ Likes DIY. ■ Dislikes pomposity and bigotry.   ■ Married to Regine Launay, has three children and lives in Hertfordshire.

RONNIE ROSS
'Discovered all over again . . .'
BORN: 2nd October 1933 in Calcutta, India. Father a contractual engineer in paper mills. **EDUCATED:** St Paul's, Darjeeling (The highest school in the world!). Perse School, Cambridge. Learnt the piano parrot-fashion at an early age; I just memorized everything and then went in for the exams.' Took clarinet lessons at Perse School and private alto sax lessons. 'No one was allowed to learn to play the saxophone

at public schools in those days!' **FIRST JOB:** Junior office job, training to be an architect. In 1951 he signed on for five years with the Grenadier Guards Band. 'TV producer Terry Henebery who was in the Grenadiers, got me interested in the Guards. What he didn't tell me about was the training school at Caterham. It nearly killed me!' He bought himself out after three years. While with the Guards he had switched to playing tenor and his first break came when he appeared with Don Rendell (qv) on *Tele Club* with Steve Race. It was a showcase for young musicians who were invited to play with anyone they chose, and Ronnie chose Don. It was the start of a working partnership that has lasted to this day. Shortly afterwards he joined the Don Rendell Sextet, and as they needed a baritone, at Don's suggestion he went out and bought one. 'That baritone was what I had been looking for all my life.'

The mid 50s, found him, along with Don Rendell, joining Tony Crombie's Band. In 1958, after touring with the MJQ, he was invited to join them for a recording session in Stuttgart to make an album called *European Windows* with the Stuttgart Symphony Orchestra, on which he was the featured soloist. When it was released in the States, it won the American Jazz Artists Award for Downbeat and Ronnie was voted the New Star Award in the Downbeat Poll for 1959. His first visit to the USA had been the previous year when he played with the International Youth Band at the Newport Jazz Festival. His next was with the band he formed with drummer Alan Ganley called The Jazzmakers. They did a coast to coast tour of America in the early 60s, making an album while they were there; *Swinging Sound of the Jazzmakers*. Back home they were named Top Jazz Band in the *Melody Maker* poll. Ronnie as a soloist topped ten *Melody Maker* polls throughout the 50s and 60s. He was also nominated on three occasions in the *Playboy* Jazz poll. The 60s found him doing an increasing amount of session work including a UK concert tour with Billy Holliday and a three-week tour with Woody Herman's Anglo American Herd. He played with Frederick Gulda on the Continent with such famous names as Tubby Hayes, J.J. Johnson and Art Farmer. 'He was a good man to work for, because he thought musicians should travel First Class everywhere!'

He also played with the bands of Maynard Ferguson, Johnny Dankworth, Dizzy Gillespie and Ted Heath, the last for recording sessions when two baritones were needed. 'Ted asked me to join the band while I was with the Jazzmakers. I'm probably the only person ever to have turned him down.' He appeared with Frank Sinatra at the special Year of the Child concert held in Cairo in the late 70s when the promoter took off with the entire proceeds and was subsequently hunted by the Mafia and the Egyptian police without ever being found. Three other European concert tours with Sinatra followed. Fronts his own Quintet and Sextet making regular broadcasts on *Jazz Club* and *Night Owls*; and although the baritone has remained his favourite instrument, he's equally happy playing alto. 'These days you accept anything and if I can't play it, I'll learn it!'

■ Highspot of career: 'There have been so many, but over the last three of four years I seem to have been discovered all over again. I played the alto solos for the Agatha Christie film *The Mirror Crack'd* in 1980 and in 1984 I recorded all the alto solos for the new television series, *Marlow*. ■ A moment to remember: 'Some years ago I did the baritone solo on Lou Reed's hit record, *Walk on The Wild Side*. It became something of a classic solo, I can't think why, as it was out of tune for one thing! Recently I was working on a television show with Wayne Sleep who was using the same tune for one of his routines. During rehearsal the director came over the me and said: "Do you think you can make that a bit more like it is on the record?" "I am the record" was my reply!' ■ Likes sunshine and ice cream. ■ Dislikes inefficiency. ■ Married to Sue, has two sons and one daughter by a previous marriage and lives in London. (His two sons are with the pop group. Immaculate Fools.)

RONNIE SCOTT
'One cannot imagine there being no Ronnie Scott's . . .'
BORN: 28th January 1927 in London. Father professional saxophonist, Jock Scott. EDUCATED: Benthall Road Elementary; Central Foundation School in the City; Edgware School;

Hendon Technical College. He always wanted to be an aeronautical engineer and a rear gunner, but after dabbling with an old soprano sax and an old cornet, his step-father bought him a tenor when he was 15. 'I took lessons from Jack Lewis, who was the father of Harry Lewis, who married Vera Lynn.' **FIRST JOB:** Selling records for Keith Prowse. He also worked in a musical instrument shop in London's West End. His first professional job as a musician came when he was 16 and had only been playing for 18 months. It was for two weeks at the Jamboree Club in Wardour Street as a fill-in between one tenor player leaving and the new one arriving. Pointing out that his playing wasn't really up to it, he was assured that all he had to do was look as if he was playing as the band's contract was for six musicians. Whether he played or not, was beside the point! After that it was back to the weddings and the bar mitzvahs, but not for long. Within a year he was on the road with the Johnny Claes Band. In 1946 he joined Ted Heath, who was a stickler for discipline and never accepted any excuses for anyone being late. After a gig in Liverpool, Ronnie decided not to take the night train back to London for the next day's engagement, but the morning plane instead. It snowed, he never made it and got the sack. In 1947, out of work, he and Tony Crombie went to New York to hear some of their jazz idols, and it was in the New York jazz clubs that he first got the glimmering of an idea of opening his own club. Back in the UK, he joined Tito Burns and also played with Ambrose, at the Nightingale in Berkeley Square, before joining what became known as Geraldo's Navy, the band on the *Queen Mary*. (Geraldo did all the booking for the boats.) He did several Atlantic crossings in 1948 which enabled him to hear such players as Miles Davis, Charlie Parker and Dizzy Gillespie during his one-night stop-overs in New York.

A spell with Jack Parnell's new band followed in 1951 in which he found himself playing alongside Pete King, the start of a partnership that was to result in him opening his first club in 1959. But first came the famous nine-piece band with Derek Humble, Benny Green, Pete King, Jimmy Deuchar, Ken Wray, Norman Stenfalt, Lennie Bush and Tony Crombie. 'It was tremendous fun and very satisfying musically. I've never laughed so much in all my life as I did with that band.' The nine-piece was replaced by a sextet which he took to the States on the first of the Anglo-American band exchanges. Back in Britain, he teamed up with Tubby Hayes to form one of the best modern jazz groups this country has produced, the Jazz Couriers. In 1959, the idea that had first occured to him 12 years previously in New York, became a reality when with Pete King, he opened his first club at 39 Gerrard Street. Although visiting American musicians would sometimes 'sit in' during their visit to the club, it wasn't until November 1961, that the first American jazz star was booked for a four-week engagement. Zoot Sims was the first of many 'greats' to play the club and help to give it a well deserved worldwide reputation. But not only is it a showcase for visiting musicians to this country, it's also *the* place to hear the best of British jazz. One cannot imagine there being no Ronnie Scott's. The club moved to new and bigger premises in Frith Street in 1965 where it has retained its intimate atmosphere. What is the secret of its success? Ronnie doesn't really know. 'I never had any idea in the beginning that it would develop like it has. I think we get the big names because they know that the club's run by a musician and they're not working for gangsters, so they'll be well treated. Also I try and create the

sort of atmosphere I like working in, because after all, I spend a lot of time there. We've always tried to keep the prices within reason, and we're still here, but it's for sure, nobody gets rich running a jazz club!'

Two weeks out of every six, he plays with his Quartet in the club, and it's not just his skill as a musician that keeps the customers happy, he's one of the wittiest compères around.

■ Highspot of career: 'I'm still waiting for it, I'm a late developer! The first time I worked with Sarah Vaughan and the visit of Sonny Rollins, Count Basie and Coleman Hawkins to the club. There have been some really great moments.' ■ A moment to remember: 'Pete King and I are law abiding chaps, but there was a time when we were raided by the police. It happened in the middle of Roland Kirk's appearance at the club one night. As well as playing his 23 or so regular instruments, he would hand out penny whistles to the audience and it was while this massed penny whistle choir was in full cry, that about 20 policemen burst in blowing their own whistles. Roland, who is blind, hadn't the remotest idea of what was going on but was obviously very pleased at the augmentation to his penny whistle section. "Tell that man to stop playing", said one policeman. "You tell him", I replied. For a few moments chaos reigned but eventually calm was restored, names and addresses were taken and we were fined for some breach of the licensing laws. After that, we applied for and got a different kind of licence.' ■ Likes Chinese food. 'I was in Hong Kong not long ago and the food was sensational.' ■ Dislikes bores. ■ Lives in London.

BETTY SMITH
'Melody Maker headline . . . Betty Smith cracks U.S. charts . . .'

BORN: 6th July 1933, in Sileby, Nr. Leicester. Father a publican. **EDUCATED:** Stoneygate College, Leicester. Plays piano, tenor saxophone and clarinet. **FIRST JOB:** Singing and playing with Archie's Juvenile Band. Has sung and played with Billy Penrose Quartet, Freddie Randall Band, and fronts her own line-up, The Betty Smith Quintet. Made her first broadcast as a singer at the age of 15 and has made numerous broadcasts over the years with a variety of bands. Did a regular Saturday series featured with the Ted Heath Band and has been featured vocalist and instrumentalist with John Dankworth, Ken Mackintosh and Sid Phillips. Did several American tours with Bill Haley. Programmes include *Saturday Club* as the resident Quintet, *Jazz Club*, *Workers Playtime*, *Mid-day Music Hall*, *Variety Band Box*, and *Radio 2 Ballroom*. As well as playing with her own Quintet she plays in The Best of British Jazz along with Jack Parnell, Kenny Baker, Don Lusher and Tony Lee. Also plays in a band fronted by her husband, bass player Jack Peberdy. Is heard regularly on Radio 2's music programmes.

■ Highspot of career: 'Playing with Bobby Hackett on Dutch Television; and being told by Ted Heath that my record of *Bewitched, Bothered and Bewildered* had made the American charts, the first time an instrumental had made them for years. The headline in the *Melody Maker* that week read . . . "Betty Smith cracks American Charts!"' ■ A moment to remember: 'I was doing a *Workers Playtime* when Bill Gates was the producer and he always liked us to announce our own numbers. So after the first song, I say "Thank you very

Stapleton, Johnny Howard and the Nelson's Column Big Band. Is a freelance session musician who does a lot of writing and arranging especially for the BBC Radio Orchestra/Radio Big Band, Also fronts his own group Seminar which is heard regularly on Radio 2's music programmes.

■ Most exciting moment of career: 'Recording the *Bones Galore* album in 1969. ■ Likes playing football and squash. ■ Dislikes bad pop groups (of which there are many). ■ Married to Eileen, has two children and lives in Kent.

much ladies and gentlemen and now I'd like to play for you . . ." My mind went a complete blank – I tried again – "Now I'm going to play . . ." looking around frantically for help from some quarter. Bill Gates rushed on and said "I think she wants to play *Over the Rainbow*. On every broadcast after that I always wrote the titles of my songs on my hand in biro!' ■ Likes drinking. ■ Dislikes smoking. ■ Married to Jack Peberdy and lives in London.

PETE SMITH
'A lot of writing . . .!'
BORN: 28th July 1937, in London. Father an artist/designer. **EDUCATED:** Westminster City School. Royal College of Music, London. Plays trombone and piano. **FIRST JOB:** Trombonist with the Denny Boyce Orchestra at the Lyceum in 1958, Made his first broadcast in December 1958 on *Music While You Work*. Has played with Bill Collins, Johnnie Gray, Cyril

KATHY STOBART
'I couldn't face the big deal, big sell attitudes in the States . . .'
BORN: 1st April 1925 in South Shields, Co. Durham. Father a policeman. Mother was one of 10 children who all became musicians. 'She was playing piano for dances and in pit orchestras when she was 12. She could read anything and was a phenomenal accompanist.' **EDUCATED:** Westoe Central School, South Shields. Attended dancing class at four, started piano lessons at seven and at nine was doing a song and dance act in a concert party playing at Seamen's Missions,

TOC H and miner's social clubs. Her mother stopped teaching her the piano because she was beginning to play by ear and she didn't approve, so her two brothers who were both classical clarinettists, suggested she take up the alto saxophone, which she did at 12. **FIRST JOB:** In a printing works for three months. Having spotted an advert saying that Don Rico and his Ladies Swing Band were holding auditions for a tenor player in Sunderland, she borrowed her brother's tenor and took the bus to Sunderland. 'I had no experience and my playing must have sounded horrible, but when I did a tap dance and my impersonation of Gracie Fields, that did it. I was put on a month's trial at 8*s.* 6*d.* a week. 'The month became a year and the salary £2 10*s.* a week. Following that she spent a year at the Oxford Galleries in Newcastle with the Peter Fielding Band, with whom she made her first broadcast. 'That's where I learnt my trade. Eleven performances a week plus a Sunday concert'. During the year in Newcastle she took lessons on tenor from Keith Bird of the Squadronaires who in November 1942 got her a job in London at the Palladium Ballroom, Ealing. He also took her to the Jamboree Club in the West End where she sat in one night with the Denis Rose Band. Two days later she was offered a job with the band.

In April 1943 joined Art Thompson at the Embassy Club where she spent the next two years and married her boss. Made her American debut in 1947 playing at Eddie Condon's Club in New York. 'I had an offer to stay in the States but I just couldn't face the big deal, big sell attitude out there, it frightened me to death, so I came home.'

With the break up of her marriage to Art Farmer, she formed her own line-up which financially was a failure so she joined Vic Lewis and got married again, to Bert Courtley. Worked as a freelance session musician while bringing up a family and in 1969 joined Humphrey Lyttelton. Eight years later was fronting her own line-up once again and has been doing so ever since. The Kathy Stobart Quintet made several trips to America playing at the Village Gate in the Salute to Women Festival in New York; with Zoot Sims at the Village Vanguard and with Marion McPartland at the Carlisle Rooms. The Quintet has played all the major European jazz festivals including two appearances at the Nice Jazz Festival. Recent record releases include *Saxploitation* and *Arbeia*.

■ Highspot of career: 'My entire playing life has been a series of peaks.' ■ A moment to remember: 'When I was playing at the Embassy Club, it was nothing unusual to see stars like Bob Hope, Bing Crosby, Frances Langford or Clark Gable among the customers. One of our regulars was Glen Miller who we got to know quite well. I think he used to enjoy listening to us as we played some jazz as well as the pops. He'd nearly always come in with a friend, I think he was his Colonel and they would come around and chat to us after we finished playing. On this particular night, Glen came in on his own and he had a fair bit to drink. He wasn't drunk but Art thought he ought to get him a taxi at the end of the evening. We found out where he was staying, put him into the taxi and said goodbye. The next morning, against everyone's advice, he got into that small plane to cross the Channel and never made it. So I guess we were about the last civilians to see him alive.' ■ Likes sewing and dressmaking, painting and travelling. ■ Dislikes . . . 'I don't think I've got any!' ■ Has three sons, one grandson and lives in London.

JOHN SURMAN
'I'm essentially not a commercial musician . . .'
BORN: 30th August 1944 in Tavistock, Devon. Father worked for GPO Telecommunications. **EDUCATED:** Ford Primary School and Devonport High School, Plymouth. London College of Music. London University. (Music Teaching Diploma).
He sang in the church choir while at school and at 15 learnt to play the clarinet. Two years later he switched to play baritone saxophone. He studied at the London College of Music 1962–65 along with Mike Westbrook, whose band he later played with. Also played with Alexis Korner in the early 60's. In 1967 he joined Humphrey Lyttelton's Big Band and made his first broadcast with them from the Paris Studio. Over the next couple of years he also played with Ronnie Scott's Band. In 1969 he moved to Belgium, where he joined forces with two American musicians, drummer Stu Martin and bassist Barre Phillips to form The Trio, working extensively throughout Europe and in Japan until the mid 70s, when he became Musical Director of The Carolyn Carlson Dance Theatre at the Paris Opera, a post he held until 1979. Between 1979 and 1982 he played with a group formed by Miroslav Vitous, founder member of Weather Report, which also included pianist John Taylor.

The majority of work in recent years has been in Europe and Scandinavia. 'There's a much more open music scene in those countries. I'm essentially not a commercial musician and we're very commercially based in this country.' As well as baritone, he also plays soprano saxophone and bass clarinet and synthesizers. 'I like working with synthesizers, they can be very interesting when you don't play bubble gum music on them.' From 1968 was named top baritone player by the *Melody Maker* Jazz Poll, every year until the poll was discontinued.

The Spring of 1984 saw him touring the UK with the John Surman Brass Project, a line-up of three trumpets, four trombones and rhythm with John as featured soloist. Has recorded with many of the jazz greats over the years including *Sonatinas* with Stan Tracey in 1978. Joined the German label ECM in 1980 and his first solo album *Upon Reflection* won the Italian Radio Critics Award. In 1982 his album with Jack DeJohnette, *The Amazing Adventures of Simon Simon* was named European Record of the Year and also won the *Jazz Forum* Readers Poll. Another recent album, *Such Winters of Memory* found him duetting vocally with singer Karin Krog, saying: 'I think my time spent in the church choir as a lad has given me some understanding of the delights and difficulties that are part and parcel of the art of singing.'

■ Highspot of career: Working with the Gil Evans Big Band at the Royal Festival Hall in the summer of 1983. ■ A moment to remember: 'On a recent recording session, they decided at the last minute that some tubular bells were needed and I should play them. They were so late arriving in the studio, that there was no time to hang them properly, which meant that when I tried to play them, they started to swing madly from side to side. So I had to hold on to the bells with one hand and play them with the other and it was then that my trousers started to fall down. There was nothing I could do about it and by the end of the piece, they were around my ankles. When I looked towards the control room, there was no one to be seen. They were all doubled up on the floor laughing.' ■ Likes living in the country and good red wine. ■ Dislikes pompous people. ■ Has one son and lives in Kent.

IAIN SUTHERLAND
'Conducting the first public concert at the Barbican . . .'
BORN: 1936 in Glasgow. Studied violin at the Royal Scottish Academy of Music, gaining his Performer's Diploma. During National Service he was Leader of the Grenadier Guards Orchestra. He then became an orchestral and session player with the major London Orchestras. He made his first broadcast with his own orchestra on *Morning Melody* in 1964. In 1966 was appointed conductor of the BBC Scottish Radio Orchestra. Moved to London as a freelance conductor in 1972 and regularly conducts the BBC Concert Orchestra. Has made many appearances at the Royal Festival Hall in the BBC International Festival of Light Music and also conducted the BBC's 60th Anniversary Concert there. Conducted the BBC Concert Orchestra in the first public concert at the new Barbican Centre. Is heard regularly on such Radio 2 programmes as *Friday Night is Music Night* and *Melodies for You*, and as a guest conductor on Radio 3. He is Vice President of the Television and Radio Industries Club; a Councillor of the British Academy of Songwriters, Composers and Authors; Patron of the Young Persons Concert Foundation and a member of the BBC Central Music Advisory Committee.

■ Highspot of career: 'Conducting the BBC Concert Orchestra at the first public concert at the Barbican Centre;

and making my debut with the Philharmonia Orchestra at the Royal Festival Hall.' ■ A moment to remember: 'While conducting the BBC Northern Ireland Orchestra during the early 70s, a freelance guitarist was booked for the afternoon recording session. Although his wife was expecting him home for supper, Billy and I went for a quick drink in the BBC Club. One drink led to another and we were the last to leave. Billy decided he would walk the 15 minutes or so to his home and by way of a peace offering to his wife, bought a large bottle of vodka to take with him, I didn't hear about his hilarious if frightening trip until some time later. After leaving the club, guitar case clutched in one hand and the vodka in a brown paper bag in the other, he had hardly gone a hundred yards through Belfast's dark curfewed streets, before he found himself spreadeagled against a wall, in a blaze of light, stuttering out his explanation of what was in the brown paper bag to the security forces sergeant. Being of a generous disposition Billy was soon handing around his peace offering to the appreciative Tommies, who having warned him to waste no time in getting home, disappeared into the darkness. The mere idea of such a thing as a field telephone never crossed his mind until he had been stopped, questioned and joined in a kerbside toast no fewer than three times, when even his befuddled brain registered the fact that the patrols seemed a bit heavy that night. As might be expected, when he explained to his wife about the visiting conductor and how he'd been stopped three times by the army, the bottle of vodka was produced from its bag — empty!' ■ Likes history, current affairs, sport (golf, soccer and rugby). ■ Dislikes trendy philistines. ■ Married to Barbara and lives in Hertfordshire.

RAY SWINFIELD
'An Australian import who plays the best jazz flute around . . .'
BORN: 14th December 1939, in Sydney, Australia. Father a garage forecourt attendant. EDUCATED: Mortlake Primary School. Homebush Boys High School, Sydney. Started on fife

at school and played in the Boys Club Fife and Drum Band. Studied theory of music at Sydney Conservatorium of Music and harmony with Australian composer Ray Hanson. Had private clarinet and saxophone lessons. Plays flutes, clarinet and alto and soprano saxophones. **FIRST JOB:** Playing with a trio for weddings and parties. Made his first broadcast for ABC in Sydney in 1960 on the *Spike Milligan Show*. His first broadcast in the UK was in 1964 when he played with the Johnnie Spence Band on the *Tommy Steele Show*. Has played with Nelson Riddle, Lalo Schifrin, Henry Mancini, Michel Le Grand, Count Basie, David Rose, Quincy Jones, Burt Bacharach, Jack Parnell, Don Sebesky, Duncan Lamont, Ted Heath, the London Symphony Orchestra and the Royal Philharmonic Orchestra. With his own group, Ray Swinfield's Argenta Ora, he is heard regularly on such programmes as *Sounds of Jazz*, and *Night Owls*. Ray's own composition *The Sydney Suite* was broadcast on *Sounds of Jazz* and is included on a highly acclaimed album by the group called The Winged Cliff. They have made two LP's, the first, *Rain Curtain* was released in 1981.

■ Highspot of career: 'Tomorrow!' ■ A moment to remember: 'On the *Spike Milligan Show*, which was my first broadcast in Sydney, Spike wasn't there when we were due to start rehearsing. He was discovered much later asleep under a loose carpet in a room adjacent to the studio. People had been walking through, but no notice had been taken of the lump under the carpet.' ■ Likes music, drinking and girls (Ret.). ■ Dislikes vacuum cleaners and people who speak while eating apples. ■ Married to Rosemarie (Head of Make-up at RADA), has one daughter, Caroline, and lives in Surrey.

JOHN TAYLOR
'An unscheduled two hour tour of Rome . . .'
BORN: 25th September 1942 in Manchester. Father a post office worker. **EDUCATED:** Hastings Grammar School. Started playing piano by ear from the age of three. 'I used to try and copy my elder sister who was a classical pianist and my

father also gave me a few hints as he taught himself to play piano.' At 15 became very interested in jazz, listening to Oscar Peterson, Bill Evans and Denny Zeitlin records. **FIRST JOB:** Civil Servant, but was playing the usual evening gigs around Hastings. His job with the Civil Service took him to London and during the three years before he turned professional he met other jazz musicians such as Tommy Whittle, Terry Smith, John Surman and Cleo Laine and John Dankworth. He made his first broadcast with Tommy Whittle in 1968 and in 1970 joined Cleo Laine and John Dankworth as their accompanist for the next two years.
In 1972 formed a sextet along with Kenny Wheeler, Chris Pyne, Stan Saltzman, Chris Laurence and Tony Levin. 1977 found him resident at Ronnie Scott's before forming another group, Azimuth, with Kenny Wheeler and vocalist Norma Winstone, (who's also his wife). They made their first record in 1977 and since then have made many tours of Europe where they have established quite a reputation on the jazz circuit. They made their first tour of Canada in 1980.

■ Highspot of career: 'Making a record in New York in May 1983 with Kenny Wheeler, American drummer Jack DeJohnette, American tenorman Michael Brecker and bassist Dave Holland. I first met Dave in 1966 when we used to room together and we had never worked together until that recording session in New York, seventeen years later!' ■ A moment to remember: 'What turned out to be a disastrous gig in the South of Italy with Ronnie Scott. The band took two taxis to Rome railway station in order to catch a train south, on what was something like a nine hour journey. We were all at one end of the station, which is enormous, while, unbeknown to us Ron Mathewson with all the luggage including the drum kit was at the other. With time getting short, we got off the train in order to search the station, no Ron. By this time, the train was due to depart and of course we missed it. So Ronnie Scott and I booked a flight and with time to spare had two hours in which to see Rome, which we did after a fashion! We got to our destination in time to meet the train, but still no Ron. So we had to borrow a drum kit, the piano was out of tune and we only had half a band. Ron eventually turned up at 3am with baggage, having missed the train and us. What a night!' ■ Likes good pianos and good Indian curries. ■ Dislikes bad pianos, motor cars and sometimes television. ■ Married to Norma Winstone (qv), has two sons and lives in London.

BARBARA THOMPSON
'In Europe she's known as Lady Saxophone . . .'
BORN: 27th July in Oxford. Father Chief Registrar of the Court of Appeal (Criminal Division). **EDUCATED:** Queen's College, Harley Street, London. Royal College of Music where she studied clarinet, piano, flute and composition. Took up the alto saxophone while still at the RCM, but although she joined the New Jazz Orchestra led by Neil Ardley, was well into her 20's before she started to take jazz seriously. Now plays all the saxes. **FIRST JOB:** Playing in the all girl band on stage in the musical *Cabaret* at the Palace Theatre in 1968. 'We had to wear high heeled shoes which I always replaced with plimsolls as soon as I came off stage. One night I forgot to change back so there I was in my flat, white plimsolls and the rest of the cast including Judi Dench doubled up. I got the sack after a year as I put Kathy Stobart in as a 'dep',

saying I was ill, but in fact I was playing at a jazz concert and they found out.'

Played with several pick up groups at the start of her jazz career. 'I believed in starting at the top, so my first regular group were the Tubby Hayes rhythm section. I don't know how they put up with me.' In 1978, with husband Jon Hiseman on drums, Bill Worral on keyboards, Dave Ball on bass guitar and Rod Dorothy on violin, formed Paraphernalia to play her kind of music, which she describes as contemporary music. 'I believe in playing one's instrument authentically and I use my classical background as part of what I do, but it's certainly not effeminate music. We have our own style which many groups in Europe try to copy. It's often very difficult for us in Britain because people always want to define our music and label it. We set out to entertain an audience and after two and a half hours on stage, we usually have to do two or three encores; in Hamburg we did five!' Their constant round of concert engagements take them all over Scandinavia, Europe and the UK.

A talented composer, Barbara writes all the music performed by Paraphernalia on both the concert platform and record. Her compositions include three major works for 20 piece jazz orchestra recorded by the BBC; a suite, *In Search of Serendib*, commissioned by the Arts Council and performed at the 1982 Bracknell Festival; music for numerous documentary and feature films including *The Challenge*, the film of the America's Cup Yacht Race. She has also written the music for a Thames Television School's Drama series and the theme for Capital Radio's main news programme.

The featured soloist in two of Andrew Lloyd Webber's television Specials, she also played for the opening performances of his hit musical *Cats* and is on the original cast album. With Paraphernalia also collaborated with Andrew Lloyd Webber on his album *Variations*. She has recorded with many different line-ups over the years, but Paraphernalia have released five albums including *Pure Fantasy*, recorded digitally in their own studio in 1984.

In 1979, just a couple of years before they built a recording studio as an extension to their house and started their own record company, Barbara, Jon and their two children were featured on a BBC Television documentary *Jazz, Rock and Marriage*. For the Hisemans, they seem to mix remarkably well.

■ Highspot of career: 'I'm still working towards it. It's one thing to be recognized in one's own field, but I'm looking forward to something broader than that.'　■ A moment to remember: 'During a Festival tour of Europe with the United Jazz and Rock Ensemble, we had a Saturday off in the middle which we thought we might spend relaxing in the South of France. But it turned out that Andrew Lloyd Webber, for whom we'd just recorded an album *Variations* had been asked to put on a concert at the Royal Festival Hall and the only night available was this Saturday. Could we make it back to London for the one night? 'Yes' we said, somewhat rashly as things turned out. The night before we were in Gdansk on the Baltic coast and there was a scheduled flight out at 8am the next morning to Warsaw with a connecting flight to Heathrow via Amsterdam. Knowing what connecting flights can be like, we asked the concert agent to fix a taxi to take us to Warsaw immediately the concert was over. We paid him an enormous amount of money but when this car turned up it was a very old Renault which didn't look as if it was going to survive the four hour trip to Warsaw. It didn't. It broke down half way and there we were at 2.30am in the middle of Poland, miles from anywhere. There was only one thing for it, shank's pony. We walked to the nearest town, got another taxi and arrived in Warsaw at 5.30am. When we got to the airport at 7.30, in walked the remainder of our tour party from Gdansk who had just flown in, so we would have made the connection easily. We also discovered that the Gdansk driver had only received a quarter of the money we had paid the agent, so it was obviously a big 'con'. But that wasn't the end of the story. We got the plane to Amsterdam, but because of industrial troubles, there were no planes to Heathrow. So now it's 2pm and we can't get out of Amsterdam! We eventually got a plane to take us to Heathrow and we made the Festival Hall by the skin of our teeth. There was a party afterwards followed by four hours sleep and then it was back on the plane to the North Sea Festival. Jon collapsed into bed that afternoon and never woke up. We got him up for that night's concert, but he doesn't remember doing it!'　■ Likes positive people, 'I admire talent.'　■ Dislikes dishonesty and hypocrisy.
■ Married to Jon Hiseman, has one son Marcus, one daughter Anna and lives in Surrey.

EDDIE THOMPSON
'I can't see, what's your excuse . . .'

BORN: 31st May 1925 in London. Father a car worker at Fords.
EDUCATED: Linden Lodge School for the Blind, Battersea. Blind from birth, he learnt to play the piano when he was five years old. **FIRST JOB:** Piano tuner. His first job as a performer was playing with the Home Guard Band at their dances on a Saturday night. His first broadcast, as far as he can remember, was on Jazz Club in the early 50's along with Stan Tracey and Tubby Hayes.

During the 50's he was guest pianist at several of the Ted Heath Sunday concerts at the London Palladium. In 1959 he followed Alan Clare into Soho's Downbeat Club. 'The four years I spent there were the happiest of my life.' Following the residency at the Downbeat, he crossed the Atlantic for a four year stint at the Hickory House on 52nd Street in New

York where he worked opposite Bill Taylor and met up with many of the American jazz greats. 'Marion McPartland and Errol Garner would often drop in and I got to know Duke Ellington very well while I was there.' He also played Birdland, The Five Spot and The Village Gate. In 1972 he returned to the UK. 'I suppose I got homesick in the end. I'm very much an Englishman.'

He spends a fair amount of time touring, playing jazz clubs around the country and appears at such top London venues as Ronnie Scott's, Pizza on the Park and Pizza Express. Most Friday lunchtimes he can be heard along with pianist Mattie Ross Kettners in Romilly Street, W.1.

Ask him if he has won any awards and he will tell you that the first award he ever won was for Ten Pin Bowling in America. 'I'm quite a good bowler!'.

He was the first person to receive the Musician of the Year Award from the BBC Staff Jazz Club.

■ Highspot of career: 'I'll tell you that when I'm dead! Meeting Duke Ellington was probably the most thrilling thing that has happened to me.' ■ A moment to remember: 'In the days before I had a guide dog, I was walking up Regent Street when I bumped into someone who started to become very offensive. I got very angry and was about to hit him with my stick when a passer by shouted: "Don't hit him mate, he's a bleedin' cripple"! There was also the time I got off the train at Waterloo station, this time with my guide dog and the ticket collector said: "Got a ticket for the dog?"; "It's a guide dog, it doesn't need one," I replied. "I don't care if it's an Alsatian, it still needs a ticket" was his reply. I've had three guide dogs and usually they are very good in recording studios, but the second of them Maeda, whom I got in the States and brought her back with me, had a habit of snoring. During one broadcast, the sound engineers couldn't think what the funny noise was until they discovered Maeda, snoring happily away underneath the grand piano. One day I'm going to write a book called, I Can't See, What's Your Excuse!' ■ Likes good food and good humour. ■ Dislikes salads and bull. ■ Married to Mary, has one son by a previous marriage and one grand daughter. 'I don't mind being a grandfather, my only objection is being married to a grandmother!' Lives in Essex.

STAN TRACEY
'It all started with a piano accordion . . .'
BORN: 30th December 1926 in London. EDUCATED: Stanley Street School, Brixton. Graveney School, Tooting. Ensham Central School, Tooting. When his school was evacuated during the war, he left, at the age of 13. Taught himself to play the accordion when he was 12. FIRST JOB: Taking the burr off mine caps in a factory in London. He also operated a printing machine in a printing works and was employed by The Scotsman in Fleet Street, 'tearing bits of paper off the Telex machine. I'll never forget how the Sub-Editor used to reek of Guinness all day!'

At 16 he joined an accordion band with ENSA and, listening to a colleague's boogie woogie records, decided he wanted to be a piano player and play boogie woogie. He was called up into the RAF and, after a year, volunteered for the RAF Gang Show on which he became accompanist on piano with a solo spot on accordion. After being demobbed, he tried forming a double act and when that failed got a job on accordion, playing with a band at the Paramount, Tottenham Court Road in London. 'The leader played several instruments hardly at all and also sang hardly at all; the bass played pizzicato on every first and third beat and the drummer would clap the high hat on every second and fourth beat.' He stuck it for a year but it was during that period that he made contact with several jazz musicians. 'After leaving the Paramount I joined Laurie Morgan who soon realized he had a frustrated jazzer for an accordion player. It was a constant battle and the jazz and the piano won.' He played with the bands of Roy Fox and Basil Kerchin before joining Ted Heath in 1957. From 1960–67 was resident pianist at Ronnie Scott's during which time he worked with almost every visiting American musician from Sonny Rollins to Jimmy Witherspoon, from Ben Webster to Roland Kirk. Also at this time he formed his own quartet and big band. Described by Humphrey Lyttelton as one of the finest jazz composers in the world, his major works are Alice in Jazzland, Under Milkwood, The Bracknell Connection, written for the Bracknell Festival in 1976, Salisbury Suite, for the Salisbury Festival in 1977, Crompton Suite, Expressly Richmond, for the 1983 Richmond Festival sponsored by American Express, Cardiff Chapter for the Cardiff Festival the same year, and Anniversary Suite to celebrate the 10th anniversary of the Newcastle Jazz Festival in 1984. The Poets Suite, composed for his 1984 tour of Northern Ireland was inspired by the work of five Ulster poets. Has undertaken many overseas tours with his own line-ups and played at most of the major jazz festivals around the world. In 1978 his Octet toured with the Gil Evans Orchestra. His recordings over the years with his Trio, Quartet, Sextet and Octet have been numerous and he has also recorded as a duo with Keith Tippett and with

John Surman. His son Clark Tracey now forms part of his regular line-ups on drums. He has topped the *Melody Maker* Poll many times as pianist, composer and arranger and in 1984 was voted Jazz Musician of the Year by *Jazz Journal International*.

■ Highspot of career: 'Working with Sonny Rollins and Roland Kirk. Also there have been certain nights with my own various groups.' ■ A moment to remember: 'When I was playing at a club in Amsterdam, I arrived to find the piano tuner at work. After a few minutes, he finished and I sat down at the piano to discover that everything was fine apart from the upper one and a half octaves which he hadn't tuned at all. He hadn't left the club so I called him over and asked him why he hadn't tuned the whole piano, to which he replied, "Oh I didn't bother with the top bit as I didn't think you'd be playing up there"!' ■ Likes most things. 'The nearest thing I've got to a hobby is taping old Laurel and Hardy films.' ■ Dislikes pomposity. ■ Married to Jackie, has one son, Clark, and one daughter and lives in London.

■ Highspot of career: 'Still waiting.' ■ A moment to remember: 'For a couple of years in the 70s, I ran a band which did occasional broadcasts. As it had ten members and was run by me it was, not unreasonably called the Dick Walter Tentette. Like all such bands, it was made up of freelance studio players and, if we were lucky, some marvellous jazz players like Kenny Wheeler and John Taylor. For years I'd been listening to records by somebody's sextet, somebody else's nonet and so the name of our band seemd self explanatory. It came as a bit of a surprise after a couple of months to receive an enquiry from a tax office addressed to "D.W. Tentette Esq . . ."' ■ Likes playing the saxophone and the Suffolk coast. ■ Married to Anne, has two children and lives in London.

ANDREW LLOYD WEBBER
'Dominating the musical stage on both sides of the Atlantic . . .'
BORN: 1948 in London. Father an organist, was Director of the London College of Music and Professor of Theory and Composition at the Royal College of Music. Mother a piano teacher. **EDUCATED:** Westminster School. Magdalen College, Oxford.
Learnt to play a miniature violin at three and went on to study piano and French Horn. Brought up on a musical diet of Mozart and Edmundo Ross, he composed his first piece of music at nine and at 12 built a toy theatre in which he staged musicals with a cast of lead soldiers operated by brother Julian. 'I knew early on I'd be a composer.'
While at Oxford he was introduced to a 20 year old law student Tim Rice who knew very little about musicals but was interested in writing pop songs. Their first collaboration, *The Likes of Us* was never commercially produced, but they were prepared to try again when they were asked to write a 15 minute musical play for the boys of St Paul's School in London. The result was *Joseph and the Amazing Technicolour Dreamcoat* which was performed for the first time by St Paul's School in March 1968. When an extended version was

DICK WALTER
'D.W. Tentette Esq . . .'
BORN: 13th December 1946, in Beckenham, Kent. Father 'something in the City'. **EDUCATED:** Beckenham and Penge Grammar School. Nottingham University. Studied piano and clarinet as a child and later added saxophone and flute. Paid his dues in writing for big bands by running and writing for the University Jazz Orchestra. **FIRST JOB:** Three hours of questionable activity in an undesirable Nottingham night club. Played lead alto with Maynard Ferguson in 1969, but from then on concentrated on writing and arranging. His first arrangement for the Radio Big Band was *The Fool on the Hill* and was broadcast in 1968. Since the early 70s he's been active mainly as a composer in TV commercials and films, but has always maintained a link with arranging through the Radio Orchestras and two singers in particular, Danny Street and Norma Winstone. His arrangements are heard on many of Radio 2's music programmes, particularly *Big Band Special*.

put on at Central Hall, Westminster a couple of months later, it was seen and given a favourable review by Derek Jewell of *The Sunday Times*. A recording was made and soon the play was being performed by schools all over the world. It has since been staged five times in London's West End and four times in America.

The next Lloyd Webber/Rice collaboration, like the first was a flop. *Come Back Richard, Your Country Needs You* never made it to the professional stage. It was Tim Rice who got the idea for their fourth musical, straight from the Bible, the story of Jesus. The two of them took themselves off to a Hertfordshire hotel for a week during which time most of the show was written. The title song, *Jesus Christ Superstar* was released first as a single in 1969. Then came the best selling double album and in October 1971 the show opened on Broadway. But it was not the kind of production they had envisaged. 'I think that opening night was the worst night I can remember. The show was a travesty.' But not so the London production some ten months later which opened at the Palace, the theatre that a decade later, he would be buying. *Jesus Christ Superstar*, which had clocked up a mere 711 performances in New York, ran for an astonishing eight years. The next Lloyd Webber musical *Jeeves* which Tim Rice dropped out of, being replaced by playwright Alan Ayckbourn, was another flop. After opening in Bristol it transferred to London for a mere 47 performances. And so if the previous form was to continue the next Lloyd Webber/Rice collaboration was due to be a hit. It was. It was also the last musical they would write together. *Evita*, like *Jesus Christ Superstar*, started life as a double album which not only made it into the album charts when it was released in 1976, but also produced the No.1 hit single *Don't Cry For Me Argentina*, sung by Julie Covington. 18 months later *Evita* opened at the Prince Edward Theatre with Elaine Page in the title role, where it is still playing to packed houses at the time of going to press. The Broadway production ran for four years. But another hit musical wasn't enough to save the partnership. Tim Rice went off to work with Stephen Oliver on *Blondel* and Andrew Lloyd Webber set to work on what was to be his biggest success yet, *Cats*, based on the poems of T.S. Elliot opened in May 1981 in London to rave reviews which were repeated in New York in the autumn of '82. It became the hit of the season with tickets hard to come by. Surprisingly enough the one hit from the show, *Memory* was composed as a mock Puccini tune for another project and the lyrics, which owed some inspiration to T.S. Elliot were written by the show's Director, Trevor Nunn. With the opening of *Song and Dance* at the Palace Theatre in 1982, he became the only composer in the history of the theatre to have three musicals running simultaneously in both London's West End and Broadway.

Following the failure of *Jeeves* in 1974, his policy of trying out his shows before an invited audience at Sydmonton, his 65 acre country estate in Hampshire, has paid off. It was there in 1979 that he first tried out his idea of a musical about a train. Richard Stilgoe who had contributed the words for the opening number of *Cats*, was brought in as lyricist and so *Starlight Express* was born. If the setting and staging of *Cats* was spectacular, *Starlight Express* went even further with the Apollo Victoria being transformed into a railway switching yard and the whole of the cast on roller skates. At a cost of 2.9 million pounds, one critic described it as 'A millionaire's folly, which happens to be open to the public'. But the public

adored it and the undoubted success of the show in London will almost certainly be repeated on Broadway.

In 1983 he turned his hand to production with the comedy *Daisy Pulls it Off* at the Globe and the following year co-produced the Rogers and Hart revival *On Your Toes* at the Palace. As the new owner of that theatre, he plans to restore it to its former Victorian splendour and plans to produce an opera there in a couple of seasons, treating it in exactly the same way as a musical. As he told *Time* magazine: 'I think opera is the best form of musical theatre; but I don't think sitting in an opera house in a dinner jacket next to someone in a tiara is a particularly satisfactory kind of theatre.'

A workaholic, he thinks about music all the time and just as Irving Berlin claimed to have written one of his songs in the back of a New York taxi, Andrew Lloyd Webber confesses to writing one in a London taxi. He is invariably working on his next show, or two and it could well be that he'll continue to dominate the musical stage on both sides of the Atlantic for many years to come. ■ Likes ruins, monuments and old buildings. ■ Has a daughter, Imogen, a son, Nicholas, and lives in London and Hampshire.

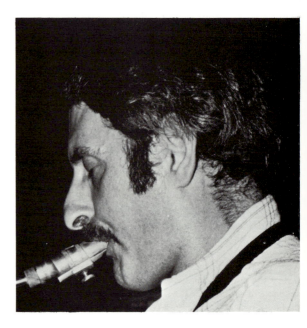

BOBBY WELLINS
'A dastardly deed at the dead of night . . .'
BORN: 1936 in Glasgow, Scotland. Father a professional musician (saxophone), Mother a vocalist who sang in the same band. **EDUCATED:** Shawlands Academy, Glasgow. 'I was playing the piano from as long ago as I can remember, but my father taught me the alto sax when I was 12. He also taught me harmony.' **FIRST JOB:** At 17 joined the RAF School of Music and for two years played with the Central Band. 'I switched to tenor from alto as I preferred the sound'. After his demob, played with Bernard Ebbinghouse at Slough Palais and also played with Malcolm Mitchell, Frank Weir and Vic Lewis. In 1979 formed his own Quartet playing Ronnie Scott's and various jazz venues in the UK and on the Continent. His 1984 album *The Endangered Species* was commissioned by the Arts Council of Great Britain and South East Arts. A

member of the New Music Sub Committee of the ACGB 1983–84.

■ Highspot of career: 'I'm still waiting! But to be fair, in musical terms, as far as jazz playing is concerned, I am lucky enough to play with some of the best improvisers in the world, so every playing night is a highspot.' ■ A moment to remember: 'I had joined Frank Weir's band and had been playing with them for about three months. Frank had made a couple of hit records playing his soprano saxophone. He suddenly had the brilliant idea of the sax section plus himself all playing soprano saxes and commissioned a special arrangement for the six sopranos and band of *In a Persian Market*. This was to be one of the band's big feature numbers. Now the rule was that the last member to join the sax section was given the worst soprano sax and I was the delegate at this time. After some weeks of frustration, attempting to play this terrible instrument, the band were booked to play at a big function given by Lord and Lady somebody who resided in the Midlands. The soiree was held in the grounds and was a huge affair. During our interval, we had consumed a fair amount of alcohol and I decided to take a stroll around the grounds. In doing so, I came across the gardener's tool shed. I decided there and then that the only way to acquire a new soprano sax from Frank would be to bury the existing one, which I did. At the end of the night the band were filing into the coach making ready for our return to London and on that occasion our coach driver decided to take a count of the instruments before moving off. He reported one soprano sax missing. The Lord and Lady of the Manor were extremely upset over the missing instrument and called the police. This was at a time when the police had just introduced their 'sniffer' dogs to track down any missing objects. Half an hour later we saw the dog and handler trotting across the lawn with the dog holding this mud-caked piece of metal in its mouth. It was the missing soprano sax. The police decided that the burglar had buried it with the intention of returning when all was quiet and retrieving the instrument.

During the following months, travelling in the band coach, I would catch Frank looking at me quizzically and I knew he was working out the dastardly plot. He never did find out the truth and I never acquired a new soprano sax, however the special arrangement for the six soprano saxes was suddenly dropped from the band's music library.' ■ Likes the sea. 'I live in Bognor Regis and really enjoy the combination of being near the sea and having some of the most beautiful scenery in the world, to enjoy at all times of the year.
■ Dislikes a lack of civility, good manners and consideration for our fellow human beings. ■ Married to Isabelle, has two daughters, Elizabeth and Fiona and lives in West Sussex.

KENNY WHEELER
'Started by playing at Polish weddings . . .'
BORN: 13 January 1930 in Toronto, Canada. Father a professional trombonist and accountant. **EDUCATED:** St Joseph's, Toronto. St Catherine's, Ontario. Learnt the piano at seven and didn't like it. He ignored music until he was 12, when he started to play the cornet. He studied harmony at the Toronto Conservatory of Music, and studied counterpoint with Bill Russo in London in the early 60s. **FIRST JOB:** Messenger in a bank; clerk in an insurance office. 'I had

numerous jobs and none of them lasted for more than three months.'
He earned his first money as a musician, playing at a Polish wedding in Toronto. 'I used to play at a lot of Polish weddings as there was a large Polish community in Toronto. They would last about two days and you would end up with a very swollen lip.'
He wandered around from job to job in Canada until 1952 when he emigrated to Britain. 'The big band era was still in progress in the UK and even if you couldn't play very well, you could find a job in some band or other and that's what I did, playing with Vic Lewis, Roy Fox, Johnny Dankworth and Carl Barriteau over the next few years.' He became a much sought-after session trumpet player in the late 60s and early 70s, but then started to travel around Europe, building up quite a reputation on the European jazz circuit. By the beginning of the 80s, 90 per cent of his work was on the Continent. 'I still do the odd session here, but my telephone stopped ringing when they found me away most of the time.' However he fronts his own big band for BBC's *Jazz Club*, once a year, and when he does find time to take in a recording session as sideman, it always proves to be quite an occasion as most of his colleagues consider him to be one of the great jazz trumpeters.
As well as a constant round of broadcasts, concerts and club appearances, has made four albums under his own name with all his own original compositions. The first, *Gnu High*, released in 1976, won a German award for the Best Jazz Record of the Year. His latest album released in 1984 is dedicated to his father who has the initials W.W., hence the title *Double Comma, Double You*. 'It's a silly play on words, but I don't like serious titles.' He rarely writes for other bands, although he has done some work for the EBU Band on occasions. 'I never really get commissioned to write for anyone else, but I don't mind it that way.'

■ Highspot of career: 'I couldn't pick any one although I get a lot of kicks out of playing with the Dave Holland Quintet. (Dave is the English bass player who left to join Miles Davis). I get as much pleasure out of that as out of anything I've ever

done.' ■ A moment to remember: 'I usually only get to remember this sort of thing when I've had a few drinks, but I do recall being in Austria a few years ago with Ronnie Scott (qv). He was talking to this Austrian lady, who had a very thick accent, and she asked him if he played chess. Well, that's what Ronnie thought she said, but what she really asked was, did he play jazz. So they had this 10-minute conversation with Ronnie explaining the finer points of his chess game, while she was discussing his finer points as a jazzman. It was quite hilarious until they each discovered what the other was talking about.' ■ Likes comedy, silly humour with people like Mel Brooks, and Laurel and Hardy. 'Women never seem to like them and I could never figure that one out. It's a great thing to have a good laugh.'
■ Dislikes people who don't leave much space. 'I don't drive, so I'm a great tube traveller and it's the people who get right up close to you who irritate me.' ■ Married to Doreen, has one son, Mark, one daughter, Louisa, and lives in Essex.

wife Barbara Jay. Fronts his own Quartet and is heard regularly on many of Radio 2's music programmes. Appears at Jazz Clubs in the UK and Europe and 1984 saw him at the Nice Jazz Festival with the Jazz Journal All Stars. Has made several albums featuring his Quartet with Barbara Jay.

■ Highspot of career: 'In 1956 I travelled on the *Queen Mary* as a passenger with my Quartet, to New York to play there in an exchange with the Gerry Mulligan Quartet. We were well received and the whole trip was very exciting.' ■ A moment to remember: 'As featured sax soloist with the BBC Showband, Cyril Stapleton would usually have me playing a fast jazz number which he always wanted to rehearse first, no matter where it came in the programme. Sometimes this would get me down as it would mean playing something frantic at maybe 9am, which I found a bit shattering to the nerves. Then one day my two children had found some keys and locked my tenor case without my knowing. As I never locked it, I never carried keys with me so on arriving at the Paris Cinema for rehearsal I couldn't open my case and had to phone for the keys to be sent by taxi. But I enjoyed it when Cyril called out "*Lester Leaps In*" as first number – he was foiled and had to rehearse a string number instead!'
■ Likes playing tennis. ■ Dislikes queues. ■ Married to vocalist Barbara Jay (qv), has two sons Martin and Sean and lives in Hertfordshire.

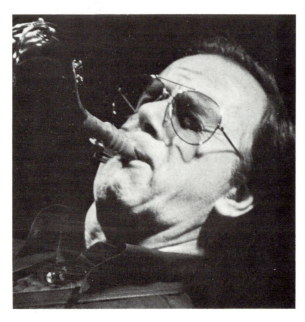

TOMMY WHITTLE
'An exchange with Gerry Mulligan . . .'
BORN: 13th October 1926, in Grangemouth, Stirlingshire. Father a river pilot on the River Forth. EDUCATED: St Aloysius College, Glasgow. Taught himself to play clarinet with a few initial lessons from Sammy McLean of Falkirk and, later in London, Aubrey Franks. When a friend loaned him his tenor saxophone, he decided to become a professional musician although his parents thought it would be much safer if he got an office job! Plays all the saxes, clarinets and flutes. FIRST JOB: Playing with the Claude Giddings Band at the Gillingham Pavillion, and the Norman Williams Band in Gillingham. Made his first broadcast with Lew Stone somewhere around 1943. Has played with Johnnie Claes, Lew Stone, Rex Owen, Carl Barriteau. Harry Hayes, Ted Heath, Geraldo, Cyril Stapleton Show Band; Jack Parnell, ATV Orchestra. Fronted his own band at the Dorchester Hotel, London for two and a half years. Was the featured soloist with the BBC Showband and was heard on the Ted Heath broadcasts and *Jazz Club*, the *Arthur Askey Show* and the *Kenneth Williams Show* with his

ROY WILLIAMS
'Jazz Journal's International Top Trombonist four years in a row . . .'
BORN: 7th March, 1937 in Manchester. Father an engineer. EDUCATED: All Saints Junior School. Harper Green Secondary Modern School, Farnworth, Nr. Bolton.
'We had a piano at home although I never had any lessons I used to plonk away at it. Then when I was 17 I heard my first jazz. I fell in love with it and wanted to play the trombone.' His parents bought him a trombone when he was 18 and he took a few lessons but soon got disillusioned with his teacher who never had any patience with him. 'One day he said to me, "Look Roy, we're wasting each other's time, why don't you try something else." Sod you, I thought, I'll show you, I'll teach myself. And I did and I taught myself to read music.'
FIRST JOB: Apprentice with an engineering firm until he was 21. He spent the next two years in the Army doing National Service and soon discovered that his trombone got him out of a lot of parades and square bashing.
After being demobbed in 1960 he was determined to

become a professional trombonist. The Trad boom had just started and he auditioned for and got a job with the Mike Peters Band in London. After nine months was asked to join the Terry Lightfoot Band and stayed with them for five years. He then joined Alex Welsh for 12 years and freelanced for a year in 1977 before joining Humphrey Lyttelton with whom he remained until 1983. Now works as a session trombonist and is a member of the five trombone line-up known as Five a Slide.

Jazz Journal International voted him Top Trombonist four years running, 1981–84, beating American Bill Watrous into second place.

■ Highspot of career: 'Being invited to play at the Denver Jazz Festival in 1978 and '79, the first Englishman to do so and playing alongside over 50 other great musicians including Benny Carter.' ■ A moment to remember: 'When drummer Lennie Hastings died, most of us at the funeral were musicians. There was Acker Bilk, Kenny Ball, George Chisholm and American trumpeter Ruby Braff to name but a few. Now Lennie used to love the singing of Richard Tauber and *You Are My Heart's Delight* was his particular favourite, so it was agreed that the organist would play this before the start of the service. So there we were, all standing quietly with eyes downcast, listening to the organ softly playing *You Are My Heart's Delight*, when suddenly there was a glaringly obvious wrong chord. All the bowed heads came up as one, and there was an audible "aah" from the congregation. Lennie would have loved it!' ■ Likes cricket, collecting books, (particularly P.G. Wodehouse), model railways. 'I'm a great fan of the steam age'. ■ Dislikes Country & Western music, bad pop and bad jazz. ■ Married to Margot, has two sons, one daughter and lives in Bedfordshire.

ROY WILLOX
'I never did get a rise . . .'

BORN: 31st August 1929 in Welwyn Garden City. Father a machine minder at the Shredded Wheat factory and also a semi-pro alto saxophone player. Mother a pianist. Together they ran a band called The Blue Lyres. **EDUCATED:** Welwyn Garden City Grammar School. Had piano lessons at seven years old but gave them up at 11. 'I wasn't a natural pianist. My Dad started me off on the alto and then sent me to Harry Hayes for lessons.' **FIRST JOB:** Playing alto with the Claude Giddings Band at Gillingham Pavilion in 1945. After nine months, Harry Hayes got him an audition with Henry Hall, whom he joined in 1946. The following year he joined the RAF for two years' National Service and on his demob played gigs on the Lyons circuit, Regent Palace etc, before joining Ronnie Pleydell at the Embassy Club. In 1950, Harry Hayes fixed an audition with the Ted Heath Band and he joined Heath in September for a stay of five years. He then switched to Geraldo on lead alto. 'I'd only played second alto with Ted and I thought if I'm going to find out if I can play lead, this is the time to do it, and Geraldo had a marvellous saxophone pad.' A spell with Jack Parnell at ATV followed before he joined the BBC Revue Orchestra under Harry Rabinowitz in 1958. After two years, with the freelance scene in good shape, he left and has been doing session work ever since. Plays alto, clarinet, flute, bass flute, piccolo and bass clarinet.

■ Highspot of career: Two of the greatest kicks I ever had was to be in the backing band for Frank Sinatra at the Royal

Albert Hall and at the same venue, playing with Henry Mancini and backing Andy Williams. I did four of Sinatra's concerts in all, then I decided to stick my neck out and ask for more money. I didn't do any more!' ■ A moment to remember: 'When I had been in Henry Hall's band for about three months, I'd been playing a few features and was a bit of the boy wonder at 16, so I thought it was about time I had a raise. When I went in for my money on the Friday morning I said, "Morning Guv'nor", (it was Mr Hall or Guv'nor, never Henry). "Guv'nor, I wondered whether you thought it was time I had a rise?" He said, "No, I don't think so. Why?" "Well I've been here a bit and I've been playing some solos and I thought maybe it was time I had more money". "No, I'll tell you when," said the Guv'nor. So I slunk out with my tail between my legs. And that was the money I stayed on until I left. I never did get a rise!' ■ Likes good big bands. 'I enjoy playing jazz, golf, [he plays off 14], and sailing a racing dinghy. I frequently fall in. Country walking. ■ Dislikes rhythm sections who can't keep time, 'and there are far too many of them – they drive me potty. I don't like the way politics are going. Things disturb me these days. I like a nice peaceful life.' ■ Married to Doreen, has two sons, one grandson and one granddaughter who live in Australia, and lives in Hertfordshire.

'Hancocked'. We started playing at 8pm, back to the pub during the break, back to the club for the next set, back to the pub and back to the club for the cabaret spot, The Bachelors. By this time I had gone completely. The street lights were spinning around and I couldn't even see the stage. All I remember is a voice saying: "Ladies and Gentlemen, the Bachelors." and as if on cue I . . . . well, never mind what I did, but all I heard was Hancock's voice behind me, saying "Well timed!" ■ Likes skiing. (Although I usually break something). Dislikes anything that's done badly, unprofessionalism and shoddy things.   ■ Has one son and one daughter and lives in London.

RAY WORDSWORTH
'They were always moaning I played too many notes . . .'
BORN: 18th November 1946 in Mexborough, Yorkshire. Father a miner. **EDUCATED:** Wisewood Secondary School, Sheffield. Played trombone in the Rawmarsh Prize Band in Sheffield at eight years old. Also learnt to play the piano. 'I still love playing the piano, although I don't play professionally. By the time he was in his teens, was playing with various Dixieland bands in the Sheffield area. **FIRST JOB:** One year management course in a store. 'My mother had a general store and knew all the store keepers and managers in the area, so she fixed up for me to go on this course.'
After a year he joined an Irish Show Band (Jack Ruane). In the late 60's moved to London and played with Monty Sunshine, Alan Elsdon and Alex Welsh. In 1970, wanting to improve his reading, he joined the Ken Mackintosh Orchestra for a year. After that it was back to Dixieland with Sid Phillips although he was also doing more studio sessions. 'I always played more mainstream to modern jazz when I was with the Dixieland line-ups, and they were always moaning that I played too many notes, especially Sid Phillips "Play what's written" he would say! The 70's saw him moving into the modern jazz field, playing with Thad Jones on his visits to the UK; playing in Norway for the Norwegian Jazz Federation and teaching at Summer Jazz Courses. He fronts his own Quartet which includes Ronnie Ross and John Horler, playing such venues as the Barbican Centre, the Royal Festival Hall and the Bull's Head at Barnes. They also make regular broadcasts on Jazz Club. Appeared in Oslo and at the Molde Jazz Festival in the summer of 1984.

■ Highspot of career: 'I don't think I've had one yet!'   ■ A moment to remember: 'In the days when Alan Downey and Dave Hancock were in the Radio Big Band, we were working one day at the Aeolian Hall and the afternoon session finished early, so Dave Hancock and I, who had a gig that night in Purfleet, set off early and went into the local pub for a drink. I should have known better. As everyone who knows him knows, if you get stoned drinking with him, you've been

The author and publishers thank the following for supplying photographs:

FIRST SECTION

A & M Records
Elkie Brooks

Danny Allmark
Barbara Jay

Dennis Austin
Norma Winston

Beds & Bucks Observer
Barron Knights

BBC Copyright
Julie Andrews
Vera Lynn

CBS
Paul Young
Picture by Andrew Catlin

EMI Records
Cliff Richard
Photograph by Brian Aris
Duran Duran
Photograph by Brian Aris
Iris Williams
David Bowie
Photograph by Denis O'Regan

EPIC
Shakin' Stevens
Photograph by Vic Prior
Barbara Dickson

Trans World Eye
Joan Savage

Beverley Lebarrow
Val Doonican

Les Leverett
Stu Stevens

Eric G Lovat
Jeanie Lambe

MPL
Paul McCartney

Oscar Creative Photography
Kelly Ford

Platform
Carole Kidd
Photograph by Sean Hudson

Polydor
The Shadows
Shakatak

Ritz
Bonnie Dobson

Rockney Records
Chas & Dave

Peter Simpkin
Sandra King

Staff Records
Madness

Ian Tilbury
Tammy Cline

Simon Fowler
Tracy Ullman

Peter Ventham
Pat Whitmore

Virgin Records
Culture Club
Picture by Andre Cstillag
Boy George
Picture by David Levine

WEA
Elaine Page

SECOND SECTION

Dennis Austin
Chris Laurence
John Taylor

Alistair A Beattie
Adrian Drover

Julia Bennett Studios
Pete Moore

Studio Cole Ltd
Gordon Langford

Chelsea Colour Studio
John Critchinson

Joseph Coomber
Cliff Adams

Peter Danson
Kenny Wheeler

Daytota Records
John Gregory

Roger J Delaney
Dave Hancock/John McLevy

Johnny Donnels
Chris Barber

William S Douse
Bobby Wellins

Andrew Dunsmore
Ray Wordsworth

ECM Records
John Surman

EMI Records
Geoff Love

Graham Forbes Gordon
Bob Burns

Hamilton Marshall Photography
Johnny Howard

Handford Photography
Barry Forgie

Peter A Harding
George French

Humphrey-Saunders Studios Ltd
Alec Gould

Jak Kilby
Graham Collier

London Weekend Television Ltd
Alyn Ainsworth
Harry Rabinowitz

Bernard Long
Humphrey Lyttelton

Tim Motion
Brian Lemon
Alan Ganley

Edward Obden
Ronnie Ross

Petrina – Photo
Steve Race

RCA
James Galway

John Rose Associates
Don Lusher

David Ross Studios
Bill Geldard

John D Sharp
Nigel Ogden

Starax Press Services
Don Rendell

Denis J Williams
Ron Mathewson
Tommy Whittle

Stephen Wolfenden Photo
Jack Parnell